Searches and enquiries
A conveyancer's guide

Searches and enquiries
A conveyancer's guide

Frances Silverman
Solicitor, Principal lecturer
at the College of Law

London
Butterworths
1985

England	Butterworth & Co (Publishers) Ltd, 88 Kingsway, LONDON WC2B 6AB
Australia	Butterworths Pty Ltd, SYDNEY, MELBOURNE, BRISBANE, ADELAIDE, PERTH, CANBERRA and HOBART
Canada	Butterworth & Co (Canada) Ltd, TORONTO and VANCOUVER
New Zealand	Butterworths of New Zealand Ltd, WELLINGTON and AUCKLAND
Singapore	Butterworth & Co (Asia) Pte Ltd, SINGAPORE
South Africa	Butterworth Publishers (Pty) Ltd, DURBAN and PRETORIA
USA	Butterworth Legal Publishers, ST PAUL, Minnesota, SEATTLE, Washington, BOSTON, Massachusetts, AUSTIN, Texas and D & S Publishers, CLEARWATER, Florida

© Butterworth & Co (Publishers) Ltd 1985

British Library Cataloguing in Publication Data

Silverman, Frances
  Searches and enquiries: a conveyancer's guide.
  1. Conveyancing—England
  I. Title
  344.2064'38 KD979

ISBN 0 406 25513 X

Made and printed in Great Britain by
Butler & Tanner Ltd, Frome and London

Preface

The making of searches and enquiries forms an integral part of every conveyancing transaction and imposes a heavy responsibility on the purchaser's solicitor who may be liable in negligence to his own client if he omits to do a search which would have been appropriate to the particular transaction and the client suffers loss by reason of this omission. The purpose of this book is to provide the conveyancing practitioner with an analysis of the usual searches, ie those which are encountered in virtually every transaction, and with a comprehensive source of reference for the less usual searches which may occasionally be required either because of the nature of the property being purchased or because of the geographical locality of the land. In all cases where a standard form is commonly used for the search that form is illustrated in the text, together with a commentary on the printed form.

In the case of the less usual searches, the circumstances in which the search should be made, the information revealed in answer to the search and practical guidance as to how and where to do these less common searches is contained in each chapter.

A search summary, containing the basic information relating to each search appears at the end of each chapter and tables showing the various searches and their relevance to specific geographical areas appear in Appendices II and III. Where search fees have been quoted, those fees were correct at the time of going to press but are subject to change and may need to be checked before submitting an application for a search.

Unless otherwise stated, the use of the word 'purchaser' in the text should be read as including mortgagee and lessee as the procedure for undertaking the various searches is, in general, relevant to all persons who are acquiring an interest for value in land.

In the course of writing this book I discovered several searches applicable to particular areas of England and Wales of which I had previously been unaware, and whilst I have made every attempt to locate 'local peculiarities' I fear there may still be some unusual searches which have evaded my detective work. If so, I apologise for their omission and would be grateful to learn of their existence so that this defect may be remedied in the next edition of the book.

I acknowledge with thanks the permission of the Solicitors' Law

Preface

Stationery Society plc to reproduce their standard forms, also the permission of the Chief Land Registrar to reproduce Practice Leaflet No 2 in ch 34 and of Unilaw to reproduce form Convey 1. I am most grateful to Kathleen Davis and Sue James for typing and correcting the manuscript and to Tony Donell whose correction of my legal and grammatical errors is much appreciated. Any errors which remain are my responsibility alone. Finally I would like to thank my publishers for their advice and assistance and my family whose memories of the long hot summer of 1984 will be coloured not by the drought but by the seemingly everlasting diet of sausages, caused by my inability to concentrate simultaneously on both writing and cooking.

The Law is stated as at 25 October 1984 and references within the text to the Law Society Conditions of Sale and National Conditions of Sale are to the 1984 revision and the 20th edition respectively.

Frances Silverman

Guildford
25 October 1984

Addendum

Since writing the main text of the book my attention has been drawn to another new version of the standard preliminary enquiry form. Although it has not been possible to include a full commentary on the contents of the three preliminary enquiry forms and client questionnaires recently published by Stat-Plus, a copy of these forms, together with a brief commentary thereon, is contained in Appendix IV, and I acknowledge with thanks the permission of Stat-Plus Ltd to reproduce their forms.

Frances Silverman

Guildford
18 February 1985

Contents

Contents

Table of statutes

References in this Table to *Statutes* are to Halsbury's Statutes of England (Third Edition) showing the volume and page at which the annotated text of the Act will be found.
In this Table references are to chapters in bold type, to paragraphs in roman type and to notes in italic type (ie **21**.3, **5** note *1*). Notes are located at the end of each chapter.

Table of statutes

List of cases

References in this List are to chapters in bold type and notes in italic type, i.e. **5** note *1*.
Notes are located at the end of each chapter.

Part I

General principles

Chapter 1

Reasons for making searches

1.1 ORIGINS OF SEARCHES

The solicitor acting for the purchaser in a sale of land transaction accepts as part of the routine of such a transaction that he will have to undertake various searches and enquiries on behalf of his client. Many of these searches take a standard form and some may even be regarded as a formality serving little useful purpose. Seldom will the solicitor have time to pause to consider why he is making the searches or to question the origins of the practice. Most of the searches which are undertaken today are comparatively recent in their origins and would have been unknown to a solicitor practising at the beginning of this century, since many, including for example the central land charges search, owe their existence to the 1925 legislation which introduced sweeping reforms into the land law of England and Wales. Some are of much more recent origin than this, as for example the commons registration search which was introduced by the Commons Registration Act 1965. Even the familiar form of preliminary enquiries was unheard of in 1900, first appearing in published form in 1944 and if contemporary conveyancing practice is to be judged by texts current at the time, their use was not widespread for several years following their publication, since Gibson's *Conveyancing* in the 1947 edition dismisses the practice of raising preliminary enquiries in a mere half-page with the comment 'It is increasingly common for preliminary enquiries to be made about matters which may affect a purchaser'.[1] In contrast to this quotation, Professor Barnsley in his recent book, *Conveyancing Law and Practice*, says 'the pre-contract inquiry (is) as important, perhaps even more so especially in relation to registered land, than the post-contract investigation of title'.[2] Although Professor Barnsley confines his remarks to pre-contract, or preliminary enquiries, it may be argued that the whole area of pre- and post-contract searches now far outweighs in importance the investigation of title stage of the transaction, since the increase in the number of registered titles and the reduction in length of the statutory root of title in recent years have both served to reduce the purchaser's solicitor's problems in the title area. Thus it may be seen that over the past half-century the 'searches' stage of a conveyancing transaction has emerged from a virtual non-existence to play a vital part in the transaction, but it remains to be explained why searches have attained

3

their present dominant role. The answer to this lies in one of the most well known of all legal maxims: caveat emptor; the buyer takes the property as it is and it is his responsibility to find out what faults or flaws exist in the property which he is purchasing. It is therefore principally for this reason that the purchaser's solicitor undertakes various searches and enquiries before permitting his client to commit himself to a contract to purchase land. However, in order to give some protection to the purchaser there exists in relation to a contract for the sale of land one major exception to the caveat emptor rule, and that exception is known as the vendor's duty of disclosure.

1.2 THE VENDOR'S DUTY OF DISCLOSURE

The nature and state of the vendor's title can only be discovered by questioning the vendor himself. For this reason the vendor is under an obligation to disclose to the purchaser any latent defects in his title which will not be removed before completion. The ambit of this duty of disclosure is not easy to define since in practice the distinction between latent and patent defects is somewhat blurred. A defect may be described as latent if it cannot be discovered by the exercise of reasonable care on the inspection of the property or if it constitutes a deficiency in the vendor's documentary title which may affect his ownership of the property or his right to deal with it. Within this category are included third-party rights which affect the property and which will not be discharged or overreached on or before completion.

1.3 PARTICULAR MATTERS WHICH MUST BE DISCLOSED

1.3.1 Restrictive covenants

All restrictive covenants which affect the property, even those created prior to the root of title, must be disclosed.

1.3.2 Leases and tenancies

Unless the contract provides to the contrary the purchaser is entitled to vacant possession on completion, thus the vendor must supply details of all leases and tenancies to which the property is subject including details of the rent, and if relevant the fact that a notice to quit has been received from the tenant.[3]

1.3.3 Easements

All easements adversely affecting the property including rights of light, drainage and rights of way should be disclosed. The courts are generally reluctant to hold that a right of way is a patent defect, even if the track or path is clearly visible to the eye, since it is generally not possible to tell from mere inspection of the land whether the right of way is public or private or who is entitled to exercise the rights over the land.[4]

1.3.4 Leasehold property

The vendor is under a duty to disclose all unusual or onerous covenants in the lease. In order to avoid difficulties encountered in defining what is unusual or onerous it is usual for the vendor to comply with this particular duty by supplying a copy of the entire lease to the purchaser at the draft contract stage in the transaction. It is also common for the contract to contain a clause protecting the vendor from liability for non-disclosure in respect of such covenants. A typical clause will provide that the purchaser having been supplied with a copy of the lease will be deemed to have bought with full notice of its contents, thus throwing the obligation of querying the contents of the lease on to the purchaser.[5]

1.3.5 Local land charges

Financial charges registered by the local authority have been held to be incumbrances over the property[6] and thus should be disclosed by the vendor. Some other local land charges, eg planning matters, do not fall within the definition of incumbrances and do not require disclosure. In practice it is unusual, except at auctions, for a vendor to disclose any local land charges to the purchaser and the contract will normally relieve him of the obligation to do so.[7] For this reason the purchaser should always make a search of the local land charges register prior to exchange of contracts (see ch 4, below). In the context of registered land local land charges will constitute overriding interests over the property (see para 1.4, below).

1.3.6 Matters registered at the Central Land Charges Registry

The Law of Property Act 1925, s 198 provides that registration of a land charge is notice of that incumbrance to all persons and for all purposes. A possible construction of the effect of s 198 on a purchaser has been mitigated by the Law of Property Act 1969, s 24 which provides that registration of a land charge shall not of itself constitute knowledge of that incumbrance to a purchaser at the pre-contract stage of the transaction, thus effectively placing the onus of disclosing such charges on the vendor.

1.3.7 Exceptions and reservations

Although these matters do not necessarily constitute incumbrances over the property they must be revealed in the contract and therefore arguably fall within the vendor's duty of disclosure.

1.3.8 *Type and tenure of title*
The nature of the vendor's title ie whether freehold or leasehold and if
the latter the terms of the lease including a statement of whether the
lease is a head lease or sub-lease, must be revealed to the purchaser
because in the absence of an express stipulation to the contrary the
purchaser is entitled to assume that the vendor is offering for sale an
unencumbered freehold title. In the case of registered land the purchaser is entitled to assume that he is being offered an absolute title
unless told otherwise, so the nature of the registered title must similarly
be revealed. These details will appear in the particulars of sale of the
contract. The remedy for any inaccuracies in these details technically
lies in misdescription rather than non-disclosure. However, these items
are mentioned here since they do fall within the general scope of matters which the vendor is under an obligation to reveal to the purchaser.

1.3.9 *Matters not within the vendor's knowledge*
The vendor's duty of disclosure has been held to extend even to matters
which were outside the vendor's own knowledge.[8] It is suggested that
to protect the vendor the contract should contain a clause restricting
liability for non-disclosure to matters which are within the vendor's
actual knowledge; National Condition 14 is worded to cover this situation but Law Society Condition 3 is not.

1.4 REGISTERED LAND
The rules of disclosure mentioned above also apply to registered land
but with some modifications. There is no registered land equivalent of
the Law of Property Act 1925, s 198 and as the land register is not
open to public inspection a purchaser is not deemed to know the
contents of the register unless he has been shown copies of the entries
or he has with the vendor's permission inspected the register itself.
Overriding interests do not appear on the register and the vendor is
under a duty to disclose latent, but not patent, overriding interests.
There is some doubt whether the rights of occupation of a person living
in the property are a latent or patent defect, but in view of the nature
of the problems which can arise in this area it would in practice be
inadvisable for the vendor to withhold such information. All local land
charges are overriding interests and thus in the registered land context
the vendor strictly is under a duty to disclose them although he may
be relieved of his obligation to do so by a contractual condition. It may
be argued that the vendor's duty of disclosure extends to all overriding
interests whether latent or patent since the Land Registration Act 1925,
s 38 permits the purchaser to bring an action under the implied covenants for title in respect of overriding interests of which he had no
notice. Thus in order to avoid such possible liability the vendor should
disclose the existence of all overriding interests to the purchaser. The

vendor's duty to disclose the nature of his registered title in the particulars of sale has been noted above (para 1.3.8).

1.5 MATTERS NOT REQUIRING DISCLOSURE

1.5.1 Patent defects in title

It follows from what has been stated above that the vendor is not under a duty to disclose patent defects in his title. A defect may be described as patent if it can be discovered either by the exercise of reasonable care on inspection of the property or if it is readily visible to the eye. The distinction between latent and patent is not always very clear particularly in the area of planning, local land charges and rights of way and if there is doubt in a particular case in deciding whether a matter is latent or patent, and possibly in any event, the most sensible course of action must be to err on the side of discretion and to make a full disclosure of the incumbrance, supported by a special condition in the contract.

1.5.2 Removeable incumbrances

Incumbrances which are to be removed prior to completion, eg a mortgage or a lease which is to be surrendered, need not be disclosed to the purchaser. However, if the incumbrance is presently protected by a central land charges registration (eg where the vendor has a second mortgage over the property which is protected by a C(1) registration), it may be wise to give notice of the existence of the incumbrance to the purchaser who will then be able to reconcile this information with the result of his central land charges search.

1.5.3 Physical defects in the property

As a general rule the vendor is under no obligation to disclose physical defects in his property so long as he does not mislead the purchaser. This general rule must be applied with some caution since there have been decided cases in which the vendor has been held liable for non-disclosure of a latent physical defect.[9] In most cases, however, the caveat emptor rule applies to physical defects and the purchaser should be urged to make a full inspection of the land and where the purchase is of a house or other buildings a structural survey of the property is to be recommended.

1.5.4 *Planning matters*

Planning is arguably not a matter affecting the vendor's legal title to the property, but neither can it be described as relating to the physical qualities of the land. The duty to disclose such matters is therefore uncertain in law, but the widely held belief is that planning matters do

7

not fall within the vendor's duty of disclosure unless the contract provides to the contrary.

1.6 CONTRACTUAL CONDITIONS AFFECTING THE DUTY OF DISCLOSURE
Since the duty to disclose incumbrances imposes a heavy burden on the vendor the contract frequently contains a condition which seeks to limit or restrict this duty and to place the onus of inquiry on to the purchaser. Both commonly used forms of contract, the Law Society's contract of sale (1984 revision) and the National Conditions of sale (20th edition) contain such conditions.

1.6.1 Law Society General Condition 3
Under sub-clause (2) the property is deemed to be sold subject to

'(a) all matters registrable by any competent authority pursuant to statute; (b) all requirements of any competent authority; (c) all matters disclosed or reasonably expected to be disclosed by searches and as a result of enquiries formal or informal, and whether made in person, by writing or orally by or for the purchaser or which a prudent purchaser ought to make; (d) all notices served on or on behalf of a reversioner, a tenant or sub-tenant, or the owner or occupier of any adjoining or neighbouring property'.

The main effect of this sub-clause is to exclude from the vendor's duty of disclosure the matters mentioned in the sub-clause, throwing the burden of enquiry in relation to these matters on to the purchaser. From the vendor's point of view this clause is a welcome inclusion in the contract since it exonerates him from his duty of disclosure in some of the more uncertain areas to which the duty applies, eg local land charges. The sub-clause is not so happily drafted when viewed from the purchaser's point of view, since it creates a heavy obligation on the purchaser to make full searches and enquiries. In view of the wide definition of 'a competent authority' within the sub-clause, and the inclusion of the words 'searches ... which a prudent purchaser ought to make' the purchaser's obligation to make searches against the property may need to be extended beyond the usual range of local authority search with additional enquiries plus preliminary enquiries, and, dependent upon the nature of the property, one or more of the less usual searches may also have to be undertaken.

In contrast to the onus placed on the purchaser by sub-clause (2), sub-clause (3) of this condition, which prevails over sub-clause (2), places a heavy burden of disclosure on the vendor, requiring him to disclose matters which are known to him or written communications received by him in relation to a wide variety of matters concerning the property including matters which are registrable against the property even though not actually registered. The onus of disclosure imposed by sub-clause (3) seems to extend beyond the ordinary common law duty and the vendor might justifiably consider amending the sub-clause to bring the requirements for disclosure back into line with those imposed by the common law.

1.6.2 National Condition 14
This condition broadly contains a restatement of the general law except that the clause is drafted so as to protect the vendor from liability for non-disclosure in circumstances where the purchaser complains of a defect of which the vendor had no knowledge. The reason for this rather curious choice of phrase in the condition is because there has been at least one reported case[10] where the implication of the decision was that the vendor could be held liable for non-disclosure even in circumstances where the matter complained of was outside the vendor's own knowledge.

1.6.3 *Leasehold property*
Law Society Condition 8(3) and National Condition 11(2) both override the vendor's duty of disclosure in relation to leasehold property by providing that once the purchaser has been supplied with a copy of the lease he shall be deemed to have knowledge of its contents. The vendor's duty to disclose breaches of covenant is also negated by the requirement that the purchaser shall buy the property in its present state and condition.

1.7 REMEDIES FOR NON-DISCLOSURE
Where the non-disclosure is of a substantial defect the purchaser will be entitled to rescind before completion although he may if he prefers complete his purchase and take his compensation through an abatement in the purchase price.

Rescission is only available as a remedy where the non-disclosed defect is so serious as to prevent the purchaser from getting substantially what he contracted to buy. In all other cases the purchaser's remedy is limited to compensation, ie he can be forced to complete subject to an abatement in the purchase price to compensate for the defect.

1.7.1 *Misdescription*
A failure to disclose a matter in relation to the type or tenure of the vendor's title or a misleading physical description of the property in the particulars of sale leads to liability in misdescription rather than non-disclosure. The remedies for misdescription are similar to those for non-disclosure in that only in circumstances where the misdescription

9

is material or results in the purchaser not getting substantially what he bargained for will the purchaser be entitled to rescind. In other cases he is entitled to compensation only.

1.7.2 *Exclusion clauses*
Contractual conditions, eg Law Society Condition 7 and National Condition 17 frequently seek to limit the purchaser's remedies for both mis-description and non-disclosure. These clauses tend to be narrowly construed by the courts and will generally not be allowed to operate so as to deprive the purchaser of his right to rescind in respect of a substantial error but they may be effective to preclude the purchaser's right to compensation.

1.7.3 *Misrepresentation*
A remedy will lie in misrepresentation in respect of an untrue statement of fact made by the vendor which has been relied on by the purchaser in entering into the contract. By its very nature a non-disclosure is an omission rather than a statement thus precluding an alternative remedy in misrepresentation. It is, however, sometimes possible to allege that a misrepresentation has occurred through silence, ie where the vendor deliberately omits to reveal a fact knowing that this omission will lead the purchaser to assume that a certain state of affairs exists. In such cases an action may lie in misrepresentation in addition to or as an alternative to the action in non-disclosure. If an action in misrepresentation can be established it may be preferable to that in non-disclosure since the remedies for the former action are now clearly defined under the Misrepresentation Act 1967 whereas the common law remedies for non-disclosure are sometimes uncertain in their effect. Furthermore the validity of clauses attempting to exclude liability for misrepresentation is subjected to the reasonableness test contained in the Unfair Contract Terms Act 1977, s 11 where the subjective nature of the reasonableness test favours the purchaser.

A misdescription will invariably also constitute a misrepresentation possibly giving the purchaser the option of suing for either remedy. For the reasons stated above it seems that an action in misrepresentation may now be preferable to that in misdescription.

1.8 Summary
The principal reason why the purchaser undertakes searches and enquiries is to discover matters relating to the property which the vendor is not by law required to disclose. As will have been seen from the above paragraphs, the vendor's duty of disclosure is in some respects both vague and uncertain, as are the purchaser's remedies for non-disclosure, so the importance of the purchaser's searches should not be underestimated.

1 At p 61.
2 (2nd edn, 1982, Butterworths) p 181.
3 *Dimmock v Hallett* (1866) 2 Ch App 21, 36 LJ Ch 146.
4 See *Yandle & Sons v Sutton* [1922] 2 Ch 199, 91 LJ Ch 567.
5 See LSC 8(3) and NC 11(2).
6 *Stock v Meakin* [1900] 1 Ch 683, 69 LJ Ch 401, CA.
7 See LSC 3(2) and NC 14.
8 *Re Brewer and Hankin's Contract* (1899) 80 LT 127, CA.
9 *Re Puckett and Smith's Contract* [1902] 2 Ch 258, 71 LJ Ch 666, CA.
10 *Re Brewer and Hankin's Contract* (1899) 80 LT 127, CA.

Chapter 2

Liability on searches

2.1 PURCHASER'S SOLICITOR

The case of *Cooper v Stephenson*[1] established that a purchaser's solicitor would be liable in negligence to his client if the client suffered loss through the solicitor's failure to make the 'usual' searches and inquiries. The word 'usual' is accepted as meaning at the least (a) a local land charges search; (b) additional inquiries of the local authority; (c) preliminary enquiries of the vendor.

These three searches should be regarded as the absolute minimum requirement of the purchaser's solicitor and should be undertaken in every transaction unless there is very good reason to do otherwise, in which case the consequences of their omission should have been fully explained to the client and his instructions to dispense with the searches should for the solicitor's protection preferably be obtained in writing.

In *G & K Ladenbau (UK) Ltd v Crawley and De Reya*[2] the purchaser's solicitors were held to be liable in negligence for having failed to make one of the less usual conveyancing searches, a commons registration search. The implication of the decision in that case is that the solicitor will probably be liable in negligence if he fails to make any of the less usual searches in a situation where such search or searches would have been appropriate. Therefore thought must always be given to the particular nature of the transaction being contemplated and to the situation of the property and where necessary an additional search or searches must be undertaken.

The solicitor's duty to his client extends beyond the mere routine of making the searches and receiving in answer the replies or search certificates. He is under an obligation to pursue thoroughly the answers to his inquiries until he achieves a satisfactory answer which accords with his client's instructions or failing that, he informs the client of the unsatisfactory result of his enquiries and takes the client's further instructions on the point. Liability in negligence to the client will be incurred if the client suffers loss as a result of the solicitor's omission to pursue diligently the search result or inquiry answers.[3]

Even where no problems emerge from the results of searches the solicitor is under a duty to inform the client of the results of the searches and will be liable in negligence if the client suffers loss through this omission.[4]

12

2.2 VENDOR'S SOLICITOR'S LIABILITY

Since the burden of undertaking searches is placed on the purchaser's solicitor it is often assumed that the vendor's solicitor has no responsibility in this area. Liability may, however, arise in relation to the vendor's solicitor's answers to preliminary enquiries where a duty of care is owed to both the vendor and purchaser.

2.2.1 Liability to own client

If the vendor's solicitor gives an erroneous answer to a preliminary enquiry as a result of which the vendor suffers loss, the solicitor may be liable to his client for either breach of contract and/or negligence. It is in order to avoid such liability that some solicitors adopt the practice of sending a copy of the purchaser's enquiries to their client with a request that the vendor fills in the replies himself. The argument supporting this course of action is that the replies as evidenced in writing are the vendor's own, and not those of his solicitor and thus liability in this area is avoided. This argument is probably fallacious since the standard preliminary enquiry form is not phrased in layman's language nor will the average client be familiar with the type of question raised on the form. It is suggested that even where this course of action has been adopted the solicitor might still be liable to his own client for breach of the duty of care in so far as the solicitor has failed to explain to the client the purpose of the enquiries or the nature of the information which the questions are designed to reveal. Where the solicitor does not have sufficient information in his possession to answer the purchaser's enquiries, he should take full instructions from his client. It will not always be possible to take the client's instructions in person and to meet this situation the solicitor may consider sending a 'layman's version' of the enquiry form to the client which, provided the questions are carefully and accurately phrased should ensure that the solicitor has discharged his duty towards his client. (See para 3.5, below for a suggested wording of a layman's version of the enquiry form.)

2.2.2 Liability to purchaser

Although direct liability between the vendor's solicitor and the purchaser is rare, it may exist. Since there is no contractual relationship between these parties any action brought would lie in negligence. A solicitor's duty of care, although not extending to the world at large can extend beyond the duty owed to his own client. This point was established in *Ross v Caunters* [5] and seems to have been followed in *Wilson v Bloomfield* [6] where the defendant's solicitor's application to be struck out as defendants in an action brought by the purchaser was refused by the Court of Appeal. It probably follows from these decisions that the vendor's solicitor's duty of care would also extend to the purchaser's mortgagee, who like the purchaser will be relying on the accuracy of the vendor's preliminary enquiry answers. As a direct result of the *Wilson* case, the wording of the disclaimer printed at the top of the standard preliminary enquiry form was altered so that the disclaimer now contains (inter alia) the following phrase 'These replies are given on behalf of the proposed vendor and without responsibility on the part of his solicitors their partners or employees'. This change in wording is intended to exonerate the vendor's solicitor from liability to the purchaser, but it is suggested that such liability may still exist unless the solicitor takes reasonable steps to ensure that his vendor client is properly advised in relation to answering the enquiries.

2.3 NATURE OF LIABILITY

2.3.1 If either vendor or purchaser establishes liability against his own solicitor the action may lie in contract or in tort for negligence. Contractual damages are awarded on the basis of attempting to place the client in the position in which he would have been had the contract been properly performed and are generally restricted to pure financial loss although an award to compensate for mental distress under the principle established in *Jarvis v Swans Tours Ltd*[7] is now possible in the context of breach of contract between solicitor and client.[8] In contrast to this, tortious damages are assessed on the basis of restoring the client to the position in which he would have been had the act or misfeasance never occurred. It is generally accepted that the tortious rules are more liberal in their approach than their contract counterparts giving a theoretically higher measure of damages in tort, but in the context of the type of action under discussion there would in most cases be little difference in financial terms between the two assessments, thus the quantum of damages is not usually an influential factor in deciding which course of action it is preferable to pursue.

2.3.2 Misrepresentation

The vendor's liability to the purchaser for an erroneous reply to a preliminary enquiry is likely to be founded in misrepresentation, where an action may lie in tort for deceit (fraudulent misrepresentation only) or under the Misrepresentation Act 1967. The tortious action will only succeed if the plaintiff can prove that the defendant made a deliberately dishonest statement within the definition of fraud contained in *Derry v Peek*.[9] Since this burden of proof is a very onerous one to discharge it is likely in most circumstances that the plaintiff will choose to treat the statement as if it were an innocent misrepresentation and to pursue his remedy under the 1967 Act which allows the plaintiff to recover damages unless the defendant can prove that he had grounds for belief and did believe the statement he made was true up until the time the contract was made. Rescission is also available as a remedy under the Act but its award remains subject to the equitable bars and it will not generally be awarded as a remedy unless the effect of the misrepresentation has been to deprive the purchaser of substantially what he contracted to buy. Damages therefore remain the most likely outcome of a successful misrepresentation action and the long standing argument over whether such damages should be assessed on a contractual or on a tortious basis seems now to have been resolved by *Chesneau v Interhome Ltd*[10] where damages, including a sum for loss of enjoyment, analagous to the principle under *Jarvis v Swans Tours Ltd*[11] were awarded on a tortious basis. Contractual clauses which seek to limit or exclude liability for misrepresentation are governed by the Misrepresentation Act 1967, s 3 as amended by the Unfair Contract Terms Act 1977, s 8 which sections only allow such a clause to stand in so far as it satisfies the reasonableness test laid down in the Unfair Contract Terms Act 1977, s 11 and Sch 1. Reasonableness has to be judged in the light of all the circumstances of the case. The test is therefore a subjective one and there is no guarantee that any such exclusion clauses, whether incorporated in a standard form of contract, or a specially drafted clause, will pass the reasonableness test until it has been litigated.

Both the forms of contract in common use contain clauses which attempt to protect the vendor from liability for misrepresentation but neither clause as currently drafted has so far been tested by the courts.

Law Society Condition 7 is widely drafted in favour of the vendor and seeks to limit the vendor's liability to material written statements only. The clause does not differentiate between liability for fraudulent and innocent statements and it is suggested that in certain circumstances this factor may influence the court in deciding against the reasonableness of the clause. National Condition 17 was redrafted following the decision in *Walker v Boyle*[12] where it was held that the exclusion clause incorporated in the previous edition of the National Conditions failed the reasonableness test on the facts of that particular case. It is, however, doubtful whether the rewording of the clause as it now appears in the 20th edition of the National Conditions has added significantly to its strength. However, unlike its Law Society counterpart, the National Condition does not seek to preclude liability for oral statements and the clause does differentiate between fraudulent and innocent statements, both of which factors may be of assistance to a vendor who is seeking to prove the reasonableness of the clause. The disclaimer at the top of the standard form of preliminary enquiries does not form part of a contractual document and is therefore not caught by the Misrepresentation Act 1967, s 3. Despite this immunity the protection afforded by the disclaimer is of dubious value since in *Walker v Boyle*[13] it was held that the vendor could not rely on the wording of the disclaimer to escape liability to the purchaser for the erroneous preliminary enquiry reply.

2.4 LOCAL AUTHORITY'S LIABILITY ON SEARCHES

2.4.1 Local land charges search

A purchaser is bound by a local land charge affecting the land which he is seeking to buy whether or not it is registered at the time when he makes the search and whether or not it is disclosed in any search made by him, but he may in certain circumstances be entitled to compensation from the registering authority if he suffers loss as a consequence of the charge being binding on him. The right to compensation is governed by the Local Land Charges Act 1975, s 10 and the definition of a purchaser in this context will include a lessee, mortgagee or subpurchaser.

Where a material personal search is made compensation is payable where at the relevant time the charge was in existence but not registered. 'Material' means a search which is made by or on behalf of the purchaser who is claiming compensation before the relevant time. 'Relevant time' generally means the date of the contract for the acquisition of the interest in the land, or if there is no contract, the date of the conveyance, lease or other disposition. Where a material official search has been made compensation is payable in respect of a charge not revealed by the search whether or not that charge was registered.

The amount of compensation is limited to the loss sustained by the purchaser but it may include lost expenditure, eg legal fees incurred in claiming compensation.

A few land charges, eg light obstruction notices under Rights of Light Act 1959, are excluded from the compensation provisions of s 10 but if the charge had been registered at the relevant time, and was not disclosed by the search it is possible that an action in negligence could be sustained against the local authority. If however the charge were not registered at the relevant time no claim could be brought against the local authority.

The compensation provisions outlined above are clearly more generous in their application to official searches than to personal searches. Further the official search affords protection to the purchaser's solicitor since s 13 of the Act provides that a solicitor will not be liable in respect of any loss occasioned by reliance on an erroneous official search certificate or an erroneous office copy of an entry in the register.

2.4.2 Additional enquiries

The printed form of additional enquiries contains a clause which excludes the local authority's liability in contract for an erroneous reply. An action in negligence against the authority will lie in respect of loss arising from erroneous replies to the standard printed Part I and Part II enquiries.

Where supplementary questions are asked by the purchaser's solicitor the local authority is free to decide for itself whether to accept liability for the replies or to attempt to exclude liability by means of a separate exclusion clause. The effect of any separate exclusion clause would depend on its wording but it should be remembered that such clauses are narrowly construed by the courts and that express words will need to be used if tortious as well as contractual liability is to be excluded.

2.5 LAND REGISTRY SEARCHES
An official certificate of search issued by the Land Registry is not conclusive in favour of the applicant, but a person who suffers loss through an error in an official search may claim compensation from the Chief Land Registrar.[14] No formal procedure for making the claim exists but the application should be submitted to the Chief Land Registrar giving details of the grounds of the claim and the amount sought in compensation. The time limit for making the claim is six years from the time when the claimant knew or ought to have known of the facts giving rise to the claim. The amount of compensation payable is limited to the value of the loss; the date on which the value is ascertained will depend on whether or not rectification of the register has also taken place. Where an actual loss of land has occurred through an error in an official search it is advisable to support the claim with an estimate of value from a competent valuer.

A personal search in the Land Registry confers no right to compensation.

2.6 CENTRAL LAND CHARGES REGISTRY SEARCHES
An official certificate of search issued by the Central Land Charges Department is conclusive in favour of the applicant provided that a proper search has been made (see ch 34 below). The applicant will therefore take free of any undisclosed charge leaving the loss to fall on the person whose registration was not revealed by the search.

Although the Registrar will in appropriate circumstances accept responsibility for loss caused through entries not being revealed by official search certificates there is no statutory right to compensation. It may, however, be possible to bring an action in negligence against the Registrar.[15]

No liability will attach to the solicitor who made the search provided a correct official search was made.[16]

2.7 OTHER SEARCHES
Except as outlined in the preceding paragraphs no statutory rights to compensation exist in relation to other searches. Where an authority or organisation offers a public search procedure it is suggested that they will owe a common law duty of care to the applicant and thus an action in negligence for breach of that duty might be sustained. Where

2.7 Liability on searches

the authority or organisation operates its search service as a matter of goodwill only, the success of an action in negligence is questionable.

1 (1852) Cox M & H 627, 21 LJQB 292.
2 [1978] 1 All ER 682, [1978] 1 WLR 266.
3 *Computastaff Ltd v Ingledew Brown Bennison and Garrett* (1983) 133 LJ 598.
4 *Lake v Bushby* [1949] 2 All ER 964.
5 [1980] Ch 297, [1979] 3 All ER 580.
6 (1979) 123 SJ 860, CA.
7 [1973] QB 233, [1973] 1 All ER 71, CA.
8 *Heywood v Wellers* [1976] QB 446, [1976] 1 All ER 300, CA.
9 (1889) 14 App Cas 337, 58 LJ Ch 864.
10 (1983) Times, 9 June.
11 [1973] QB 233, [1973] 1 All ER 71, CA.
12 [1982] 1 All ER 634, [1982] 1 WLR 495.
13 [1982] 1 All ER 634, [1982] 1 WLR 495.
14 Land Registration Act 1925, s 83(3).
15 See *Ministry of Housing and Local Government v Sharp* [1970] 2 QB 223, [1970] 1 All ER 1009, CA.
16 Land Charges Act 1972, s 12.

Part II

The usual searches

Chapter 3

Preliminary enquiries of the vendor

3.1 Preliminary enquiries of the vendor are one of the pre-contract searches made by the purchaser's solicitor which fall into the category of 'usual searches' and thus should normally be undertaken in every transaction. The search is usually made on form Con 29 or CONVEY 1 although other forms do exist which cater for particular types of transaction (see paras 3.10–3.14, below). Some solicitors prefer to substitute their own version of preliminary enquiries in place of or in addition to the standard form.

3.2 PURPOSE OF SEARCH
The traditional purpose of this search is to elicit from the vendor information about the property which he is not by law bound to disclose. The vendor's duty of disclosure is principally confined to latent defects in title (para 1.2) and does not in general extend to the disclosure of physical defects in the property. It follows therefore that the main area of investigation at which preliminary enquiries are directed is in relation to the physical qualities of the property. Since the purchaser's enquiries are directed at matters which the vendor is under no legal obligation to disclose it also follows that the vendor would in law be entitled to refuse to answer the purchaser's questions and to insist that the purchaser makes his own independent enquiries about the property. It would, however, be extremely unusual for the vendor to take such an attitude towards preliminary enquiries and his refusal to reply might be construed as an attempt to conceal defects in the property which could in turn result in the purchaser withdrawing from the transaction. A more modern explanation of the function of preliminary enquiries would be to say that their purpose is to discover information about the physical qualities of and amenities enjoyed by the property which might affect the purchaser's decision to proceed with his purchase. Whichever view is taken of the purpose of preliminary enquiries it is clear that their primary function is in connection with the physical state of the property and they should not be used as a vehicle for raising queries about the vendor's legal title although in practice it is common to find that questions arising out of the form of the draft contract have been added as supplementary questions on the standard form.

3.3 APPROACH TO PRELIMINARY ENQUIRIES

3.3.1 Purchaser's solicitor

The procedure of raising preliminary enquiries is sometimes regarded by the purchaser's solicitor as a routine operation which serves little useful purpose in the context of the conveyancing transaction as a whole, and two copies of the standard form are submitted to the vendor's solicitor with little thought as to the relevance of the questions on that form or to the necessity for raising supplementary questions. In all cases questions which are clearly inapplicable to the nature of the transaction being undertaken should be deleted from the standard form, to save the vendor from having to spend time in answering irrelevant questions. Similarly questions to which the answer is already known or is not needed to be known should be deleted. Some thought should be given to the raising of supplementary questions which are pertinent to the particular transaction. Attention should be directed towards any peculiarities in the neighbourhood of the property, eg rivers, railways, industrial premises, and any peculiarities in the property itself, eg the age of the property, its occupiers, availability of services. A discussion of Con 29 (supplementary) which deals with additional enquiries is contained in para 3.8, below and of additional questions not appearing on the printed forms of enquiry in para 3.10, below. Although the purchaser's desire to obtain as much information as possible about the property is understandable, some restraint should be exercised in the area of supplementary questions and these should be raised only in connection with matters which are relevant to the particular property being purchased. The practice of appending several pages of supplementary questions in every transaction is not appreciated by the vendor's solicitor who has to answer them. Neither should preliminary enquiries be used as a general fishing expedition to obtain information which could readily be obtained elsewhere; for example questions relating to the structural state of the property could be resolved by obtaining a surveyor's report, and since questions of this nature are unlikely to elicit more than a very guarded reply from the vendor, little seems to be achieved by asking them.

Although theoretically preliminary enquiries should not be raised in connection with matters affecting the vendor's legal title to the property, the standard forms of preliminary enquiry do provide a useful medium through which to raise queries relating to the form of the draft contract, and it is probably sensible to postpone the raising of preliminary enquiries until such time as the draft contract is received since some matters which will form the basis of valid supplementary enquiries will only come to light on perusal of this document.

3.3.2 Vendor's solicitor

The vendor's solicitor's approach to answering preliminary enquiries must of necessity be a cautious one, bearing in mind his own and his client's potential liability in misrepresentation for erroneous replies (see para 2.2, above). It would, however, be wrong to take the view that the protection of the client from such liability was the prime objective in answering the purchaser's questions. To do so would be to defeat the object of the enquiries and to render the whole procedure useless from the purchaser's point of view. Since the vendor's solicitor must be fully aware from the outset of the transaction that he will be asked to answer the purchaser's queries about the property he should take steps when taking instructions from his client to ensure that his instructions cover the subject matter of the questions which will inevitably be raised on the standard form. It should then be possible to give the purchaser clear and unambiguous answers to the questions without fear of liability in misrepresentation. The practice of sending the standard preliminary enquiry form to the client with a request that the client fills in the replies is not to be advocated since the nature and wording of many of the questions on the standard form may be misleading to the vendor client unless their context is explained clearly to him. Where it is not possible to obtain the client's instructions in person a possible solution is for the vendor's solicitor to prepare a layman's version of the enquiry form to be sent to the client, and then to construct the answers to the preliminary enquiry form from the information supplied by the client (see para 3.5.20, below). Where supplementary questions are raised by the purchaser, the vendor's specific instructions should be obtained before a reply is made, unless the answer to the supplementary question is clear from information already in the solicitor's possession.

Since the procedure of the submission of and reply to preliminary enquiries is a routine step in the normal conveyancing transaction, the vendor's solicitor would both assist the purchaser and help to minimise delay in the transaction if he were prepared to send the answers to the standard form of preliminary enquiries to the purchaser at the same time as the draft contract is submitted to him; any supplementary matter could be dealt with later.

3.4 FORM CON 29 (LONG)
This form is reproduced on pp 24–27, below.

3.4 *Preliminary enquiries of the vendor*

re...

Parties ....

to...

ENQUIRIES

BEFORE CONTRACT

In cases of property subject to a
tenancy, forms **Con 291** (general
business and residential tenancies)
or **Con 292** (agricultural tenancies)
should also be used.

**These enquiries are copyright
and may not be reproduced**

Replies are requested to the following enquiries.

**Please strike out enquiries
which are not applicable**

The replies are as follows.

....

Proposed purchaser's solicitors.

Date.. 198 ....

GENERAL ENQUIRIES

....

Proposed vendor's solicitors.

Date.. 198...

REPLIES

These replies, except in the case of any enquiry expressly requiring a reply
from the Vendor's solicitors, are given on behalf of the proposed Vendor
and without responsibility on the part of his solicitors their partners or
employees. They are believed to be correct but the accuracy is not
guaranteed and they do not obviate the need to make appropriate
searches, enquiries and inspections.

1. Boundaries

(A) To whom do all the boundary walls, fences, hedges and ditches
belong?

(B) If no definite indications exist, which has the Vendor maintained or
regarded as his responsibility?

2. Disputes

(A) Is the Vendor aware of any past or current disputes regarding
boundaries, easements, covenants or other matters relating to the
property or its use?

(B) During the last three years, has the Vendor complained or had
cause to complain about the state and condition, or the manner of
use, of any adjoining or neighbouring property? If so, please give
particulars.

3. Notices

Please give particulars of all notices relating to the property, or to
matters likely to affect its use or enjoyment, that the Vendor (or to his
knowledge, any predecessor in title) has given or received.

4. Guarantees etc.

(A) Please supply a copy of any of the following of which the
Purchaser is to have the benefit:

agreement, covenant, guarantee, warranty, bond, certificate,
indemnity and insurance policy,
relating to any of the following matters:

the construction of the property, or any part of it, or of any
building of which it forms part;
any repair or replacement of, or treatment or improvement to the
fabric of the property;
the maintenance of any accessway;
the construction costs of any road (including lighting, drainage
and crossovers) to which the property fronts, and the charges for
adopting any such road as maintainable at the public expense;
a defective title;
breach of any restrictive covenant.

(B) (i) What defects or other matters have become apparent, or
adverse claims have been made by third parties, which might give
rise to a claim under any document mentioned in (A)?
(ii) Has notice of such defect, matter or adverse claim been
given? If so, please give particulars.
(iii) Please give particulars of all such claims already made,
whether or not already settled.

LEASEHOLD ENQUIRIES

1. General

(A) Is the lease under which the property is held a head lease or an underlease?

(B) Please state the names and addresses of the lessor, any superior lessors, their respective solicitors, and the receivers of the rent.

(C) Please supply copies of all licences granted by the lessor, other than licences to assign.

(D) What steps have been taken to obtain the lessor's consent to the proposed assignment? Please supply a copy of any licence granted.

II. Covenants

(A) Has the lessor complained of any breach of covenant?

(B) Has any obligation in the lease to paint or do any other work by or at a particular time been strictly fulfilled? If not, please give details.

(C) Has the Vendor had cause to complain of any breach of the lessor's covenants?

III. Service Charge

(A) Please give details of service charge payments for the last three years, with any supporting accounts or vouchers that the Vendor has.

(B) Has the Vendor, or to his knowledge any predecessor in title, exercised a statutory right to obtain information? If so, with what result?

IV. Insurance

(A) Who effected the insurance policy currently covering the property?

(B) Please give particulars: insurers' and any insurance brokers' name and address, policy number, insured's name(s), risks covered, for what amount, premium, and date to which the property is insured.

V. Reversionary Title

Is there with the title deeds a marked abstract or office copy of the freehold title and of any superior lease?

ADDITIONAL ENQUIRIES

© 1984 **oyez** The Solicitors' Law Stationery Society plc, Oyez House, 237 Long Lane, London SE1 4PU

Conveyancing 29 (Long)

Revised 9-84 F4278
* * * * *

25

5. Services

(A) Does the property have drainage, water, electricity and gas services? Which of them are connected to the mains?

(B) Is the water supply metered?

(C) Do any of the services (except where part of the mains) pass through or over property not included in the sale?

(D) If so, please give details of route and particulars of any easement, grant, exception, reservation, wayleave, licence or consent authorising this.

(E) Please supply a copy of any licence to abstract water and of any consent or licence relating to drainage, issued in respect of the property or the activities carried on there.

6. Facilities

(A) Except in the case of public rights or where particulars have already been given, what rights are there for the use of the following facilities, whether enjoyed by the owner or occupier of the property, or over the property for the benefit of other property:

- — Access for light and air;
- — Access for pedestrians and vehicles;
- — Emergency escape routes;
- — Pipes and wires for services not dealt with in Enquiry 5.
- — Access and facilities for repair, maintenance and replacement.

Please supply copies of any relevant documents.

(B) Has any person taken any action to stop (whether immediately or at some future time) the use of any facility? If so, please give particulars.

(C) In respect of maintenance, repair or replacement work on any land or fixtures affording any facility:

(i) What work has been done by the Vendor (or, to his knowledge, any predecessor in title), and when?

(ii) What work has the Vendor been called upon to do which has not yet been done?

(iii) What sums has the Vendor contributed to work done by others, and when? Is any demand for such sums still outstanding?

(iv) What sums has the Vendor called upon others to contribute, and when? Is any demand still outstanding?

7. Adverse Rights

(A) Is the Vendor aware of any rights or informal arrangements specifically affecting the property, other than any disclosed in the draft contract or immediately apparent on inspection, which are exercisable by virtue of an easement, grant, wayleave, licence, consent, agreement relating to an ancient monument or land near it, or otherwise or which are in the nature of public or common rights?

(B) (i) Please give the full names, and ages if under 18, of all persons in actual occupation of the property.

(ii) What legal or equitable interest in the property has each of those persons?

(C) Is the Vendor aware of any other overriding interests as defined by the Land Registration Act 1925, s. 70(1)?

8. Restrictions

(A) Have all restrictions affecting the property or its use been observed up to the date hereof? If not, please give details.

(B) Where such restrictions have in the past required any person's consent or approval of plans, does the Vendor have written evidence of that consent or approval?

9. Planning etc.

(A) (i) When did the present use of the property commence?

(ii) Has this use been continuous since it commenced?

(B) During the four years immediately prior to receipt of these enquiries:

(i) Were any of the buildings on the property erected, or have any been altered or added to?

(ii) Have any other building, engineering, mining or other operations been carried out in, on, over or under the property?

(iii) Has any condition or limitation on any planning permission not been complied with?

If so, please give details.

(C) Please supply a copy of:

(i) Any planning permission authorising or imposing conditions upon the present use of the property, and the erection or retention of the buildings now on it.

(ii) Any bye-law approval or building regulation consent relating to those buildings.

(iii) Any current fire certificate.

10. Fixtures, Fittings etc.

(A) Does the sale include all of the following items now on the property, and attached to or growing in it?

Trees, shrubs, plants, flowers, and garden produce. Greenhouses, garden sheds and garden ornaments. Aerials. Fitted furniture and shelves. Electric switches, points and wall and ceiling fittings.

(B) What fixtures and fittings affixed to the property are not included in the sale?

(C) If the property has any fixed oil burning appliance, what arrangements are proposed for the sale to the purchaser on completion of any stock of oil?

11. Outgoings

(A) (i) What is the rateable value of the property?

(ii) Have any works been carried out at the property which might result in a revision of this?

(B) Does the hereditament, in which the property to be sold is included for rating purposes, also include any other property?

(C) What annual or periodic charges, other than general and water rates, affect the property or its occupier?

12. Completion

(A) How long after exchange of contracts will the Vendor be able to give vacant possession of the whole of the property?

(B) The Purchaser's solicitors wish to complete by adopting the Law Society's Code for Completion by Post (1984 edition). Do the Vendor's solicitors agree?

13. Development Land Tax

Is the usual place of abode of the Vendor, or any other person disposing of an interest for the purposes of the Development Land Tax Act 1976, outside the United Kingdom?

14. New Properties

(A) Will the Vendor pay all charges for construction and connection of the drainage system and the services?

(B) Are all the following included in the purchase price: fencing all boundaries, laying all paths and drives, and levelling and clearing the garden area? If not, please give particulars.

ADDITIONAL ENQUIRIES

For Leasehold Enquiries and further Additional Enquiries see over

27

3.5 COMMENT ON FORM CON 29 (LONG)

3.5.1 This version of the preliminary enquiry form is frequently used in practice. The form should be completed in duplicate with any supplementary questions typed in the space provided on the reverse of the form (or on a separate sheet of paper if necessary) and irrelevant enquiries deleted.

3.5.2 Although the standard form bears a disclaimer of liability the disclaimer has to be treated as a non-contractual exclusion clause and as such is subject to the reasonableness test contained in the Unfair Contract Terms Act 1977, s 11. The wording of the disclaimer has been altered since the decision in *Wilson v Bloomfield*[1] but it is doubtful whether the amended form of wording affects the liability of the vendor, and care should be exercised in replying to the enquiries in order to avoid liability in either misrepresentation or negligence.

3.5.3 An analysis of the questions on the standard form appears in the following sub-paragraphs.

3.5.4 Boundaries
3.5.4.1

> 1. Boundaries
> (A) To whom do all the boundary walls, fences, hedges and ditches belong?
> (B) If no definite indications exist, which has the Vendor maintained or regarded as his responsibility?

3.5.4.2 Unless clear evidence of the ownership of boundaries is shown in the title deeds, and copies of the relevant documents have already been supplied to the purchaser, the vendor should endeavour to answer this question in specific terms.

Where evidence relating to the ownership of the boundaries is unclear some thought may be given to the application of the common law presumptions (see ch 25, below).

3.5.4.3 Both Law Society Condition 13 and National Condition 13 relieve the vendor of his obligation precisely to define the extent of his boundaries. It is therefore essential that the purchaser obtains all necessary information relating to boundaries before exchange of contracts since by virtue of both the above mentioned conditions he will be precluded from raising queries about the boundaries to the property once contracts have been exchanged.

3.5.5 Disputes
3.5.5.1

2. Disputes
(A) Is the Vendor aware of any past or current disputes regarding boundaries, easements, covenants or other matters relating to the property or its use?
(b) During the last three years, has the Vendor complained or had cause to complain about the state and condition, or the manner of use, of any adjoining or neighbouring property? If so, please give particulars.

3.5.5.2 Although the vendor may be reticent to disclose details of past or present disputes relating to the property it should be borne in mind that failure to disclose such matters may lead to liability in misrepresentation, or at worst to the rescission of the contract. Information revealed in response to part (B) of the question might affect the purchaser's decision to proceed with his purchase and would be particularly relevant to the purchase of a flat or a house in a high density development.

3.5.6 Notices
3.5.6.1

3. Notices
Please give particulars of all notices relating to the property, or to matters likely to affect its use or enjoyment, that the Vendor (or to his knowledge, any predecessor in title) has given or received

3.5.6.2 This question is extremely widely drafted and in the form of wording printed above could refer to anything from a rates demand to a notice received relating to a planning application affecting a neighbouring property. To safeguard the vendor all notices, however irrelevant they may seem, should be disclosed in answer to this question. It should also be noted that the question encompasses notices given by the vendor as well as those received by him.

3.5.6.3 *Examples of notices where rights be revealed in response to this question*
(a) rate demands;
(b) notice of planning application affecting a neighbouring property;
(c) notice of listing of a building as of architectural or historic interest;
(d) enforcement or stop notices under the Town and Country Planning Act 1971;
(e) notice of draft compulsory purchase order or notice to treat;
(f) purchase or blight notices;

(g) notice to abate a statutory nuisance;

(h) notice of intention to carry out work under the Building Regulations;

(i) notice requiring the provision of maintenance of sanitary appliances at places of entertainment;

(j) notice to repair an unfit house, or closing order;

(k) notice requiring a fire certificate;

(l) notice to quit (tenanted property);

(m) notice to exercise option;

(n) notice under the Law of Property Act 1925, s 146 (breach of covenant, leasehold property);

(o) notice to operate rent review (leasehold property);

(p) notice exercising rights under the Leasehold Reform Act 1967;

(q) notice to terminate a business tenancy under the Landlord and Tenant Act 1954, Part II;

(r) notice of increase in rent;

(s) tenant's counter-notice under the Leasehold Property (Repairs) Act 1938;

(t) notice that mandatory grounds for possession may apply (regulated tenancies under the Rent Act 1977);

(u) notice to effect improvements (leasehold property).

3.5.7 Guarantees etc
3.5.7.1

4. Guarantees etc.

(A) Please supply a copy of any of the following of which the Purchaser is to have the benefit:

agreement, covenant, guarantee, warranty, bond, certificate, indemnity and insurance policy;

relating to any of the following matters;

the construction of the property, or any part of it, or of any building of which it forms part;

any repair or replacement of, or treatment or improvement to the fabric of the property;

the maintenance of any accessway;

the construction costs of any road (including lighting, drainage and crossovers) to which the property fronts, and the charges for adopting any such road as maintainable at the public expense;

a defective title;

breach of any restrictive covenant.

(B) (i) What defects or other matters have become apparent, or adverse claims have been made by third parties, which might give rise to a claim under any document mentioned in (A)?

(ii) Has notice of such defect, matter or adverse claim been given? If so, please give particulars.

(iii) **Please give particulars of all such claims already made, whether or not already settled**

3.5.7.2 This question requires the vendor to supply the purchaser with a copy of any document which relates to the construction of or repair to the fabric of the property including guarantees and certificates issued in respect of such matters as woodworm and dry rot treatment, but does not include planning consent which is separately dealt with in question 9 (para 3.5.12, below).

An insurance policy covering a defective title or breach of a restrictive covenant must also be disclosed. The question relates to the construction of sewers underneath roads serving the property, but not to the construction of the sewers serving the property itself.

3.5.7.3 *NHBC Scheme*
Most builders of new dwellings are registered with the National House Builders Council whose minimum standards of building must be adhered to in the construction of the dwelling. Where the builder is so registered the purchaser will receive the benefit of the NHBC Scheme which in effect provides an insurance policy against structural defects in the property for the first ten years after its completion in the event of the insolvency of the builder. Question 4 (A) is therefore of relevance to the purchaser of a house which is currently under construction or which has been erected within the past few years since the benefit of the policy can be assigned to a subsequent purchaser. The question does not deal with the assignment of the policy to a second or subsequent purchaser of a recently erected dwelling and a supplementary question may be raised in connection with this although in practice the NHBC will allow a subsequent purchaser to take the benefit of a policy despite lack of formal assignment. The formal assignment of the policy should be executed on form HB12. Most building societies insist on the property being covered by the NHBC Scheme as a condition of granting a mortgage for the purchase of a dwelling which is under construction. Although this requirement is not so stringently enforced in relation to subsequent purchasers the existence of an NHBC policy does provide a safeguard for the subsequent purchaser and the absence of such a policy should be investigated. The NHBC Scheme does not apply to converted properties.

3.5.7.4 The details of any insurance policy, indemnity or guarantee revealed in response to question 4 (A) should be checked to ensure the cover provided is adequate. Policies and guarantees are normally assignable and notice of the assignment should be given to the insurers or guarantors.

3.5.7.5 Question 4 (A) also relates to the maintenance of private rights of way. In the absence of express provision in the deeds the common law places no obligation to repair on either the grantor or grantee of the right.

3.5.7.6 An agreement and supporting bond under the Highways Act 1980, s 38 is normally to be expected in connection with a property which is in the course of construction or which has recently been built, since the local highway authority will frequently not formally adopt the road until all construction works on the site have been completed and the road has been maintained by the developer for a period of one year. The existence of the agreement and the adequacy of the bond should be checked, although in practice it may be difficult to ascertain whether the amount secured by the bond is adequate to cover the cost of the outstanding roadworks. The absence of an agreement or bond in such a situation may involve the purchaser in maintenance payments for the road. The reply to this question may also be checked against the replies to the additional enquiries of the local authority where question 1 (para 5.9.1, below) also enquires as to the existence of such an agreement and bond. The bond is made in favour of the highway authority and is only enforceable by that authority.

3.5.7.7 The disclosure of any defects or claims in response to part (B) of the question will obviously be of concern to the purchaser and any information revealed should be carefully investigated.

3.5.8 Services
3.5.8.1

5. Services
(A) Does the property have drainage, water, electricity and gas services? Which of them are connected to the mains?
(B) Is the water supply metered?
(C) Do any of the services (except where part of the mains) pass through or over property not included in the sale?
(D) If so, please give details of route and particulars of any easement, grant, exception, reservation, wayleave, licence or consent authorising this.
(E) Please supply a copy of any licence to abstract water and of any consent or licence relating to drainage, issued in respect of the property or the activities carried on there.

3.5.8.2 The information relating to part (A) of this question is purely factual but the lack of a mains supply to one of the essential services may be of concern to the purchaser and should be reported to him. Information relating to the drainage of the property will also be detailed in response to question 5 on the standard form of additional enquiries of the local authority (para 5.9.5, below). Where mains services are not available the land owner can frequently insist on a connection to mains services being made by the public authority concerned but may have to contribute towards the cost of the connection. The route of the service is often unknown to the vendor but may sometimes be discovered on a full structural survey of the property or by making enquiries of the appropriate statutory bodies (see chs 21 and 22, below). Where the route of services passes through a neighbouring property difficulty is sometimes encountered in the maintenance of the pipeline or cable, and in some cases there may be a liability on the landowner to contribute towards the cost of maintenance.

3.5.8.3 Where a water supply is metered the owner will pay for his water supply according to the amount of water used. Few domestic properties are currently metered.

3.5.8.4 A licence is needed under the Water Resources Act 1963 in order to abstract water from its natural source in, eg a well or a river, but this requirement does not apply to the abstraction of water for domestic purposes. The licence can usually be assigned to the purchaser provided that notice of the assignment is given to the water authority within one month of the change of ownership. Failure to notify renders the licence void and there is no guarantee that a new licence will be granted to the purchaser (see ch 21, below).

3.5.9 Facilities
3.5.9.1

6. Facilities

(A) Except in the case of public rights or where particulars have already been given, what rights are there for the use of the following facilities, whether enjoyed by the owner or occupier of the property, or over the property for the benefit of other property:

—Access for light and air;
—Access for pedestrians and vehicles;
—Emergency escape routes;
—Pipes and wires for services not dealt with in Enquiry 5;
—Access and facilities for repair, maintenance and replacement.

Please supply copies of any relevant documents.

(B) Has any person taken any action to stop (whether immediately or at some future time) the use of any facility? If so, please give particulars.

(C) In respect of maintenance, repair or replacement work on any land or fixtures affording any facility:

(i) What work has been done by the Vendor (or, to his knowledge, any predecessor in title), and when?
(ii) What work has the Vendor been called upon to do which has not yet been done?
(iii) What sums has the Vendor contributed to work done by others, and when? Is any demand for such sums still outstanding?
(iv) What sums has the Vendor called upon others to contribute, and when? Is any demand still outstanding?

3.5.9.2 The vendor is requested by this question to disclose whether any of the rights mentioned in the question, whether exclusively enjoyed by the property or shared with another property, are the subject of any licence, agreement, easements or prescriptive rights. If the purchaser intends to develop the property he will be concerned to ensure that no third party has rights over the property which may impede his development plans. Where a property is built close to the boundaries of its own land it may be necessary to have a right of access to a neighbouring property in order to effect repairs to parts of the building which are close to the boundary. Although the wording of the question would encompass this situation it may be prudent to raise a specific additional enquiry relating to this matter in order to draw it to the vendor's attention.

3.5.9.3 Whatever rights and liabilities are disclosed in response to the question the purchaser should consider the following points:

(a) the extent of the rights enjoyed and whether they are sufficient for his intended use of the property;

(b) whether the rights are capable of being terminated or curtailed by a third party;

(c) who is responsible and to what extent for maintenance, repairs etc.;

(d) the cost of maintenance and repairs.

3.5.9.4 Where a right of way is granted 'for all purposes', its use may be changed or altered from its present use provided that the new user does not unreasonably interfere with the enjoyment of the rights by others who are entitled to use it.[2] One user of a shared right of way may have a right against the other for obstruction but not for damage to the surface.[3] The benefit of the user of a right of way or other shared facility may be, and frequently is, made dependent on contributing towards its maintenance.[4]

3.5.10 Adverse rights
3.5.10.1

7. Adverse Rights

(A) Is the Vendor aware of any rights or informal arrangements specificially affecting the property, other than any disclosed in the draft contract or immediately apparent on inspection, which are exercisable by virtue of an easement, grant, wayleave, licence, consent, agreement relating to an ancient monument or land near it, or otherwise or which are in the nature of public or common rights?

(B) (i) Please give the full names, and ages if under 18, of all persons in actual occupation of the property.

(ii) What legal or equitable interest in the property has each of those persons?

(C) Is the Vendor aware of any other overriding interests as defined by the Land Registration Act 1925, s 70(1)?

3.5.10.2 The vendor is required by the wording of this question to disclose details of any adverse rights affecting the property of which he is aware. This question has been the focus of much attention since the case of *Williams & Glyn's Bank Ltd v Boland.*[5] It seems to be widely accepted that the implications of the *Boland* decision extend beyond the registered land context in which that case was set; obviously the concept of an overriding interest has no direct parallel in unregistered conveyancing, but what can and may exist in the unregistered situation is an equitable interest in favour of a non-owning spouse or other occupier. As regards registered land, the Land Registration Act 1925, s 70(1)(g) says that the purchaser is bound by the rights of every person in actual occupation of the land except where enquiry is made of that person and the rights are not disclosed. In unregistered land, the doctrine of constructive notice applies, and in the light of the *Williams & Glyn's* decision it is possible that the judiciary may decide to interpret the doctrine of constructive notice to produce a result which is analogous to that now pertaining to registered land. A distinction between the two situations is that the unregistered equitable interest can at least be overreached provided that the purchase price is paid to two trustees, whilst the overriding interest probably cannot. Thus in either situation it is vital to have precise information about the occupants of the premises and their status so that the appropriate steps may be taken in the contract to deal with the problem.

The Law Commission report on *Boland*[6] suggested that to be effective all such interests should be protected by registration but there is as yet no sign that these proposals are to be enacted. The printed question mainly focuses attention on the equitable or overriding interest problems and does not deal with registrable interests under the Matrimonial Homes Act 1983. A pertinent supplementary question, if it can be tactfully worded, would be to enquire as to the existence or likelihood of a registration under this Act.[7] As it stands, the printed question simply refers to overriding interests as defined by the Land Registration Act 1925, s 70(1). That definition encompasses a wide variety of third party interests including local land charges, knowledge of which is fixed on the purchaser by the Law of Property Act 1925, s 198. The vendor in reply to this question may therefore choose to exclude his liability to disclose registered local land charges and refer the purchaser to his local search.

3.5.10.3 A list of overriding interests as shown in the Land Registration Act 1925, s 70(1) is set out below:

(a) rights of common, drainage rights, customary rights (until extinguished), public rights, profits à prendre, rights of sheepwalk, rights of way, watercourses, rights of water, and óther easements not being equitable easements required to be protected by notice on the register;

(b) liability to repair highways by reason of tenure, quit-rents, crown rents, heriots, and other rents and charges (until extinguished) having their origin in tenure;

(c) liability to repair the chancel of any church;

(d) liability in respect of embankments, and sea and river walls;

(e) payments in lieu of tithe, and charges or annuities payable for the redemption of tithe rentcharges;

(f) subject to the provisions of that Act, rights acquired or in the course of being acquired under the Limitation Acts;

(g) the rights of every person in actual occupation of the land, or in receipt of the rents and profits thereof, save where enquiry is made of such person and the rights are not disclosed;

(h) in the case of possessory, qualified or good leasehold title, all estates, rights, interests, and powers excepted from the effect of registration;

(i) rights under local land charges unless and until registered or protected on the register in the prescribed manner;

(j) rights of fishing and sporting, seignorial and manorial rights of all descriptions (until extinguished), and franchises;

(k) leases for any term or interest not exceeding 21 years, granted at a rent without taking a fine;

(l) in respect of land registered before 1 January 1926, rights to mines and minerals, and rights of entry, search, and user, and other rights and reservations incidental to or required for the purpose of giving full effect to the enjoyment of rights to mines and minerals or of property in mines or minerals, being rights which, where the title was first registered before 1 January 1898, were created before that date, and where the title was first registered after 31 December 1897, were created before the date of first registration.

3.5.11 Restrictions
3.5.11.1

8. Restrictions

(A) Have all restrictions affecting the property or its use been observed up to the date hereof? If not, please give details.

(B) Where such restrictions have in the past required any person's consent or approval of plans, does the Vendor have written evidence of that consent or approval?

3.5.11.2 The question on restrictions is generally understood as referring to restrictive covenants but as worded its scope is wider than this and would also include tenant's covenants, planning restrictions and other statutory restrictions on the use of the property, examples of which are listed below:

(a) prohibition of a particular use of the property under the terms of a closing order or fire certificate;

(b) prohibition of use of a property which is normally used for the preparation or handling of food where the premises fall below the prescribed hygiene standards;

   (c) restrictions imposed in the interests of air safety;

   (d) conditions attached to a licence to store petroleum.

3.5.11.3 Details of the restrictions and of any non-observance revealed in response to this question should be investigated. Restrictive covenants other than those between landlord and tenant affecting unregistered land which were entered into before 1926 depend for their enforceability against a purchaser on the doctrine of notice. Such covenants which were entered into since 1925 are enforceable against a purchaser only if registered as class D(ii) land charges and a central land charges search may be made either at this stage of the transaction or shortly before completion to check whether or not the covenants have been registered (see ch 34, below). Restrictive covenants affecting registered land will be set out in the charges register of the title.

3.5.12 Planning
3.5.12.1

  9. Planning etc.

  (A) (i) When did the present use of the property commence?

     (ii) Has this use been continuous since it commenced?

  (B) During the four years immediately prior to receipt of these enquiries:

     (i) Were any of the buildings on the property erected, or have any been altered or added to?

     (ii) Have any other building, engineering, mining or other operations been carried out in, on, over or under the property?

     (iii) Has any condition or limitation on any planning permission not been complied with?

If so, please give details.

  (C) Please supply a copy of:

     (i) Any planning permission authorising or imposing conditions upon the present use of the property, and the erection or retention of the buildings now on it.

     (ii) Any bye-law approval or building regulation consent relating to those buildings.

     (iii) Any current fire certificate.

3.5.12.2 Any 'development' of land, the definition of which, contained in the Town and Country Planning Act 1971 s 22, includes both building works and the change of use of land, prima facia requires planning permission. Since the penalities for breach of planning control are stringent the answers to this question are of vital concern to any purchaser and the information revealed in response to the question should be checked against the answers to the planning enquiries on the local search (ch 4, below) and on the form of additional enquiries of the local authority (para 5.9, below).

3.5.12.3   Fire certificates are required for most hotels and boarding houses, factories, shops, offices and railway premises.

3.5.13   Fixtures, fittings etc
3.5.13.1

> 10. Fixtures, Fittings etc.
> (A) Does the sale include all of the following items now on the property, and attached to or growing in it?
> Trees, shrubs, plants, flowers, and garden produce. Greenhouses, garden sheds and garden ornaments. Aerials. Fitted furniture and shelves. Electric switches, points and wall and ceiling fittings.
> (B) What fixtures and fittings affixed to the property are not included in the sale?
> (C) If the property has any fixed oil burning appliance, what arrangements are proposed for the sale to the purchaser on completion of any stock of oil?

3.5.13.2   The removal of fixtures and fittings by the vendor gives rise to a frequent source of contention between the parties and it is an area where the costs of litigation will usually outweigh the value of the disputed fittings. It is therefore important to define clearly as between the parties, which items presently attached to the property will be included in the sale and which will be removed. Although legal definitions of both 'fixtures' and 'fittings' exist it is not always easy to say with certainty into which category a particular item falls.

As a general guideline fixtures are items which are either secured to the land or to the structure of the building and which automatically pass to the purchaser unless the vendor expressly reserves the right to remove them. Fittings are not attached to the structure and the vendor has the right to remove them unless he has agreed not to do so. These general guidelines are not easy to apply in practice to, eg a bathroom cabinet or mirror which is actually fixed to the wall.

There is also some legal doubt as to the status of such items as external television aerials and garden ornaments which have been held variously in decided cases to come within either classification. In order to avoid future contention it should be made quite clear which items the vendor does intend to remove and which items are to remain on the property for the purchaser's benefit, and if required a special condition may be added to the contract to deal with this matter. The purchaser's solicitor, in taking instructions from his client should ascertain from his client the nature of any items within the broad definition of 'fixtures and fittings' which the client does expect to be left at the property, and if such items are not included in the list contained in this question a specific additional preliminary enquiry should be raised.

Where fittings are to be included in the purchase price of the property it is common for a small proportion of the price to be apportioned to represent the value of the fittings. Where such an apportionment is desired and has not been made on the draft contract it is courteous to seek the vendor's consent to the amendment. This may be dealt with by raising a supplementary preliminary enquiry. The standard enquiry deals with the purchase of any stock of oil on the premises. Where relevant the question could be amended to apply to stocks of coal, calor gas or logs. Form Q3 (reproduced in Appendix IV, post) may be used to ascertain from the client which fixtures and fittings are intended to be included in or excluded from the sale.

3.5.14 Outgoings
3.5.14.1

> 11. Outgoings
> (A) (i) What is the rateable value of the property?
> (ii) Have any works been carried out at the property which might result in a revision of this?
> (B) Does the hereditament, in which the property to be sold is included for rating purposes, also include any other property?
> (C) What annual or periodic charges, other than general and water rates, affect the property or its occupier?

3.5.14.2 Improvements which have been made to the property, for example the addition of a garage, are likely to affect the rateable value of the property. The valuation officer may seek to increase the rateable value of the property by making a proposal to alter the valuation list at any time, except where the alterations to the premises were necessitated for the installation of a central heating system or where the proposed increase in the gross value would not exceed £30.

The answer to this question should therefore be read in conjunction with the information supplied in answer to question 9 and where recent improvements or alterations have been made to the property it should be borne in mind that a reassessment of the rateable value may be made.

3.5.14.3 Where a property is for rating purposes treated as part of a larger property and is not separately assessed, the occupier of part of the property may in some circumstances be liable for the rates for the whole property. The ratepayer may at any time make application to have the individual parts of the property separately rated.

3.5.14.4 Examples of annual or periodic charges affecting the property would include the following:

(a) rent and service charge and other payments reserved by a lease;
(b) water rates;
(c) drainage charges;
(d) annual maintenance charges in respect of a private road or foot-path.

3.5.14.5 Since water rates and sewerage charges are now assessed and collected separately from general rates, and can constitute a heavy annual charge on the property it may be pertinent to raise a specific supplementary question asking the amount of such payments.

3.5.15 Completion
3.5.15.1

12. Completion
(A) How long after exchange of contracts will the Vendor be able to give vacant possession of the whole of the property?
(B) The Purchaser's solicitors wish to complete by adopting the Law Society's Code for Completion by Post (1984 edition). Do the Vendor's solicitors agree?

3.5.15.2 The question on vacant possession is rarely capable of being precisely answered by the vendor at this stage of the transaction. Where vacant possession is to be given the contract normally makes express provision for vacant possession to be given on completion; the date of completion being arranged shortly before exchange of contracts and inserted in the contract itself.

3.5.15.3 It is unlikely that the purchaser's solicitor will know at this stage in the transaction whether he will wish to complete through the post and part (B) of this question may be more appropriately raised as a requisition on title. For information purposes the text of the Law Society's code for completion by post is set out below.

3.5.15.4 The Law Society's Code for Completion by Post (1984 Edition). The following was published in The Law Society's Gazette of Wednesday, March 28, 1984, at pages 858 and 859.

> 'As was announced in [1983] *Gazette*, 16 November, 2882, The Society's Land Law and Conveyancing Committee have been considering completion practice, where the purchaser's solicitor does not attend at the vendor's solicitor's office. In doing so, they have taken account of the Privy Council case of *Edward Wong Finance Co Ltd v Johnson, Stokes and Master*, originally reported in [1983] *The Times*, 8 November and later in [1984] 2 WLR 1.
>
> That case concerned a finding of negligence against a firm of solicitors in Hong Kong where, in accordance with the general practice of the profession in Hong Kong, solicitors acting for a mortgagee paid over the advance money to the vendors' solicitors against his undertaking to forward the documents of title. The vendors' solicitors absconded with the money and the mortgagee's solicitors were held to be negligent.

The Law Society's code for completion by post (1984 edition) ("the code") has now been approved for publication by the Council's Non-Contentious Business Committee and is set out below. The attention of practitioners is drawn, in particular, to the notes that are published with it.

The Law Society's Code for Completion by Post (1984 Edition)

Preamble
The code provides a procedure for postal completion which practising solicitors may adopt by reference.
First, each solicitor must satisfy himself that no circumstances exist that are likely to give rise to a conflict between this code and the interests of his own client (including where applicable a mortgagee client). The code, where adopted, will apply without variation except so far as recorded in writing beforehand.

The Code
1 Adoption hereof must be specifically agreed by all the solicitors concerned and preferably in writing.
2 On completion the vendor's solicitor will act as agent for the purchaser's solicitor without fee or disbursements.
3 The vendor's solicitor undertakes that on completion, he:
   (1) will have the vendor's authority to receive the purchase money; and
   (2) will be the duly authorised agent of the proprietor of any charge upon the property to receive the part of the money paid to him which is needed to discharge such charge.
4 The purchaser's solicitor shall send to the vendor's solicitor instructions as to:
   (1) documents to be examined and marked;
   (2) memoranda to be endorsed;
   (3) deeds, documents, undertakings and authorities relating to rents, deposits, keys, etc; and
   (4) any other relevant matters.
In default of instructions, the vendor's solicitor shall not be under any duty to examine mark or endorse any documents.
5 The purchaser's solicitor shall remit to the vendor's solicitor the balance due on completion specified in the vendor's solicitor's completion statement or with written notification; in default of either, the balance shown due by the contract. If the funds are remitted by transfer between banks, the vendor's solicitors shall instruct his bank to advise him by telephone immediately the funds are received. The vendor's solicitor shall hold such funds to the purchaser's solicitor's order pending completion.
6 The vendor's solicitor, having received the items specified in paras 4 and 5, shall forthwith, or at such later times as may have been agreed, complete. Thereupon he shall hold all documents and other items to be sent to the purchaser's solicitor as agent for such solicitor.

7 Once completion has taken place, the vendor's solicitor shall as soon as possible thereafter on the same day confirm the fact to the purchaser's solicitor by telephone or telex and shall also as soon as possible send by first class post or document exchange written confirmation to the purchaser's solicitor, together with the enclosures referred to in para 4 hereof. The vendor's solicitor shall ensure that such title deeds and any other items are correctly committed to the post or document exchange. Thereafter, they are at the risk of the purchaser's solicitor.

8 If either the authorities specified in para 3 or the instructions specified in para 4 or the funds specified in para 5 have not been received by the vendor's solicitor by the agreed completion date and time, he shall forthwith notify the purchaser's solicitors and request further instructions.

9 Nothing herein shall override any rights and obligations of parties under the contract or otherwise.

10 Any dispute or difference which may arise between solicitors that is directly referable to a completion agreed to be carried out in accordance herewith, whether or not amended or supplemented in any way, shall be referred to an arbitrator to be agreed, within one month of any such dispute or difference arising between the solicitors who are party thereto, and, in default of such agreement, on the application of any such solicitor, to an arbitrator to be appointed by the President of The Law Society.

11 Reference herein to vendor's solicitor and purchaser's solicitor shall, where appropriate, be deemed to include solicitors acting for parties other than vendor and purchaser.

Notes

1 The object of the code is to provide solicitors with a convenient means for completion, on an agency basis, that can be adopted for use, where they so agree beforehand, in completions where a representative of the purchaser's solicitors is not attending at the office of the vendor's solicitors for the purpose.

2 As with The Law Society's formulae for exchange of contracts by telephone/telex (republished in [1984] *Gazette*, 18 January 1982), the code embodies professional undertakings and is, in consequence, only recommended for adoption between solicitors.

3 Cl 2 of the code expressly provides that the vendor's solicitor will act as agent for the purchaser's solicitor without fee or disbursements. It is envisaged that, in the usual case, the convenience of not having to make a specific appointment on the day of completion for the purchaser's solicitor to attend for the purpose will offset the agency work that the vendor's solicitor has to do and any postage he has to pay in completing under the code, and on the basis that most solicitors will from time to time act both for vendors and purchasers. If, nevertheless, a vendor's solicitor does consider that charges and/or disbursements are necessary in a particular case, as such an arrangement represents a variation in the code, it should be agreed in writing beforehand.

4 Having regard to the decision in *Edward Wong Finance Co Ltd v Johnson, Stokes and Master (supra)*, cl 3(2) of the code requires the vendor's solicitor

to confirm, before he agrees to use the code, that he will be the duly authorised agent of the proprietor of any charge upon the property (typically but not exclusively the vendor's building society) to receive that part of the money paid to him which is needed to discharge such charge.

5 Cl 9 of the code expressly provides that nothing therein shall override any rights and obligations of parties under the contract or otherwise.

The above notes refer only to some of the points in the code that practitioners may wish to consider before agreeing to adopt it. It is emphasised that it is a matter for the solicitors concerned to read the code in full, so that they can decide beforehand whether they will make use of it as it stands or with any variations agreed in writing beforehand, whether or not they are referred to in the above notes, as the case may be.'

3.5.16 Development Land Tax
3.5.16.1

13. Development Land Tax
Is the usual place of abode of the Vendor, or any other person disposing of an interest for the purposes of the Development Land Tax Act 1976, outside the United Kingdom?

3.5.16.2 The Development Land Tax Act 1976, s 40 (as amended by the Finance Act 1984) requires a purchaser of land within the United Kingdom (whether or not that land is development land) from a vendor whose usual place of abode is outside the United Kingdom to make a deduction of 40% from the purchase price on account of any liability of the vendor to development land tax and to pay this sum to the Inland Revenue unless the transaction is below one of the thresholds from time to time specified in relation to s 40 (currently £75,000 or £150,000 for dwelling houses) or the Inland Revenue otherwise directs. If he fails to make this deduction the purchaser will still be liable to account for the tax and the purchaser's solicitors will be liable in negligence to their client for having overlooked this problem.

3.5.17 New properties
3.5.17.1

14. New Properties
(A) Will the Vendor pay all charges for construction and connection of the drainage system and the services?
(B) Are all the following included in the purchase price: fencing all boundaries, laying all paths and drives, and levelling and clearing the garden area? If not, please give particulars.

3.5.17.2 The builder of a new property will frequently enter an agreement with the regional water authority under the Public Health Act 1936, s 18 for the construction of the sewerage system serving the property. Under the terms of such an agreement the water authority will usually take over the ownership of the drains and sewers on the completion of the construction works and thereafter maintain them at public expense. Where such an agreement exists the vendor may be asked to supply a copy of the agreement and any supporting bond. This point is not covered by the wording of this question, but the vendor may have supplied copies under question 4 (para 3.5.7, above).

Although the information revealed by part (B) of the question is purely factual, it is important for the purchaser to know this in order to estimate the extent of his financial commitment on purchasing the property.

3.5.18 Leasehold enquiries

3.5.18.1 *General*

I. General
(A) Is the lease under which the property is held a head lease or an underlease?
(B) Please state the names and addresses of the lessor, any superior lessors, their respective solicitors, and the receivers of the rent.
(C) Please supply copies of all licences granted by the lessor, other than licences to assign.
(D) What steps have been taken to obtain the lessor's consent to the proposed assignment? Please supply a copy of any licence granted.

3.5.18.2 The relevance of part (A) of the question is that the title which a purchaser of a leasehold property can require to be deduced differs depending whether the lease is a head lease or a sub-lease.[8] The landlord may under the terms of the lease have granted a licence to the tenant to effect improvements or alterations to the property or otherwise to vary the terms of the lease (part (C)). Where a licence to assign is required contracts should not normally be exchanged until it is certain that the landlord's consent will be forthcoming.

National Condition 11(5) and Law Society Condition 8(4) deal with the time limits within which the vendor must obtain the licence.

3.5.18.3 *Covenants*

II. Covenants
(A) Has the lessor complained of any breach of covenant?
(B) Has any obligation in the lease to paint or do any other work by or at a particular time been strictly fulfilled? If not, please give details.
(C) Has the Vendor has cause to complain of any breach of the lessor's covenants?

3.5.18.4 The vendor will usually require the inclusion in the assignment or transfer of a clause which modifies his liability on the covenants for title implied by the Law of Property Act 1925, s 76 so that the purchaser will be unable to recover damages from the vendor in relation to the vendor's breach of a repairing covenant in the lease. Law Society Condition 8(5) and National Condition 11(7) both provide to this effect. In view of this limitation of liability any breach of covenant disclosed by the vendor should either be remedied or formally waived by the landlord prior to completion, since neither the purchaser nor his mortgagee will wish to assume liability under a lease which is liable to be forfeited. Where the lease contains an option the terms of which are expressed to be dependent on the due observance of the covenants in the lease, the landlord may be able to refuse the exercise of the option unless the covenants in the lease have been strictly complied with.[9]

It is implicit from the wording of part (C) of the question that the vendor should reveal any complaint which he has made in relation to both the landlord's express and implied covenants under the lease. Breaches of repairing covenants or of the covenant for quiet enjoyment would be of particular concern to a purchaser.

3.5.18.5 *Service charge*

> III. Service Charge
> (A) Please give details of service charge payments for the last three years, with any supporting accounts or vouchers that the Vendor has.
> (B) Has the Vendor, or to his knowledge any predecessor in title, exercised a statutory right to obtain information? If so, with what result?

3.5.18.6 In relation to flats a service charge is defined by the Housing Act 1980, Sch 19 as an amount payable as part of or in addition to the rent for services, repairs, maintenance, or insurance or the landlord's costs of management the whole or part of which varies or may vary according to the relevant costs (as defined).

The amount of the service charge is usually expressed in the lease as being a proportion of the total charges expended by the landlord over the period to which the charge relates, relative to the number of flats in the block, or units in the landlord's estate. The amount of the charge may vary considerably from year to year, depending (partly) on the cost of the repairs which the landlord has had to effect during that period; thus the purchaser will need to see at least three years' accounts in order to estimate the amount of his potential liability. It is now possible for a landlord to demand a proportion of the service charge in advance and so set up· a sinking fund to cover future major expenditure on the property.[10]

The tenant of a flat is entitled to a written summary of the expenditure to which his service charge relates in any accounting year. The summary must be certified by a qualified accountant unconnected with the landlord. To exercise this right the tenant must make a written request to the landlord within one year of the end of the calendar year affected and the landlord must comply with this request either within one month of the receipt of the request, or within six months of the end of the accounting period whichever is later.

The right to demand this information under the Housing Act 1980. Such a request is deemed to be served on the landlord if served on any agent of the landlord named as such in the rent book or other similar document, or on the person who receives the rent on behalf of the landlord. A person on whom a request is so served must forward it to the landlord.

The apportionment of a service charge on completion is dealt with by Law Society Condition 19(6) and National Condition 6(5).

3.5.18.7   *Insurance*

IV. Insurance
(A) Who effected the insurance policy currently covering the property?
(B) Please give particulars: insurers' and any insurance brokers' name and address, policy number, insured's name(s), risks covered, for what amount, premium, and date to which the property is insured.

3.5.18.8   Despite the fact that the lease contains a tenant's covenant to insure it may sometimes be found that the insurance policy has in fact been effected by the landlord. In such a case the tenant cannot insist that the landlord maintains the policy.[11]

Both National Condition 21(1) and Law Society Condition 11(4) require the vendor to maintain his insurance policy after exchange of contracts only in circumstances where the vendor has covenanted under the terms of the lease to insure. Where one of the above conditions applies the purchaser should, strictly speaking, have his interest noted on the vendor's policy on exchange of contracts because at that stage in the transaction the beneficial ownership of the property passes to the purchaser.

The terms of any policy covering the property should be checked to ensure that:

(a) the policy is valid and subsisting;

(b) its terms comply with the covenant for insurance contained in the lease;

(c) the risks and amount insured are adequate;

(d) the terms of the policy comply with the purchaser's mortgagee's requirements for insurance.

3.5.18.9   *Reversionary title*

V. Reversionary Title
Is there with the title deeds a marked abstract or office copy of the freehold title and of any superior lease?

3.5.18.10   The Law of Property Act 1925, s 44 stipulates the title to which the purchaser is entitled to call on the grant or assignment of a lease or sub-lease. A purchaser's solicitor is probably negligent if he does not insist on his client's minimum entitlement to title under this section.[12] In the absence of express condition to the contrary the grantee of a head lease is not entitled to inspect the freehold reversionary title. This rule is from the purchaser's point of view most unsatisfactory in the context of the grant of a long lease (eg over 21 years) or when a premium is to be paid for the grant, and the purchaser should ensure that the contract makes express provision for the deduction of the reversionary title in such circumstances. Law Society Condition 8(2) provides for the deduction of the reversionary title in limited circumstances on the assignment of a lease. There is no equivalent condition contained in the National Conditions. The purchaser of or grantee of a lease which will on completion be required to be registered under the Land Registration Acts 1925–71 should ensure that the reversionary title is deduced and made available to HM Land Registry at the time of the application to register the lease. Failure to produce the reversionary title will result in the lease being registered with good leasehold title only. Some mortgagees are reluctant to lend money on the security of a lease where the reversionary title has not been investigated.

3.5.19   Answering preliminary enquiries

3.5.19.1   Some of the information which is needed in order to answer the questions on the preliminary enquiry form will be available to the vendor's solicitor from either the title deeds or the estate agent's particulars but since most of the questions on the standard form relate to the physical qualities of the property much of the information can only be obtained from the client himself. In view of the potential liability which may be incurred through an erroneous reply to a preliminary enquiry it would be unwise for the vendor's solicitor to complete the replies without having obtained his client's instructions. Ideally the client's instructions should be obtained in person but it is recognised that this will not always be practicable. Possibly the least satisfactory way of obtaining the requisite information is by sending a printed copy of the standard enquiry form to the client with a request that the client completes and returns the form, since the information obtained in this way may be either incomplete or inaccurate, simply because the form is designed for use by solicitors and is phrased in such a way that the meaning of some of the questions will not be apparent to the average

3.5.19.1 *Preliminary enquiries of the vendor*

lay client. One way of surmounting this problem is to prepare a layman's version of the enquiries to send to the client, and then to compile the answers to the standard form from the information supplied by the client. Firms who employ this procedure say that it works well. Others, who disapprove of this procedure base their disapproval on the grounds that sending a 'form' to the client, however simple that form may be, destroys the personal relationship which exists between a solicitor and his client. For the advocates of this method of obtaining information a suggested 'layman's version' of the enquiries is set out below. It should be noted that the questionnaire deals only with seeking information to answer the standard preliminary enquiries and does not deal with other matters which may be relevant to the vendor's side of the transaction, eg capital gains tax liability. Questionnaires similar to that set out below are published by Stat-Plus. Examples of their forms are reproduced in Appendix IV, post.

3.5.19.2 *Layman's version of preliminary enquiries for client's use*

CLIENT:

PROPERTY:

We would be grateful if you would read through this questionnaire and answer the questions to the best of your ability. All the questions on the form concern matters relating to your house the answers to which are not contained in your title deeds but which the purchaser will want to know about. Please return the completed form to us as quickly as possible so that we may supply the purchaser with this information.

QUESTIONS   REPLIES

1 Which of your boundary walls do you own or have you maintained during your ownership of the property? (It may be easiest to answer this by drawing a rough sketch plan of the property opposite and marking your boundaries on the plan.)

2 Have you at any time had a dispute with your neighbours or anyone else (eg the local council) about:

(a) fences or boundaries;

(b) any other matter relating to the property, eg use of a shared driveway? If so, please give details, including the result of any court action.

3 Please let us have copies of any official letter or notice which you have received from anyone relating to the property, eg any notice from the local

authority relating to the use of the
property

4 Have you had any work carried out
on the property relating to:
  (a) cavity wall insulation;
  (b) woodworm or dry rot treatment;
  (c) any other structural repairs?
If so, please supply a copy of any
guarantee or certificate relating to such
work.

5 If the answer to question 4 was 'Yes'
please give details of any defect in the
property which has emerged as a result
of this work being unsatisfactory and of
any action which you have taken in
respect of your complaint.

6 If the property was built within the
last ten years and is covered by a
National House Builders Certificate,
have you had any cause to complain to
either the builder or the NHBC about
structural defects in the property? If so,
please give details.

7 Does the property have:
  (a) mains electricity;
  (b) mains gas;
  (c) mains water;
  (d) main drainage?

8 Do you know whether the routes of
water electricity and gas pipes and
cables serving your property join the
mains directly, or do the routes of the
pipes and cables cross through someone
else's property before joining the mains
supply?
If you are aware of the route of the
pipelines etc please draw a diagram
showing the routes.

9 Have you had any problems with
the drainage system? If so what?

10 When were the drains last inspected?

11 Do you have any formal or informal
arrangements with another person
(other than the statutory supply
companies) relating to your use of
water, electricity, gas or a right of way
or any other matter affecting the use of
the property? If so, please give details.

3.5.19.2 *Preliminary enquiries of the vendor*

12 Is there any shared access to the
property over a driveway, footpath etc?
If so, please give details including
whether you have to pay any
contribution towards its maintenance.

13 Are any of the services to the
property, eg gas supply, water etc
shared by another property? If so,
please supply details including whether
you pay any contribution towards
maintenance.

14 Does anyone else have a right of
way over your property? If so whom,
and to what extent?

15 Are there any wayleave agreements,
eg for electricity or telephone cables,
which affect your property?

16 Have you received any complaints
from anyone concerning your use of the
property?

17 Has the property, so far as you
know always been used as a private
dwelling house? If not, for what other
purpose has it been used and for how
long?

18 Have any structural alterations
additions or improvements been made
to the property since it was built? If so,
please supply details.

19 If alterations etc have been made
within the last five years did you obtain
planning permission and building
regulation consent for the alterations?
Please let us have copies of any such
consents.

20 How old is the property?

21 Are you intending to remove any
of the following items from the
property:
   (a) trees plants or garden produce;
   (b) greenhouse, garden shed, or
garden ornaments;
   (c) external TV or radio aerial;
   (d) fitted cupboards or shelves;
   (e) electric switches or points or light
fittings?

22 Are there any other items not
included in question 21 which you

QUESTIONS

intend to remove from the property
when you move? If so, please give
details.

23 Have you agreed to sell any fittings,
eg carpets and curtains, to the
purchaser? If so, please supply a list.
Are these items included in the
purchase price of the property or is the
purchaser to pay an additional sum for
them, if so, how much?

24 Please confirm that there is no
outstanding hire-purchase credit or loan
agreement relating to fittings which the
purchaser is to buy, or relating to any
other alteration or improvement to the
property, eg double glazing, central
heating. If there is such an agreement
please let us have a copy of it.

25 What is the rateable value of the
property?

26 How much are the present water
rates on the property? (We will at some
stage need to see the rates and water
rates receipts and it would be helpful if
you could let us have these documents
either now or later.)

27 Apart from rates and water rates
and insurance do you pay any other
annual outgoings on the property eg for
maintenance of a private road. If so,
please let us have copies of any relevant
demands or receipts.

28 Have you agreed any date with the
purchaser for completion of the sale? If
not, what date (approximately) would
suit you?

29 Please supply the full names and
ages (if under 18) of anyone who lives
at the property with you.

30 If anyone other than your wife and
children lives at the property what is
their status, eg mother-in-law, lodger,
and do they pay rent?

31 Does the property have a garage? If
so when was it built?

32 If there is no garage what
arrangements are there for the parking
of vehicles?

33 Is the road in which the property is

REPLIES

3.5.19.2 *Preliminary enquiries of the vendor*

QUESTIONS   REPLIES

situated maintained by the local
authority?

34 Have you or (if known) the previous
owners of the property ever experienced
problems relating to any of the
following matters? If so please supply
details:
  (a) flooding;
  (b) subsidence;
  (c) woodworm damp or rot;
  (d) defective electric wiring.

35 When was the property last rewired
for electricity? Is the supply the
standard 240 volt?

36 Please confirm that your normal
place of residence is within the United
Kingdom.

37 Is your water supply metered?

The following questions relate to
leasehold property only:

A. Have you received any notice of any
sort from your landlord. If so please
supply a copy.

B. Please let us have the last receipt for
rent.

C. Please let us have any documents
relating to the payment of service
charge for the past three years.

D. When was the property last painted:
  (a) outside;
  (b) inside?

E. Have you any complaints about the
landlord? If so what have you done
about them?

F. Please let us have a copy of the
insurance policy for the property and
the receipt for the last premium
payment.

G. Please supply the name and address
of:
  (a) the landlord;
  (b) the person to whom rent is paid;
  (c) the secretary of the residents'
association or management company;
  (d) the insurance brokers through
whom the insurance on the property is
effected.

3.6 FORM CON 29 (SHORT)

Short description
of the property

re ....

Parties ....

ENQUIRIES

BEFORE CONTRACT

to ....

**These enquiries are copyright
and may not be reproduced**

**Please strike out enquiries
which are not applicable**

Replies are requested to the following enquiries.

....

Proposed purchaser's solicitors.

Date ....198 ....

ENQUIRIES

The replies are as follows.

....

Proposed vendor's solicitors.

Date ....198 ....

REPLIES

These replies, except in the case of any enquiry expressly requiring a reply
from the Vendor's solicitors, are given on behalf of the proposed Vendor
and without responsibility on the part of his solicitors their partners or
employees. They are believed to be correct but the accuracy is not
guaranteed and they do not obviate the need to make appropriate
searches, enquiries and inspections.

1. Boundaries

(A) To whom do all the boundary walls, fences, hedges and ditches belong?

(B) If no definite indications exist, which has the Vendor maintained or regarded as his responsibility?

2. Disputes

Is the Vendor aware of any past or current disputes regarding boundaries or other matters relating to the property or its use, or relating to any neighbouring property?

3. Notices

Please give particulars of all notices relating to the property, or to matters likely to affect its use or enjoyment, that the Vendor (or, to his knowledge, any predecessor in title) has given or received.

4. Guarantees etc.

(A) Please supply a copy of any of the following of which the Purchaser is to have the benefit:

agreement, covenant, guarantee, warranty, bond, certificate, indemnity and insurance policy,

relating to any of the following matters, and affecting the property, any part of it, or any building of which it forms part:

construction, repair, replacement, treatment or improvement of the fabric; maintenance of any accessway; construction costs of any road (including lighting, drainage and crossovers) to which the property fronts, and adoption charges for such a road; defective title; breach of restrictive covenant.

(B) What has become apparent, which might give rise to a claim under any document mentioned in (A), and what claims have third parties made, and has notice of such a claim been given?

5. Services and Facilities

(A) Does the property have drainage, water, electricity and gas services and are they all connected to the mains?

(B) Are any of the following facilities either shared, or enjoyed by exercising rights over other property?

access for light and air; access for pedestrians and vehicles; emergency escape routes; access and facilities for repair, maintenance and replacement; pipes and wires for services not mentioned in (A).

If so, please give particulars (including copies of relevant documents; liabilities for carrying out work and for making payment; work proposed, in hand, and completed but not paid for).

6. Adverse Rights

(A) Please give details of any rights or facilities over the property to which anyone other than the owner is entitled, or which any such person currently enjoys.

(B) (i) Please give the full names, and ages if under 18, of all persons in actual occupation of the property.

(ii) What legal or equitable interest in the property has each of those persons?

(C) Is the Vendor aware of any other overriding interests as defined by the Land Registration Act 1925, s. 70(1)?

7. Restrictions

Have all restrictions affecting the property or its use been observed up to the date hereof? If not, please give details.

8. Planning and Development Land Tax

(A) When did the present use of the property commence?

(B) Please supply a copy of any planning permission authorising or imposing conditions upon this use, and authorising the erection or retention of the buildings now on the property.

(C) Please supply a copy of any bye-law approval or building regulations consent relating to the buildings now on the property.

(D) Is the Vendor's usual place of abode outside the United Kingdom?

9. Fixtures, Fittings etc.

(A) Does the sale include all of the following items now on the property, and attached to or growing in it?

Trees, shrubs, plants, flowers, and garden produce. Greenhouses, garden sheds and garden ornaments. Aerials. Fitted furniture and shelves. Electric switches, points and wall and ceiling fittings.

(B) What fixtures and fittings affixed to the property are not included in the sale?

(C) If any central heating or other oil is to be sold to the purchaser, what arrangements are proposed?

10. Outgoings

(A) (i) What is the rateable value of the property?

(ii) Have any works been carried out at the property which might result in a revision of this?

(B) What annual or periodic charges, other than general rates and water charges, affect the property or its occupier from time to time?

11. Completion

(A) How long after exchange of contracts will the Vendor be able to give vacant possession of the whole of the property?

(B) The Purchaser's solicitors wish to complete by adopting the Law Society's Code for Completion by Post (1984 edition). Do the Vendor's solicitors agree?

3.7 COMMENT ON FORM CON 29 (SHORT)

3.7.1 This form is a shortened version of form Con 29 and may be used as an alternative to the long form. The main differences between these two forms are tabulated below.

The short form of enquiries may conveniently be used in conjunction with one of the specialised preliminary enquiry forms (eg Con 291, general tenancy enquiries) or in a situation where it is contemplated that a large number of supplementary questions will be raised.

3.7.2 **Comparison of forms Con 29 (long) and Con 29 (short)**

Topic	Con 29 (long) question no	Con 29 (short) question no	Differences
Boundaries	1	1	—
Disputes	1	2	2(B) is omitted from the short form.
Notices	3	3	—
Guarantees	4	4	The wording of this question is different on each form but similar information is required by both.
Services	5	5	The questions on services and facilities on the long form are combined in one question on the short form. Less information will be revealed in response to the short form enquiry.
Facilities	6	5	
Adverse rights	7	6	Question 7 on the long form is more specific in detail than Question 6 on the short form.
Restrictions	8	7	8 (B) on the long form does not appear on the short form.
Planning	9	8	This question is differently worded on the two forms. Less information will be obtained if Con 29 (short) is used.
Fixtures	10	9	Part (C) is differently worded on the short form but approximately the same information would be forthcoming.
Outgoings	11	10	No difference in 11A. 11B omitted from short form. 11C (long) is the equivalent of 10B (short).

55

3.7.2 *Preliminary enquiries of the vendor*

Topic	Con 29 (long) question no	Con 29 (short) question no	Differences
Completion	12	11	—
Development Land Tax	13	8D	Difference in wording, but the same information is required.
New properties	14	—	These are omitted from the short form.
Leasehold enquiries	I-V	—	

3.8 SUPPLEMENTARY QUESTIONS

3.8.1 Form Con 29 (Supplementary)
This form is reproduced on pp 57–58, below.

3.8.2 This form comprises a set of queries grouped under five main headings covering matters which are not dealt with by the printed questions on forms Con 29 (long) or (short) but which solicitors frequently need to raise as supplementary preliminary enquiries. The subject matter of the questions is general in nature and does not purport to provide a comprehensive list of all possible supplementary questions. It is intended that the form should be used in conjunction with either of forms Con 29 (long) or (short). Further supplementary questions may if necessary be added to the end of the supplementary enquiry form. Questions to which the answer is already known, or to which an answer is not required should be deleted from the form before sending it to the vendor's solicitors.

3.8.3 Property
3.8.3.1

Property
(a) Please give details of any of the following which have at any time affected the property:
    (i) Structural defects;
    (ii) Drainage defects;
    (iii) Defective foundations;
    (iv) Rising damp, dry or wet rot;
    (v) Infestation by wood boring insects.
(b) Has the property or the site been subject to:
    (i) Flooding?
    (ii) Landslip?
    (iii) Subsidence or heave?
(c) Is the property situated in an area where mining or underground mineral extraction is carried on?

SUPPLEMENTARY ENQUIRIES
BEFORE CONTRACT

To be attached to form **Con 29
(Long)** or form **Con 29 (Short)**

**These enquiries are copyright
and may not be reproduced**

**Please strike out enquiries
which are not applicable**

Property

(a) Please give details of any of the following which have at any time affected the property:

    (i) Structural defects;

    (ii) Drainage defects;

    (iii) Defective foundations;

    (iv) Rising damp, dry or wet rot;

    (v) Infestation by wood boring insects.

(b) Has the property or the site been subject to:

    (i) Flooding?

    (ii) Landslip?

    (iii) Subsidence or heave?

(c) Is the property situated in an area where mining or underground mineral extraction is carried on?

Services

(d) When was the electrical system:

    (i) Last tested and approved by the local electricity board?

    (ii) Comprehensively rewired?

(e) Please give details of the service provided by the local authority for emptying any private drainage system.

(f) When the central heating system was last in use, did it function completely satisfactorily?

(g) Please give details of the operation of any fixed burglar alarm system.

(h) Please supply copies of any contracts for regular maintenance or servicing of fixed appliances, which the Purchaser could take over.

Vehicles

(i) Was the garage on the property erected at the same time as the dwelling, or, if later, when?

(j) Do parking restrictions apply to the road in front of the property, or have the police objected to vehicles being parked there?

Chattels and fixtures

(k) A copy of the estate agents' sale particulars is attached. Is any item mentioned there not included in the sale?

(l) Please confirm that no moveable or detachable item included in the sale is subject to any lease, hire, hire purchase or loan agreement, or lien or any other claim by a third party.

(m) Do the telephone instruments on the property belong to British Telecommunications?

Financial

(n) What is the current annual amount payable in respect of the property for:

(i) General rate?

(ii) Water charges (including drainage and environmental charges)?

(o) Does this sale depend on the Vendor contracting to purchase another property?

(p) Please confirm that the Vendor will arrange for the appropriate authorities to read the electric, gas, water and telephone meters on the day of actual completion.

3.8.3.2   Question (a) asks the vendor to give details of defects which have at any time affected the structure of the property. Disclosure of these matters is probably outside the vendor's common law duty of disclosure and he may therefore be reluctant to supply such information (even if in his possession) and may choose to ask the purchaser to rely on a surveyor's report. Where remedial work has been done on the property a guarantee covering the work may exist and this would be disclosed in reply to question 4(a) on Con 29 (long) or (short) (para 3.5.7).

Information disclosed in reply to questions (b) or (c) of this question may indicate to the purchaser that further searches eg for mining, or with the water authority, should be undertaken.

3.8.4   Services
3.8.4.1

Services
(d) When was the electrical system:
   (i) Last tested and approved by the local electricity board?
   (ii) Comprehensively rewired?
(e) Please give details of the service provided by the local authority for emptying any private drainage system.
(f) When the central heating system was last in use, did it function completely satisfactorily?
(g) Please give details of the operation of any fixed burglar alarm system.
(h) Please supply copies of any contracts for regular maintenance or servicing of fixed appliances, which the Purchaser could take over.

3.8.4.2   It should not be necessary to ask question (d) in relation to a new or recently built or converted property, nor where the purchaser has commissioned a full structural survey of the property. Similarly question (e) is only of relevance to properties known or thought not to have mains drainage. Any answer given to question (f) must be read as a subjective view of the state of the central heating system and if there is doubt as to the adequacy of the system the purchaser should obtain an independent report from a heating engineer. Obviously question (g) should be deleted if it is known that the property is not fitted with a burglar alarm system. Question (h) is a useful question to ask since the purchaser may wish to take over the benefit of service contracts relating to such matters as the central heating system. Any copy contract supplied in response to this question should be carefully checked to ensure that it is capable of assignment and that its terms are satisfactory to the purchaser. Where an assignment is effected it may be necessary to consider the apportionment of the annual charge on the completion statement.

3.8.5 Vehicles
3.8.5.1

Vehicles
(i) Was the garage on the property erected at the same time as the dwelling, or, if later, when?
(j) Do parking restrictions apply to the road in front of the property, or have the police objected to vehicles being parked there?

3.8.5.2 If the garage at the property was erected after the property was built the purchaser should ensure that any necessary planning consent and building regulation consent for its construction were obtained. Similar information may be obtained under question 9 on form Con 29 (long) although question 9 is restricted to buildings erected during the last four years.

Any extension to the original property when built (or after 1 July 1948 in the case of older properties) will have the effect of using up in whole or in part the concession given by the General Development Order to extend the property within the limits laid down by the Order and the erection of a garage may therefore affect the purchaser's ability to further extend the property in the future without the need to obtain express planning permission.

Question (j) is of particular relevance to inner city houses and flats where parking space is at a premium.

3.8.6 Chattels and fixtures
3.8.6.1

Chattels and fixtures
(k) A copy of the estate agents' sale particulars is attached. Is any item mentioned there not included in the sale?
(l) Please confirm that no moveable or detachable item included in the sale is subject to any lease, hire, hire purchase or loan agreement, or lien or any other claim by a third party.
(m) Do the telephone instruments on the property belong to British Telecommunications?

3.8.6.2 Question (k) supplements question 10 on Con 29 (long) and question 9 on Con 29 (short).

Question (l) is a sensible precautionary question aimed at avoiding problems which may arise out of undischarged credit agreements over fittings. The question might be extended by asking whether any credit agreements exist over fixtures, eg double glazing, and to seek express confirmation that any subsisting credit agreements or third-party rights over fixtures or fittings will be discharged on or before completion.

A subsisting hire-purchase or credit agreement over fixtures does not present a legal problem for the purchaser because title to the fixtures will have passed to the vendor when the fixtures were installed, but the purchaser will avoid the practical problems involved in fending off the finance company if he takes the trouble to seek confirmation from the vendor that any such credit agreements will be discharged before completion. As far as fittings such as carpets are concerned, the purchaser is much more vulnerable, because under a conventional hire-purchase agreement, title to the goods does not pass to the buyer until all the instalments under the agreement have been paid and a repossession order could be sought by the finance company against the purchaser. If the credit agreement was either a credit sale or conditional sale agreement title may already have passed to the buyer, but this again should be checked.

3.8.6.3 Question (m) relates to the telephone installation at the property. If the telephone equipment is not owned by British Telecom enquiries should be raised as to its ownership and maintenance. The vendor should also be asked to confirm that the telephone will not be disconnected.

3.8.7 Financial
3.8.7.1

Financial
(n) What is the current annual amount payable in respect of the property for:
  (i) General rate?
  (ii) Water charges (including drainage and environmental charges)?
(o) Does this sale depend on the Vendor contracting to purchase another property?
(p) Please confirm that the Vendor will arrange for the appropriate authorities to read the electric, gas, water and telephone meters on the day of actual completion.

3.8.7.2 Question (n) supplements question 11 on form Con 29 (long) (question 10 Con 29 (short)) and may provide useful information relating to the actual outgoings on the property. In some cases the vendor may well refer the purchaser to the agent's particulars.

3.8.7.3 The purpose of question (o) is to obtain information which will enable the purchaser to estimate or anticipate any delay in the transaction which may be caused where several sales and purchases are dependent on one another. Where the sale is part of a chain of transactions the vendor should be asked to supply any information in his possession relating to the approximate number of transactions involved in the chain.

3.8.7.4 Question (p) concerns a purely practical matter and needs no comment.

3.9 ENQUIRIES PRIOR TO CONTRACT ON FORM CONVEY 1
3.9.1 Form Convey 1

ENQUIRIES PRIOR TO CONTRACT FOR SALE
(This form and the enquiries herein are copyright and may not be reproduced without written permission of the publisher)

Property ....

....

Proposed Vendor ....

Proposed Purchaser ....

Please answer the following enquiries:

The replies are as stated hereunder

Solicitor for proposed purchaser

Date

Solicitor for proposed vendor

Date

ENQUIRIES	REPLIES
	The replies hereunder are given on behalf of the proposed vendor. Whilst they are believed to be accurate and correct the vendor's solicitors, their partners and employees can give no guarantee in this respect and cannot accept any responsibility for them. You are reminded to make the necessary searches, enquiries and inspections in any event.

1. Boundaries and disputes

(a) Please supply a plan showing the property indicating the maintenance of the boundaries with "T" marks.

(h) Please show on the plan, with "H" marks, any party walls and indicate their length.

(c) When were the boundary fences last repaired?

(d) Has the Vendor had any problems with the adjoining owners over the ownership of any of the boundaries?

(e) If so give details and send us all the attendant correspondence.

(f) Has the Vendor erected a fence on a boundary which a neighbour is supposed to maintain? If so, has the Vendor carried out this work with the neighbour's consent?

(g) Has the property mooring rights attached to its river boundary?

(h) If the property is under construction, please confirm that the plot will be fenced by the Vendor before completion as part of the purchase price and please confirm the dimensions of the plot.

2. Notices

(a) Has the Vendor received any notice from the local authority about the property?

(b) Has the Vendor received any notices about the property or affecting the property from any neighbour, local or national body or group or any other person whatsoever?

(c) If the answer to (a) or (b) is yes, please give full details and let us have copies of the relevant correspondence.

3. Works carried out at the Property

(a) Please state which of the following improvements the Vendor has carried out to the Property within the last 5 years

    (i) new kitchen fitments (ii) new bathroom equipment (iii) re-wiring (iv) extensions at ground level (v) loft room built (vi) garage (vii) extensions above ground level (viii) additional rooms, outhouses

(b) Are there any other improvements which have been made. If so, please attach list.

(c) Please state whether the items mentioned in either (a) or (b) above require planning permission. If so, then state whether permission was unconditional.

(d) Please supply copies of *all* planning permissions affecting the Property.

(e) Has the property the benefit of

(i) a NHBC agreement,with top up cover.

(ii) guarantee for work carried out for weatherproofing, damp proofing, dry rot, wet rot or any insect infestation.

(iii) guarantees for any building works or extensions or roof repairs or renewals

(iv) guarantees for any central heating or electrical wiring

(f) Please confirm that the Vendor will assign the benefit of any of the above guarantees.

4. Services to Property

(a) is there mains water

mains electricity

gas

drainage

(b) If so, please supply plan showing the running of these services if it is not already dealt with in the contract.

(c) Has the Vendor the relevant rights to grant the relevant easements over adjoining land? If so, please supply title to these if different from title to Property.

(d) Has the Vendor granted similar rights to any other person?

(e) If so, how many and to whom?

(f) Do these others have to contribute to the cost?

(g) If so how much?

5. Adverse rights; restrictions etc.

(a) (i) Does the Vendor know of any person having adverse rights over the property?

(ii) If so, how are these rights exercised?

(b) (i) How many persons inhabit the property?

(ii) Who are they?

(iii) What age?

(iv) Has any person other than the Vendor any equitable or registrable right over the Property?

(v) If so, please confirm that the persons having such rights will be parties to the contract.

(vi) Please confirm that all persons in present occupation of the Property agree to vacate on completion.

(c) Please state which, if any, of the following affect the Property:

(i) Restrictive covenants

(ii) Positive convenants

(iii) Rent Charges

(iv) Chancel Repair liability

(v) Corn Rents

(vi) Declarations

If so, please send full details.

(d) Is the Property being sold subject to

(i) any bridle paths?

(ii) foot paths?

(iii) foot paths or bridle paths in the course of being incorporated in the definitive maps?

(iv) rights of way?

(v) rights for timber extraction?

(vi) rights to extract water?

(vii) rights of common?

If so, please give all relevant details.

(e) Is the Property in

(i) a coal mining area?

(ii) a salt mining area?

(iii) a tin mining area?

(iv) a natural gas or oil exploration area?

If so, please confirm in each case that there are

(a) no outstanding leases

(b) no liability which is not covered by compensation by the relevant authority

(c) no compensation has been paid

(f) Is the Property sold with the benefit of
    (i)   rights of access
    (ii) rights of air and light
    (iii) rights of common over other land.
If so, please let us have details.

6. Fixtures and fittings
Please list all items of fixtures and fittings which are being *taken*.

7. *For semi-detached and terraced houses only*
Does the Vendor know whether the adjoining owner has made any improvements to the adjoining house which could affect the property e.g. demolition of internal load bearing walls without replacing an RSJ to support.

8. Outgoings
Please state whether the Vendor pays
(a) general rates – when due – and how much
(b) water rates – when due – and how much
(c) drainage rates – when due – and how much
(d) cesspit cleaning – how often – and how much
(e) licence fees for access
(f) licence fees for water abstraction – when due – and how much
(g) Any other items. Please list.

9. Residency
Is the Vendor resident outside UK?

10. Completion
(a) When does the Vendor require completion?
(b) Please confirm that the Vendor and all other occupiers will be out of house before 12 noon.

11. Please see that there is no rubbish left on the property at completion.

LEASEHOLD ENQUIRIES
    (Reference to 'lease' in these enquiries include an underlease.)

12.
(a) (i)   Please supply a copy of the lease if this has not already been supplied.
    (ii) Please supply copies of the documents forming any superior title which are with the deeds.
(b) (i)   Please confirm that the Lessor mentioned in the Lease is the present Lessor and please confirm his present address.
    (ii) If not the present Lessor, please give details of the present Lessor and his address.
    (iii) Please supply details of the Lessor's solicitors and agents.
(c) Please supply details of all superior Lessors and their respective solicitors and agents.
(d) (i)   Please confirm that the Lessor has given consent to all assignments (if this is required under the terms of the lease).
    (ii) Please confirm that the Vendor has obtained consent or will obtain consent to this sale by the date of exchange of contracts.
(e) Please confirm that the Lessor has given consent to any of the improvements made to the Property and please supply details.
(f) Please supply a copy of the insurance policy relating to the property and state any premiums paid by the Vendor.
(g) Please supply details of the service charge and supply copies of the accounts for the last three years.
(h) Is there a maintenance fund to cover large items of repair and redecoration? If so please supply details.
(i) Please advise of any breach of covenant complained of by the Lessor or any superior Lessor.

ADDITIONAL ENQUIRIES

Printed and published by *UNILAW*

Unilaw members: Services to Lawyers Limited; Stephen Cox & Co. Limited; Meredith Ray & Littler Limited; Dennis Welbourn Limited; Jordan & Sons Limited; Holbrook & Gration Limited.

3.9.2.1 This form of preliminary enquiries which was first published in October 1984 contains questions of a very similar nature to those contained in form Con 29 and also deals with a number of matters which are the subject of questions on form Con 29 (supplementary). A brief comment on each of the questions on this form appears below and a comparative table of the questions contained in forms Convey 1 and Con 29 is set out in para 3.9.14, below.

Since many of the questions on form Convey 1 are similar in wording to their equivalent questions on form Con 29 the general comments and background law stated in para 3.5 relating to form Con 29 have not been repeated here but a cross-reference has been made to the relevant sections of para 3.5.

The replies column to the form is headed with an exclusion clause. For a discussion of the not dissimilar provision in form Con 29, see para 2.3.2, above.

3.9.3 Boundaries and disputes
3.9.3.1

1. Boundaries and disputes
(a) Please supply a plan showing the property indicating the maintenance of the boundaries with 'T' marks.
(b) Please show on the plan, with 'H' marks, any party walls and indicate their length.
(c) When were the boundary fences last repaired?
(d) Has the Vendor had any problems with the adjoining owners over the ownership of any of the boundaries?
(e) If so give details and send us all the attendant correspondence.
(f) Has the Vendor erected a fence on a boundary which a neighbour is supposed to maintain? If so, has the Vendor carried out this work with the neighbour's consent?
(g) Has the property mooring rights attached to its river boundary?
(h) If the property is under construction, please confirm that the plot will be fenced by the Vendor before completion as part of the purchase price and please confirm the dimensions of the plot.

3.9.3.2 This detailed question asks the vendor to supply information relating to his ownership and maintenance of boundaries and also information regarding any disputed boundary. The request to supply a plan will be helpful to the purchaser, if an accurate response is forthcoming.

It should be noted that the disclosure of disputes is limited to ownership of boundaries only and not to other disputes with adjoining owners. Part (g) of this question will not often be of relevance but it is useful to have such a question on the standard form so that mooring rights are not overlooked in the cases where there is a river boundary to the property. Fishing rights are not mentioned in part (g) and do not appear elsewhere on this form.

3.9.3.3 For general comments on boundaries and disputes see paras 3.5.4 and 3.5.5, above. Chapter 25 also discusses liability for the maintenance of boundaries.

3.9.4 Notices
3.9.4.1

2. Notices
(a) Has the Vendor received any notice from the local authority about the property?
(b) Has the Vendor received any notices about the property or affecting the property from any neighbour, local or national body or group or any other person whatsoever?
(c) If the answer to (a) or (b) is yes, please give full details and let us have copies of the relevant correspondence.

3.9.4.2 Question 2 requires the vendor to supply copies of all notices and related correspondence received by him about the property, but he is not required to disclose details of any notices served by him. Examples of the type of notice to which this question might relate are contained in para 3.5.6.3, above.

3.9.5 Works carried out at the property
3.9.5.1

3. Works carried out at the Property
(a) Please state which of the following improvements the Vendor has carried out to the Property within the last 5 years.
   (i) new kitchen fitments (ii) new bathroom equipment (iii) re-wiring (iv) extensions at ground level (v) loft room built (vi) garage (vii) extensions above ground level (viii) additional rooms, outhouses.
(b) Are there any other improvements which have been made. If so, please attach list.
(c) Please state whether the items mentioned in either (a) or (b) above require planning permission. If so, then state whether permission was unconditional.
(d) Please supply copies of *all* planning permissions affecting the Property.
(e) Has the property the benefit of
   (i) a NHBC agreement with top up cover.
   (ii) guarantee for work carried out for weatherproofing, damp proofing, dry rot, wet rot or any insect infestation.
   (iii) guarantees for any building works or extensions or roof repairs or renewals.
   (iv) guarantees for any central heating or electrical wiring.

(f) Please confirm that the Vendor will assign the benefit of any of the above guarantees.

3.9.5.2 The period of five years mentioned in this request does not appear to be of any direct legal significance. An enforcement notice or stop notice to enforce a breach of planning control can in general only be served within four years of the breach, the major exception to this four-year rule being in relation to breaches caused by a change of use of the premises where enforcement proceedings may normally be brought at any time. One purpose of this question is to bring to the purchaser's attention any alterations or additions to the property which might have required planning permission. The question requires the vendor to supply copies of all planning permissions, not just those obtained within the last five years, but does not refer at all to building regulation consent which may have been required even in circumstances where planning permission was not needed. A further purpose of this question is to inform the purchaser which of the major internal fittings, eg kitchen and bathroom equipment have been installed within the last five years. Although this information may have been self-evident to the purchaser on his initial inspection of the property, confirmation of the information may be useful.

No questions are asked relating to the authorised use of the property, nor is there any requirement to supply copies of current fire certificates. For general comments on planning see para 3.5.12.2 above, and chs 4 and 5, below (planning matters revealed by local authority search and additional enquiries).

3.9.5.3 Part (e) of this question asks whether the property has the benefit of the various certificates and guarantees listed in the question but does not require the vendor to supply copies. NHBC agreements and notices of insurance entered into since the scheme was modified several years ago do not require the top up cover mentioned in question (e) (i). An explanation of the NHBC Scheme is contained in para 3.5.7.3, above.

3.9.6 Services to property
3.9.6.1

4. Services to Property
(a) is there mains water
           mains electricity
           gas
           drainage
(b) If so, please supply plan showing the running of these services if it is not already dealt with in the contract.
(c) Has the Vendor the relevant rights to grant the relevant easements over adjoining land? If so, please supply title to these if different from title to Property.

    (d) Has the Vendor granted similar rights to any other person?
    (e) If so, how many and to whom?
    (f) Do these others have to contribute to the cost?
    (g) If so how much?

3.9.6.2 As drafted part (a) of the question simply requires the vendor to disclose whether there is gas and drainage serving the property, without disclosing whether these services are connected to the mains. The remainder of this question will supply information relating to the routes of these services, and the rights and obligations connected with their maintenance. See also paras 3.5.8.2 and 3.5.9.3, above.

3.9.7 Adverse rights; restrictions etc
3.9.7.1

    5. Adverse rights; restrictions etc.
    (a)   (i) Does the Vendor know of any person having adverse rights over the property?
        (ii) If so, how are these rights exercised?
    (b)   (i) How many persons inhabit the property?
        (ii) Who are they?
      (iii) What age?
      (iv) Has any person other than the Vendor any equitable or registrable right over the Property?
       (v) If so, please confirm that the persons having such rights will be parties to the contract.
      (vi) Please confirm that all persons in present occupation of the Property agree to vacate on completion.
    (c) Please state which, if any, of the following affect the Property:
       (i) Restrictive covenants
      (ii) Positive covenants
     (iii) Rent Charges
     (iv) Chancel Repair liability
      (v) Corn Rents
     (vi) Declarations
If so, please send full details.
    (d) Is the Property being sold subject to
       (i) any bridle paths?
      (ii) foot paths?
     (iii) foot paths or bridle paths in the course of being incorporated in the definitive maps?
     (iv) rights of way?
      (v) rights for timber extraction?
     (vi) rights to extract water?
    (vii) rights of common?
If so, please give all relevant details.
    (e) Is the Property in
       (i) a coal mining area?

> > (ii) a salt mining area?
> > (iii) a tin mining area?
> > (iv) a natural gas or oil exploration area?
>
> If so, please confirm in each case that there are
>
> > (a) no outstanding leases
> > (b) no liability which is not covered by compensation by the relevant authority
> > (c) no compensation has been paid
>
> (f) Is the property sold with the benefit of
>
> > (i) rights of access
> > (ii) rights of air and light
> > (iii) rights of common over other land
>
> If so, please let us have details.

3.9.7.2 Part (a) of this long question deals with adverse rights and third-party interests over the property and requires the vendor to disclose the names of all persons who have an equitable or registrable interest in the property, thus including persons who have a registrable estate contract or rights under the Matrimonial Homes Act 1983 as well as persons who have an overriding interest in registered land. The question refers to persons who currently *have* such an interest and therefore does not cover persons who may potentially have such an interest and the purchaser may choose to amend the wording of the question slightly to cover this point.

3.9.7.3 Restrictive and positive covenants and rent charges should be revealed by the terms of the draft contract and thus questions (c) (i), (ii) and (iii) may be asking for information already known to the purchaser. It is not clear what is meant by 'declarations' in question (c) (vi). If this term is intended to refer to declarations in a previous conveyance or transfer relating to such matters as the maintenance of, eg party walls then the answer to this question may duplicate information already given in response to question 1(b). Declarations of trust in a previous conveyance or transfer may also be included in this term but these would only be of concern to a purchaser if the beneficial interests were not to be overreached on completion, in which case this matter would have to be dealt with in the draft contract.

3.9.7.4 Chancel repair liability and liability to pay corn rent are not commonly encountered but may exist in situations where the purchaser's solicitor would not have thought to raise the question. Questions (c) (iv) and (v) are therefore sensible inclusions on a standard form of enquiries in appropriate cases. Corn rent liability is discussed in ch 16 below, and ch 17 below, deals with chancel repair liability.

3.9.7.5 Part (d) of the question is designed to reveal details of rights of way and other rights over the property which may need to be investigated further by the purchaser by means of further searches or enquiries. Water authority searches are dealt with in ch 21, below and commons registration searches in ch 9, below.

3.9.7.6 A solicitor acting for a purchaser who is buying property outside the area in which the solicitor practices may be unaware of local peculiarities which affect the area in which the property to be purchased is situated. Part (e) of this question is intended to alert the purchaser to the fact that one of the less usual searches may also have to be undertaken before exchange of contracts. Four of the most common types of mining and drilling are covered by this question but gravel extraction and clay and limestone mining are not mentioned in the standard question. Further details of mining searches are contained in chs 27–32, below.

3.9.7.7 Rights to which the property is subject are dealt with by the question in part (d), and rights which benefit the property are the subject of question (f). Rights of common can be checked by making a commons registration search (ch 9, below). The existence and extent of other rights of way air and light must also be carefully checked (see para 3.5.9.3, above).

3.9.8 Fixtures and fittings
3.9.8.1

> 6. Fixtures and fittings
> Please list all items of fixtures and fittings which are being *taken*.

3.9.8.2 It is intended that the vendor should in reply to this question list the fixtures and fittings which he is going to remove from the property on or before completion thus allowing the purchaser to assume that any items not included in the list will be left at the property. The question neither defines nor gives examples of what is meant by the phrase 'fixtures and fittings' and this lack of definition may lead to ambiguity or confusion. For further comment see para 3.5.13.2, above.

3.9.9 Semi-detached and terraced houses
3.9.9.1

> 7. For semi-detached and terraced houses only
> Does the Vendor know whether the adjoining owner has made any improvements to the adjoining house which could affect the property eg demolition of internal load bearing walls without replacing an RSJ to support.

3.9.9.2 Although this question is only stated to be applicable to semi-detached and terraced houses it seems that the subject matter of the question could equally well apply to flats, large houses which have been converted into separate units and in some cases also to office suites and other commercial premises. If the question is going to be asked it should be extended to apply to all properties which are not totally detached.

71

3.9.10   Outgoings
3.9.10.1

> 8. Outgoings
> Please state whether the Vendor pays
> (a) general rates – when due – and how much
> (b) water rates – when due – and how much
> (c) drainage rates – when due – and how much
> (d) cesspit cleaning – how often – and how much
> (e) licence fees for access
> (f) licence fees for water abstraction – when due – and how much
> (g) Any other items. Please list.

3.9.10.2   This is a clear and comprehensively drafted request which could yield useful information for the purchaser.

3.9.11   Residency
3.9.11.1

> 9. Residency
> Is the Vendor resident outside UK?

3.9.11.2   The relevance of this question relates to the vendor's liability for Development Land Tax. See para 3.5.16.2, above.

3.9.12   Completion
3.9.12.1

> 10. Completion
> (a) When does the Vendor require completion?
> (b) Please confirm that the Vendor and all other occupiers will be out of house before 12 noon.
> 11. Please see that there is no rubbish left on the property at completion.

3.9.12.2   Although it will not normally be possible to arrange a definite completion date at this stage of the transaction the answer to part (a) of question 10 will give the purchaser some idea of the anticipated completion date.

Part (b) of question 10 could equally well be asked at the stage when requisitions on title are raised and may need to be repeated at that stage in order to remind the vendor of this requirement. The only significance of this question is to try to ensure that the vendor physically vacates the property at a reasonable hour on the day of actual completion and thus allows the purchaser to move into the property on the same day should he wish to do so. The time limit of 12 noon mentioned in the question will not necessarily be the same as the actual time of completion, which is a matter which will be dealt with in the draft contract. (See Law Society Condition 21 and National Condition 5.)

The vendor will not, strictly speaking, have complied with his contractual condition relating to vacant possession unless all rubbish is removed from the premises. In this respect question 11 is a valid preliminary enquiry and does have legal significance. From the purchaser's point of view the practical aspect of the question is far more important since it would be extremely inconvenient for the purchaser to have to deal with the disposal of the vendor's rubbish.

3.9.13 Leasehold enquiries
3.9.13.1

12.
(a) (i) Please supply a copy of the lease if this has not already been supplied.
   (ii) Please supply copies of the documents forming any superior title which are with the deeds.
(b) (i) Please confirm that the Lessor mentioned in the Lease is the present Lessor and please confirm his present address.
   (ii) If not the present Lessor, please give details of the present Lessor and his address.
   (iii) Please supply details of the Lessor's solicitors and agents.
(c) Please supply details of all superior Lessors and their respective solicitors and agents.
(d) (i) Please confirm that the Lessor has given consent to all assignments (if this is required under the terms of the lease).
   (ii) Please confirm that the Vendor has obtained consent or will obtain consent to this sale by the date of exchange of contracts.
(e) Please confirm that the Lessor has given consent to any of the improvements made to the Property and please supply details.
(f) Please supply a copy of the insurance policy relating to the property and state any premiums paid by the Vendor.
(g) Please supply details of the service charge and supply copies of the accounts for the last three years.
(h) Is there a maintenance fund to cover large items of repair and redecoration? If so please supply details.
(i) Please advise of any breach of covenant complained of by the Lessor or any superior Lessor.

3.9.13.2 The purpose of this detailed question is to obtain information relating to the lease or sub-lease under which the property is held and details of any outgoings which are specifically connected with the lease, such as service charge and insurance premiums. A matter which is worthy of particular comment in this question is that part (d) (ii) of the question asks the vendor to obtain any necessary consent to the assignment by the date of exchange of contracts. Part (h) of the question asks for details of any sinking fund or reserve fund maintained by the landlord to meet contingent repairs but does not raise an enquiry about the existence of a management company and any obligations to hold shares in such a company, neither does the question refer to the tenant's statutory right to obtain information under the Housing Act 1980, s 136 and Sch 19 where the demised premises are a flat.

Since the covenants for title implied by the Law of Property Act 1925, s 76 (the Land Registration Act 1925, s 24 in relation to registered land) are likely to be modified by the terms of the draft contract (see Law Society Condition 8 (5) and National Condition 11 (7)) it would be prudent to ask the vendor to confirm that all repairing obligations under the lease have been strictly complied with. In all other respects this question is similarly worded to the leasehold enquiries on form Con 29 (long) and an explanation of the general law applicable to those enquiries may be found in para 3.5.18, above.

3.9.14 Comparative table of questions on forms Convey 1, Con 29 and E1 (Form E1 is reproduced in Appendix IV)

Topic	Convey 1	Con 29 (long)	Con 29 (short)	Con 29 (supplementary)	E1
Boundaries	1	1	1	–	10
Supply of plan	1 (a)	–	–	–	10 (e)
Party walls	1 (b)	–	–	–	10 (c)
Boundary disputes	1 (d)	2	2	–	15
General neighbourhood disputes	–	2	2	–	15
Mooring rights	1 (g)	–	–	–	–
Notices received	2	3	3	–	16
Notices given	–	3	3	–	16
Improvements made in last five years	3	(4 years) 9 (B)	–	–	12 (c)
Use of property	–	9 (A)	8 (A)	–	12 (a)
Building Regulation consent	–	9 (C)	8 (C)	–	12 (d)
Copy of planning permission	3 (a)	9 (C)	8 (C)	–	12 (d)
NHBC	3 (e)	4	4	–	9
Guarantees for structural etc repairs	3 (e)	4	4	–	9
Assignment of guarantees	3 (f)	4	4	(h)	–
Mains services	4 (a)	5 (A)	5 (A)	–	7
Metering of water	–	5 (B)	–	–	–
Routes of services	4 (b)	5 (C)	–	–	7
Easements for services	4 (c)	5 (D)	5 (B)	–	7, 8
Adverse rights	5 (a) and (b)	7 (A)	6	–	3

Topic	Convey 1	Con 29 (long)	Con 29 (short)	Con 29 (supple-mentry)	E1
Overriding interests	–	7 (C)	6 (C)	–	3
Covenants	5 (c)	8	7	–	4
Rent charges	5 (c)	–	–	–	–
Chancel repairs	5 (c)	–	–	–	–
Corn rents	5 (c)	–	–	–	–
Declarations	5 (c)	–	–	–	–
Footpaths, bridleways and rights of way	5 (d)	–	–	–	–
Timber extraction	5 (d)	–	–	–	–
Water extraction	5 (d)	–	–	–	–
Rights of common	5 (d) and 5 (f)	7 (A)	–	–	–
Mining searches	5 (e)	–	–	(c)	–
Oil and gas exploration	5 (e)	–	–	–	–
Rights of access and light	5 (f)	6	5 (B)	–	6
Fixtures and fittings	6	10	9	(k) & (1)	13
Sale of oil	–	10 (C)	9 (C)	–	13 (f)
Improvements to adjoining property	7	–	–	–	16 (6)
Rates	8 (a)	11	10 (A)	(n)	17
Water rates	8 (b)	–	–	(n)	17 (d)
Drainage rates	8 (c)	11 (C)	10 (B)	(n)	–
Cesspit charges	8 (d)	11 (C)	10 (B)	(e)	–
Licence fees for access	8 (e)	11 (C)	10 (B)	–	6 (d)
Water abstraction	8 (f)	5 (e)	–	–	–
Development Land Tax	9	13	8 (D)	–	18
Date of completion	10 (a)	12 (A)	11 (A)	–	19
Vendor vacate by noon	10 (b)	–	–	–	–
Postal completion	–	12 (B)	11 (B)	–	–
Removal of rubbish	11	–	–	–	–
Copy of lease	12 (a) (i)	–	–	–	20 (a)
Reversionary title	12 (a) (ii)	V	–	–	24
Details of landlord and superior landlord	12 (b) and (c)	I (B)	–	–	20 (c)
Licence to assign	12 (d)	I (D)	–	–	20 (d)
Consent to improvements	12 (e)	I (C)	–	–	–
Details of tenants breach of covenant	–	II (A) and (B)	–	–	22 (a)
Insurance of leaseholds	12 (f)	IV	–	–	23
Service charge	12 (g) and (h)	III	–	–	21
Landlord's breach of covenant	12 (i)	II (C)	–	–	22 (b)
Drainage system to new property	–	14 (A)	–	–	–

Topic	Convey 1	Con 29 (long)	Con 29 (short)	Con 29 (supple-mentary)	E1
Fencing etc new property	1 (h)	14 (B)	–	–	14 (a)
Structural etc defects	–	–	–	(a)	11 (a)
Flooding and subsidence	–	–	–	(b)	11 (a)
Electric wiring	–	–	–	(d)	13 (e)
Central heating	–	–	–	(f)	13 (f)
Burglar alarm	–	–	–	(g)	–
Garage and parking	–	–	–	(j)	–
Telephone	–	–	–	(m)	13 (g)
Chain of transactions	–	–	–	(o)	1 (b)
Meters to be read on completion	–	–		(p)	–
Vacant possession	–	–	–	–	1 (a)
Details of tenancies	–	–	–	–	2
Discharge of mortgages	–	–	–	–	5
Fire certificate	–	9 (c)	–	–	12 (a)
Enfranchisement of lease	–	–	–	–	25
Residents Association	–	–	–	–	26

3.10 ADDITIONAL ENQUIRIES NOT ON THE PRINTED FORMS

3.10.1 The number and type of additional enquiries which *could* be raised in any given situation is limitless and certainly the purchaser's solicitor should in each transaction consider the necessity of raising additional enquiries before sending the standard preliminary enquiry forms to the vendor. It is no doubt tempting for an office to compile its own standard list of additional enquiries which thereafter are submitted in every transaction, but if one is to expect the vendor to answer these additional enquiries fully and with courtesy some discretion must be used in the selection of the questions asked, and care taken only to ask such questions as are totally relevant to the circumstances of the particular transaction. Some peculiarities relating to the property, its use, or the area in which it is situated may have emerged through the client's instructions, the estate agent's particulars, or the draft contract, and these should be followed up by raising appropriate additional enquiries. It is also accepted that the purchase of newly built properties or leasehold properties may legitimately give rise to a large number of additional enquiries.

Set out below is a table of some suggested additional enquiries which may be of relevance in certain circumstances. It is not suggested that the table contains a comprehensive list of all possible enquiries, neither should the table be treated as a blueprint for a firm's 'standard list' of additional enquiries. The table is provided as an outline checklist to jog the purchaser's solicitor's memory about matters which should validly be raised as additional enquiries.

3.10.2 Table of suggested additional enquiries

Topic	*Nature of question*	*Relevance of question*
NHBC agreement	Ask the vendor to confirm that he will assign the benefit of an existing NHBC agreement without cost to the purchaser.	A formal assignment of the agreement should be made to comply with the Law of Property Act 1925 s136 although in practice the NHBC do not insist that this provision be complied with.
Age of property	Ask when the property was first built, (if this information is not already known to purchaser).	The age of the property may be relevant when considering planning matters, eg whether the vendor has used up his limit to extend the property under the terms of the General Development Order. It may also have some bearing on the type of survey the client is advised to undertake, eg an older property may need expensive structural repairs.
Access to neighbouring property	Enquire whether the vendor is permitted access to neighbouring property in order, eg to inspect and repair gutters and whether the neighbours enjoy similar reciprocal rights.	This will be of relevance where a property is built close to the boundaries of its own land and it may not be possible to effect repairs without venturing on to neighbouring property.
Deposit	Ask whether the vendor will accept payment of a deposit of less than 10% of the purchase price.	This is a frequently raised supplementary question, since the payment of a deposit of less than 10% of the purchase price is now quite common.
Telephone	Ask the vendor to confirm that the telephone will not be disconnected.	Apart from the inconvenience and cost of having to arrange for reconnection of the telephone, in some areas, where there is a scarcity of available lines, the purchaser may experience considerable delay before the telephone is re-connected.

Topic	Nature of question	Relevance of question
Rights under Matrimonial Homes Act	Seek confirmation from vendor that no such rights exist, or that if they do, that the person with the benefit will join in the contract to release his or her rights.	This question is only necessary where the legal estate is held in the name of one spouse alone. Question 7 on form Con 29 deals with adverse rights generally, but does not specifically refer to rights under this Act.
Water abstraction licences	Seek confirmation that the licence will be assigned to the purchaser.	A water abstraction licence can usually be assigned to the purchaser provided that notice of the assignment is given to the water authority within one month of the change of ownership. Failure to notify renders the licence void and there is no guarantee that a new licence will be granted to the purchaser (see ch 21, below).
Stocks of coal, calor gas, logs etc	Ask whether the vendor's stocks of such items may be bought by the purchaser at completion.	Enquiry 10(C) on form Con 29 deals with oil supplies on the premises. It would seem sensible in appropriate cases for the purchaser also to be able to take over stocks of coal calor gas or logs.
Removal of rubbish	Seek the vendor's confirmation that all rubbish will be removed from the property and all outbuildings.	This is not strictly a preliminary enquiry, but serves as a reminder to the vendor that he should remove all his possessions, whether wanted or otherwise, from the property, otherwise he will not have complied with the contractual condition relating to the giving of vacant possession. Question 11 on Convey 1 asks this question.

Topic	*Nature of question*	*Relevance of question*
Names of previous estate owners	Ask the vendor to supply the full names of all estate owners since 1925 for whom he does not hold clear central land charges search certificates.	This question is more in the nature of a requisition on title than a preliminary enquiry, but may be raised in relation to unregistered land where the purchaser intends to make a full central land charges search before exchange of contracts.
Fixtures and fittings	(a) Ask whether the vendor will agree to an apportionment of the purchase price between the land and the chattels.	Chattels do not attract stamp duty and so the purchase price may legitimately be apportioned in order to deduct the value of the chattels. The vendor will doubtless agree to the apportionment but it is courteous to seek his permission to make this adjustment to the price.
	(b) Seek a warranty from the vendor that in removing fixtures from the property he will cause no unnecessary damage and will make good any damage caused.	This enquiry should not strictly be necessary but serves as a reminder to the vendor that he should not vandalise the property before completion. Breach of this warranty may be actionable as a collateral contract.
Newly built property	(a) Ask for a copy of the Public Health Act 1936, s18 agreement and bond.	This is often not supplied by the vendor in answer to question 4(A) on form Con 29.
	(b) Seek confirmation that a letter in lieu of a habitation certificate will be supplied by the vendor on completion.	This letter confirms that the construction of the house has been completed to the satisfaction of the local building inspector. This question may be premature at the preliminary enquiry stage and may equally well be raised as a requisition.

Topic	Nature of question	Relevance of question
	(c) Request the vendor to supply a letter from the Post Office confirming the correct postal address of property which will probably at this stage only be identified by its plot number.	This letter may not be available until nearer completion.
	(d) Seek confirmation that the builder will replace all top soil in the garden and will remove all builders' rubbish and equipment from the plot before completion.	This enquiry should not strictly be necessary but may serve as a reminder to the vendor about these matters.
	(e) Ask for precise details of the builder's obligation to remedy minor defects which occur after completion has taken place.	This information is often not contained either in the contract nor in the details of the property supplied by the builder to the purchaser.
	(f) Ask for the approximate date when it is anticipated that the whole estate will be completed.	Where the purchase is of a single plot on a large estate the dates given in answer to (f) and (g) may be as much as two years ahead, during which time the purchaser will suffer a small amount of inconvenience through the noise of nearby works and traffic, and of rough road surfaces.
	(g) Ask for the approximate date for the final making up and adoption of the roads and footpaths.	Little can be done to hasten the builder's departure from the site but the knowledge of the approximate date of final completion of the estate may make the inconvenience a little more tolerable from the purchaser's point of view.

Topic	Nature of question	Relevance of question
Tenanted property	(a) Ask whether the landlord receives any part of the tenant's rent directly from the local authority through a rent allowance scheme. (b) Specific questions relating to protected shortholds or assured tenancies.	This question appears on form Con 292 (agricultural enquiries) but not on form Con 291 (general tenancy enquiries) (see para 3.13.6, below). Form Con 291 (general tenancy enquiries) does not contain any questions specifically relating to either of these types of tenancy (see generally para 3.11.14, below).
Leasehold property	(a) Where relevant ask when and at whose expense the licence to assign is to be obtained. (b) Specific questions may be raised in relation to the compliance with painting and repairing obligations under the lease. (c) Ask whether the tenant is required to become a shareholder of a management company. If so, ask for copies of the memorandum and articles and confirmation that the consideration for the share transfer is included in the purchase price of the property. (d) Ask whether the vendor is aware of any proposals which the landlord may have for major repairs or reconstruction of the property.	Question I(D) on form Con 29 does not deal with these points. Question II (B) on form Con 29 deals with this topic in general but not specific terms (see para 3.5.17.3, above). Tenants under long leases are often required to become shareholders in a management company or residents association. None of the questions on form Con 29 or form Convey 1 deal with this matter. The cost of such works may have a bearing on the amount of the tenant's future service charge.
Leasehold flats	(a) Ask what arrangements are made for the disposal of the tenant's rubbish, eg communal dustbin. (b) A detailed question should be raised in	This question is asked for information purposes only. The amount of a service charge can be quite

Topic	Nature of question	Relevance of question
	connection with service charges.	substantial and the purchaser should seek as much information about the charge as possible. Question III on form Con 29 deals briefly with service charges (para 3.5.17.5, above) but a much more detailed question appears on form Con 291 (para 3 11 19, below) which could be adapted for use when acting for the purchaser of the lease.
Long leases of houses	(a) Ask what the rateable value of the property was at the date of the grant of the lease. (b) Ask how long the vendor has been resident in the house. (c) Ask whether the vendor has served any notice on the landlord purporting to exercise his rights under the Leasehold Reform Act 1967. If so, ask for a copy of the notice and whether the vendor will assign the benefit of the notice to the purchaser.	The tenant of a long lease of a house may be able to exercise the right to an extension of his lease or to purchase the reversion under the Leasehold Reform Act 1967. These questions should reveal whether the house falls within the limits set by the 1967 Act and whether any steps have been taken to exercise the rights given by the Act (see generally para 3.11.19, below).

3.11 FORM CON 291 (TENANTED PROPERTY)

This form is reproduced on pp 83–86, below.

3.11.1 Comment on form Con 291
3.11.1.1   This form of preliminary enquiries is intended to be used in conjunction with either form Con 29 (long) or Con 29 (short) where the purchase is of tenanted residential or business premises. In order to avoid the duplication of information it would seem sensible to use form Con 29 (short) when form Con 291 is also used. The form is divided into three sections, the first of which contains general enquiries relevant to all properties, the second part contains questions relating only to business premises and the final section relates to residential tenancies.

Short description re ....
of the property

Parties ....

to ....

**These enquiries are copyright
and may not be reproduced**

**GENERAL
TENANCY
ENQUIRIES**
FOR USE WITH ENQUIRIES BEFORE
CONTRACT WHERE ALL OR PART
OF THE PROPERTY IS LET OR
OCCUPIED ON LICENCE
*(For Agricultural Holdings and
Agricultural Tied Cottages, use
Agricultural Tenancy Enquiries).*

**Please strike out enquiries which
are not applicable**

Replies are requested to the following additional enquiries.
Please reply separately for each part of the property to be sold which is
separately let.
The words 'landlord' and 'tenant' should be construed to include
predecessors in title wherever possible.

Licensees If all or any part of the property is occupied by a licensee,
please reply to the appropriate enquires in respect of that occupation,
making it clear that the agreement is a licence. In that case, read
'tenancy' and 'letting' as licence, 'tenant' as 'licensee', 'landlord' as
licensor, and 'rent' as sum contracted to be paid under the licence.

....
Proposed purchaser's solicitor

Date .... 198...........

The replies are as follows.

....
Proposed vendor's solicitor

Date .... 198......

REPLIES

**These replies are given on behalf of the proposed vendor and
without responsibility on the part of his solicitors their partners or
employees. They are believed to be correct but the accuracy is
not guaranteed and they do not obviate the need to make
appropriate searches, enquiries and inspections.**

GENERAL INQUIRIES

A. Tenant

What are the full names and address of the tenant?

B. Terms of letting

(1) Please supply a copy of the lease, tenancy agreement and any other
document evidencing all or any of the terms of letting, and any variations
thereof.

(2) Unless shown on any copy document supplied:
    (i) What part of the property to be sold is let to the tenant, and
what rights has the tenant over other parts of the property?
    (ii) When was the tenancy originally granted?
    (iii) What is the period of the letting?
    (iv) How much is the rent, on what days or dates is it payable, in
advance or in arrear?
    (v) What express repairing and other obligations have been
undertaken respectively by the landlord and the tenant?
(3) What licences or consents have been given by the landlord to the
tenant?

C. Sub-letting

If the vendor is aware of any sub-letting of all or part of the demised
premises, what are:
    (i) the full names and address of the sub-tenant?
    (ii) the terms of the sub-letting?

D. Insurance

If the tenant or a sub-tenant insures the demised premises, please
give particulars of the existing cover, stating insurers' name and address,
policy number, insureds' name(s), risks covered, for what amount,
premium and date to which the property is insured.

E. Orders, etc.

Please supply copies of any of the following which relate to or affect
the term of the letting or which affect the use of the property when let:

    (i) orders of any court, tribunal or local authority;
    (ii) notices served on or by the local authority, and any acknowl-
edgement received from the local authority;
    (iii) undertakings given by the landlord or the tenant.

83

F.   Disputes

(1) Have the terms of the tenancy or any dispute between landlord and tenant been the subject of proceedings before any court, tribunal or arbitrator, or are any such proceedings pending? If so, please give particulars.

(2) Is the tenant now, or has he previously been, in arrear in paying the rent?

(3) Of what other breaches of convenant by the tenant, continuing or past, is the vendor aware?

(4) Has the tenant complained of any breach of the landlord's obligations?

G.   Rent revision

(1) Please give particulars of the result of any rent review determined under the lease, including the award of any arbitrator or valuer.

(2) Have the landlord and the tenant concluded any agreement as to the rent payable for any future period? If so please give particulars.

(3) Has the tenant or any sub-tenant made any improvement to the demised premises which is to be ignored in agreeing or determining any future rent?

BUSINESS TENANCY ENQUIRIES

Please reply to enquiries in this section if the letting may be affected by the Landlord and Tenant Act 1954, Pt. II.

H.   Duration of business

Since what date have the demised premises been occupied for the purposes of the business now carried on by the tenant?

I.   Improvements

(1) Is the tenant entitled on quitting the demised premises at the termination of the tenancy to any compensation for improvements?

(2) Has the tenant made any improvement which is to be ignored in determining a new rent, under the Landlord and Tenant Act 1954, s. 34 (1) (c) as amended by the Law of Property Act 1969?

J.   New tenancy

Have terms been agreed for any new tenancy to be granted to the tenant? If so, please supply a copy of any written agreement or particulars of any oral agreement.

RESIDENTIAL TENANCY ENQUIRIES

Please reply to enquiries in this section if any part of the property is used for residential purposes. It may be necessary to raise additional enquiries in respect of tenancies granted by housing associations, housing trusts and the Crown Estate Commissioners.

K.   Application of statutory rules

(1) Is the tenancy:
   (i) regulated?
   (ii) a restricted contract?
   (iii) treated as a restricted contract, because there is a resident landlord?

(2) What was the retable value of the demised premises on:
   (i) 23rd March 1965?
   (ii) 22nd March 1973?
   (iii) 1st April 1973?

(3) Has any agreement been reached between landlord and tenant apportioning the rateable value of the demised and other premises? If so please give particulars.

(4) Has a reduced rateable value for the purposes of the Leasehold Reform Act 1967 been agreed or determined? If so, please give particulars.

(5) Has there been a statutory transmission of the tenancy? If so, please give particulars.

L.   Rent

(1) Is a rent registered for all or any part of the demised premises? If so, please state:
   (i) amount of rent;
   (ii) amount shown as attributable to services;
   (iii) date of registration, and effective date if different;
   (iv) extent of premises affected;
   (v) any other registered details.

(2) If the current recoverable rent is restricted by the operation of statutory phasing provisions, please state:
   (i) the previous rent limit;
   (ii) the service element.

M. Terms of letting

(1) If the present rent contains any amount in respect of the cost, or the increased cost to the landlord or a superior lessor of rates, improvements, furniture, or the provision of services, please give full particulars.

(2) What furniture used by the tenant is supplied by the landlord, and on what terms?

(3) What services is the landlord contractually obliged to supply to the tenant?

N. Resident landlord

If it is considered that the tenancy falls within the Rent Act 1977, s. 12 (lettings by resident landlords):

(1) Did the landlord occupy as his residence (as defined by the Rent Act 1977, Sched. 2, para. 5) another dwellinghouse in the same building when the tenancy was granted to the tenant?

(2) Has the landlord continuously occupied another such dwellinghouse even since?

(3) If the answer to (1) or (2) is No, please give details of the grounds on which it is believed that the provisions apply.

(4) Immediately before the grant of the current tenancy, did the tenant occupy the demised premises, or some other dwellinghouse in the same building? If so, on what terms?

O. Long tenancies

Where the letting was originally for over 21 years, or is otherwise within the statutory definition for a long tenancy:

(1) How long has the present tenant, and any member of his family from whom he inherited the property, been in possession?

(2) Have terms been agreed with the tenant for a statutory tenancy pursuant to the Landlord and Tenant Act, 1954, Pt I, and if so, on what terms?

(3) Was the lease granted on the exercise of a secure tenant's right to buy?

P. Service charges

If the demised premises are a flat let on a long lease and the tenant pays a service charge as defined by the Housing Act 1980, Sched. 19:

(1) Is there a recognised tenants' association for the tenants of flats in the building containing the demised premises?

(2) If so:

(i) was it recognised by the landlord or by a certificate of a rent assessment committee member?

(ii) please give the name and address of its secretary.

(3) Has the tenant, or the secretary of the tenants' association, served a request for a written summary of costs with which the vendor has not yet complied?

(4) Please confirm that on completion the vendor will hand over particulars of the relevant costs, with accounts and receipts to vouch them, competitive estimates obtained and evidence of consultations with tenants and any tenants' association or (as the case may be) of compliance with the requirements for works whose cost exceeded the prescribed amount, for the current and previous accounting years.

(5) In respect of items included in the service charge, the full cost of which has not yet been recovered:

(i) please supply copies of estimates obtained before the liabilities were incurred;

(ii) please supply evidence of compliance with the requirements for works whose cost exceeded the prescribed amount or reasons for non-compliance;

(iii) please supply copies of accounts paid by or rendered to the vendor;

(iv) has the tenant, or tenants' association, expressed dissatisfaction at the standard of, or the amount payable for, any such item?

FOR ADDITIONAL ENQUIRIES, SEE OVER.

ADDITIONAL ENQUIRIES

oyez The Solicitors' Law Stationery Society plc. Oyez House, 237 Long Lane, London SE1 4PU ★ ★ ★

Conveyancing 291
FOURTH EDITION
May, 1983

The headnote to the form requests the vendor to reply separately to each question in respect of each part of the property which is separately let and to reveal information in relation to licences as well as tenancies. A commentary on the individual questions on the form appears below.

3.11.2   Tenant
3.11.2.1

> A. Tenant
> What are the full names and address of the tenant?

3.11.2.2   This question is self-explanatory.

3.11.3   Terms of letting
3.11.3.1

> B. Terms of letting
> (1) Please supply a copy of the lease, tenancy agreement and any other document evidencing all or any of the terms of letting, and any variations thereof.
> (2) Unless shown on any copy document supplied:
>> (i) What part of the property to be sold is let to the tenant, and what rights has the tenant over other parts of the property?
>> (ii) When was the tenancy originally granted?
>> (iii) What is the period of the letting?
>> (iv) How much is the rent, on what days or dates is it payable, in advance or in arrear?
>> (v) What express repairing and other obligations have been undertaken respectively by the landlord and the tenant?
> (3) What licences or consents have been given by the landlord to the tenant?

3.11.3.2   The purchaser will need to obtain precise details relating to the nature of any tenancy to which the property is subject and this question is designed to reveal such information.

The date when the tenancy was originally granted may affect the nature of the security of tenure afforded to the tenant and, in the case of business premises, the tenant's entitlement to compensation. It should be remembered that in the case of residential or mainly residential tenancies of houses or flats for a term of less than seven years, the Housing Act 1961, ss 31 and 32 will impose certain repairing obligations on the landlord in addition to any express covenants contained in the lease or tenancy agreement.

3.11.4 Sub-letting

C. Sub-letting
If the vendor is aware of any sub-letting of all or part of the demised premises, what are:
   (i) the full names and address of the sub-tenant?
   (ii) the terms of the sub-letting?

3.11.4.1 Where a sub-letting of the property has taken place it should be ascertained whether the sub-letting has been effected in accordance with the terms of the superior lease. If the vendor is aware of a sub-letting which has taken place without the necessary consent or licence, enquiries should be made as to whether the vendor by his conduct has waived the requirement for a consent or licence and thus has acquiesced in the sub-letting, or whether any steps have been taken by the landlord in respect of the breach. A statutory tenancy under the Rent Act 1977 is incapable of being assigned without the landlord's consent, and the same applies to a sub-letting of the whole of the premises. In certain cases (eg residential property where the superior landlord is the Crown) a sub-tenant may be able to claim security of tenure against his immediate landlord despite the fact that the superior tenant has no such rights.

3.11.5 Insurance

D. Insurance
If the tenant or a sub-tenant insures the demised premises, please give particulars of the existing cover, stating insurers' name and address, policy number, insureds' name(s), risks covered, for what amount, premium and date to which the property is insured.

3.11.5.1 This question asks for details of property insurance effected by the tenant or sub-tenant. Details of the existing cover will be revealed, but the question does not specifically require the vendor to supply a copy of the policy itself.

3.11.6 Orders etc
3.11.6.1

E. Orders, etc.
Please supply copies of any of the following which relate to or affect the term of the letting or which affect the use of the property when let:
   (i)   orders of any court, tribunal or local authority;
   (ii) notices served on or by the local authority, and any acknowledgement received from the local authority;
   (iii) undertakings given by the landlord or the tenant.

3.11.6.2 The nature of the orders, notices and undertakings which could be revealed in response to this question might include the following:

  (a) orders relating to the rent recoverable for the property;
  (b) possession orders;
  (c) notices served by the local authority in relation to planning matters, closing orders, notices relating to houses in multiple occupation, orders relating to fire certificates;
  (d) undertakings in relation to repairs to the property.

As worded, the question only requires the vendor to disclose orders and notices which relate to the terms of the letting or which affect the *use* of the property and therefore example (d) above would not strictly speaking have to be disclosed. It is clearly in the purchaser's interests to discover and investigate all notices or orders which might affect the property which he is intending to buy and thus consideration may be given to widening the scope of the question by deleting the words 'the use of'. The word 'notice' in E(ii) suggests that the vendor is only obliged to disclose formal notices which he has received from the local authority. The purchaser should require him also to disclose informal notices and letters received from the local authority.

3.11.7 Disputes

F. Disputes
  (1) Have the terms of the tenancy or any dispute between landlord and tenant been the subject of proceedings before any court, tribunal or arbitrator, or are any such proceedings pending? If so, please give particulars.
  (2) Is the tenant now, or has he previously been in arrear in paying the rent?
  (3) Of what other breaches of covenant by the tenant continuing or past, is the vendor aware?
  (4) Has the tenant complained of any breach of the landlord's obligations?

3.11.7.1 It is clearly in the purchaser's interest to know of any circumstances affecting the tenancy which have been or which might give rise to proceedings and this question is intended to reveal such information. Any current disputes, or breaches of covenant by the tenant should be required to be settled or remedied prior to completion. Where a current breach of covenant by the tenant is disclosed or suspected, an additional enquiry should be raised asking the vendor what steps, if any, he has taken to require the tenant to remedy the breach.

Forfeiture actions to enforce a breach of covenant (other than for non-payment of rent) must generally be preceded by the service of a notice under the Law of Property Act 1925, s146.

Where the Leasehold Property (Repairs) Act 1938 applies to a breach of a tenant's repairing covenant, the above requirement extends also to an action for damages for non-repair and the tenant has a right to serve counter-notice under the 1938 Act requiring the landlord to obtain leave of the court before proceeding with his remedy.

3.11.8   Rent revision

G. Rent revision
(1) Please give particulars of the result of any rent review determined under the lease, including the award of any arbitrator or valuer.
(2) Have the landlord and the tenant concluded any agreement as to the rent payable for any future period? If so please give particulars.
(3) Has the tenant or any sub-tenant made any improvement to the demised premises which is to be ignored in agreeing or determining any future rent?

3.11.8.1   A rent review provision contained in a lease should be carefully examined to ensure that it contains a certain method of assessing the new rent and a workable notice procedure to enable the clause to take effect. The clause will often specify that improvements effected by the tenant, except where made pursuant to a contractual obligation, are to be ignored in assessing the amount of rent payable under the review clause. 'Improvements' are often defined by reference to the Landlord and Tenant Act 1954, s34 which lays down the criteria on which the court will rely in assessing the rent for a new lease ordered by the court under Part II of the Landlord and Tenant Act 1954.

It should be noted that effectively the power to increase the rent in relation to tenancies protected by the Rent Act 1977 is limited by the Rent Act itself.

3.11.9   Business tenancies
3.11.9.1   Questions H, I and J on the standard form are the only questions which relate exclusively to business premises.

3.11.10   Duration of business
3.11.10.1

H. Duration of business
Since what date have the demised premises been occupied for the purposes of the business now carried on by the tenant?

3.11.10.2   The length of time during which the tenant has occupied the premises for his business will affect the tenant's entitlement to compensation for disturbance on quitting the premises.

The tenant is only entitled to such compensation where he is required to vacate the premises as a result of the landlord's successful claim under grounds (e) (f) or (g) of the Landlord and Tenant Act 1954, s30. The amount of compensation is generally the rateable value of the premises multiplied by $2\frac{1}{4}$. In cases where that business has been carried on for at least 14 years, the amount of compensation is $2\frac{1}{4} \times$ the rateable value $\times 2$. In this case the business user may have been carried on either by the tenant or by his predecessor in title. Although the question as drafted extends to predecessors in title this could be made clearer. From 7 May 1985 the multiplier is increased from $2\frac{1}{4}$ to 3.

3.11.11   Improvements
3.11.11.1

   I. Improvements
   (1) Is the tenant entitled on quitting the demised premises at the termination of the tenancy to any compensation for improvements?
   (2) Has the tenant made any improvement which is to be ignored in determining a new rent, under the Landlord and Tenant Act 1954, s34 (1) (c) as amended by the Law of Property Act 1969?

3.11.11.2   The tenants entitlement to compensation for improvements to business premises will normally depend on his having given notice of his intention (under the terms of the Landlord and Tenant Act 1927 as amended) to effect the improvements prior to commencing the work. Further, a claim for compensation must generally be made to the landlord within three months of the service of the notice (whether given by landlord or tenant) or other act which purports to determine the tenancy.

Subject to these two conditions, the amount of the compensation, payable when the tenant actually quits the property, is either the value which the improvements have added to the capital value of the premises or the cost of effecting the improvements at the date when the tenant leaves. No compensation is payable for improvements which have been effected by the tenant under a contractual obligation, nor for 'improvements' which are in the nature of tenant's fixtures which the tenant is entitled to remove from the premises.

When the court settles the rent for a new lease under the Landlord and Tenant Act 1954, Part II certain factors, listed in s34(1)(c) of the Act (as amended) must be ignored by the court in determining the new rent. These factors include any effect on the rent of an improvement carried out by the current tenant, or his predecessor in title, provided that the improvement was not carried out pursuant to a contractual obligation to the immediate landlord.

3.11.12   New tenancy
3.11.12.1

> J. New tenancy
> Have terms been agreed for any new tenancy to be granted to the
> tenant? If so, please supply a copy of any written agreement or
> particulars of any oral agreement.

3.11.12.2   A lease of business premises continues despite expiry of the
contractual term unless and until determined in one of the ways specified by the Landlord and Tenant Act 1954, s24. On determination of
the lease the tenant has the right to the grant of a new lease unless the
landlord can establish one of the grounds for possession listed in s30 of
the Act. The terms of the new lease are agreed by the parties with
resort to the court in default of agreement. Any purchaser of tenanted
business premises will need to know what terms, if any, have already
been agreed between the landlord and tenant for the grant of a new lease.

3.11.13   Exemption of premises from the Landlord and Tenant Act 1954, Part II
3.11.13.1   The headnote to the business tenancy enquiries asks the
vendor to reply to these questions if the letting *may* be affected by the
1954 Act.

In certain circumstances leases of business premises may be either
exempted from the protection afforded by the Act, or ineligible to
claim its protection. The principle exceptions are listed below:

(a) where the court has granted an order exempting a fixed term
lease from the security of tenure provisions of the Act;

(b) most public houses;

(c) fixed term tenancies not exceeding six months provided the tenant has not been in possession for more than 12 months and there is
no provision for extension beyond six months;

(d) agricultural holdings;

(e) mining leases;

(f) a written tenancy granted to an employee stating the purpose of
the letting and which continues only so long as the tenant is employed;

(g) tenancies at will;

(h) a tenancy where the tenant is carrying on business in breach of
a general prohibition against business use contained in the lease,
unless the breach has been waived.

A proposed purchaser of business premises will wish to know if the
premises are potentially covered by the security provisions of the 1954
Act and a supplementary question asking the vendor whether he is
aware of any circumstances relating to the tenancy which might exempt it from the provisions of the Act may be considered.

3.11.14 Residential tenancies

3.11.14.1 Questions K–P inclusive on this form relate to residential tenancies. None of the questions in this section specifically apply to assured tenancies as defined by the Housing Act 1980, s56.

Assured tenancies are in general long leases of residential property which have been constructed or converted to such use after 8 August 1980 and where the landlord is a housing association or other body approved by regulations made under the Housing Act 1980. Security of tenure under these tenancies is provided by the Landlord and Tenant Act 1954, Part II as modified by the Housing Act 1980. If it is thought that the property being acquired may be subject to such a tenancy consideration should be given to raising specific additional enquiries.

Further, these questions do not specifically relate to protected shorthold tenancies and extra enquiries may be necessary in relation to this type of tenancy.

For a protected shorthold tenancy of a dwelling to exist the following conditions must be satisfied:

(a) the letting must be for a fixed term of not less than one year nor more than five years and be incapable of premature determination by the landlord except where the tenant is in breach of covenant;

(b) a prescribed form of notice, informing the tenant that the tenancy is a protected shorthold must have been given to the tenant before the tenancy commenced;

(c) the tenancy is not granted to someone who prior to the grant of this tenancy was the protected or statutory tenant of those premises;

(d) in the case of a shorthold tenancy granted before 1 December 1981, or a shorthold tenancy granted at any time of premises within Greater London the rent must be registered or a certificate of fair rent issued before the commencement of the tenancy (see para 3.11.16, below).

3.11.15 Application of statutory rules
3.11.15.1

K. Application of statutory rules
(1) Is the tenancy
  (i) regulated?
  (ii) a restricted contract?
  (iii) treated as a restricted contract, because there is a resident landlord?
(2) What was the ratable value of the demised premises on
  (i) 23rd March 1965?
  (ii) 22nd March 1973?
  (iii) 1st April 1973?
(3) Has any agreement been reached between landlord and tenant

apportioning the rateable value of the demised and other premises? If so please give particulars.

(4) Has a reduced rateable value for the purposes of the Leasehold Reform Act 1967 been agreed or determined? If so please give particulars.

(5) Has there been a statutory transmission of the tenancy? If so, please give particulars.

3.11.15.2   *Regulated tenancies*

A regulated tenancy is a tenancy of a house or part of a house which enjoys the full protection of the security of tenure provisions contained in the Rent Act 1977 as amended by the Housing Act 1980.

To be a regulated tenancy the following conditions must be satisfied:

(a) there must be a tenancy (not a licence) of a house or part of a house which is let as a separate dwelling;

(b) the rateable value of the premises must fall within certain limits (para 3.11.15.6, below);

(c) the rent payable must equal or exceed two-thirds of the rateable value on a certain date;

3.11.15.3   *Principle exceptions from the Act*

Some tenancies which satisfy the conditions set out in the preceding paragraph are nevertheless excluded from the full protection of the Rent Act 1977. The principle exceptions are listed below:

(a) premises which are let together with more than 2 acres of agricultural land;

(b) where the rent includes payment in respect of board or substantial payments in respect of attendance;

(c) a tenancy granted to a student by an institution specified by the Secretary of State (eg university accommodation);

(d) where the right of occupation is for the purpose of a holiday;

(e) agricultural holdings;

(f) premises with an off-licence for liquor;

(g) where the landlord is resident in the same building or shares essential living accommodation with the tenant (see para 3.11.15.4, below);

(h) where the immediate landlord is the Crown, a local authority, housing association or one of various other public bodies;

(i) business premises;

(j) parsonage houses of the Church of England.

3.11.15.4   *Restricted contracts*

A restricted contract exists where (no protected tenancy being created) a tenancy or licence fulfills the conditions in (a) below or where a tenancy is excluded from being a regulated tenancy only by reason of the fact that one of the situations listed in (b) and (c) below applies:

(a) the rent payable for the premises includes payment for the use of furniture or in relation to services provided by the landlord. 'Services' includes attendance, lighting, heating and the supply of hot water, but not a cold water supply or sanitary accommodation;

(b) the tenant shares essential living accommodation (eg kitchen, living room) with his landlord;

(c) the landlord is resident in the same house. To fall within this category all of the following conditions must be satisfied:

  (i) the dwelling house which is the subject of the contract must form part only of a building, which building is not a purpose built block of flats;

  (ii) the tenancy was granted on or after 14 August 1974. Where the tenancy was granted before this date a restricted contract can exist only in relation to fully furnished premises;

  (iii) at the time when the tenancy commenced the landlord was resident in another part of the same building;

  (iv) the landlord's residence has been continuous since the tenancy was granted. There are however certain exceptions to this rule, eg on a sale of the house or on the landlord's death.

(See Sch 2 to the 1977 Act as amended by the Housing Act 1980, s65(2).)

If the conditions of the exceptional cases are not met, the tenancy will cease to be a restricted contract and will receive the benefit of the full security of tenure provisions applicable to regulated tenancies.

Rent control provisions apply to restricted contracts (reasonable rents) as to regulated tenancies (fair rents), but the security of tenure available under a restricted contract is limited and takes effect as a postponement of the operation of a notice to quit (in the case of contracts entered into before 28 November 1980). Where the contract was granted on or after this date the only power is in the courts to order a postponement of the execution of a possession order for such period, not exceeding three months, as it thinks fit.

3.11.15.5 *The statutory tenancy*

On the termination of the contractual tenancy (protected tenancy) of a house with full Rent Act protection a statutory tenancy arises which entitles the tenant to remain in possession of the premises until such time as he vacates the premises voluntarily or the landlord obtains a court order for possession, having first established one of the grounds for possession listed in Sch 15 to the 1977 Act.

The statutory tenancy is the form of security of tenure given to the tenant under a regulated tenancy and is personal to the tenant in that it cannot be assigned or sublet as to the whole although the court has power to order the transfer of the statutory tenancy in the course of matrimonial proceedings. The statutory tenancy is dependent on the tenant's occupation of the premises as his residence and will end if he ceases to occupy the premises as his home. The provisions of the original contract continue to apply during the statutory tenancy, except where inconsistent with the provisions of the Rent Act 1977. A statutory tenancy does not vest in personal representatives on the death of the tenant (para 3.11.15.7, below), although it may pass by operation of law to a member of the family of the deceased.

3.11.15.6   *Rateable value limits*
Section 4(1) of the Rent Act 1977 provides that a tenancy is not a protected (regulated) tenancy if the dwellinghouse falls within one of the classes listed in s4(2) which is set out below. The 'appropriate day' is generally 23 March 1965 or the date when the property was first entered on the valuation list if later.

> **s4 (2)** Where alternative rateable values are mentioned in this subsection, the higher applies if the dwellinghouse is in Greater London and the lower applies if it is elsewhere.
>
> *Class A*
>
> The appropriate day in relation to the dwellinghouse falls or fell on or after 1st April 1973 and the dwellinghouse on the appropriate day has or had a rateable value exceeding £1,500 or £750.
>
> *Class B*
>
> The appropriate day in relation to the dwellinghouse fell on or after 22nd March 1973, but before 1st April 1973, and the dwellinghouse—
> (a) on the appropriate day had a rateable value exceeding £600 or £300, and
> (b) on 1st April 1973 had a rateable value exceeding £1,500 or £750.
>
> *Class C*
>
> The appropriate day in relation to the dwellinghouse fell before 22nd March 1973 and the dwellinghouse—
> (a) on the appropriate day had a rateable value exceeding £400 or £200, and
> (b) on 22nd March 1973 had a rateable value exceeding £600 or £300, and
> (c) on 1st April 1973 had a rateable value exceeding £1,500 or £750.

(3) If any question arises in any proceedings whether a dwellinghouse falls within a Class in subsection (2) above, by virtue of its rateable value at any time, it shall be deemed not to fall within that Class unless the contrary is shown.

The rateable value limits for restricted contracts are governed by the Rent Act 1977, s19 (3) and (4) set out below. 'Appropriate day' has the meaning given above.

s19 (3) A contract is not a restricted contract if the dwelling falls within one of the Classes set out in subsection (4) below.

(4) Where alternative rateable values are mentioned in this subsection the higher applies if the dwelling is in Greater London and the lower applies if it is elsewhere.

Class D

The appropriate day in relation to the dwelling falls or fell on or after 1st April 1973 and the dwelling on the appropriate day has or had a rateable value exceeding £1,500 or £750.

Class E

The appropriate day in relation to the dwelling fell before 1st April 1973 and the dwelling—

(a) on the appropriate day had a rateable value exceeding £400 or £200, and

(b) on 1st April 1973 had a rateable value exceeding £1,500 or £750.

3.11.15.7 *Transmission of regulated tenancies*

On the death of a statutory tenant, under the Rent Act the tenancy does not vest in the tenant's personal representatives or pass under his will or intestacy. The tenant's spouse, if resident with the tenant at the time of the death, or if there is no such spouse a member of the tenant's family who had been living with the tenant for a period of at least six months immediately preceding the death, may claim a transmission of the tenancy and may continue to occupy the premises as his or her residence in place of the deceased tenant.

'Member of the family' is not defined by the Act but may include parents, brothers and sisters, children (including adopted and step-children), grandchildren and nephews and nieces. Recent cases have also established that a common law husband or wife may, provided the relationship was established and permanent, fall within this category.[13]

A second transmission, on a similar basis, is possible on the death of the first transmittee. There can even be a transmission of a statutory tenancy where the deceased was a protected (or contractual) tenant at his death in which event any rights of a beneficiary of the deceased to the protected tenancy are deferred to the rights of the transmittee.

3.11.15.8   *Leasehold Reform Act 1967*
This Act, which in certain circumstances gives the tenant the right to claim an extension of his lease by a term of 50 years and or the right to buy the freehold reversion, applies where (inter alia) the rateable value of a house, let on a long lease was below a certain limit on a particular date. These limits are set out below. In some cases the rateable value of the premises may be notionally reduced for the purposes of the 1967 Act, to exclude the effect of improvements made or paid for by the tenant. This notional reduction may have the effect of bringing the premises within the scope of the Act (see also para 3.11.19).

3.11.15.9   *Rateable value limits for the purposes of the Leasehold Reform Act 1967*

A. Where the lease was granted on or before 18 February 1966.

	Greater London	*Elsewhere*
Appropriate day before 1 April 1973	£400 on the appropriate day or £1,500 on 1 April 1973 if the first limit was exceeded	£200 on the appropriate day or £750 on 1 April 1973 if the first limit was exceeded
Appropriate day on or after 1 April 1973	£1,500 on the appropriate day	£750 on the appropriate day

B. Where the lease was granted after 18 February 1966.

	Greater London	*Elsewhere*
Appropriate day before 1 April 1973	£400 on the appropriate day	£200 on the appropriate day
Appropriate day on or after 1 April 1973	£1,000 on the appropriate day	£500 on the appropriate day

The appropriate day is 23 March 1965 or (if the house had no rateable value on that date), the first date on which a rateable value for it appears on the valuation list.

3.11.16 Rent
3.11.16.1

L. Rent

(1) Is a rent registered for all or any part of the demised premises? If so, please state:

   (i) amount of rent;

   (ii) amount shown as attributable to services;

   (iii) date of registration, and effective date if different;

   (iv) extent of premises affected;

   (v) any other registered details.

(2) If the current recoverable rent is restricted by the operation of statutory phasing provisions, please state.

   (i) the previous rent limit;

   (ii) the service element.

3.11.16.2 *Rent control (regulated tenancies)*

There is no limit on the rent recoverable under a regulated tenancy unless a rent is registered. On registration the registered rent becomes the maximum rent legally recoverable for the premises and this sum cannot in general be altered for a period of two years following the registration. The landlord and tenant either alone or on a joint application may apply to the rent officer for the area to have a rent registered for the property. Appeal from the rent officer's decision lies to the rent assessment committee within 28 days. In assessing a fair rent all the circumstances of the case (other than personal circumstances) will be taken into account although there are certain matters (eg the effect of a housing shortage) which must be ignored by the rent officer in reaching his decision.

Any person who intends to let property on a protected tenancy may, prior to the commencement of the letting apply to the rent officer for a certificate specifying what would be a fair rent for the property (certificate of fair rent).

When the rent limit for an existing tenant is increased the landlord cannot immediately recover the full amount of the increase. Any sum in the increased rent which is attributable to the increase in the cost of services provided by the landlord is recoverable in full immediately, but subject to this the increased rent is subject to phasing and the landlord may recover one-half of the increase immediately, but can only recover the full amount of the increase at the end of one year from the date of the increase.

3.11.16.3 *Restricted contracts*

The rent control provisions applicable to these contracts are similar to those affecting regulated tenancies (outlined in the preceding paragraph) except that the reasonable rent (cf fair rent for regulated tenancies) is assessed by the Rent Tribunal which is not bound by the statutory criteria for assessment which apply to regulated tenancies.

3.11.16.4 *Protected shortholds*
The rent control provisions applicable to these tenancies are similar to those affecting regulated tenancies (para 3.11.16.2, above). In the case of a shorthold tenancy granted before 1 December 1981 or a shorthold tenancy granted at any time of premises within Greater London, either a fair rent must be registered at the time of the grant of the tenancy, or a certificate of fair rent must have been issued by that time. In the latter case, an application for the registration of the rent must be made within 28 days of the commencement of the term.

3.11.16.5 Where the vendor cannot supply details of the registered rent, or in any case where the purchaser wishes to check the accuracy of the details supplied a search may be undertaken with the rent officer (regulated tenancies) or rent assessment committee (restricted contracts) (see ch 15, below).

3.11.17 Terms of letting
3.11.17.1

> M. Terms of letting
> (1) If the present rent contains any amount in respect of the cost or the increased cost to the landlord or a superior lessor of rates, improvements, furniture or the provision of services, please give full particulars.
> (2) What furniture used by the tenant is supplied by the landlord, and on what terms?
> (3) What services is the landlord contractually obliged to supply to the tenant?

3.11.17.2 This question asks the vendor to give details of the amount contained in the rent which relates to the supply of services, or improvements, the use of furniture or the rates on the property.

In so far as such amounts relate to the supply of services or to the rates on the property, increases in these sums are not subject to the phasing provisions on the increase of rent (para 3.11.16.2, above).

The use of furniture and supply of services may be relevant in deciding whether the tenant has a restricted contract (para 3.11.15.4, above).

3.11.18 Resident landlord
3.11.18.1

> N. Resident landlord
> If it is considered that the tenancy falls within the Rent Act 1977, s12 (lettings by resident landlords).

(1) Did the landlord occupy as his residence (as defined by the Rent Act 1977, Sched. 2, para 5) another dwellinghouse in the same building when the tenancy was granted to the tenant?
(2) Has the landlord continuously occupied another such dwelling-house ever since?
(3) If the answer to (1) or (2) is No, please give details of the grounds on which it is believed that the provisions apply.
(4) Immediately before the grant of the current tenancy, did the tenant occupy the demised premises or some other dwellinghouse in the same building? if so, on what terms?

3.11.18.2 This question is designed to elicit information relating to tenancies which may fall within the resident landlord exception under the Rent Act 1977, s12 and which may therefore be treated as restricted contracts. An explanation of the provisions relating to restricted contracts is contained in para 3.11.15.4, above.

3.11.18.3 Where the tenancy was granted before 14 August 1974, unless the premises were a fully furnished letting, the tenant may enjoy the full protection of the Rent Act 1977 under a regulated tenancy.

3.11.19 Long tenancies
3.11.19.1

O. Long tenancies
Where the letting was originally for over 21 years, or is otherwise within the statutory definition for a long tenancy:
(1) How long has the present tenant and any member of his family from whom he inherited the property, been in possession?
(2) Have terms been agreed with the tenant for a statutory tenancy pursuant to the Landlord and Tenant Act 1954, Pt 1, and if so, on what terms?
(3) Was the lease granted on the exercise of a secure tenant's right to buy?

3.11.19.2 A long tenancy is generally one where the original lease was granted for a term exceeding 21 years. In cases where the Leasehold Reform Act 1967 applies a tenancy for an initial period of less than 21 years, but which contains an option to renew, which having been exercised takes the total term of the lease over 21 years, is also treated as a long lease.

3.11.19.3 *Leasehold Reform Act 1967*
This Act applies to a tenant who occupies a house (not a flat) as his main residence under a long lease at a low rent (rent less than two-thirds rateable value) and in certain circumstances gives such a tenant the right to obtain a 50-year extension of his lease or to acquire the freehold. The rateable value of the premises must fall within certain limits (para 3.11.15.8, above).

The tenant must have occupied the premises as his only or main residence for a period of three years immediately preceding the service of the notice exercising his rights under the Act. Alternatively the tenant must be in occupation and have occupied the premises for periods totalling three years out of the previous ten years. If the tenant dies a member of his family who succeeds to the tenancy can treat the deceased's period of residence as his own to the extent that the member of the family also lived in the house during the deceased's occupation and was resident with him at the time of the death. Where the lease is held by trustees, they may exercise the rights given under the Act, dependent on the residence qualifications of a beneficiary.

A tenant who has obtained a 50-year extension of his lease may at any time up to the term date of the original lease also exercise the right to buy the freehold.

On the expiry of the 50-year extension the lease comes to an end and there is no right to a further extension of the lease and no security of tenure for the tenant.

Contracting out of the Act is generally not possible although the Act does not bind the Crown and the freehold may not be acquired where the landlord is the National Trust.

In limited circumstances (see the Leasehold Reform Act 1967, ss17 and 18) the landlord may defeat the tenant's claim on the grounds that the landlord requires possession of the premises for his own occupation, or occupation by a member of his family, or for redevelopment. Additional questions may be raised here, asking the landlord to supply the rateable value of the premises at the time when the lease was granted, and asking whether the tenant has served any notice of his intention to exercise his rights under the Act.

3.11.19.4 *Landlord & Tenant Act 1954, Part I*

This Act provides security of tenure for the tenants of long leases of dwelling houses (including flats) at a low rent (less than two-thirds rateable value). Many of the tenancies which would previously have fallen within the scope of this Act have now either been converted into statutory tenancies within the Rent Act 1977 or have ceased to exist as tenancies because the tenant has exercised his right to buy the freehold under the Leasehold Reform Act 1967. There are however some premises to which Part I of the 1954 Act still applies.

For the Act to apply, the tenancy when originally granted must have been for a term in excess of 21 years at a rent of less than two-thirds of the rateable value. Except for the latter matter the tenancy must be one which would otherwise satisfy the conditions for a tenancy regulated under the Rent Act 1977 (para 3.11.15.2, above).

The contractual tenancy continues in force, even after expiry of the contractual term date, until determined by the service of a notice in the prescribed form by either landlord or tenant.

The notice procedure is similar to that applicable to business tenancies under Part II Landlord and Tenant Act 1954 except that the landlord must in his notice either state that he requires possession on one of the grounds specified in the Act (s12(1)(a) and Sch 3 as amended) or make proposals for a regulated statutory tenancy between the landlord and tenant.

3.11.19.5 *Secure tenancies*

Secure tenancies are tenancies similar to regulated tenancies or restricted contracts but where the landlord is one of a number of public bodies specified in the Housing Act 1980, s28, as amended, eg a local authority, housing association or the housing corporation. The security of tenure afforded to secure tenants is similar to that given to tenants of regulated tenancies except that additionally a secure tenant may have the right to acquire the freehold or a long lease of his property. Subject to exceptions contained in the Housing Act 1980, s2 a secure tenant who has occupied premises within the Act for a period or periods together totalling two years has the right to purchase the freehold or if the dwelling house is a flat, to be granted a long lease. The price the tenant pays for the property may be reduced by a discount, and the tenant generally has the right to leave the whole or a part of the purchase price outstanding on the security of a first mortgage.

Long leases or freeholds acquired under these provisions are subject to compulsory registration of title.

3.11.20 Service charge
3.11.20.1

P. Service charges
If the demised premises are a flat let on a long lease and the tenant pays a service charge as defined by the Housing Act 1980, Sch. 19.
(1) Is there a recognised tenants' association for the tenants of flats in the building containing the demised premises?
(2) If so:
  (i) was it recognised by the landlord or by a certificate of a rent assessment committee member?
  (ii) please give the name and address of its secretary.
(3) Has the tenant, or the secretary of the tenants' association, served a request for a written summary of costs with which the vendor has not yet complied?
(4) Please confirm that on completion the vendor will hand over particulars of the relevant costs, with accounts and receipts to vouch them, competitive estimates obtained and evidence of consultations with tenants and any tenants' association or (as the case may be) of

compliance with the requirements for works whose cost exceeded the prescribed amount, for the current and previous accounting years.

(5) In respect of items included in the service charge, the full cost of which has not yet been recovered

- (i) please supply copies of estimates obtained before the liabilities were incurred;
- (ii) please supply evidence of compliance with the requirements for works whose cost exceeded the prescribed amount or reasons for non-complance;
- (iii) please supply copies of accounts paid by or rendered to the vendor;
- (iv) has the tenant, or tenants association, expressed dissatisfaction at the standard of, or the amount payable for, any such item?

3.11.20.2   The tenant of a flat is given the right to certain information about the sums which make up his service charge by the Housing Act 1980, Sch 19. The same Schedule imposes a statutory limit on the amount recoverable by the landlord as a service charge. A service charge is a variable sum payable as part of the rent or in addition to rent and is defined to include charges for services, repairs, maintenance, insurance and the landlord's cost of management. The rights given by Sch 19 do not apply to short leases (ie not exceeding 21 years) granted by a public authority (eg a local authority) or in general to premises which comprise a regulated tenancy under the Rent Act 1977.

3.11.20.3   *The right to information*
The tenant of a flat is entitled to a written summary of costs incurred in the 12 months accounting period ending last before the tenant's request for information showing a breakdown of the costs comprised in the service charge. Where there are more than four flats in the building which includes the demised premises the summary must be certified as fair and accurate by a qualified accountant who is independent of the landlord. The request for information may be made by the tenant or by the secretary of a recognised tenants' association. Failure to comply with the request within one month, or within six months of the end of the accounting period, whichever is later, is an offence punishable by a fine of up to £1,000.

3.11.20.4   *Limit on service charge payments*
When a sum demanded by way of service charge relates to costs which have not yet been incurred, the sum demanded must be reasonable.

Charges in respect of costs already incurred must relate to reasonably incurred costs in that the services or repairs which have been done must have been completed to a reasonable standard and at an economical price. If the costs of carrying out work on a building exceed a prescribed limit the landlord will be unable to recover costs in excess of the prescribed limit unless he has, before carrying out the works, complied with the following notice procedure:

(a) the landlord must obtain at least two estimates for the proposed works. At least one of these estimates must be obtained from a person or company who is unconnected with the landlord;

(b) copies of the estimates together with an explanation of the proposed works must be sent to each tenant and to the secretary of any recognised tenants' association. The tenants and secretary of the tenants' association must be allowed at least one month in which to make representations to the landlord relating to his proposals;

(c) unless the works are urgently needed, the works on the building must not commence until the time allowed for the tenants to make their representations has elapsed and the landlord must have regard to the representations made by the tenants or by the secretary of the tenants' association.

The 'prescribed limit' on expenditure is the greater of £500 or £25 per flat in the building.

3.11.20.5 *Recognised tenants' associations*

A tenants' association is 'recognised' if either:

(a) the landlord has given notice to this effect to the secretary of the association. Six months' notice must be given to the secretary if the landlord wishes to withdraw his recognition, or;

(b) there is in force a certificate issued by a member of the rent assessment panel for the area.

3.12 FORM CON 292 (agricultural tenancies)

This form is reproduced on pp 106–109, below.

3.13 COMMENT ON FORM CON 292

3.13.1 This form is designed to supplement form Con 29 (long) or (short) where all or part of the land to be purchased is let either as an agricultural holding or as an agricultural tied cottage. The form is divided into three sections the first of which deals with general enquiries relevant to all tenanted property, followed by a section specifically applicable to tied cottages. The final section of the form is relevant to agricultural holdings. The general enquiries section is very similar to the general enquiries section of form Con 291. A commentary on the wording of those questions is contained in para 3.11 above, and is not repeated below.

3.13.2 **Tied cottage enquiries: Application of statutory rules**

H. Application of statutory rules

(1) Is the tenancy

Short description
of the property

re ....

Parties ....

to ....

These enquiries are copyright and may not be reproduced.

AGRICULTURAL
TENANCY ENQUIRIES

FOR USE WITH ENQUIRIES BEFORE
CONTRACT WHERE ALL OR PART
OF THE PROPERTY IS LET AS AN
AGRICULTURAL HOLDING OR AN
AGRICULTURAL TIED COTTAGE

**Please strike out enquiries which
are not applicable.**

Replies are requested to the following additional enquiries.
Please reply separately for each part of the property to be sold which
is separately let.
The words 'landlord' and 'tenant' should be construed to include
predecessors in title wherever possible.
In the case of an agricultural tied cottage, these enquiries are
intended to extend to a licence to occupy. 'Tenancy' and 'tenant'
should be read to include 'licence' and 'licensee' where appropriate,
and 'landlord' should be given the extended meaning assigned to it
by the Rent (Agriculture) Act 1976.

....
Proposed purchaser's solicitor

Date.. 198 ....

REPLIES

These replies are given on behalf of the proposed Vendor and without
responsibility on the part of his solicitors their partners or employees. They
are believed to be correct but the accuracy is not guaranteed and they do
not obviate the need to make appropriate searches, enquiries and
inspections.

The replies are as follows.

....
Proposed vendor's solicitor

Date..198 .....

GENERAL ENQUIRIES

A. Tenant
(1) What are the full names and address of the tenant?
(2) How old is the tenant?

B. Terms of letting
(1) Please supply a copy of the lease, tenancy agreement and any
other documents evidencing all or any of the terms of letting.
(2) Unless shown on any copy document supplied:
    (i) What part of the property to be sold is let to the tenant, and
what rights has the tenant over other parts of the property?
    (ii) When was the tenancy originally granted?
    (iii) What is the period of the letting?
    (iv) How much is the rent, on what days or dates is it payable,
in advance or in arrear?
    (v) What express repairing and other obligations have been
undertaken respectively by the landlord and the tenant?
(3) What licences or consents have been given by the landlord to
the tenant?

C. Sub-letting
If the vendor is aware of any sub-letting of all or part of the
demised premises, what are:
    (i) The full names and address of the sub-tenant?
    (ii) The terms of the sub-letting?

D. Insurance
If the tenant insures the demised premises, please give
particulars of the existing cover, stating name and address of
insurers and any brokers, policy number, insureds' name(s), risks
covered, for what amount, premium and date to which the property
is insured.

E. Orders, etc.
Please supply copies of any of the following which relate to or
affect the terms of the letting or which affect the use of the property
when let:
    (i) Orders or directions of any court, tribunal or local
authority, or arbitration awards;
    (ii) Notices served on or by the local authority, and any
acknowledgment received from the local authority;
    (iii) Undertakings given by the landlord or the tenant.

F. Disputes

(1) Have the terms of the tenancy or any dispute between landlord and tenant been the subject of proceedings before any court, tribunal or arbitrator, or are any such proceedings pending? If so, please give particulars.

(2) Is the tenant now, or has he previously been, in arrear in paying the rent?

(3) Of what other breaches of covenant by the tenant, continuing or past, is the vendor aware?

(4) Has the tenant complained of any breach of the landlord's obligations?

G. Rent revision

Have the landlord and the tenant concluded any agreement as to the rent payable for any future period? If so, please give particulars.

TIED COTTAGE ENQUIRIES

Please reply to enquiries in this section if any part of the property is used for residential purposes.

H. Application of statutory rules

(1) Is the tenancy

(i) a relevant licence or a relevant tenancy (as defined by the Rent (Agriculture) Act 1976, Sched. 2)?

(ii) a statutory tenancy?

(2) What was the rateable value of the demised premises on:

(i) 23rd March 1965?

(ii) 22nd March 1973?

(iii) 1st April 1973?

(3) Is the tenant a qualified worker (as defined by the Rent (Agriculture) Act 1976, Sched. 3), or successor to one?

(4) Have the premises, at any time during the tenancy, been in qualifying ownership (as defined by the Rent (Agriculture) Act 1976, Sched. 3)?

(5) Has there been a statutory transmission of the tenancy? If so, please give particulars.

I. Rent

(1) Please supply a copy of any agreement fixing the rent payable, under the Rent (Agriculture) Act 1976, s. 11.

(2) If the rent is based on rateable value, under the Rent (Agriculture) Act 1976, s. 12, please give particulars.

(3) Is a rent for all or any part of the demised premises registered by the rent officer? If so, please state:

(i) Amount of rent;

(ii) Whether determined by the rent officer or a rent assessment committee;

(iii) Amount shown as attributable to services;

(iv) Date of registration, and effective date if different;

(v) Extent of premises affected;

(vi) Any other registered details.

(4) If the current recoverable rent is restricted by the operation of statutory phasing provisions, please state:

(i) The previous rent limit;

(ii) The service element.

J. Terms of letting

(1) Please supply a copy of any agreement varying any provisions of the statutory tenancy, under the Rent (Agriculture) Act 1976, Sched. 5, para. 12.

(2) What furniture used by the tenant is supplied by the landlord, and on what terms?

(3) What services or facilities is the landlord obliged to supply to the tenant either by contract, or as a term of the statutory tenancy, under the Rent (Agriculture) Act 1976, Sched. 5, para. 5?

K.   Rent allowances

(1)   Has the tenant been supplied with the statutory particulars of the local rent allowance scheme?

(2)   Has the landlord received payment of the tenant's rent allowance direct from the local authority?

L.   Rehousing

(1)   Has the vendor, or any predecessor in title, applied to the housing authority to rehouse the tenant, under the Rent (Agriculture) Act 1976, s. 27?

(2)   If so, what was the result?   Please supply copies of the advice of the agricultural dwellinghouse advisory committee and the decision of the authority.

AGRICULTURAL TENANCY ENQUIRIES

Please reply to enquiries in this section if any part of the property constitutes an agricultural holding for the purposes of the Agricultural Holdings Act 1948.

M.   Excluding renewal

Before the grant of the tenancy, did the Minister

(i) Approve it for the purposes of the Agricultural Holdings Act 1948, s. 2?

(ii) Approve an agreement that s. 3 should not apply to it, under s. 3B?

If so, please supply a copy of that approval.

N.   Improvements and fixtures

(1)   (i) Did the tenant carry out any improvements of the classes specified in the Agricultural Holdings Act 1948, Sched. II or Sched. V, which were begun before 1st March 1948?

(ii) If so, was the tenant obliged to carry them out by the terms of a tenancy agreement made before 1st January 1921, did the landlord consent in writing to their execution or did the tenant give notice of intention to carry them out?

(2)   (i) Has the tenant carried out any improvements of the classes specified in the Agricultural Holdings Act 1948, Sched. III, Sched. IV, pt. 1, or Sched. V, which were begun on or after 1st March 1948?

(ii) If so, did the landlord give written consent or has the tenant applied for or obtained the consent of the county executive committee or the Agricultural Land Tribunal?

(3)   What buildings, engines, machinery, fencing or other fixture was erected or fixed to the property by the tenant (excluding any erected or fixed in pursuance of an obligation, or to replace a building or fixture belonging to the landlord)?

O.   Compensation

(1)   Have the landlord and the tenant agreed that compensation shall be payable to the tenant for any matter or in any circumstances not covered by the Agricultural Holdings Act 1948 (as amended)?

(2)   For the purposes of claiming compensation for tenant right, did the tenant enter into occupation before 1st March 1948?

(3)   Is any compensation, or any sum agreed or awarded under the Agricultural Holdings Act 1948, due to the tenant but not paid?

(4)   (i) Has any compensation been awarded either to the tenant or to the landlord under the Agriculture (Miscellaneous Provisions) Act 1976?   If so, please give particulars.

(ii) Is any such compensation due but unpaid?

P.   Tenant's death

(1)   Has the tenant, or have all the joint tenants, to whom the tenancy was originally granted died?

(2)   If the last tenant of the holding has died and no new tenancy has yet been granted:

(i) On what date did the tenant die?

(ii) On what date did the landlord receive notice of the death?

(iii) Has any notice to quit thereby been rendered ineffective? If so, please supply a copy.

(iv) Is there anyone whom the Vendor believes to be a person eligible to succeed to a tenancy of the holding on the tenant's death?

(v) Has any person made an application to the Agricultural Land Tribunal?   If so, please give particulars.

Q.   Statutory succession

(1) (i) Was the tenancy granted on or after 12th July 1984?

(ii) If so, does it fall within the Agricultural Holdings Act 1984, s. 2(2) (new tenancies to which statutory succession rights still apply)?

(2) Was either

(i) the present tenancy, or

(ii) the tenancy which preceded it

granted as a result of a tribunal direction under the Agriculture (Miscellaneous Provisions) Act 1976 (succession to deceased tenant) or the Agricultural Holdings Act 1984, Sched. 2, para. 5 (succession on tenant's retirement) or by agreement in lieu thereof?

(3) Has the tenant ever nominated a successor to succeed him on retirement under the Agricultural Holdings Act 1984, Sched. 2? If so, please give particulars.

R.   General

(1) Has either the landlord or the tenant required the making of a record in respect of the condition of the holding under the Agricultural Holdings Act 1948, s. 16? If so, please supply a copy.

(2) Has application been made for a certificate of bad husbandry, and, if so, when and with what result?

(3) Who has the right to kill and take wild animals and birds on the property?

(4) Has an agreement been entered into under the Ancient Monuments and Archaeological Areas Act 1979, or legislation replaced thereby, in respect of any part of the property? If so, please supply a copy.

ADDITIONAL ENQUIRIES

(i) a relevant licence or a relevant tenancy (as defined by the Rent (Agriculture) Act 1976, Sched. 2)?

(ii) a statutory tenancy?

(2) What was the rateable value of the demised premises on:

(i)   23 March 1965?

(ii) 22 March 1973?

(iii) 1 April 1973?

(3) Is the tenant a qualified worker (as defined by the Rent (Agriculture) Act 1976, Sched. 3), or successor to one?

(4) Have the premises, at any time during the tenancy, been in qualifying ownership (as defined by the Rent (Agriculture) Act 1976, Sch. 3)?

(5) Has there been a statutory transmission of the tenancy? If so, please give particulars.

3.13.3 *The Rent (Agriculture) Act 1976*

A farm worker who occupies a tied cottage will generally be excluded from the protection given by the Rent Act 1977 either because the amount of rent (if any) payable under the tenancy agreement is less than two-thirds of the rateable value of the property or because his right to occupy is based on a licence and not a tenancy. Subject to various qualifying conditions outlined below, the Rent (Agriculture) Act 1976 provides such a tenant or licensee (a 'protected occupier') with security of tenure and a measure of rent control similar to that afforded to regulated tenancies under the Rent Act 1977. To fall within the 1976 Act, there must be a relevant licence or tenancy (the 'protected occupancy'). A relevant tenancy is a tenancy which would be a protected tenancy within the Rent Act 1977 except for the fact that:

(a) the rent is less than two-thirds of the rateable value; or

(b) the dwelling house forms part of an agricultural holding which is occupied by the person responsible for the farming.

A relevant licence is any licence under which a person has the right to exclusive occupation of a house as a separate dwelling and which if it were a tenancy and not a licence, would be a relevant tenancy as defined above.

3.13.3.1 *The statutory tenancy*

On the termination of the relevant licence or tenancy, security of tenure is provided in the form of the statutory tenancy which in nature and application is similar to the statutory tenancy which arises under the Rent Act 1977 on termination of a Rent Act protected tenancy (see para 3.11.15.5, above) subject to the following differences:

(a) if the protected occupany had been a licence, the statutory tenancy takes effect as a weekly tenancy, with an implied covenant by the landlord for quiet enjoyment;

(b) the repairing obligations imposed on the landlord by the Housing Act 1961, s32 are implied;

(c) if the tenant wishes to give up possession he must give at least four weeks' notice to his landlord, or any longer period of notice required by the original contract;

(d) if no rent is registered for the property, the maximum annual rent recoverable must not exceed one and a half times the rateable value of the house.

3.13.3.2 The rateable value limits under the Rent (Agriculture) Act 1976 are the same as those for the Rent Act 1977 (see para 3.11.15.6, above).

3.13.3.3 A qualifying worker is a person who has worked full-time in agriculture for not less than 91 out of the last 104 weeks. Any absence from work on account of sickness or injury may be counted towards the calculation of this total.

3.13.3.4 Qualifying ownership exists where the occupier of the house is employed in agriculture and his employer is either:

the owner of the house; or

the employer has made arrangements with the owner of the house for it to be used to house an agricultural employee.

3.13.3.5 On the death of the protected occupier or statutory tenant a transmission of the tenancy may take place to a member of the tenant's family. This is a similar, but not identical provision to that contained in the Rent Act 1977 (see para 3.11.15.7, above) but under the 1976 Act only *one* transmission of the tenancy may take place.

3.13.4 Rent
3.13.4.1

I. Rent

(1) Please supply a copy of any agreement fixing the rent payable, under the Rent (Agriculture) Act 1976, s. 11.

(2) If the rent is based on rateable value, under the Rent (Agriculture) Act 1976, s. 12, please give particulars.

(3) Is a rent for all or any part of the demised premises registered by the rent officer? Is so, please state:

   (i) amount of rent;

   (ii) whether determined by the rent officer or a rent assessment committee;

   (iii) amount shown as attributable to services;

   (iv) date of registration, and effective date if different;

   (v) extent of premises affected;

   (vi) any other registered details.

(4) If the current recoverable rent is restricted by the operation of statutory phasing provisions, please state:

>   (i)   the previous rent limit;
>   (ii)   the service element.

3.13.4.2   During the term of the relevant licence or tenancy the rent payable for the property is not capable of being registered and the amount of rent is such as is agreed between the parties. Once the statutory tenancy has arisen an application may be made to register the rent, and once registered, the registered rent becomes the maximum legally recoverable amount for the premises. If no rent is registered for the statutory tenancy the annual rent must not in any event exceed one and a half times the rateable value of the property. The provisions relating to the registration of rent and for phasing are similar to those under the Rent Act 1977 relating to regulated tenancies (para 3.11.16.2, above).

3.13.5   Terms of letting
3.13.5.1

>   J. Terms of letting
>   (1) Please supply a copy of any agreement varying any provisions of the statutory tenancy, under the Rent (Agriculture) Act 1976, Sched. 5, para. 12.
>   (2) What furniture used by the tenant is supplied by the landlord, and on what terms?
>   (3) What services or facilities is the landlord obliged to supply to the tenant either by contract, or as a term of the statutory tenancy, under the Rent (Agriculture) Act 1976, Sched. 5, para. 5?

3.13.5.2   Certain terms are implied into statutory tenancies which arise on the termination of the contractual licence or tenancy (see para 3.13.3.3, above). These implied terms may be varied by agreement made between the parties at any time except that it is not permissible to:

(a) vary the terms as to payment to rent so as to conflict with the terms of the 1976 Act;

(b) add substantially to the land or premises which the statutory tenant is entitled to occupy;

(c) exclude the repairing obligations imposed on the landlord under the Housing Act 1961, s 32;

(d) alter the circumstances in which the statutory tenant can give notice to quit;

(e) include any term which relates to the employment by the landlord of the tenant, or any other term unrelated to the occupation of the dwelling house.

3.13.5.3   Schedule 5 to the 1976 Act lays down the terms of the statutory tenancy. Paragraph 5 of that Schedule requires the landlord to continue to provide the occupier with any services or facilities which were provided to the occupier before the commencement of the statutory tenancy, whether under contractual obligation or otherwise where those services or facilities are reasonably necessary for any person occupying the house as a statutory tenant but which such a tenant cannot reasonably be expected to provide for himself, eg electricity, water supplies or sewage disposal facilities.

3.13.6 Rent allowances
3.13.6.1

K. Rent allowances
(1) Has the tenant been supplied with the statutory particulars of the local rent allowance scheme?
(2) Has the landlord received payment of the tenant's rent allowance direct from the local authority?

3.13.6.2 A tenant may be entitled to a rent allowance under the provisions of the Housing Finance Act 1972. There is no statutory obligation on the landlord to supply the tenant with details of the rent allowance scheme, but the Rent Book (Forms of Notice) Regulations 1982[14] require the landlord of premises which are let to a statutory tenant who is protected under the Rent (Agriculture) Act 1976 to supply the tenant with a rent book containing certain prescribed information which includes the following statement: 'You may be entitled to get help to pay your rent. Apply to your local Council for details of the rent allowance and rent rebate schemes'.

3.13.7 Rehousing
3.13.7.1

L. Rehousing
(1) Has the vendor, or any predecessor in title, applied to the housing authority to rehouse the tenant, under the Rent (Agriculture) Act 1976, s. 27?
(2) If so, what was the result? Please supply copies of the advice of the agricultural dwellinghouse advisory committee and the decision of the authority.

3.13.7.2 Where a dwelling house of the type under discussion is occupied by an occupant whose occupancy is protected by either the Rent (Agriculture) Act 1976 or the Rent Act 1977, the landlord may apply to the local housing authority to rehouse the occupant on the grounds that vacant possession of the premises is required in order to house a person who is to be employed in agriculture by the applicant, and the applicant is unable to provide suitable alternative accommodation for the occupant and that the authority ought, in the interests of efficient agriculture to provide suitable alternative accommodation for the occupant. When such an application is made it may be referred to an agricultural dwelling house advisory committee at the request of the housing authority, the applicant or the occupant. The committee will consider the case and will submit advice to the housing authority who must take full account of the committee's report when making their decision on the application.

3.13.8   Agricultural tenancy enquiries: Excluding renewal

M. Excluding renewal
Before the grant of the tenancy, did the Minister
 (i) approve it for the purposes of the Agricultural Holdings Act 1948, s. 2?
 (ii) approve an agreement that s. 3 should not apply to it, under s. 3B?
If so, please supply a copy of that approval.

3.13.8.1   A licence to occupy agricultural land, or the grant of a tenancy which creates an interest less than a tenancy from year to year is by the Agricultural Holdings Act 1948, s 2, converted into a yearly tenancy and thus attracts the security of tenure provisions of that Act. It is, however, possible to exclude such licence or tenancy from security provisions of the Act provided that the approval of the Minister was obtained prior to the commencement of the arrangement.

3.13.8.2   Section 3B of the Act, which was added to s 3 of the 1948 Act by the Agricultural Holdings Act 1984 provides that where the proposed tenancy is to be the grant of a fixed term of not less than two nor more than five years, the parties to the agreement may, prior to the commencement, make a joint application to the Minister for his approval of the agreement. If such approval is granted the security of tenure provisions of s 3 of the Act will not apply and the tenancy will in due course expire by effluxion of time. Where this provision applies the contract of tenancy must be in writing and must contain a statement within it or endorsed on it to the effect that s 3 of the Act does not apply to the tenancy.

3.13.9   Improvements and fixtures
3.13.9.1

N. Improvements and fixtures
 (1) (i) Did the tenant carry out any improvements of the classes specified in the Agricultural Holdings Act 1948, Sched. II or sched. V, which were begun before 1st March 1948?
    (ii) If so, was the tenant obliged to carry them out by the terms of a tenancy agreement made before 1st January 1921, did the landlord consent in writing to their execution or did the tenant give notice of intention to carry them out?
 (2) (i) Has the tenant carried out any improvements of the classes specified in the Agricultural Holdings Act 1948, Sched. III, Sched. IV, pt. I, or Sched. V, which were begun on or after 1st March 1948?

(ii) If so, did the landlord give written consent or has the tenant applied for or obtained the consent of the county executive committee or the Agricultural Land Tribunal?

(3) What buildings, engines, machinery, fencing or other fixture was erected or fixed to the property by the tenant (excluding any erected or fixed in pursuance of an obligation, or to replace a building or fixture belonging to the landlord)?

N.B. The expression 'agricultural holding' has been redefined by the Agricultural Holdings Act 1984.

3.13.9.2 The Agricultural Holdings Act 1948, Sch II specifies a list of improvements for which compensation is payable where the work was commenced before 1 March 1948. The right to compensation is generally dependent on the landlord having been notified of the improvements or having given his consent thereto. Schedule V to the Act contains a similar list of improvements to market gardens for which compensation may be payable.

There is no right to compensation for improvements where the tenancy agreement was made before 1 January 1921 and it imposed an obligation to do the work.

3.13.9.3 *Agricultural Holdings Act 1948, Sch II*

PART I

IMPROVEMENTS FOR WHICH COMPENSATION IS PAYABLE IF CONSENT OF LAND-LORD WAS OBTAINED TO THEIR EXECUTION

1. Erection, alteration or enlargement of buildings.
2. Formation of silos.
3. Laying down of permanent pasture.
4. Making and planting of osier beds.
5. Making of water meadows or works or irrigation.
6. Making of gardens.
7. Making of improvement of roads or bridges.
8. Making or improvement of watercourses, ponds, wells or reservoirs or of works for the application of water power or for supply of water for agricultural or domestic purposes.
9. Making or removal of permanent fences.
10. Planting of hops.
11. Planting of orchards or fruit bushes.
12. Protecting young fruit trees.
13. Reclaiming of waste land.
14. Warping or weiring of land.
15. Embankments and sluices against floods.
16. Erection of hop gardens.
17. Provisions of permanent sheep-dipping accommodation.
18. In the case of arable land, the removal of bracken, gorse, tree roots, boulders or other like obstructions to cultivation.

PART II
IMPROVEMENTS FOR WHICH COMPENSATION IS PAYABLE IF NOTICE WAS GIVEN
TO LANDLORD BEFORE EXECUTION THEREOF

19. Drainage.

PART III
IMPROVEMENTS FOR WHICH COMPENSATION IS PAYABLE WITHOUT EITHER
CONSENT OF OR NOTICE TO LANDLORD OF THEIR EXECUTION

20. Chalking of land.
21. Clay-burning.
22. Claying of land or spreading blaes upon land.
23. Liming of land.
24. Marling of land.
25. Application to land of purchased artificial or other purchased manure.
26. Consumption on the holding by cattle, sheep or pigs, or by horses other than those regularly employed on the holding, of corn, cake or other feeding stuff not produced on the holding.
27. Consumption on the holding by cattle, sheep, or pigs, or by horses other than those regularly employed on the holding, of corn proved by satisfactory evidence to have been produced and consumed on the holding.
28. Laying down temporary pasture with clover, grass, lucerne, sainfoin, or other seeds, sown more than two years prior to the termination of the tenancy, in so far as the value of the temporary pasture on the holding at the time of quitting exceeds the value of the temporary pasture on the holding at the commencement of the tenancy for which the tenant did not pay compensation.
29. Repairs to buildings, being buildings necessary for the proper cultivation or working of the holding, other than repairs which the tenant is himself under an obligation to execute.

3.13.9.4 *Agricultural Holdings Act 1948, Sch V*

MARKET GARDEN IMPROVEMENTS FOR WHICH COMPENSATION MAY BE PAYABLE

1. Planting of standard or other fruit trees permanently set out.
2. Planting of fruit bushes permanently set out.
3. Planting of strawberry plants.
4. Planting of asparagus, rhubarb and other vegetable crops which continue productive for two or more years.
5. Erection, alteration or enlargement of buildings for the purpose of the trade or business of a market gardener.

3.13.9.5 Compensation may also be payable for the improvements listed in Schs III, IV or V to the 1948 Act which were commenced after 1 March 1948. The right to compensation is generally dependent on the appropriate consent to the improvement having been obtained where necessary.

3.13.9.6   *Agricultural Holdings Act 1 948, Sch III*

PART I

IMPROVEMENTS TO WHICH CONSENT OF LANDLORD REQUIRED

1. Making or planting of osier beds.
2. Making of water meadows or works of irrigation.
3. Making of watercress beds.
4. Planting of hops.
5. Planting of orchards or fruit bushes.
6. Warping or weiring of land.
7. Making of gardens.

PART II

IMPROVEMENTS TO WHICH CONSENT OF LANDLORD OR APPROVAL OF THE AGRICULTURAL LAND TRIBUNAL REQUIRED

8. Erection, alteration or enlargement of buildings, and making or improvement of permanent yards.
9. Construction of silos.
10. Claying of land.
11. Marling of land.
12. Making or improvement of roads or bridges.
13. Making or improvement of water courses, culverts, ponds, wells or reservoirs, or of works for the application of water power for agricultural or domestic purposes or for the supply of water for such purposes.
14. Making or removal of permanent fences.
15. Reclaiming of waste land.
16. Making or improvement of embankments or sluices.
17. Erection of wirework for hop gardens.
18. Provision of permanent sheep-dipping accommodation.
19. Removal of bracken, gorse, tree roots, boulders or other like obstruction, to cultivation.
20. Land drainage (other than mole drainage and works carried out to secure the efficient functioning thereof).
21. Provisions or laying-on of electric light or power.
22. Provision of means of sewage disposal.
23. Repairs to fixed equipment, being equipment reasonably required for the proper farming of the holding, other than repairs which the tenant is under an obligation to carry out.
24. The growing of herbage crops for commercial seed production.

3.13.9.7 *Agricultural Holdings Act 1948, Sch IV*

PART I
IMPROVEMENTS

1. Mole drainage and works carried out to secure the efficient functioning thereof.
2. Protection of fruit trees against animals.
4. Clay burning.
5. Liming [(including chalking)]¹ of land.
6. Application to land of purchased [manure and fertilizer, whether organic or inorganic]¹.
7. Consumption on the holding of corn (whether produced on the holding or not) or of cake or other feeding stuff not produced on the holding, [by horses, cattle, sheep, pigs or poultry]¹.

[Paragraph 3 was omitted by the Agricultural Holdings Act 1948 (Variation of Fourth Schedule) Order 1978 (SI 1978/742).
¹ *Substituted by The Agricultural Holdings Act 1948 (Variation of Fourth Schedule) Order 1978 (SI 1978/742.]*

PART II
OTHER MATTERS

8. Growing crops and severed or harvested crops and produce, being in either case crops or produce grown on the holding in the last year of the tenancy, but not including crops or produce which the tenant has a right to sell or remove from the holding.
9. Seeds sown and cultivations, fallows and acts of husbandry performed on the holding at the expense of the tenant.
10. Pasture laid down with clover, grass, lucerne, sainfoin or other seeds, being either—
    (a) pasture laid down at the expenses of the tenant otherwise than in compliance with an obligation imposed on him by an agreement in writing to lay it down to replace temporary pasture comprised in the holding when the tenant entered thereon which was not paid for by him; or
    (b) pasture paid for by the tenant on entering on the holding.
[11. Acclimatisation, hefting or settlement of hill sheep on hill land.]
[12.—(1) Where a holding is situated in a district in which the growing of a succession of tillage crops on the same arable land is normal farming practice, the residual fertility value of the sod of the excess qualifying leys on the holding, if any: Provided that—
    (a) the qualifying leys comprising the excess qualifying leys shall be those indicated to be such by the tenant; and
    (b) qualifying leys laid down at the expense of the landlord without reimbursement by the tenant or any previous tenant of the holding or laid down by and at the expense of the tenant pursuant to agreement by him with the landlord for the establishment of a specified area of leys on the holding as a condition of the landlord giving consent to the ploughing or other destruction of permanent pasture or pursuant

to a direction given by an arbitrator on a reference under section 10(1) of this Act, shall not be included in the excess qualifying leys.
(2) In this paragraph—
'leys' means land laid down with clover, grass, lucerne, sainfoin or other seeds, but does not include permanent pasture;
'qualifying leys' means—
(a) leys continuously maintained as such for a period of three or more growing seasons since being laid down excluding, if the leys were undersown or autumn-sown, the calendar year in which the sowing took place, and
(b) arable land which within the three growing seasons immediately preceding the termination of the tenancy was ley continuously maintained as aforesaid before being destroyed by ploughing or some other means for the production of a tillage crop or crops:
Provided that for the purpose of paragraph (a) above the destruction of a ley (by ploughing or some other means) followed as soon as practicable by re-seeding to a ley without sowing a crop in the interval between such destruction and such reseeding shall be treated as not constituting a break in the continuity of the maintenance of the ley;
'the excess qualifying leys' means the area of qualifying leys on the holding at the termination of the tenancy which is equal to the area (if any) by which one third of the aggregate of the areas of leys on the holding on the following dates, namely,
(a) at the termination of the tenancy,
(b) on the date one year prior to such termination, and
(c) on the date two years prior to such termination,
exceeds the accepted proportion at the termination of the tenancy;
'the accepted proportion' means the area which represents the proportion which the aggregate area of the leys on the holding would be expected to bear to the area of the holding, excluding the permanent pasture thereon, in accordance with normal farming practice in the district or if a greater proportion is provided for by or under the terms of the tenancy, that proportion.]

3.13.9.8 The tenant is entitled on quitting the holding to remove agricultural fixtures placed on the land by him, provided he is not entitled to compensation for them as improvements. The landlord has the option of purchasing such items from the tenant.

3.13.10 Compensation
3.13.10.1

O. Compensation
(1) Have the landlord and the tenant agreed that compensation shall be payable to the tenant for any matter or in any circumstances not covered by the Agricultural Holdings Act 1948 (as amended)?
(2) For the purposes of claiming compensation for tenant right, did the tenant enter into occupation before 1 March 1948?
(3) Is any compensation, or any sum agreed or awarded under the Agricultural Holdings Act 1948, due to the tenant, but not paid?

(4) (i) Has any compensation been awarded either to the tenant or to the landlord under the Agriculture (Miscellaneous Provisions) Act 1976? If so, please give particulars.
(ii) Is any such compensation due but unpaid?

3.13.10.2 A tenant who quits an agricultural holding may in certain circumstances be entitled to compensation under the general law or under the Agricultural Holdings Act 1948 (as amended) for improvements, tenant-right, and disturbance. During the tenancy a claim may also be made for compensation for damage done by any wild animals or birds which the tenant has not permission in writing to kill.

The amount of the compensation for improvements varies dependent on:

(a) whether any necessary consent to the improvement was obtained;

(b) the nature of the improvement;

(c) the date when it was effected.

3.13.10.3 Tenant right covers the matters for which an outgoing tenant of an agricultural holding will be compensated by either his landlord or the incoming tenant and constitutes payment for the benefit of labour and materials invested in the land by the outgoing tenant which will accrue to the new tenant. The items included in this head of compensation are specified in the Agricultural Holdings Act 1948 and include compensation for growing crops, seeds sown, pasture laid down to grass, clover etc., acclimatisation, hefting or settlement of hill sheep. If the tenant entered into occupation before 1 March 1948 statutory compensation is only payable where the tenant gives written notice to his landlord before the tenancy ends, electing for such compensation. The amount of compensation is prescribed by statute or may be agreed between the parties.

3.13.10.4 The Agriculture (Miscellaneous Provisions) Act 1976 gave the right to certain eligible persons to succeed to the holding on the death of the tenant. In the case of a dispute over the succession the matter was to be referred to the Agricultural Land Tribunal.

These rights of succession have been altered by the Agricultural Holdings Act 1984 but without prejudice to tenancies granted before 12 July 1984.

3.13.11 Tenant's death
3.13.11.1

P. Tenant's death
(1) Has the tenant, or have all the joint tenants, to whom the tenancy was originally granted died?
(2) If the last tenant of the holding has died and no new tenancy has yet been granted:
(i) on what date did the tenant die?
(ii) on what date did the landlord receive notice of the death?

(iii) has any notice to quit thereby been rendered ineffective? If so please supply a copy.

(iv) is there anyone whom the vendor believes to be a person eligible to succeed to a tenancy of the holding on the tenant's death?

(v) has any person made an application to the Agricultural Land Tribunal? If so, please give particulars.

3.13.11.2   *Tenancies granted before 12 July 1984*

On the death of the sole or last surviving tenant of the holding a relative of the deceased may be eligible to apply to the Agricultural Land Tribunal within three months of the tenant's death for a direction entitling him to a tenancy of the holding.

Certain conditions must be satisfied:

(a) at the date of the tenant's death the tenancy agreement must have been a yearly tenancy or a fixed term with no more than 27 months of the fixed term still unexpired. A fixed term of more than one year but less than two years does not fall within this category;

(b) the applicant must be 'eligible', ie he or she must be the wife, husband, brother, sister or child of the deceased tenant and have derived his or her livelihood from the holding for five years out of the previous seven years;

(c) the applicant must be 'suitable' to take over the tenancy having regard to his or her age, training, practical experience, health, and financial standing.

Where more than one person applies to succeed to the holding the matter is arbitrated by the Agricultural Land Tribunal. Only two successions on death are allowed under these provisions. If before the tenant's death a notice to quit had been served by the landlord, and had been unchallengeable the right to succession on death is excluded.

A tenant whose holding is subject to statutory succession under the 1976 Act may by the Agricultural Holdings Act 1984, Sch 2 nominate a person to succeed the tenant on his retirement.

3.13.11.3   *Tenancies granted on or after 12 July 1984*

The statutory succession provisions outlined above do not in general apply to tenancies granted on or after 12 July 1984 (Agricultural Holdings Act 1984, s 2) although the 1984 Act in effect preserves existing rights of succession. It is, however, possible for the parties to exclude the effect of s 2 of the 1984 Act in the contract of tenancy. Where rights of succession are preserved then by s 4 of and Sch 2 to the 1984 Act the tenant of an agricultural holding may nominate a person to succeed to the holding on his retirement. The nominee may apply to the Agricultural Land Tribunal for a direction entitling him to a tenancy of the holding. The nominee must be eligible and suitable (similar to the meanings given to these words in para 3.13.11.2, above) and have derived his livelihood from the holding for five out of the past seven years.

3.13.12   Statutory succession
3.13.12.1

Q. Statutory succession
(1)   (i) Was the tenancy granted on or after 12 July 1984?
      (ii) If so, does it fall within the Agricultural Holdings Act 1984,
           s 2(2) (new tenancies to which statutory succession rights
           still apply)?
(2) was either
     (i) the present tenancy, or
     (ii) the tenancy which preceded it
granted as a result of a tribunal direction under the Agricultural
(Miscellaneous Provisions) Act 1976 (succession to deceased tenant) or the Agricultural Holdings Act 1984, Sched. 2, para. 5
(succession on tenant's retirement) or by agreement in lieu thereof?
(3) has the tenant ever nominated a successor to succeed him on
retirement under the Agricultural Holdings Act 1984, Sched. 2? If so
please give particulars.

3.13.12.2   The statutory succession provisions on the death or retirement of the tenant are outlined in para 3.13.11, above.

3.13.13   General
3.13.13.1

R. General
(1) Has either the landlord or the tenant required the making of a
record in respect of the condition of the holding under the Agricultural Holdings Act 1948, s 16? If so please supply a copy.
(2) Has application been made for a certificate of bad husbandry,
and, if so, when and with what result?
(3) Who has the right to kill and take wild animals and birds on the
property?
(4) Has an agreement been entered into under the Ancient Monuments and Archaeological Areas Act 1979, or legislation replaced
thereby, in respect of any part of the property? If so, please supply
a copy.

3.13.13.2   The Agricultural Holding Act 1948, s 16 as amended by the
Agricultural Holdings Act 1984, s 10(1) and Sch 3, para 8 entitles the
landlord or tenant of an agricultural holding at any time during the
tenancy to require the making of a record of the fixed equipment on
the holding and of the general condition of the holding itself. The
tenant is also entitled to require the making of a record of existing
improvements executed by him or in respect of the execution of which
the tenant, with the landlord's written consent, paid compensation to

an outgoing tenant and of any fixture or building which the tenant is entitled to remove from the holding.

3.13.13.3 A certificate of bad husbandry may be obtained by the landlord from the Agricultural Land Tribunal where the tribunal is satisfied that the tenant is not fulfilling his responsibilities to farm in accordance with the rules of good husbandry.

Having obtained such a certificate the landlord is then entitled within six months of the date of the certificate to give the tenant notice to quit the holding on the grounds of bad husbandry and the tenant is not entitled in these circumstances to serve a counter-notice on his landlord. The tenant's right to compensation for disturbance is lost where the tenancy is terminated on these grounds. The Agricultural Land Tribunal has a discretion to shorten the period of a notice to quit where a certificate of bad husbandry has been issued.

3.13.13.4 Game is defined by the Agricultural Holdings Act 1948, s 14 as amended by the Agricultural Holdings Act 1984, s 10(1) and Sch 3, para 7 as any wild animals or birds. Where the right to kill game on the land is vested in the landlord, or anyone other than the tenant claiming under the landlord, and the tenant does not have the landlord's written permission to kill the wild animals or birds, the tenant may be entitled to compensation for damage done to the land by game.

3.13.13.5 An agreement under the Ancient Monuments and Archaeological Areas Act 1979 may be made to preserve and maintain a site of archaeological interest or an ancient monument. Planning permission for such a site will be almost impossible to obtain and farming over that piece of land will be restricted. Such an agreement may be registered as a local land charge under Part IV of the register.

3.14 FORMS CON 293 AND CON 294 (PURCHASE OF BUSINESSES)

3.14.1 These forms contain preliminary enquiries relating to the sale of a company (Con 293) and enquiries relating to the acquisition of an unincorporated business. Where the purchase of the business or company includes the purchase of land these forms may be used in conjunction with forms Con 29 (long) or (short) or where no land is being bought, the forms may be used independently of forms Con 29 (long) and (short). Since neither form contains any question specifically relating to the acquisition of an interest in land it is thought that a commentary on their contents would be beyond the scope of this book and for that reason alone has been omitted.

3.14.2 FORM CON 293
This form is reproduced on pp 124–127, below.

Name of company

re .... Limited

Parties ....

to ....

————oyez————

ENQUIRIES

BEFORE CONTRACT
FOR SALE OF A COMPANY

For enquiries relating to land, use
form **Con 29 (Long).**

**Please strike out enquiries
which are not applicable.**

Replies are requested to the following enquiries.

The replies are as follows.

....

....

Proposed purchaser's solicitor.

Proposed vendor's solicitor.

Date..19 ....

Date..19 ....

GENERAL ENQUIRIES

REPLIES

These replies do not obviate the need to obtain warranties. If replies have
been, or are to be, supplied under separate cover, please indicate this in
the Replies column, stating "Already supplied" or "To be supplied", as
appropriate, and giving details such as the description and date of the
relevant documentation containing the requested reply.

1. Share Capital

(A) What is the present:

    (i) authorised share capital?

    (ii) issued share capital?

(B) Was all issued share capital issued for cash? If not, give details.

(C) Are any shares under option or agreed to be under option?
If so, give details.

(D) Will the vendor agree to a reorganisation of the company's share
capital prior to completion in order to mitigate stamp duty?

2. Taxation

(A) To what date have tax returns been made?

(B) To what extent have tax returns been agreed?

(C) What matters are in dispute with the Inland Revenue?

(D) To what extent has tax deducted under PAYE been accounted for
and paid over?

(E) To what date has VAT been accounted for and paid over?

(F) Is the company now, or has it ever been, a "close" company?

(G) (i) Is the company a trading company or a member of a trading
group? If yes, what income does the company receive other than
trading income.

    (ii) State the financial periods for which clearances have been
obtained against statutory apportionment of the income of the
company.

    (iii) Are any directions for statutory apportionment of the
company's income anticipated for any financial period for which
the company's tax returns are not agreed and for the current
financial period and, if so, to what extent?

(H) Has any death occurred in respect of which a charge for CTT
against the company or any of its subsidiaries could arise? If so,
please give details.

(I) Are there any outstanding loans from the company to directors or
any participator or associate? If so, please give details.

(J) Is the company a member of a group of companies? If so, please
give details.

(K) Please supply details of all direct or indirect interests of the
company in any controlled foreign company (within the meaning of
Sections 82-91 of the Finance Act 1984).

3. Trading

(A) Has any trading occurred since the last audited balance sheet date when the company's normal margins have not been applied or where the company has made or is likely to make a loss or otherwise is out of the normal course of the company's business? If so, please specify.

(B) Please confirm that the business of the company will be managed as a going concern until completion.

(C) Please supply details of:

(i) All outstanding capital commitments.

(ii) Any hire-purchase, credit sale or leasing contracts.

(iii) Any long-term contract for the supply and/or sale of goods or services involving a future commitment in excess of £1,000.

(iv) Any agreement or licence under which any part of the company's business is conducted or in respect of which a fee, commission or royalty is paid.

(v) Any sales, agency or distributorship agreements of the company.

(vi) Any litigation or arbitration in which the company is engaged.

(vii) Any agreement or arrangement with trades unions or other bodies relating to the employment of labour by the company.

4. Accounts

(A) Do the last audited accounts:

(i) give a true and fair view of the company in all respects?

(ii) fully disclose all the assets and liabilities of the company as at their date?

(B) Please confirm that all slow-moving, redundant or obsolete stock was written down appropriately and the value attributed to the remaining stock did not exceed the lower of direct cost or net realisable value at the accounts date.

5. Outstanding Debts

(A) Please confirm that at completion no amount due from the debtors of the company will be overdue by more than four weeks.

(B) Please confirm that, since the last audited accounts, no debt has been released on terms that the debtor pays less than the full value of his debt.

(C) Please confirm that no debt is likely to prove irrecoverable.

6. Employees

(A) Please supply details of:

(i) Directors' remuneration and terms of engagement.

(ii) Pay and terms and duration of employment of all employees.

(iii) All retirement benefit and assurance schemes and all pensions payable.

(B) (i) Are all pensions and other retirement benefit arrangements:
   (a) approved by the Inland Revenue?
   (b) adequately funded?

(ii) Is there a contracting-out certificate issued pursuant to the Social Security Pensions Act 1975?

(C) Please confirm that, since the last audited accounts, the company has not paid and, pending completion, will not pay, or agree to pay, any compensation or redundancy payment to past or present directors or employees.

7. Insurance

(A) Please supply details of all insurances and produce the receipts for the last premiums.

(B) Please specify any outstanding insurance claims.

8. Statutory and General

(A) Please supply copies of the Memorandum and Articles of Association, together with all resolutions and consents required by law to be attached thereto.

(B) Please supply full names and addresses of shareholders, directors, secretary and auditors.

(C) (i) Have all documents required by law to be registered with the Registrar of Companies been properly registered?

(ii) Have any loans been made by the company? If so, please give full details.

(iii) Have any loans secured or unsecured been made to the company? If so, please give full details.

(iv) Please supply details of:

(a) the company's bankers;

(b) the company's banking facilities;

(c) authorised signatories on all accounts;

(d) all relevant documents relating to the company's banking arrangements.

9. Subsidiaries

(A) Please specify all subsidiary companies.

(B) Please specify all guarantees or indemnities given by the company in respect of the liabilities of any subsidiary.

(C) Please answer all the above enquiries (numbers 1–8) as if they related to each subsidiary.

10. Conveyancing

Please answer all enquiries on form Conveyancing 29 (Long) in respect of all freehold and leasehold properties held by the company.

ADDITIONAL ENQUIRIES

ADDITIONAL ENQUIRIES

Conveyancing 293

Revised 12-84 F3292
* * * * *

3.14.3 *Preliminary enquiries of the vendor*

3.14.3 FORM CON 294

Name of Business

re ....

Parties   ....

to ....

ENQUIRIES

BEFORE CONTRACT
**FOR ACQUISITION OF AN
UNINCORPORATED
BUSINESS**
For enquiries relating to land, use
form **Con 29 (Long).**

**These enquiries are copyright
and may not be reproduced**

**Please strike out enquiries which
are not applicable.**

Replies are requested to the following enquiries.

....
Proposed purchaser's solicitor.

Date .... 19 .....

The replies are as follows.

....
Proposed vendor's solicitor.

Date .... 19 .....

GENERAL ENQUIRIES

1. Please supply details of:

(A) All contracts, licences or other arrangements subject to which the business or any part has been conducted and necessary for future trading or in respect of which a fee, commission or royalty is paid.

(B) Any sales, agency or distributorship agreements relating to products or services forming part of the business.

(C) Any long-term or outstanding contracts for the supply and/or sale of goods or services which are to be assigned or are necessary for the continuance of the business.

(D) Any patents, trade-marks, know-how or other confidential information or data owned by the Vendor and used in the business.

(E) Any disputes and litigation concerning the business which would be relevant to the continuation of the business by the Purchaser in succession to the Vendor.

2. Please give a precise apportionment of the price between goodwill, premises and other assets to be acquired.

3. Please supply an inventory of all fixtures, fittings, furniture, machinery, plant and equipment included in the sale and confirm whether they are owned unencumbered by the Vendor. If not, give details of any hire-purchase, credit sale or leasing contracts.

4. Give particulars of all employees proposed to be offered employment by the Purchaser with details of job description, pay, terms of employment, pension rights and duration of employment.

5. If book debts are included in the sale, confirm that they will all be collectable at face-value. Specify any book debts likely to prove bad or difficult to collect.

6. In respect of outstanding orders to be assigned to the Purchaser:

(A) State any reasons why novation by the Purchaser is unlikely to be possible.

(B) Whether any advance payments or deposits have been taken by the Vendor.

(C) Whether any such orders are likely to produce a loss or less than the usual profit margin.

REPLIES

If replies have been, or are to be, supplied under separate cover, please indicate this in the Replies column, stating "Already supplied" or "To be supplied", as appropriate, and giving details such as the description and date of the relevant documentation containing the requested reply.

7. Please confirm the business will be managed as a going concern until completion.

8. Please supply details of all insurances and confirm that they will be kept in force until completion, and the Purchaser's interest noted.

9. (A) Provide a list with addresses of all regular or account customers.

(B) Provide a list with addresses of all suppliers, identifying type(s) of goods or services supplying. State whether there is any reason why such suppliers should not continue business with the Purchaser on same terms.

(C) Does the Vendor propose to set up in competition to the business within a radius of twenty miles?

(D) Please confirm that there is no dispute concerning the use of the Business Name of the business by the Vendor and that the Vendor will not use or authorise any other party to use such Business Name in connection with any other business activity.

10. (A) Do the last accounts of the business submitted to the Inland Revenue give a true and fair view of the business in all respects?

(B) Confirm that since the said accounts date the financial position and prospects of the business have not worsened and that they will not worsen pending completion.

(C) Specify any unusual classes of turnover or profit in the said accounts, to which the Purchaser will not become entitled.

11. Please specify:

(A) Approximate value of stock.

(B) How much stock is older than twelve months.

(C) Outstanding orders for stock proposed to be assigned to the Purchaser.

12. (A) State duration of existing business from the premises by the Vendor and predecessors.

(B) Are any of the leasehold premises of the business subject to a court order of exemption from the security of tenure premises of the Landlord and Tenant Act 1954, Part II?

ADDITIONAL ENQUIRIES

©1984 **oyez** The Solicitors' Law Stationery Society plc, Oyez House
237 Long Lane, London SE1 4PU   F4388—8-84
Conveyancing 294   ★ ★ ★ ★ ★

129

3.15 SEARCH SUMMARY

Application	Usually form Con 29 (long) in duplicate or Convey 1 in duplicate or form E1 in duplicate
Plan	No
Fee	—
Address	To Vendor's Solicitors
Special points	—
Areas affected	Most transactions

N.B. Forms E1, E1 (Short) and E2 are reproduced in Appendix IV below, together with a brief commentary on these forms.

1 (1979) 123 Sol Jo 860.
2 *Jelbert v Davis* [1968] 1 All ER 1182, [1968] 1WLR 589.
3 *Weston v Lawrence Weaver Ltd* [1961] 1QB 402, [1961] 1 All ER 478.
4 *Halsall v Brizell* [1957] Ch 169, [1957] 1 All ER 371.
5 [1979] Ch 312, [1979] 2 All ER 697, affd [1981] AC 487, [1980] 2 All ER 408, HL.
6 Law Com No 115 (Cmnd 8636 August 1982).
7 See also para 7.2, below.
8 Law of Property Act 1925, s44.
9 *West Country Cleaners (Falmouth) Ltd v Saly* [1966] 3 All ER 210, [1966] 1 WLR 1485, CA; *Bassett v Whiteley* (1983) 45 P & CR 87, CA.
10 Housing Act 1980, Sch 19, para 1.
11 *Argy Trading Development Co Ltd v Lapid Developments Ltd* [1977] 3 All ER 785, [1977] 1 WLR 444.
12 *Hill v Harris* [1965] 2 QB 601, [1965] 2 All ER 385, CA.
13 *Dyson Holdings Ltd v Fox* [1976] QB 503, [1975] 3 All ER 1030, CA; *Watson v Lucas* [1980] 3 All ER 647, [1980] 1 WLR 1493, CA.
14 SI 1982/1474.

Chapter 4

Local land charges

4.1 WHEN TO MAKE THE SEARCH

A local land charges search should be made with the local authority in virtually every transaction. The search should be submitted to the appropriate local authority, together with the form of additional enquiries of the local authority (see ch 5, below) as soon as firm instructions to proceed with the proposed transaction have been received. For the reasons outlined below (para 4.2) it is extremely unwise to exchange contracts without either having made this search at all, or having submitted an application, without having received the official certificate of search. The register of local land charges is not yet fully computerised and some local authorities are slow to process search applications. It is therefore essential to submit the search application at the earliest possible moment in the transaction.

If time does not permit an official search to be made a personal search of the register should be undertaken. Only in circumstances where the client is entering into a short lease or tenancy agreement without paying a premium for its grant and where there is no potential for a premium to be demanded on a future assignment of the lease or tenancy may consideration be given to dispensing with this search.

In practice the phrase 'the local search' is used to encompass both the local land charges search and the form of additional enquiries of the local authority, since the two searches are invariably made at the same time and of the same authority. This chapter deals solely with the local land charges search. Additional enquiries are discussed in ch 5, below.

4.2 REASONS FOR MAKING THE SEARCH

Matters which are registered as local land charges bind the land, and any purchaser of the land, irrespective of notice. In registered land local land charges take effect as overriding interests under the Land Registration Act 1925, s 70(1)(i). Although the existence of a registered local land charge would rank as a latent defect in title, the vendor is frequently relieved of his burden of disclosing such matters by an express condition in the contract.[1] The majority of local land charges will either impose a financial obligation on the property, or will impose restrictions on the use of the property. It is therefore imperative that the client is aware of the existence and effect of such registered charges (if any) before he enters into a binding contract to acquire an interest in the land.

4.3 HOW TO MAKE THE SEARCH

4.3.1 Official search
Form LLC1 should be completed in duplicate and sent with a cheque for the fee to the appropriate district council or London borough council. The address of the appropriate council may be ascertained from (inter alia) *The Directory of Local Authorities* (Oyez). If there is doubt as to whether a property falls within the area of a particular authority, a telephone call should be made before sending off the search application to check that the property does lie within that authority's area. The making of such a telephone call is an advisable precaution to avoid undue delay in obtaining the result of the search. Where a property straddles the areas of two authorities separate searches must be made for the part of the land which lies within the area of each respective authority.

4.3.2 Delay
A delay of some weeks in receiving the certificate of result of this search is not uncommon, the period of delay becoming even longer where, as is the usual practice, the local land charges search application and form of additional enquiries of the local authority are submitted together. Where time is short the following suggestions may be considered in order to minimise the delay:

(a) submit the applications for the local land charges search and the additional enquiries of the local authority *separately*, because the local land charges search can usually be dealt with and returned more quickly than the form of additional enquiries. Although ideally an exchange of contracts should not be undertaken until the answers to both searches have been received and scrutinised it is suggested that the information revealed by the local land charges search is the more important of the two searches and thus in an emergency consideration may be given to effecting an exchange in reliance on the result of the local land charges search alone;

(b) in a covering letter submitted with both the local land charges search and the form of additional enquiries, request the local authority to return the official certificate of search for the local land charges search as soon as it has been prepared and to return the answers to the additional enquiries at a later stage. This course of action will obviously achieve the same result as (a) above;

(c) submit the local land charges application and form of additional enquiries together with a covering letter requesting the local authoprity to expedite both searches. Some local authorities will accede to this request;

(d) before submitting the search application, telephone the local authority for an estimate of the likely period of delay. If the period of delay is considerable, apart from the steps suggested above, consideration may be given to undertaking a personal search either personally or through local agents;

(e) where there is to be a considerable delay in receipt of the official certificate of search and the vendor is pressing for an early exchange of contracts, the purchaser may choose to ask the vendor to accept an exchange of contracts which is conditional upon the receipt of satisfactory results of the local search and additional enquiries. The vendor is, however, unlikely to agree readily to this request and it should be remembered that a conditional contract can be problematical from the point of view of both vendor and purchaser.

4.3.3 Personal search

Local authorities are required by the Local Land Charges Act 1975, s 8 to allow any person to make a personal search of the register. In order to make a personal search it is necessary to attend at the offices of the appropriate authority with a completed form LLC1 (in duplicate) and the search fee. The applicant should be prepared to make notes of any relevant entries which are discovered. Charges in the local land charges register are entered against particular pieces of land and the first step in making a personal search is to look at the index for the property concerned. The index may be in written form, or in the form of a map, or computerised. Having investigated the index it should be possible to trace any entries relevant to the property being searched against. However, it is permissible for the authority to note an entry in the register by cross-referring the entry to another public record or document which the local authority is by statute required to maintain. In such cases a search of these other public records or documents will also be necessary (para 4.10, below). If the register and/or index is computerised an official of the local authority will either show the searcher how to operate the computer, or will make the search himself, allowing the searcher to view the result of the search on a screen. If a print-out of the information revealed on the screen is required this may be obtained on payment of a fee.

The procedure for making a personal search is not straightforward and there is an obvious danger of overlooking a relevant entry. An official search is therefore to be preferred and a personal search should only be undertaken where the pressure of time is most acute.

A solicitor who undertakes a personal search is not afforded the protection of the Local Land Charges Act 1975, s 13, whereby a solicitor who makes an official search is exonerated from liability for an error in an official search certificate or in an office copy of a register entry. Neither does the client enjoy the full benefits of the right to compensation for errors in the search certificate which is given when an official search is made. The disadvantages of making a personal search should be explained to the client before such a search is undertaken and the client may be asked to accept that the result of the search will incur no liability either on behalf of the person who actually made the search or on the firm. Without such a disclaimer of liability the person making the search could incur liability on his own behalf, or through the firm if an error in the result of the search caused loss to the client.

4.3.4 Fees

It is customary for the local land charges search and form of additional enquiries of the local authority to be submitted simultaneously with one cheque to cover the fees for both searches. The current fees for the local land charges search alone are set out below. All fees must be prepaid by cheque, money order, postal order or Giro.

(a)	Search in any part of the register	£1.05
(b)	Search in the whole of the register in relation to one parcel of land	£2.65
(c)	Where several parcels of land are included in one requisition for search, whether of the whole or part of the register, for each additional parcel of land	£0.40
	(subject to a maximum fee of £9.00)	
(d)	Office copy of a register entry (not including plans or documents)	£0.75
(e)	Office copy of plan or document	Fee fixed by authority

4.4 FORM LLC 1

This form is reproduced on pp 135–136, below.

4.5 COMMENT ON FORM LLC 1

The form must be completed in duplicate and sent to the appropriate local authority. It is necessary to state whether a search is required in the whole register or of only part, and if a part search is required, of which particular parts. The 12 parts of the register are listed on the reverse of the form and their contents are outlined in para 4.9, below. If a search is required in more than two single parts of the register it is cheaper to make a search of the whole register (see para 4.3.4, above). Partly for this reason, and also because it is not easy to identify with absolute certainty the individual parts of the register which will

Form LLC1. *(Local Land Charges Rules 1977 Schedule 1, Form C)*

The duplicate of this form must also be completed: a carbon copy will suffice

For directions, notes and fees see overleaf

Insert name and address of registering authority in space below

┌─────────────────────────────┐
│   │
│   │
│   │
│   │
└─────────────────────────────┘

Official Number_____
(To be completed by the registering authority)

Register of local land charges

Requisition for search and official certificate of search

---

fold

Requisition for search
(A separate requisition must be made in respect of each parcel of land except as explained overleaf)

An official search is required in *Part(s)*_____*of* [1]
the register of local land charges kept by the above-named
registering authority for subsisting registrations against the land
[defined in the attached plan and][2] described below.

Description of land sufficient to enable it to be identified

Name and address to which certificate is to be sent

┌─────────────────────────────┐
│   │
│   │
│   │
│   │
└─────────────────────────────┘

Signature of applicant *(or his solicitor)*

_____

Date

_____

Telephone number

_____

Reference

_____

Enclosure
Cheque/Money Order/Postal Order/Giro

To be completed by
authorised officer

Official certificate of search

It is hereby certified that the search requested above reveals
no subsisting registrations[3]

*or the*_____registrations described in the Schedule
hereto[3] up to and including the date of this certificate.

Signed ....

On behalf of ....

Date

---

1 Delete if inappropriate. Otherwise insert Part(s) in which
   search is required.

2 Delete if inappropriate. (A plan should be furnished
   in duplicate if it is desired that a copy should be returned.)

3 Delete inapplicable words. (The Parts of the Schedule should
   be securely attached to the certificate and the number of
   registrations disclosed should be inserted in the space provided.
   Only Parts which disclose subsisting registrations should be sent.)

4 Insert name of registering authority.

Directions and notes

1 This form and the duplicate should be completed and sent by post to or left at the office of the registering authority.

2 A separate requisition for search should be made in respect of each parcel of land in respect of which a search is required except where, for the purpose of a single transaction, a certificate is required in respect of two or more parcels of land which have a common boundary or are separated only by a road, railway, river, stream or canal.

3 'Parcel of land' means land (including a building or part of a building) which is separately occupied or separately rated or, if not occupied or rated, in separate ownership. For the purpose of this definition an owner is the person who (in his own right or as trustee for any other person) is entitled to receive the rack rent of land, or, where the land is not let at a rack rent, would be so entitled if it were so let.

4 The certificate of the result of an official search of the register refers to any subsisting registrations, recorded against the land defined in the application for search, in the Parts of the register in respect of which the search is requested. The Parts of the register record:

Part 1	General financial charges.
Part 2	Specific financial charges.
Part 3	Planning charges.
Part 4	Miscellaneous charges.
Part 5	Fenland ways maintenance charges.
Part 6	Land compensation charges.
Part 7	‸New towns charges.
Part 8	Civil aviation charges.
Part 9	Opencast coal charges.
Part 10	Listed buildings charges.
Part 11	Light obstruction notices.
Part 12	Drainage scheme charges.

5 An office copy of any entry in the register can be obtained on written request and on payment of the prescribed fee.

Fees

Official search (including issue of official certificate of search)	
in any one Part of the register	£1.05
in the whole of the register	£2.65
and in addition, but subject to a maximum additional fee of £9.00, in respect of each parcel above one, where several parcels are included in the same requisition (see notes 2 and 3 above) whether the requisition is for search in the whole or any part of the register	40p
Office copy of any entry in the register (not including a copy or extract of any plan or document filed by the registering authority)	75p
Office copy of any plan or other document filed by the registering authority	Such reasonable fee as may be fixed by the registering authority according to the time and work involved.

All fees must be prepaid

be relevant to any particular property, a search is invariably made in the whole register. Where a search of the whole register is being made the words 'Part(s) ... of' should be deleted from the form and substituted by the word 'All' or the words 'the whole'.

A description of the land sufficient to enable it to be identified must be inserted in the form. In many cases the postal address of the property will suffice, but if there is any doubt over the identification of the land by its postal address then in order to avoid unnecessary delay, the land should be clearly marked on a plan attached to the search form. It is only necessary to submit two copies of the plan where the applicant requires a copy of the plan to be returned to him with the result of the search.

Although it is usual to sign both copies of the form the local authority will accept a requisition for a search where only the top copy has been signed.

4.6 THE RESULT OF THE SEARCH

The official certificate of search, which is printed at the foot of form LLC 1 will be signed and dated by an official on behalf of the local authority and returned to the applicant. The certificate will state either that there are no subsisting registrations or that there are a stated number of registrations the details of which are appended in a schedule to the search certificate. A brief outline of the matters which are capable of registration as local land charges and which may therefore appear in the schedule to the search certificate is contained in para 4.9, below. **4.6.1** An office copy of any entry revealed by the search may be obtained by applying to the local authority. A fee of £0.75 is charged for the supply of a copy of an entry, but higher fees may be charged for the supply of documents.

It will often be necessary to obtain copies of register entries which relate to such matters as planning consents. Where it is anticipated that entries will be revealed by the search of which copies will be required, then in order to avoid delay in obtaining the copies a letter addressed to the local authority may be enclosed with the search application, requesting that the authority send copies of the relevant entries with the search certificate and giving an undertaking to pay the requisite fees for the copies. The letter should specify the type of entry of which a copy will be required, and in case there are a large number of entries of this type registered, it may be prudent to place an upper financial limit on the undertaking to pay for the copies.

4.6.2 Details revealed by the search

4.6.2.1 In general where a registered charge is revealed by the search certificate, the following details of the entry will be revealed:

  (a) a reference to the statute under which the charge is imposed;

137

(b) a description of the land affected;

(c) the date of registration of the charge.

4.6.2.2 In some cases, where relevant, the following additional information may be revealed:

(a) the date when the charge was made and/or becomes operative;

(b) the amount of a financial charge or compensation payment and rate of interest applicable;

(c) the address of the place where the document which created the charge, or a map showing the area affected by the charge, can be inspected.

4.7 THE EFFECT OF REGISTRATION OF A LOCAL LAND CHARGE

Provided that a matter which is registered as a local land charge would otherwise be enforceable under the general law, a purchaser or other person dealing with land which is affected by a registered charge is bound by that charge whether or not he made a search of the register.

Even where a search of the register has been made (whether personal or official) a charge which is registered binds the land. This is so even where the charge was registered at the time when the search was made but the entry was not revealed by the search. All registered local land charges bind the land (and the purchaser) by virtue of their registration and a purchaser must take subject to any charges which are registered between the date of issue of the search certificate and the date of completion; ie no period of 'protection' or of exemption from the effects of charges registered subsequent to the date of issue of the search certificate is offered by this search. In these circumstances the purchaser will not usually have recourse to a remedy against his own vendor. If a charge is registered between the dates of contract and completion the purchaser will be obliged to proceed to complete his purchase.[2]

The official certificate of search is therefore not conclusive in favour of a purchaser. In limited circumstances where the charge was registered at the time of an official search, but was not disclosed by the search certificate, the purchaser may claim compensation under the Local Land Charges Act 1975, s 10(4). The right to compensation exists for most but not all registered land charges.

4.7.1 Advantages of official certificate of search

Since the official certificate of search is not conclusive in favour of the purchaser the only real advantage to be obtained by making an official search lies in the circumstances in which compensation may be claimed by a purchaser who sustains loss as a result of an error in an official certificate. Limited rights to compensation exist where a personal search is made.[3] There is also the danger with a personal search that the searcher, being unfamiliar with the contents of the various registers, may unwittingly overlook a relevant entry.

A solicitor is not liable in respect of any loss occasioned by any error in an official search certificate nor by an erroneous office copy of an entry in the register.[4]

4.7.2 Liability of registering authorities

No civil or criminal liability will attach to any officer of a registering authority for any mistakes or errors which are made in the maintenance of a register or in the issue of any official certificate of search. Compensation for errors in the certificate of search is available in limited circumstances under the Local Land Charges Act 1975 s 10. This section has replaced the former common law liability in negligence which was established in *Ministry of Housing and Local Government v Sharp*.[5] Following the introduction of s 10 a successful action in negligence against an officer of the registering authority will be very rare.

4.7.3 A general discussion of liability on searches is contained in ch 2, above.

4.8 UPDATING THE SEARCH

The result of the search only reveals the state of the registers at the time of issue of the search certificate (which will usually be shortly before exchange of contracts). Since the contents of the registers may change between the date of the issue of the search certificate and the date of completion, in theory a further search should be undertaken prior to completion. Given that the interval between exchange of contracts and completion is normally very short, and that there is frequently a delay of some weeks between the submission of a search application and the receipt of the certificate, a further search is usually considered to be impracticable. A further search should, however, be undertaken where there is to be a protracted interval between exchange of contracts and completion (see para 36.1, below).

4.9 THE REGISTER OF LOCAL LAND CHARGES

4.9.1 The purpose of the register

The system of registration of local land charges was introduced by the Land Charges Act 1925 to provide readily available information for an intending purchaser of land about charges which would be enforceable by the local authority against successive owners of the land. Since 1925 various statutes have created new charges which are also registrable by the local authority and which have resulted today in there being a very large number of registrable charges of various types which together are classified as local land charges. The current legislation governing local land charges is the Local Land Charges Act 1975 and the Local Land Charges Rules 1977 (SI 1977/985).

4.9.2 Definition of a local land charge

A precise definition of a local land charge is to be found in ss 1 and 2 of the 1975 Act. In general terms a local land charge may be defined as a restriction placed on a particular piece of land in order either to secure the payment of money, or to limit the use to which the land may be put. Further the charge must be binding on successive owners of the land. A matter which falls within this definition is registrable as a local land charge.

4.9.3 The form of the register

The register itself is commonly maintained on a card index system, although a register maintained on a computer is now permissible by virtue of the Local Government (Miscellaneous Provisions) Act 1982, s 34 and a number of local authorities have taken advantage of this system and maintain their register in this manner.

The register itself is divided into the twelve parts which are listed on the reverse of form LLC 1 (para 4.4, above). Brief details of the contents of each part of the register are outlined in the following sub-paragraphs.

4.9.4 Part 1: general financial charges

The following are registrable in this part of the register:

(a) the registration of provisional apportionments of private street works expenses under Part XI Highways Act 1980;

(b) charges similar to (a) but which arise under various local Acts, eg a charge to provide sewers to public streets at the expense of the frontagers;

(c) some works schemes made under Coast Protection Act 1949;

(d) Unascertained expenses of the local authority, which expenses would, when ascertained, entitle the authority to create a charge on the land. An entry of this type is rare.

4.9.5 Part 2: specific financial charges

Sums recoverable against successive owners or occupiers of the land by a local authority or water authority or a new town development corporation under the Public Health Acts or Highways Acts are registrable in this part of the register and include the following:

(a) charges registered under the Public Health Act 1875. (Since 1980 newly created charges which would formerly have been registrable under this head now fall under the Highways Act 1980);

(b) charges registered under the Private Street Works Act 1892. (Since 1980 these come within the Highways Act 1980, s 212 but remain registrable within this part of the register);

(c) charges under the Public Health Act 1936. These charges mainly relate to the costs of supplying, maintaining or repairing sewers, drains and lavatories but also encompass a number of miscellaneous matters, eg the provision of access to public buildings, the provision of fire escapes, the cost of removing or pulling down buildings erected in contravention of building regulations, the cost of water supply and the cost of abating a public nuisance;

(d) charges under the Public Health (Drainage of Trade Premises) Act 1937;

(e) some charges under the Coast Protection Act 1949;

(f) expenses incurred by a local authority under the Prevention of Damage by Pests Act 1949 in connection with the control of vermin;

(g) a proportion of the expenses reasonably incurred by the local authority under the Clean Air Act 1956 in the adaptation of premises in smoke control areas;

(h) expenses incurred by the local authority under the Housing Act 1957 in repairing a house which is unfit for human habitation;

(i) charges under the Public Health Act 1961. These comprise a miscellany of charges including payment in respect of the construction of a new public sewer and expenses incurred in dealing with dangerous or dilapidated buildings;

(j) expenses incurred by a local authority under the Housing Act 1961 in carrying out works to a house in multiple occupation;

(k) expenses incurred by the local authority in carrying out works under some sections of the Housing Act 1964;

(l) a surcharge on rates under the General Rate Act 1967, s 17A;

(m) expenses incurred by a local authority under the Housing Act 1974 in carrying out works in default of compliance with an improvement notice;

(n) charges under the Highways Act 1980. A variety of different charges are registrable under the statute, almost all of which are charges in favour of the local authority for expenses incurred by the authority in repairing streets, buildings, footpaths, bridleways, stiles, fences and gates when there has been default after service of a notice on the owner requiring such repairs to be carried out;

(o) expenses due to a local authority by virtue of an agreement entered into by the authority under the Public Health Acts or similar statutes;

(p) some charges are registrable within this part in relation to expenses incurred by the local authority under a local act.

4.9.6 Part 3: planning charges

The majority of the local land charges relating to planning matters are registrable in this part of the register. Among those which are registrable are the following which all arise under the Town and Country Planning Act 1971 or by regulations made under that Act:

(a) conditions attached to the grant of planning permission;

(b) the revocation or modification of a planning permission;

(c) an order for the discontinuance of use of a building, for the removal of buildings or for the suspension of mineral workings. The power to make these three dissimilar orders is given to the local authority under the Town and Country Planning Act 1971, s 51;

(d) planning agreements under the Town and Country Planning Act 1971, s 52. These are agreements made between the local authority and a landowner whereby the landowner agrees (usually) to carry out certain works to his land. The agreements are often entered into in consideration of planning permission being granted to the landowner and are commonly found in relation to the development of recreation areas within new housing estates. A similar type of agreement may be entered into under the Local Government (Miscellaneous Provisions) Act 1982, s 33 which is registrable in Part 4 of the register;

(e) conditions attached to a planning permission to carry out works to a listed building;

(f) a building preservation notice. Such a notice is served by the local authority where a building which is not a 'listed building' but is nevertheless of architectural or historic interest is believed to be in danger of demolition or alteration. The notice will 'protect' the building for a period of six months during which time the Secretary of State may decide to make the building a listed building;

(g) tree preservation orders. Breach of a tree preservation order is an offence of strict liability punishable by a fine of up to £1,000 on summary conviction;

(h) a notice served by the local authority requiring a landowner to restore the condition of a garden, vacant site or other open land. Such a notice, served under the Town and Country Planning Act, 1971, s 65 is generally known as a 'waste land notice';

(i) enforcement notices and stop notices in relation to breaches of planning control served under ss 87 and 90 respectively of the Town and Country Planning Act 1971;

(j) listed building enforcement notices served under the Town and Country Planning Act 1971, s 96. These are similar to (i) above but relate to listed buildings;

(k) where a payment of compensation for the refusal of planning permission or for the grant of planning permission subject to conditions has been made and has exceeded £20 a compensation notice is registered in this part of the register. A similar notice is registered in relation to compensation paid where a planning permission has been revoked or modified;

(l) a notice of payment made by way of compensation for war damaged land. The relevance of this entry is that the amount of compensation which was paid may be recoverable by the Secretary of State on the subsequent grant of planning permission for the site;

(m) the designation of an area as a conservation area;

(n) an article 4 direction revoking the Town and Country Planning General Development Order 1977 (SI 1977/289) in whole or in part;

(o) an order designating an 'area of special control' under the Town and Country Planning (Control of Advertisements) Regulations 1984 (SI 1984/421). Under these regulations some advertisements may be displayed without the need to obtain express planning permission. An order making an 'area of special control' has a similar effect to an article 4 direction made under the General Development Order and places strict control over advertising within that area.

4.9.7 Part 4: miscellaneous charges

As the name suggests, Part 4 is the residuary part of the register containing a miscellany of charges which are not specifically registrable under any other part of the register. Among the various charges which appear in this part of the register are a number of charges which relate to planning matters which are not registrable under Part 3 due to the narrow definition of a 'planning charge' applicable to Part 3 entries.

Charges which may be registered under Part 4 are as follows:

4.9.7.1 *Planning charges*

(a) a compulsory purchase order after notice to treat has been served under the Acquisition of Land Act 1981;

(b) access agreements and orders under the National Parks and Access to the Countryside Act 1949. Where such an agreement or order is in force only limited works may be carried out on the land affected, and the area to which the public have access must not be substantially reduced;

(c) notice of intention to make a general vesting declaration under the Compulsory Purchase (Vesting Declarations) Act 1981;

(d) agreements made between the local authority and a landowner relating to the carrying out of works or development on land under the Local Government (Miscellaneous Provisions) Act 1982, s 33. These agreements are similar in nature to agreements made under the Town and Country Planning Act 1971, s 52 (registrable under Part 3);

(e) five separate charges under the Ancient Monuments and Archaeological Areas Act 1979 as follows:

    (i) the inclusion of a monument in a schedule of ancient monuments (similar to 'listed building' protection);

    (ii) a notice of payment of compensation where scheduled monument consent is refused or is granted subject to conditions;

    (iii) a guardianship deed placing the care of an ancient monument under the control of the local authority or Secretary of State;

(iv) easements over land in the vicinity of a monument in respect of which a guardianship deed has been made;

(v) the designation of an area as an area of archaeological importance (AAI);

(f) orders vesting land in an Urban Development Corporation under the Local Government, Planning and Land Act 1980. These are similar in effect to general vesting declarations;

(g) agreements relating to the development of land abutting highways made under the New Towns Act 1981. Such an agreement will usually restrict the development of the land in order, eg to preserve sight lines or to reserve land for future road widening schemes. These agreements are *not* restricted to use only in the area of new towns;

(h) the designation of an area as a site of Special Scientific Interest (SSSI) or the making of a management agreement in relation to such an area. These charges arise under the Wildlife and Countryside Act 1981 and are discussed further in ch 13, below.

(i) conditions or restrictions imposed in a planning consent for the erection of a building over a sewer or drain under the Public Health Act 1936, s 25.

4.9.7.2 *Other charges*

(a) Statutory implied conditions in mortgages made under the Small Dwellings Acquisition Act 1899;

(b) conditions applying to a house to which a subsidy has been paid under the Housing &c. Act 1923;

(c) conditions attaching to dwellings which have been subsidised under the Housing (Rural Workers) Act 1926 and the Housing (Rural Workers) Amendment Act 1938. These conditions were only enforceable for a period of 20 years from the time when the house first became fit for occupation and will rarely be encountered today.

(d) the designation of premises under the Civil Defence Act 1939, s 2;

(e) the designation of an area under the War Damage Act 1943;

(f) the designation of streets as prospectively maintainable highways under the Public Utilities Street Works Act 1950;

(g) conditions applied to a cottage where a grant has been made under the Hill Farming Act 1954 as amended. These grants are similar to improvement grants made under the Housing Acts;

(h) closing orders, demolition orders and clearance orders made under the Housing Act 1957;

(i) conditions imposed on the sale of council houses by the local authority under the Housing Act 1957. This does *not* apply to council house sales made under the Housing Act 1980;

(j) some restrictive covenants imposed on the sale of land or houses by the local authority. Such covenants may alternatively be registered as class D(ii) charges in the Central Land Charges Registry but many authorities prefer to register the covenants as *local* land charges where this is permissible;

(k) wayleave orders for oil pipe lines under the Land Powers (Defence) Act 1958;

(l) a charge registerable under the Weeds Act 1959 after non-compliance with a notice served on a landowner requiring specified action to be taken to prevent the spreading of injurious weeds;

(m) orders made by the local authority where houses in multiple occupation are in an unsatisfactory state;

(n) control orders entitling the local authority to take possession of houses under the Housing Act 1964, s 73;

(o) authorisation orders for the storage of gas;

(p) certain conditions and notices under the Agriculture Act 1967;

(q) management schemes under the Leasehold Reform Act 1967;

(r) orders made under the Pastoral Measure 1968 for the sale or lease of redundant burial grounds;

(s) conditions imposed relating to the height of a chimney under the Clean Air Act 1968, s 6;

(t) housing action areas and priority neighbourhoods under the Housing Act 1974;

(u) improvement notices and conditions imposed in improvement grants under the Housing Act 1974;

(v) an order made by the magistrates' court under the Food and Drugs (Control of Food Premises) Act 1976, closing food premises which are considered to be dangerous to health;

(w) various charges under the Highways Act 1980 including the following:

(i) covenants contained in agreements for the provision of walkways over, under or through parts of a building;

(ii) the prescription of a building or improvement line;

(iii) notices imposing restrictions on the use of land near a bend or junction in a public highway;

(iv) agreements for the construction of cattle grids;

(v) conditions attached to licences to construct bridges over highways or to place overland cables along or across a highway;

(vi) new street orders;

(vii) some notices relating to the making up of private streets.

4.9.8 Part 5: fenland ways maintenance charges

The only charge registerable in this part of the register is a charge in favour of the county council for expenses incurred in maintaining works to fenland ways.

4.9.9 Part 6: land compensation charges
Certain matters relating to compensation under the Land Compensation Act 1973 were registrable in this part of the register. Since this statute has now been repealed any entries which remain in this part of the register are ineffective.

4.9.10 Part 7: new towns charges
This part of the register only contains charges arising under the New Towns Act 1981 or previous similar legislation. Two types of charges are registrable:
(a) the designation of an area as the site of a new town;
(b) compulsory purchase orders made by new town development corporations and highway authorities but only *after* notice of the confirmation of the order has been given to affected landowners.

4.9.11 Part 8: civil aviation charges
This part of the register contains charges arising under the Civil Aviation Acts 1949, 1968 and 1971 which are enforceable by the Secretary of State for Trade and Industry. The charges all relate to the use of land in connection with civil aviation and will include, eg the creation of easements over such land, or orders or directions restricting the use of the land.

4.9.12 Part 9: opencast coal charges
Compulsory purchase orders and compulsory rights orders relating to open cast mining and enforceable by the National Coal Board are the only entries registrable in this part of the register.

4.9.13 Part 10: listed building charges
This part of the register contains a list of buildings of special architectural or historic interest under the Town and Country Planning Act 1971, s 54. Depending on the grading of the listed building planning permission to alter the building may be difficult or impossible to obtain. The details of planning permissions granted in relation to listed buildings appear in Part 3 of the register.

4.9.14 Part 11: light obstruction notices
Light obstruction notices under the Rights of Light Act 1959 contained in this part of the register are enforceable by the private individuals in whose favour the notice has been registered. The purpose of a light obstruction notice is to determine the right to the access of light to a building. Such a notice can only be registered in certain circumstances and the application for registration must be accompanied by a certificate issued by the Lands Tribunal.

There is no right to compensation for errors in an official search of this part of the register.

4.9.15 Part 12: drainage scheme charges

Entries in this part of the register are confined to land drainage schemes made by a local authority for the drainage of an area of land which is capable of improvement by drainage works but where it would not be practical to create an internal drainage board for this purpose because of the small area of the land affected.

4.9.16 Planning matters

When investigating planning matters, particular attention will be paid to Part 3 of the register which is specifically headed 'Planning Charges'. It should, however, be remembered that some planning matters may be registered in other parts of the register and parts 4, 7 and 10 should also be investigated.

4.9.17 Property within Greater London

Within Greater London the LLC 1 form is submitted to the appropriate London borough council. Although the procedure for making a local land charges search and the fees payable are the same within Greater London as for other areas of the country, the detail of some of the entries revealed by the search will be different. This is due to the fact that much of the substantive law creating land charges within Greater London is different from that applicable to the remainder of England and Wales. These differences in detail will appear in entries made in Parts 1, 2 and 4 of the register. Entries registered in Parts 3 and 6–12 inclusive of the register are not affected by these differences. Entries under Part 5 of the register would never arise in relation to land in London.

In addition to these differences there are some types of local land charges which are peculiar to the London area and which do not affect land elsewhere in England and Wales, eg charges prohibiting building made under the London Building Acts (Amendment) Act 1939, or charges registered under the Covent Garden Market Act 1961.

4.9.18 Further reading

The preceding sub-paragraphs contain only a brief outline of the matters which are capable of registration as local land charges. A full discussion of this topic is contained in J.F. Garner *Local Land Charges* (9th edn, 1982, Shaw & Sons).

4.10 OTHER STATUTORY REGISTERS

An entry in the land charges register may be made by referring to an entry in another register which is required by statute to be maintained by a local authority, and kept open for public inspection. The following registers may need to be referred to in the course of making a local land charges search in person, or otherwise during the course of making searches on behalf of a prospective purchaser of land. A personal search *only* of these registers is permitted during the normal office hours of the local land charges section of the local authority offices.

4.10.1 Public sewers map

A map showing the route of public sewers other than those vested in the local authority before 1 October, 1937 is open to inspection without payment of a fee. Although the ownership of public sewers is now vested in the water authority the map is kept at the offices of the local authority. Inspection of the map will not show the route of old sewers (ie those vested in the local authority before 1 October 1937) and it is unfortunately these which may be the most difficult to locate by a site inspection of the property.

4.10.2 List of highways maintainable at public expense

This register is kept by London borough councils, but outside London is found at the offices of the appropriate *county* council and is available for inspection free of charge.

4.10.3 Register of planning applications

A register of all applications for planning permission is maintained under the Town and Country Planning Act 1971, s 34 and is available for inspection by the public at all reasonable hours.

4.10.4 Register of applications for permission to display advertisements

A register is maintained which contains all applications for consent to display advertisements under the Town and Country Planning (Control of Advertisements) Regulations 1984. This register is very similar to the register of planning applications (para 4.10.3, above) and is usually open to public inspection but is not required to be so by statute.

4.11 SEARCH SUMMARY

Application	Form LLC 1
Plan	Only required where land cannot clearly be identified by postal address
Fee	Official search in all parts of the register— one parcel of land £2.65 each additional parcel £0.40 (max. £9.00)

Address	Appropriate District Council or London Borough Council

Special points

Area affected	All transactions to acquire an interest for value in land except perhaps the grant of a short lease where no premium is payable.

1 See Law Society Condition 3, National Conditions 15 and 16.
2 See Law Society Condition 3 and National Conditions 14, 15 and 16.
3 Local Land Charges Act 1975, s 10.
4 Local Land Charges Act 1975, s 13.
5 [1970] 2 QB 223, [1970] 1 All ER 1009.

Chapter 5

Additional enquiries of the local authority

5.1 WHEN TO MAKE THE SEARCH
This search should be made in virtually every transaction and is normally sent to the appropriate local authority (district council or London borough council) with the local land charges search (ch 4, above). Since delay is frequently experienced in receiving the result of the search, the application form should be despatched as soon as firm instructions to proceed with the transaction have been received. In normal circumstances contracts should not be exchanged before the result of this search has been obtained and analysed. Where time does not permit an official search to be made, a personal search should where possible be undertaken. Only in circumstances where the client is entering into a short lease without payment of a premium, and there is no possibility of a premium being obtained on a future possible assignment may consideration be given to dispensing with this search.

In practice the local land charges search and form of additional enquiries of the local authority are together spoken of as 'the local search'. This chapter deals only with the form of additional enquiries; the local land charges search is discussed in ch 4, above.

5.2 REASONS FOR MAKING THE SEARCH
The reasons for making this search are ancillary to the reasons cited for making the local land charges search (para 4.2, above). It is necessary to make further enquiries of the local authority in addition to the local land charges search because the information obtained from the result of the local land charges search is limited in two respects. The first limitation is that the local land charges search only reveals such information as the local authority is bound to register in one of the twelve parts of the local land charges register; the information revealed by the form of additional enquiries is wider in scope, since many of the questions on the standard form are directed at information which the local authority holds, but which it is not by statute obliged to record on a statutory register. The second limitation of the local land charges search is that it will only reveal the state of the local land charges register at the precise time at which the search is carried out; whereas the replies to the standard form of additional enquiries will reveal information relating to matters which have affected the property in the

past, eg the results of previous planning applications, and future proposals which may involve the property, but which have not yet reached
the stage of becoming registrable as land charges, eg proposals for the
compulsory acquisition of the property. Information about the previous
planning history of the property can be extremely useful to a purchaser
who is proposing to develop the land, and information relating to
proposed compulsory purchase orders would be of interest to any intending purchaser. The form of additional enquiries is in fact the only
early warning of such proposals which can be obtained, since compulsory purchase orders are not generally registered as local land charges
until after a notice to treat has been served on the landowner. The
form of additional enquiries is probably the most comprehensive single
source of information about the property and this search is therefore of
the utmost importance in the early stages of a conveyancing transaction.

5.3 HOW TO MAKE THE SEARCH

5.3.1 Official search

An official search may be made by sending two copies of Form Con
29A (Con 29D in Greater London) together with the fee to the appropriate district council or London borough council. Con 29A and Con
29D are known as the 'long' forms of enquiry. Short versions of these
forms (Con 29AX and Con 29DX) may be used in the alternative and
their use is discussed in para 5.8, below. The address of the appropriate
local authority may be ascertained from (inter alia) the *Directory of
Local Authorities* (Oyez). If in doubt as to whether a property lies within
the area of a particular local authority some delay will be avoided if a
telephone call is made to the authority to check that the property does
lie within its area prior to submission of the application. Where a
property is situate partly in the area of one authority and partly in the
area of another two separate searches must be made.

Normally the form of additional enquiries is submitted simultaneously with the local land charges search application. The local authority may often have to seek information from other sources (eg the
county council) in order to answer some of the questions on the additional enquiries form and this causes delay in the return of the search
to the applicant. If time is short the period of delay in receiving the
answers to both searches may to some extent be lessened by submitting
the two search applications separately (see para 4.3.2, above). It may
also be sensible, when time is short, to telephone the authority before
submitting the application for an estimate of the likely time which they
will take to process the search and where the delay is likely to be
considerable, consideration may be given to making a personal search.

5.3.2 Personal search

A telephone call should always be made to the appropriate local authority prior to embarking on a personal search since some authorities will not permit personal searches to be made. Where such a search is permitted the applicant should attend at the offices of the local authority with a completed search application form and fee. An officer of the authority will then obtain the answers to the questions on the form from information in the authority's possession. The information which is needed to answer the enquiries will be kept by various different departments of the local authority and by the county council. In order to obtain a full set of answers to the additional enquiry form the applicant may have to attend at several different departments, situated in different buildings at some distance apart from each other which will inevitably be a time consuming operation, and will therefore probably only be undertaken in exceptional circumstances.

5.3.3 Fees

(a) Standard Part I enquiries for one parcel of land £9.65

(b) Part I enquiries for each additional parcel of land £2.40

(c) For each printed Part II enquiry £0.75

(d) For each supplementary question not printed on the form £1.80

5.4 FORM CON 29A

This form is reproduced on pp 153–159, below.

5.5 COMMENT ON FORM CON 29A

Two completed copies of this form should be submitted to the appropriate local authority. Except where Part II or supplementary enquiries are raised, the only information to be supplied by the applicant appears on the front page of the standard form. A clear description of the property to be searched should be inserted in the box at the top right hand corner of the front page. In most cases it is only necessary to send a plan with the search application where the property cannot properly be identified by its postal address, but it should be noted that the local authority effectively disclaims liability for any inaccuracies in the result of the search due to their lack of knowledge of the boundaries because of the failure to supply a plan with the search application. Where a plan is used it should be submitted in duplicate and should contain sufficient detail to enable the local authority to identify the property by reference to an ordnance survey map.

Only the road or street which comprises part of the postal address of

1982 EDITION

To be submitted in duplicate

ENQUIRIES OF DISTRICT COUNCILS
(NOT LONDON BOROUGHS)

NAME AND ADDRESS OF DISTRICT COUNCIL (IN BLOCK LETTERS) TO WHICH THIS FORM IS TO BE SENT

Description of the Property

RE ....

....

....

Relevant roadways, footpaths and footways (see Enquiry 1) in addition to those specified in the above address, on which information is sought.

....

....

....

Fees of ....are enclosed, including fees for an Official Search.

Signed ....

Dated ....   *Solicitors.*

HEADNOTES

(1) This Form of Enquiry is approved by the Law Society, the Association of County Councils, the Association of District Councils and the Association of Metropolitan Authorities and is published by their authority.

(2) Under the arrangements made between the District Council and the County Council the Replies below to certain Enquiries cover knowledge and actions of both the District Council and the County Council. References to "the Council" are intended to include reference to a predecessor Council and to a Committee or Sub-Committee of the Council or of a predecessor Council acting under delegated powers, and to any other body or person taking action under powers delegated by the Council or a predecessor Council.

(3) The Replies below are furnished after appropriate enquiries and in the belief that they are in accordance with the information at present available to the officers of the respective Councils, but on the distinct understanding that neither the District Council nor the County Council, nor any officer of either Council, is legally responsible therefor, except for negligence. Any such liability for negligence shall extend not only to the person by or on whose behalf these Enquiries are made but also to a person (being a purchaser for the purposes of Section 10(3) of the Local Land Charges Act 1975) who or whose agent had knowledge, before the relevant time as defined in the said Section, of the Replies to these Enquiries.

(4) It is pointed out that so far as the Replies may relate to proposals they may yet change.

(5) References to the property concerned in the Enquiries and Replies are intended to include reference, where appropriate, to any part of the property.

(6) References to any Act, Regulation or Order are intended to include reference to (i) any statutory provision replaced thereby and (ii) any amendment or re-enactment thereof.

(7) References to any Town and Country Planning Act, Order or Regulation are abbreviated, e.g. "T&CP Act 1971".

(8) Where no plan of the property is furnished with the Requisition for Official Search or this Form of Enquiry, neither the District Council nor the County Council can be expected to know the boundaries of the property, and the Replies are given on the basis of the information as to these available to the Councils in their offices. The furnishing of a plan in duplicate will help the Councils to give accurate replies and may save time. The Councils must reserve the right in any particular case to call for a plan in duplicate sufficient to enable the boundaries of the property to be identified on the ordnance survey map before furnishing Replies.

CURRENT FEES

It should be noted that the following fees are liable to change during the currency of this edition. Enquiries submitted on a form which is up-to-date apart from the information concerning fees will be answered provided the current fees are tendered.

PART I ENQUIRIES:—

    (a) Where relating to one parcel of land only, as defined in Rule 2(2) of the Local Land Charges Rules, 1977 ..   ..   ..   £ p   9.65

    (b) Where relating to several parcels of land (which a single Requisition for Official Search would cover) and delivered on a single form:—

        For the first parcel of land 9.65

        For each additional parcel of land 2.40

        provided that where the fee on that basis would exceed £100, the amount is to be fixed by arrangement between the solicitors and the proper officer of the District Council.

    The above fees cover all the Enquiries in Part I.

PART II ENQUIRIES:—

    Where relating to one parcel of land only or to several parcels (as above-mentioned) and delivered on a single form:—

        For each printed Enquiry numbered in the form 0.75

        For any and each further Enquiry added by solicitors and which the proper officer of the Council is willing to answer ..   1.80

    No maximum fee.

NAME AND ADDRESS (IN BLOCK LETTERS) TO WHICH THIS FORM IS TO BE RETURNED

SOLICITORS' REFERENCE.....................................

....

TELEPHONE NUMBER ....

....

TELEX ....

CON. 29A. ENGLAND AND WALES (EXCLUDING LONDON)

oyez The Solicitors' Law Stationery Society plc, Oyez House, 237 Long Lane, London SE1 4PU

GM Set 255   **COPYRIGHT RESERVED**

F3981 :1.83
★ ★ ★ ★

5.4 *Additional enquiries of the local authority*

ENQUIRY PART I	REPLY
1. (A) Are all the roadways, footpaths and footways referred to in the Description of the Property maintainable at the public expense within the meaning of the Highways Act 1980?	1. (A)
(B) If not, please state whether the Council have passed any resolution either to:—	(B)
(i) make up any of such roadways, footpaths or footways at the cost of the frontagers, or	(i)
(ii) adopt any of them without cost to the frontagers.	(ii)
(C) (i) Have the Council entered into any outstanding agreement relating to the adoption of any such roadway, footpath or footway?	(C) (i)
*(ii) If so, is such an agreement supported by a bond?	*(ii)
2. (A) Have the Council been notified by the appropriate Secretary of State of:—	2. (A)
(i) any order, draft order or scheme for the construction of a new trunk or special road, or	(i)
(ii) any proposals for the alteration or improvement of an existing road, involving the construction, whether or not within existing highway limits, of a subway, underpass, flyover, footbridge, elevated road or dual carriageway the centre line of which in either case is within 200 metres of the property?	(ii)
†(B) Have the Council approved any proposals by themselves for:—	†(B)
(i) the construction of a new road, or	(I)
(ii) the alteration or improvement of an existing road, involving the construction, whether or not within existing highway limits, of a subway, underpass, flyover, footbridge, elevated road or dual carriageway the limits of construction of which in either case are within 200 metres of the property?	(ii)
(C) Have the Council approved, or have they been notified by the appropriate Secretary of State, of any proposals for highway construction or improvement that involve the acquisition of the property?	(C)
(D) Has either the Secretary of State or the Council published for the purposes of public consultation any proposals for the construction of a new road indicating a possible route the centre line of which would be likely to be within 200 metres of the property? [N.B. See Enquiry 21 for metropolitan roads.]	(D)
3. Are there any outstanding statutory or informal notices (other than notices shown in the Official Certificate of Search and notices served consequent on an order made or a resolution passed to acquire the property recorded in reply to Enquiry 14), which have been issued by the Council under the Public Health Acts, Housing Acts or Highways Acts or (Inner London Boroughs only) London Building Acts?	3.
4. Have the Council authorised any proceedings in respect of an infringement of the Building Regulations? [N.B. This Enquiry is not applicable to Inner London Boroughs.]	4.

* If the Reply is "yes", the enquirer should satisfy himself of the adequacy of the bond.
† This Enquiry refers to the Council's own proposals and not those of other developers.

REPLY	ENQUIRY
5. (A) (i) (a)*	5. (A) (i) (a)* Does foul drainage from the property drain to a public sewer?
(b)	(b) If the Reply to (a) above is "Yes", please indicate whether the connection to the public sewer is effected by:
(1)	(1) drain and private sewer;
(2)	(2) drain alone.
(ii) (a)	(ii) (a) Does surface water from the property drain to a public sewer?
(b)	(b) Does surface water from the property drain to a highway drain or sewer the subject of an agreement under s.21(1)(a) of the Public Health Act 1936?
(c)	(c) If the Reply to either (a) or (b) above is "Yes", please indicate whether the connection to the appropriate sewer or highway drain is effected by:
(1)	(1) drain and private sewer;
(2)	(2) drain alone.
(iii)	(iii) Is there in force in relation to any part of the drainage of the property an agreement under s.38 of the Public Health Act 1936?
(B) (i)	(B) (i) To the Council's knowledge is any sewer serving, or which is proposed to serve, the property the subject of an agreement under s.18 of the Public Health Act 1936?
†‡(ii)	†‡(ii) If the Reply to (i) above is "Yes", is the agreement supported by a bond?
(C)	(C) Is any public sewer to which the property drains a sewer of a kind described in s.24(4) of the Public Health Act 1936?
(D)	(D) If the Reply to either Enquiry (A) (i) (a) or (ii) (a) above is "No", do the Council know whether there is a foul or surface water sewer (as appropriate) within 100 feet of the property and at a level which makes it reasonably practicable to construct a drain from the property to that sewer? [N.B. If the Council cannot reply in the affirmative, the applicant must make his own survey.]
‡(E)	‡(E) Are the Council aware of any resolution affecting the property:
(i)	(i) under s.12 or s.13 of the Public Health Act 1961, or
(ii)	(ii) under any local Act as to the recovery from frontagers of the expense of sewering highways?
6. (A)	6. (A) Except as shown in the Official Certificate of Search, or in the Register kept pursuant to s.92A of the T&CP Act 1971, has any enforcement or stop notice under s.87 or s.90 of the T&CP Act 1971 been authorised by the Council for issue or service (other than notices which have been withdrawn or quashed)?
(B)	(B) Are there any entries in the Register kept pursuant to s.92A of the T&CP Act 1971?
(C)	(C) Where can that Register be inspected?
*(D)	*(D) If an enforcement notice has been served or issued, has it been complied with to the satisfaction of the Council?

* This Enquiry will be replied to unless that would necessitate an inspection by the Council's agents. It will be so stated, if it is the case.
† If the Reply is "yes", the enquirer should satisfy himself of the adequacy of the bond.
‡ Even if the Council do reply, enquiry should also be made of the Regional Water Authority.

3

5.4 *Additional enquiries of the local authority*

ENQUIRY	REPLY
*7. (A) Are the Council aware of any proposals by the Greater London Council for the alteration of the Greater London Development Plan (the Structure Plan)?	*7. (A)
(B) (i) What stage has been reached in the preparation of local plans for the area which includes the property?	(B) (i)
(ii) Have the Council made public any proposals for the alteration of an adopted local plan?	(ii)
(iii) Do any of the proposals made public by the Council in relation to local plans:	(iii)
(a) indicate the primary use for the area which includes the property?	(a)
(b) include any provisions for the property?	(b)
(C) (i) Is the Initial Development Plan for Greater London still in force in the area which includes the property?	(C) (i)
(ii) If so, does that plan:	(ii)
(a) indicate the primary use for the area?	(a)
(b) include any provisions for the property?	(b)
(D) (i) Have the Council made public any proposals for the preparation or modification of a non-statutory plan for the area which includes the property?	(D) (i)
(ii) If so:	(ii)
(a) what stage has been reached?	(a)
(b) do any of the proposals indicate the primary use of the area or include any provisions for the property?	(b)
(E) Is the property included in any of the categories of land specified in s.71 of the Land Compensation Act 1973?	(E)
†8. Except as shown in the Official Certificate of Search, have the Council resolved to make a direction under Article 4 of the T&CP General Development Order 1977 relating to the restriction of permitted development?	†8.
9. Except as shown in the Official Certificate of Search, have the Council resolved to make any order under s.45, s.51 or s.60 of the T&CP Act 1971?	9.
10. Has compensation been paid by the Council under s.169 of the T&CP Act 1971?	10.
11. (A) Are there any entries relating to the property in Part I or Part II of the Register kept pursuant to s.34 of the T&CP Act 1971?	11. (A)
(B) Where can that Register be inspected?	(B)
‡12. Is the property within a conservation area designated under s.277 of the T&CP Act 1971 prior to 31 August 1974?	‡12.

* Replies given to Enquiry 2 will not be repeated.
† The Reply to this Enquiry will include information obtained from the Greater London Council.
‡ Conservation areas designated on or after 31/8/74 are registrable as local land charges.

4

REPLY	ENQUIRY
*13.	*13. Have the Council authorised the service of a building preservation notice under s.58 of the T&CP Act 1971?
14.	14. Except as shown in the Official Certificate of Search, have the Council made any order (whether or not confirmed by the appropriate Secretary of State) or passed any resolution which is still capable of being implemented for the compulsory acquisition of the property?
15. (A)	15. (A) Is the property included in a programme of slum clearance which has been submitted, or been the subject of a resolution to submit, to the Department of the Environment, or has otherwise been adopted by resolution of the Council?
(B)	(B) Except as shown in the Official Certificate of Search, have the Council resolved to define the area in which the property is situated as a General Improvement Area?
16. (A)	16. (A) Except as shown in the Official Certificate of Search, is the property included in an area for which the Council have passed a resolution to make or vary a smoke control order under s.11 of the Clean Air Act 1956?
(B)	(B) If the property is in the City of London, please supply particulars of any order made under s.4(2) of the City of London (Various Powers) Act 1954 affecting the property and state whether any exemption from, or deferment of, the provisions of s.4 has been made under s.4(6) or (7).

17. (A)
 	
(i)
(ii)
(iii)
 	
(B)
	17. (A) Is a resolution in force bringing into operation Schedule 1 to the General Rate Act 1967, as to rating of unoccupied property? If so, please specify:
	   (i) the categories of properties affected;
	   (ii) the effective date of the resolution;
	   (iii) the proportion of the rate due.
	(B) If the property is in the City of London (in addition to replying to (A) above), is it liable to be rated under s.177 of the City of London Sewers Act 1848, as amended by s.42 of the City of London Sewers Act 1851 and the City of London (Union of Parishes) Act 1907?

18.	18. As the property is situated in an area where registration of title under the Land Registration Acts is compulsory on sale, please specify the District Registry and the date of compulsory registration.

Replies to the remaining Part I Enquiries have been obtained from the Greater London Council by the proper officer

19.	19. Are there any outstanding statutory or informal notices (other than notices shown in the Official Certificate of Search and notices served consequent on an order made or a resolution passed to acquire the property recorded in reply to Enquiries 14 or 20) which have been issued by the Council under the Public Health Acts, Housing Acts, Highways Acts or London Building Acts?

*The Reply to this Enquiry will include information obtained from the Greater London Council.

5

157

ENQUIRY	REPLY
PART II	
NOTE.—*If the applicant wishes to make any of the following Enquiries, he should place his initials clearly against those concerned. Enquiries not initialled will not be replied to. For fees, see first page.*	
I. Has any public path or road used as a public path or byway which abuts on or crosses the property been shown in a draft, provisional or definitive map or a draft revision or revised map, whichever may be the later, prepared under Part IV of the National Parks and Access to the Countryside Act 1949, Schedule 3 to the Countryside Act 1968 or Part III of the Wildlife and Countryside Act 1981? [N.B. See headnote (8) as to the furnishing of plans.]	I.
II. Have the Council approved any proposals for the stopping up or diversion of any of the roads or footpaths referred to in the Description of the Property?	II.
III. (A) Are there any entries relating to the property in the Register kept by the Council pursuant to the T&CP (Control of Advertisements) Regulations 1969?	III. (A)
(B) Where can that Register be inspected?	(B)
(C) Except as shown in the Official Certificate of Search:	(C)
(i) has any notice been given by the Secretary of State or served under Regulation 15 of the Regulations?	(i)
(ii) have the Council resolved to serve a discontinuance notice under Regulation 16?	(ii)
*(iii) if a discontinuance notice has been served, has it been complied with to the satisfaction of the Council?	*(iii)
(iv) have the Council resolved to make an order defining the area which includes the property as an area of special control under Regulation 26?	(iv)
IV. (A) Have the Council or the Secretary of State granted or refused any listed building consents under s.55 of the T&CP Act 1971?	IV. (A)
(B) Except as shown in the Official Certificate of Search, have the Council resolved to serve a listed building enforcement notice under s.96 of the T&CP Act 1971?	(B)
*(C) If a listed building enforcement notice has been served, has it been complied with to the satisfaction of the Council?	*(C)
V. (A) To the knowledge of the Council, has the service of a repairs notice under s.115 of the T&CP Act 1971 been authorised?	V. (A)
(B) If the Council have authorised the making of an order for the compulsory acquisition of the property under s.114 of the T&CP Act 1971, is a "minimum compensation" provision included, or intended to be included, in the order?	(B)
VI. Have the Council resolved to terminate any of the planning permissions in force by means of a completion notice under s.44 of the T&CP Act 1971?	VI.

*This Enquiry will be replied to unless that would necessitate an inspection by the Council's agents. It will be so stated, if it is the case.

6

158

REPLY	ENQUIRY
VII.	VII. Has any order under s.87 of the National Parks and Access to the Countryside Act 1949, been made relating to an area which includes the property?
VIII.	VIII. Has a map been deposited under s.35 of the Pipe-lines Act 1962, or s.39 of the Gas Act 1972, showing a pipe-line within 100 feet of the property?
IX.	IX. Is the property included in a registration of houses scheme (houses in multiple occupation) under s.22 of the Housing Act 1961, containing control provisions as authorised by s.64 of the Housing Act 1969?
X. (A)	X. (A) Have the Council made, or resolved to make, any noise abatement zone order under s.63 of the Control of Pollution Act 1974 for the area which includes the property?
(B)	(B) Is there any entry in relation to the property recorded in the Noise Level Register kept pursuant to s.64 of the Control of Pollution Act 1974?
(C)	(C) Where can that Register be inspected?
*XI.	*XI. If the property is situated in an area designated as an urban development area under Part XVI of the Local Government, Planning and Land Act 1980, please specify the name of the urban development corporation and the address of the principal office.
XII.	XII. Is the property situated in an area designated as an enterprise zone under Part XVIII of the Local Government, Planning and Land Act 1980?
XIII.	XIII. Have the Council resolved to define the area in which the property is situated as an improvement area under s.4 of the Inner Urban Areas Act 1978?

Signed...
          Proper officer

Dated...19.......

* Information on the functions allocated to an urban development corporation should be sought from that authority.

7

the property will automatically be searched under enquiry 1. Where the property is bordered by other roads, streets or footpaths which are not mentioned in the property's postal address, the identity of these other roads, streets or footpaths must be inserted in the space headed 'Relevant roadways footpaths and footways ...' in order to include them in the search which is made under enquiry 1 (see para 5.9, below). It may therefore be necessary to contact the vendor's solicitors to ascertain the precise location of the property and the identity of adjoining roads or footpaths before sending off the search application.

The fees may be paid by cheque, postal order, money order or Giro and must be included with the search application. Cheques should be made payable to the appropriate district council or London borough council. The space on the form for inclusion of the amount of the fees presupposes that the form of additional enquiries will be submitted simultaneously with the local land charges search application. If this is not the case, the wording should be altered accordingly.

Although it is customary to sign both copies of the search application form, the local authority will accept the search if only the top copy of the application is signed. The questions in Part II of the standard form will only be answered where the applicant has placed his initials in the margin against the individual questions which he requires to be answered and has paid the appropriate fee. The Part II enquiries will not be relevant to all transactions but should always be carefully considered in each transaction and the appropriate questions raised. It is possible to raise supplementary questions of the local authority, which are not contained on the printed form but which it is thought are relevant to the particular transaction. Where space permits, supplementary questions should be typed on to the end of the page containing the Part II enquiries, otherwise they should be typed (in duplicate) on a separate sheet of paper which is headed with the description of the property and the solicitor's name, address and-reference, and stapled to the search form. An additional fee is payable for each supplementary question raised. Since the local authority is under no statutory duty to answer any of the additional enquiry questions, even those on the printed form, some authorities exercise their right to decline to answer supplementary questions and others discourage the practice of raising them. An analysis of all the printed questions on this form appears in para 5.9, below.

5.6   FORM CON 29D
This form is reproduced on pp 161–168, below.

5.7   COMMENT ON FORM CON 29D
This form is used for searches with the Greater London area and is submitted in duplicate to the relevant London borough council. The

1982 EDITION

To be submitted in duplicate

**LONDON BOROUGH COUNCILS OR THE
CORPORATION OF LONDON**

ENQUIRIES OF
LOCAL AUTHORITY

NAME AND ADDRESS OF LOCAL AUTHORITY (IN
BLOCK LETTERS) TO WHICH THIS FORM IS TO BE SENT

Description of the Property

RE ....

....

....

....

Relevant roadways, footpaths and footways (see Enquiry 1) in addition to those specified in the above address, on which information is sought.

....

....

....

Fees of .... are enclosed, including fees for an Official Search.

Signed ....

Dated .... *Solicitors.*

HEADNOTES

(1) This Form of Enquiry is approved by The Law Society, the London Boroughs Association, the Greater London Council, and the Corporation of London, and is published by their authority.

(2) The Replies below are furnished after appropriate enquiries and in the belief that they are in accordance with the information at present available to the officers of the Council, but on the distinct understanding that neither the Common Council, nor the London Borough Council, nor the Greater London Council nor any officer of those Councils is legally responsible therefor, except for negligence. Any such liability for negligence shall extend not only to the person by or on whose behalf these Enquiries are made but also to a person (being a purchaser for the purposes of Section 10(3) of the Local Land Charges Act 1975) who or whose agent had knowledge, before the relevant time as defined in the said Section, of the Replies to these Enquiries.

(3) It is pointed out that so far as the Replies may relate to proposals they may yet change.

(4) References to the property concerned in the Enquiries and Replies are intended to include reference, where appropriate, to any part of the property.

(5) References to any Act, Regulation or Order are intended to include reference to (i) any statutory provision replaced thereby and (ii) any amendment or re-enactment thereof.

(6) References to "the Council" are intended to include reference to a predecessor Council and to a Committee or Sub-Committee of the Council or of a predecessor Council acting under delegated powers, and to any other body or person taking action under powers delegated by the Council or a predecessor Council.

(7) References to any Town and Country Planning Act, Order or Regulation are abbreviated, e.g. "T&CP Act 1971".

(8) Where no plan of the property is furnished with the Requisition for Official Search or this Form of Enquiry, neither the Greater London Council nor the Borough Council nor the Corporation of London can be expected to know the boundaries of the property, and the Replies are given on the basis of the information as to these available to the Councils/Corporation in their offices. The furnishing of a plan in duplicate will help the Councils/Corporation to give accurate Replies and may save time. The Councils/Corporation must reserve the right in any particular case to call for a plan in duplicate sufficient to enable the boundaries of the property to be identified on the ordnance survey map before furnishing Replies.

CURRENT FEES

It should be noted that the following fees are liable to change during the currency of this edition. Enquiries submitted on a form which is up-to-date apart from the information concerning fees will be answered provided the current fees are tendered.

PART I ENQUIRIES:—

		£ p
(a)	Where relating to one parcel of land only, as defined in Rule 2(2) of the Local Land Charges Rules, 1977	9.65
(b)	Where relating to several parcels of land (which a single Requisition for Official Search would cover) and delivered on a single form:—	
	For the first parcel of land	9.65
	For each additional parcel of land	2.40
	provided that where the fee on that basis would exceed £100, the amount is to be fixed by arrangement between the solicitors and the proper officer of the Council.	

The above fees cover all the Enquiries in Part I.

PART II ENQUIRIES:—

Where relating to one parcel of land only or to several parcels (as above-mentioned) and delivered on a single form:—

	£ p
For each printed Enquiry numbered in the form	0.75
For any and each further Enquiry added by solicitors and which the proper officer of the Council is willing to answer	1.80

No maximum fee.

NAME AND ADDRESS (IN BLOCK LETTERS) TO
WHICH THIS FORM IS TO BE RETURNED

SOLICITORS' REFERENCE ....

TELEPHONE NUMBER ....

TELEX ....

CON. 29D. LONDON ONLY   **GM Set 255**

oyez The Solicitors' Law Stationery Society plc, Oyez House, 237 Long Lane, London SE1 4PU

161

5.6 Additional enquiries of the local authority

ENQUIRY PART I	REPLY
1. (A) Are all the roadways, footpaths and footways referred to in the Description of the Property maintainable at the public expense within the meaning of the Highways Act 1980?	1. (A)
(B) If not, please state whether the Council have passed any resolution either to:—	(B)
(i) make up any of such roadways, footpaths or footways at the cost of the frontagers, or	(i)
(ii) adopt any of them without cost to the frontagers.	(ii)
(C) (i) Have the Council entered into any outstanding agreement relating to the adoption of any such roadway, footpath or footway?	(C) (i)
*(ii) If so, is such an agreement supported by a bond?	*(ii)
2. (A) Have the Council been notified by the appropriate Secretary of State of:—	2. (A)
(i) any order, draft order or scheme for the construction of a new trunk or special road, or	(i)
(ii) any proposals for the alteration or improvement of an existing road, involving the construction, whether or not within existing highway limits, of a subway, underpass, flyover, footbridge, elevated road or dual carriageway the centre line of which in either case is within 200 metres of the property?	(ii)
†(B) Have the Council approved any proposals by themselves for:—	†(B)
(i) the construction of a new road, or	(i)
(ii) the alteration or improvement of an existing road, involving the construction, whether or not within existing highway limits, of a subway, underpass, flyover, footbridge, elevated road or dual carriageway the limits of construction of which in either case are within 200 metres of the property?	(ii)
(C) Have the Council approved, or have they been notified by the appropriate Secretary of State of, any proposals for highway construction or improvement that involve the acquisition of the property?	(C)
(D) Has either the Secretary of State or the Council published for the purposes of public consultation any proposals for the construction of a new road indicating a possible route the centre line of which would be likely to be within 200 metres of the property?	(D)
3. Are there any outstanding statutory or informal notices (other than notices shown in the Official Certificate of Search and notices served consequent on an order made or a resolution passed to acquire the property recorded in reply to Enquiry 14), which have been issued by the Council under the Public Health Acts, Housing Acts or Highways Acts?	3.
4. Have the Council authorised any proceedings in respect of an infringement of the Building Regulations?	4.

* If the Reply is "yes", the enquirer should satisfy himself of the adequacy of the bond.
† This Enquiry refers to the Council's own proposals and not those of other developers.

2

REPLY	ENQUIRY
5. (A) (i) (a)*	5. (A) (i) (a)* Does foul drainage from the property drain to a public sewer?
(b)	(b) If the Reply to (a) above is "Yes", please indicate whether the connection to the public sewer is effected by:
(1)	(1) drain and private sewer;
(2)	(2) drain alone.
(ii) (a)	(ii) (a) Does surface water from the property drain to a public sewer?
(b)	(b) Does surface water from the property drain to a highway drain or sewer the subject of an agreement under s.21 (1) (a) of the Public Health Act 1936?
(c)	(c) If the Reply to either (a) or (b) above is "Yes", please indicate whether the connection to the appropriate sewer or highway drain is effected by:
(1)	(1) drain and private sewer;
(2)	(2) drain alone.
(iii)	(iii) Is there in force in relation to any part of the drainage of the property an agreement under s.38 of the Public Health Act 1936?
(B) (i)	(B) (i) To the Council's knowledge is any sewer serving, or which is proposed to serve, the property the subject of an agreement under s.18 of the Public Health Act 1936?
†‡(ii)	†‡(ii) If the Reply to (i) above is "Yes", is the agreement supported by a bond?
(C)	(C) Is any public sewer to which the property drains a sewer of a kind described in s.24(4) of the Public Health Act 1936?
(D)	(D) If the Reply to either Enquiry (A) (i) (a) or (ii) (a) above is "No", do the Council know whether there is a foul or surface water sewer (as appropriate) within 100 feet of the property and at a level which makes it reasonably practicable to construct a drain from the property to that sewer? [N.B. If the Council cannot reply in the affirmative, the applicant must make his own survey.]
‡(E)	‡(E) Are the Council aware of any resolution affecting the property:
(i)	(i) under s.12 or s.13 of the Public Health Act 1961, or
(ii)	(ii) under any local Act as to the recovery from frontagers of the expense of sewering highways?
6. (A)	6. (A) Except as shown in the Official Certificate of Search, or in the Register kept pursuant to s.92A of the T&CP Act 1971, has any enforcement or stop notice under s.87 or s.90 of the T&CP Act 1971 been authorised by the Council for issue or service (other than notices which have been withdrawn or quashed)?
(B)	(B) Are there any entries in the Register kept pursuant to s.92A of the T&CP Act 1971?
(C)	(C) Where can that Register be inspected?
*(D)	*(D) If an enforcement notice has been served or issued, has it been complied with to the satisfaction of the Council?

* This Enquiry will be replied to unless that would necessitate an inspection by the Council's agents. It will be so stated, if it is the case.
† If the Reply is "yes", the enquirer should satisfy himself of the adequacy of the bond.
‡ Even if the Council do reply, enquiry should also be made of the Regional Water Authority.

3

ENQUIRY	REPLY
*7. (A) (i) What stage has been reached in the preparation of a structure plan for the area which includes the property?	*7. (A) (i)
(ii) Have the Council made public any proposals for the alteration of an approved structure plan?	(ii)
(B) (i) What stage has been reached in the preparation of local plans for the area which includes the property?	(B) (i)
(ii) Have the Council made public any proposals for the alteration of an adopted local plan?	(ii)
(iii) Do any of the proposals made public by the Council in relation to local plans:	(iii)
(a) indicate the primary use for the area which includes the property?	(a)
(b) include any provisions for the property?	(b)
(C) (i) Is an old style development plan in force in the area which includes the property?	(C) (i)
(ii) If so, does the plan:	(ii)
(a) indicate the primary use for the area?	(a)
(b) include any provisions for the property?	(b)
(D) (i) Have the Council made public any proposals for the preparation or modification of a non-statutory plan for the area which includes the property?	(D) (i)
(ii) If so:	(ii)
(a) what stage has been reached?	(a)
(b) do any proposals indicate the primary use of the area or include any provisions for the property?	(b)
(E) Is the property included in any of the categories of land specified in s.71 of the Land Compensation Act 1973?	(E)
8. Except as shown in the Official Certificate of Search, have the Council resolved to make a direction under Article 4 of the T&CP General Development Order 1977 relating to the restriction of permitted development?	8.
9. Except as shown in the Official Certificate of Search, have the Council resolved to make any order under s.45, s.51 or s.60 of the T&CP Act 1971?	9.
10. Has compensation been paid by the Council under s.169 of the T&CP Act 1971?	10.
11. (A) Are there any entries relating to the property in Part I or Part II of the Register kept pursuant to s.34 of the T&CP Act 1971?	11. (A)
(B) Where can that Register be inspected?	(B)
†12. Is the property within a conservation area designated under s. 277 of the T&CP Act 1971 prior to 31 August 1974?	†12.

* Replies given to Enquiry 2 will not be repeated.
† Conservation areas designated on or after 31/8/74 are registrable as local land charges.

4

REPLY	ENQUIRY
13.	13. Have the Council authorised the service of a building preservation notice under s.58 of the T&CP Act 1971?
14.	14. Except as shown in the Official Certificate of Search, have the Council made any order (whether or not confirmed by the appropriate Secretary of State) or passed any resolution which is still capable of being implemented for the compulsory acquisition of the property?
15. (A) (B)	15. (A) Is the property included in a programme of slum clearance which has been submitted, or been the subject of a resolution to submit, to the Department of the Environment, or has otherwise been adopted by resolution of the Council? (B) Except as shown in the Official Certificate of Search, have the Council resolved to define the area in which the property is situated as a General Improvement Area.
16.	16. Except as shown in the Official Certificate of Search, is the property included in an area for which the Council have passed a resolution to make or vary a smoke control order under s.11 of the Clean Air Act 1956?
17. (i) (ii) (iii)	17. Is a resolution in force bringing into operation Schedule 1 to the General Rate Act 1967, as to rating of unoccupied property? If so, please specify: (i) the categories of properties affected; (ii) the effective date of the resolution; (iii) the proportion of the rate due.
18.	18. Is the property situated in an area where registration of title under the Land Registration Acts is compulsory on sale? If so, please specify the District Registry and the date of compulsory registration.

5.6 *Additional enquiries of the local authority*

ENQUIRY	REPLY
20. Has any order been made (whether or not confirmed by the appropriate Secretary of State) other than an order referred to in Enquiry V (B) in Part II or has any resolution been passed which would involve the acquisition of the property?	20.
21. (A) Have any proposals (other than such as are referred to in Enquiry 2) for the improvement, widening, alteration or construction of a metropolitan road been approved, which, if implemented, would involve the acquisition of the property?	21. (A)
(B) Have any proposals for the construction of a new metropolitan road been approved, the centre line of which is within 200 metres of the property?	(B)

PART II

NOTE.—*If the applicant wishes to make any of the following Enquiries, he should place his initials clearly against those concerned. Enquiries not initialled will not be replied to. For fees, see first page.*

I. Has any public path or road used as a public path or byway which abuts on or crosses the property been shown in a draft, provisional or definitive map or a draft revision or revised map, whichever may be the later, prepared under Part IV of the National Parks and Access to the Countryside Act 1949, Schedule 3 to the Countryside Act 1968 or Part III of the Wildlife and Countryside Act 1981? [N.B. See headnote (8) as to the furnishing of plans.]	I.
II. Have the Council approved any proposals for the stopping up or diversion of any of the roads or footpaths referred to in the Description of the Property?	II.
III. (A) Are there any entries relating to the property in the Register kept by the Council pursuant to the T&CP (Control of Advertisements) Regulations 1969?	III. (A)
(B) Where can that Register be inspected?	(B)
(C) Except as shown in the Official Certificate of Search:	(C)
(i) has any notice been given by the Secretary of State or served under Regulation 15 of the Regulations?	(i)
(ii) have the Council resolved to serve a discontinuance notice under Regulation 16?	(ii)
*(iii) if a discontinuance notice has been served, has it been complied with to the satisfaction of the Council?	*(iii)
(iv) have the Council resolved to make an order defining the area which includes the property as an area of special control under Regulation 26?	(iv)
IV. (A) Have the Council or the Secretary of State granted or refused any listed building consents under s.55 of the T&CP Act 1971?	IV. (A)
(B) Except as shown in the Official Certificate of Search, have the Council resolved to serve a listed building enforcement notice under s.96 of the T&CP Act 1971?	(B)
*(C) If a listed building enforcement notice has been served, has it been complied with to the satisfaction of the Council?	*(C)

*This Enquiry will be replied to unless that would necessitate an inspection by the Council's agents. It will be so stated, if it is the case.

6

166

REPLY	ENQUIRY
V. (A) (B)	V. (A) To the knowledge of the Council, has the service of a repairs notice under s.115 of the T&CP Act 1971 been authorised? (B) If the Council have authorised the making of an order for the compulsory acquisition of the property under s.114 of the T&CP Act 1971, is a "minimum compensation" provision included, or intended to be included, in the order?
VI.	VI. Have the Council resolved to terminate any of the planning permissions in force by means of a completion notice under s.44 of the T&CP Act 1971?
VII.	VII. Has any order under s.87 of the National Parks and Access to the Countryside Act 1949, been made relating to an area which includes the property?
VIII.	VIII. Has a map been deposited under s.35 of the Pipe-lines Act 1962, or s.39 of the Gas Act 1972, showing a pipe-line within 100 feet of the property?
IX.	IX. Is the property included in a registration of houses scheme (houses in multiple occupation) under s.22 of the Housing Act 1961, containing control provisions as authorised by s.64 of the Housing Act 1969?
X. (A) (B) (C)	X. (A) Have the Council made, or resolved to make, any noise abatement zone order under s.63 of the Control of Pollution Act 1974 for the area which includes the property? (B) Is there any entry in relation to the property recorded in the Noise Level Register kept pursuant to s.64 of the Control of Pollution Act 1974? (C) Where can that Register be inspected?
*XI.	*XI. If the property is situated in an area designated as an urban development area under Part XVI of the Local Government, Planning and Land Act 1980, please specify the name of the urban development corporation and the address of the principal office.
XII.	XII. Is the property situated in an area designated as an enterprise zone under Part XVIII of the Local Government, Planning and Land Act 1980?

*Information on the functions allocated to an urban development corporation should be sought from that authority.

7

167

5.6 *Additional enquiries of the local authority*

ENQUIRY	REPLY
XIII. Have the Council resolved to define the area in which the property is situated as an improvement area under s.4 of the Inner Urban Areas Act 1978?	XIII.

Signed..
Proper officer

Dated..19........

Common Council of the City of London is the appropriate authority for properties situate within the boundaries of the City of London itself. Apart from this distinction the form is completed in the same way as form Con 29A and the remarks contained in para 5.5, above apply equally to the completion of form Con 29D. The fees payable for the search are identical to those payable for form Con 29A (para 5.3.3, above). Some of the questions on form Con 29D are differently numbered or worded from their counterparts on form Con 29A. A comparative table of the numbering of the questions appears below and an analysis of each individual question is contained in para 5.9, below.

5.7.1 Comparative table of questions contained in forms Con 29A and Con 29D

Note: An asterisk placed against a question in the Con 29D column below indicates a difference in wording between the two comparative questions.

Con 29A (*outside London*)	Con 29D (*London*)	Con 29A (*outside London*)	Con 29D (*London*)
Part I enquiries		*Part I enquiries*	
1	1	11	10
2	2, 21	12	12
3	3*	13	13*
4	4*	14	14, 20
5	5	15	15
6	6	16	16*
7	7*	17	17*
8	8*	18	18*
9	9	—	19 (outstanding notices)
10	10	—	20 (compulsory acquisition)
		—	21 (metropolitan roads)
Part II enquiries		*Part II enquiries*	
I	I	VII	VII
II	II	VIII	VIII
III	III	IX	IX
IV	IV	X	X
V	V	XI	XI
VI	VI	XII	XII

5.8 SHORT FORM ENQUIRIES

Two short form enquiry forms were introduced when the current edition of the form of additional enquiries was published in 1982. These forms do not set out the wording of any of the printed questions from forms Con 29A or Con 29D but incorporate those printed questions by reference and provide a space in which to indicate which (if any) of the Part II questions are required to be answered. The form assumes that the applicant will wish to obtain answers to all the Part I printed enquiries. A space on the reverse side of the form is provided in which supplementary questions may be typed. The description of the property and relevant roadways and other information must be inserted in the same manner as is required for the long form of enquiries (see para 5.5, above). The only advantages to using the short form of enquiry are that the form may be marginally quicker to fill in and because it comprises only a single sheet of paper is less expensive to purchase and to post than the long form of enquiries. The local authority's replies to the enquiries, whether made on the long or short form, will frequently be typed or printed on a single sheet which refers to the questions which are being answered by number only. This method of supplying the answers to the enquiries does raise a disadvantage in connection with the use of the short form of enquiries because on receipt of the local authority's replies it will usually be necessary to refer to a copy of the long form of the questions in order to check the answers. Since the replies to the enquiries should be stored with the deeds for future reference a long form of the questions will also have to be placed in the file, otherwise it will be impossible to identify the questions to which the answers relate. It is therefore arguable that any cost saving which might have been achieved by using the short form of enquiries is negated because a long form of enquiries will in any event have to be placed in the file for future reference.

The two published short forms of enquiries are illustrated below.

5.8.1 Form Con 29AX (outside London)
This form is reproduced on pp 171–172, below.

1982 EDITION

To be submitted in duplicate

REQUISITION FOR ENQUIRIES OF DISTRICT COUNCILS

(NOT LONDON BOROUGHS)

NAME AND ADDRESS OF DISTRICT COUNCIL (IN BLOCK LETTERS) TO WHICH THIS FORM IS TO BE SENT

Description of the Property

RE..
....
....
....

Relevant roadways, footpaths and footways (see Enquiry 1) in addition to those specified in the above address, on which information is sought.
....
....
....

Fees of £ ....are enclosed, including fees for an Official Search.

Replies are requested to the following Enquiries contained in the 1982 Edition of form CON 29A ENGLAND AND WALES (EXCLUDING LONDON), subject to the headnotes and footnotes set out on that form:

Signed .... (*Solicitors*)   Dated ....19..............

PART I

All Enquiries

PART II

The following Enquiries (tick box(es) as required):

☐ **I** (Public paths, etc., map)

☐ **II** (Stopping up/diversion of roads etc.)

☐ **III** (Advertisements)

☐ **IV** (Listed buildings)

☐ **V** (Repairs notice/"minimum compensation")

☐ **VI** (Completion notice)

☐ **VII** (National Parks etc. Act 1949, s. 87 Order)

☐ **VIII** (Pipe-lines)

☐ **IX** (Registration of houses scheme)

☐ **X** (Noise)

☐ **XI** (Urban development area)

☐ **XII** (Enterprise zone)

☐ **XIII** (Improvement area)

For the fees relating to Part II Enquiries, see overleaf

NAME AND ADDRESS (IN BLOCK LETTERS) TO WHICH THIS FORM IS TO BE RETURNED

SOLICITORS' REFERENCE...

TELEPHONE NUMBER...

TELEX...

5.8.1 *Additional enquiries of the local authority*

The following additional Enquiries:

CURRENT FEES

It should be noted that the following fees are liable to change during the currency of this edition. Requisitions submitted on a form which is up-to-date apart from the information concerning fees will be answered provided the current fees are tendered.

	£ p
PART I ENQUIRIES:—	
(a) Where relating to one parcel of land only, as defined in Rule 2(2) of the Local Land Charges Rules, 1977	9.65
(b) Where relating to several parcels of land (which a single Requisition for Official Search would cover) and delivered on a single form:—	
For the first parcel of land	9.65
For each additional parcel of land	2.40
provided that where the fee on that basis would exceed £100, the amount is to be fixed by arrangement between the solicitors and the proper officer of the District Council.	

The above fees cover all the Enquiries in Part I.

PART II ENQUIRIES:—

Where relating to one parcel of land only or to several parcels (as above-mentioned) and delivered on a single form:—	
For each printed Enquiry numbered in the form	0.75
For any and each further enquiry added by solicitors and which the proper officer of the Council is willing to answer	1.80

No maximum fee.

CON. 29AX. ENGLAND AND WALES (EXCLUDING LONDON)

oyez The Solicitors Law Stationery Society plc. Oyez House. 237 Long Lane. London SE1 4PU

172

5.8.2 Form Con 29DX (London only)

1982 EDITION

To be submitted in duplicate

LONDON BOROUGH COUNCILS OR THE CORPORATION OF LONDON

REQUISITION FOR ENQUIRIES OF LOCAL AUTHORITY

NAME AND ADDRESS OF LOCAL AUTHORITY (IN BLOCK LETTERS) TO WHICH THIS FORM IS TO BE SENT

Description of the Property

RE..

....

....

Relevant roadways, footpaths and footways (see Enquiry 1) in addition to those specified in the above address, on which information is sought.

....

Fees of £..are enclosed, including fees for an Official Search.

Replies are requested to the following Enquiries contained in the 1982 Edition of form CON 29D LONDON ONLY, subject to the headnotes and footnotes set out on that form:

Signed .... *(Solicitors)* Dated .... 19..............

PART I

All Enquiries

PART II

The following Enquiries (tick box(es) as required):

☐ **I** (Public paths, etc., map)

☐ **II** (Stopping up/diversion of roads etc.)

☐ **III** (Advertisements)

☐ **IV** (Listed buildings)

☐ **V** (Repairs notice/"minimum compensation")

☐ **VI** (Completion notice)

☐ **VII** (National Parks etc. Act 1949, s. 87 Order)

☐ **VIII** (Pipe-lines)

☐ **IX** (Registration of houses scheme)

☐ **X** (Noise)

☐ **XI** (Urban development area)

☐ **XII** (Enterprise zone)

☐ **XIII** (Improvement area)

For the fees relating to Part II Enquiries, see overleaf

NAME AND ADDRESS (IN BLOCK LETTERS) TO WHICH THIS FORM IS TO BE RETURNED

SOLICITORS' REFERENCE ....

TELEPHONE NUMBER ....

TELEX........................

173

5.8.2 *Additional enquiries of the local authority*

If space is insufficient, continue on separate sheet, headed with description of property and solicitors' reference, and attach securely hereto.

The following additional Enquiries:

CURRENT FEES

It should be noted that the following fees are liable to change during the currency of this edition. Requisitions submitted on a form which is up-to-date apart from the information concerning fees will be answered provided the current fees are tendered.

£ p

PART I ENQUIRIES:—

(a) Where relating to one parcel of land only, as defined in Rule 2(2) of the Local Land Charges Rules, 1977 ..   9.65

(b) Where relating to several parcels of land (which a single Requisition for Official Search would cover) and delivered on a single form:—

     For the first parcel of land 9.65

     For each additional parcel of land 2.40

     provided that where the fee on that basis would exceed £100, the amount is to be fixed by arrangement between the solicitors and the proper officer of the Council.

The above fees cover all the Enquiries in Part I.

PART II ENQUIRIES:—

Where relating to one parcel of land only or to several parcels (as above-mentioned) and delivered on a single form:—

     For each printed Enquiry numbered in the form.. .. ..   0.75

     For any and each further enquiry added by solicitors and which the proper officer of the Council is willing to answer 1.80

No maximum fee.

CON. 29DX. LONDON ONLY

oyez The Solicitors' Law Stationery Society plc, Oyez House, 237 Long Lane, London SE1 4PU

5.9 ANALYSIS OF PART I ENQUIRIES ON FORMS CON 29A AND CON 29D

Note: The wording of each question as it appears on form Con 29A is set out below, immediately preceding the discussion of that question. Where form Con 29D differs from the wording given, the differences are noted in the text.

5.9.1 Question 1 (roads)

5.9.1.1
1. (A) Are all the roadways, footpaths and footways referred to in the Description of the Property maintainable at the public expense within the meaning of the Highways Act 1980?
(B) If not, please state whether the Council have passed any resolution either to:
 (i) make up any of such roadways, footpaths or footways at the cost of the frontagers, or
(ii) adopt any of them without cost to the frontagers.
(C) (i) Have the Council entered into any outstanding agreement relating to the adoption of any such roadway, footpath or footway?
(ii) If so, is such an agreement supported by a bond?

5.9.1.2 Where a roadway, footpath or footway is maintainable at the public expense, the purchaser of the property will not be under any obligation to contribute towards the cost of maintenance of the roadway, etc unless a financial charge is registered as a local land charge. Each local authority keeps a list of streets in their area which are maintainable at the public expense and this may be inspected free of charge. In certain areas where a highway is not maintainable at public expense the local authority may resolve to make the highway up to a suitable standard and thereafter maintain it at public expense, but in the majority of cases where a highway is to be adopted, the cost of making the road up to the required standard will fall on the frontagers. This cost may impose a heavy financial burden on the frontagers. The local authority cannot generally be compelled to take over the maintenance of private streets except where there is an agreement to do so under the Highways Act 1980, s 38.

The developer of, eg a new housing estate will often enter into a s 38 agreement with the local highway authority. Under the terms of this agreement the developer will agree to make up the roads which are the subject of the agreement to the standard required by the local authority and to maintain them for a specified time, after which the local authority will adopt the roads and maintain them at no cost to the frontagers. Provided that the developer carries out his obligations under the agreement the purchasers of individual plots on the estate will not have to pay road charges, but liability for road charges would exist if the developer defaulted under the agreement. To cover such contingent

175

liability the s 38 agreement is normally supported by a bond or guarantee from a bank or insurance company. The purchaser of a property which is under construction or which has been recently built should ensure that a s 38 agreement and supporting bond exists. A footnote to question 1(C)(iii) states that where the answer to this sub-question is 'yes', ie a bond exists, the purchaser should satisfy himself as to the adequacy of the bond. Although this advice is sensible, in practice it may be very difficult to ascertain with any accuracy the value of the outstanding roadworks and to compare this with the value of the bond. The printed question only refers to highways which are maintainable at the public expense under the Highways Act 1980 and will not give details of roadways which are maintainable by the local authority in some other capacity, eg as landowner or as housing authority.

5.9.2 Question 2 (new roads)

5.9.2.1

2. (A) Have the Council been notified by the appropriate Secretary of State of:
 (i) any order, draft order or scheme for the construction of a new trunk or special road, or
 (ii) any proposals for the alteration or improvement of an existing road, involving the construction, whether or not within existing highways limits, of a subway, underpass, flyover, footbridge, elevated road or dual carriageway

the centre line of which in either case is within 200 metres of the property?
(B) Have the Council approved any proposals by themselves for:
 (i) the construction of a new road, or
 (ii) the alteration or improvement of an existing road, involving the construction, whether or not within existing highway limits, of a subway, underpass, flyover, footbridge, elevated road or dual carriageway

the limits of construction of which in either case are within 200 metres of the property?
(C) Have the Council approved, or have they been notified by the appropriate Secretary of State of, any proposals for highway construction or improvement that involve the acquisition of the property?
(D) Has either the Secretary of State or the Council published for the purposes of public consultation any proposals for the construction of a new road indicating a possible route the centre line of which would be likely to be within 200 metres of the property?

5.9.2.2 This question is concerned with proposals for new roads within a radius of 200 metres of the property. The distance of 200 metres given in this question is of no legal significance, but is a purely arbitrary limit based on the assumption that roadworks beyond this distance would be unlikely to affect the property to its detriment. Although the construction of a new road at a distance of, eg 250 metres from the property would be unlikely to result in the compulsory acquisition of the property, it is suggested that the value of the property might still be adversely affected because of the resultant increased traffic noise. If, however, the applicant wishes to obtain information about proposals for the construction of roads at a greater distance than 200 metres from the property a supplementary question will have to be raised. It should also be noted that the local authority in response to this question is only obliged to reveal proposals for new roads which will be maintained at public expense. Proposals for new private roads, even if known to the local authority, will not be disclosed in answer to this question.

A trunk road is a major road which, when designated as such, vests in the Secretary of State who exercises all the powers of construction, maintenance and improvement in relation to that road which were previously exercisable by the local authority. A special road is a road designated to carry traffic of a particular class, eg a motorway. The Secretary of State exercises powers over special roads in a similar fashion to his powers over trunk roads. Where proposals for the construction or improvement of trunk or special roads are revealed in response to this question enquiries concerning the proposals will have to be raised with the Secretary of State.

Property with a frontage on to a trunk or special road, or in the close vicinity of such a road may also suffer certain disadvantages which should be borne in mind by a proposed purchaser. For example:

(a) the value of the property may be adversely affected by the amount of traffic or noise caused by traffic;

(b) such roads are more susceptible to roadworks and improvement schemes than smaller roads; which may result in interference with the property for roadworks or perhaps the compulsory purchase of part of the property for the purpose of an improvement scheme;

(c) it will be extremely difficult to obtain planning permission for an additional or altered vehicular access to such a road.

5.9.2.3   A separate enquiry on form Con 29D deals with proposals for metropolitan roads (para 5.9.21, below).

5.9.3   Question 3 (outstanding notices)

5.9.3.1

3. Are there any outstanding statutory or informal notices (other than notices shown in the Official Certificate of Search and notices served consequent on an order made or a resolution passed to acquire the property recorded in reply to Enquiry 14), which have been issued by the Council under the Public Health Acts, Housing Acts or Highways Acts?

5.9.3.2   This question is deliberately drafted widely in order to obtain information about matters which might affect the property but which would not otherwise be revealed in response to the local land charges search nor in response to other specific questions on forms Con 29A or D. Although an affirmative reply to this question is unusual there are potentially a very large number of matters which could be revealed in response to this question and where any such matter is disclosed its significance should be carefully checked by reference to the relevant statutory provisions.

5.9.3.3 Question 3 on form Con 29D varies slightly from the wording given above in that the London Building Acts are added to the list of Statutes referred to in the question. The London Building Acts only affect Inner London boroughs where they serve the same purpose as the Building Regulations.

5.9.4 Question 4 (breach of Building Regulations)

5.9.4.1
4. Have the Council authorised any proceedings in respect of an infringement of the Building Regulations?

5.9.4.2 The erection of any building on land will generally require building regulation consent from the local authority under the Building Regulations 1985 regardless of whether planning consent is also necessary. An offence is committed if the Building Regulations are contravened. A maximum period of one year is allowed in which the local authority may bring proceedings for this offence.

5.9.4.3 The Building Regulations do not apply to Inner London boroughs, where the London Building Acts apply instead.

5.9.5 Question 5 (drains and sewers)

5.9.5.1
5. (A)(i) (a) Does foul drainage from the property drain to a public sewer?
(b) If the Reply to (a) is 'Yes', please indicate whether the connection to the public sewer is effected by:
(1) drain and private sewer;
(2) drain alone.
(ii) (a) Does surface water from the property drain to a public sewer?
(b) Does surface water from the property drain to a highway drain or sewer the subject of an agreement under s 21(1) of the Public Health Act 1936?
(c) If the Reply to either (a) or (b) above is 'yes', please indicate whether the connection to the appropriate sewer or highway drain is effected by:
(1) drain and private sewer;
(2) drain alone.

(iii) is there in force in relation to any part of the drainage of the property an agreement under s 38 of the Public Health Act 1936?
(B) (i) To the Council's knowledge is any sewer serving, or which is proposed to serve, the property the subject of an agreement under s 18 of the Public Health Act 1936?
(ii) If the Reply to (i) above is 'Yes', is the agreement supported by a bond?
(C) Is any public sewer to which the property drains a sewer of a kind described in s 24(4) of the Public Health Act 1936?
(D) If the Reply to either Enquiry (A) (i)(a) or (ii) (a) above is 'No', do the Council know whether there is a foul or surface water sewer (as appropriate) within 100 feet of the property and at a level which makes it reasonably practicable to construct a drain from the property to that sewer?
B. If the Council cannot reply in the affirmative, the applicant must make his own survey.)
(E) Are the Council aware of any resolution affecting the property:
(i) under s 12 or s 13 of the Public Health Act 1961, or
(i) (ii) under any local Act
as to the recovery from frontagers of the expense of sewering highways?

5.9.5.2 This complex question is designed to elicit all the information in the local authority's possession relating to drains and sewers, but additional enquiries may need to be raised with the vendor and/or with the regional water authority.

5.9.5.3 *Terminology*
(a) *Drain.* A drain drains a single building or property.
(b) *Sewer.* A sewer is a drain which serves more than one property.
(c) *Public sewer.* A public sewer is a sewer vested in the regional water authority.
5.9.5.4 The Public Health Act 1936, s 21 (1)(a) refers to agreements made between county councils and local authorities relating to the use of sewers. A sewer which is the subject of a s 21 agreement may for practical purposes be regarded as a public sewer.
5.9.5.5 An agreement under the Public Health Act 1936, s 38 relates to properties which enjoy combined drainage with another property. Charges for repairs and maintenance of the combined drain may have to be paid where a s 38 agreement exists.
5.9.5.6 An agreement under the Public Health Act 1936 will be made between a developer and the regional water authority (or local authority to whom the regional water authority has delegated its power) in connection with the construction and maintenance of new drains and sewers. A purchaser would expect to receive an affirmative

reply to question 5(B) where he is buying property on a new estate. The s 18 agreement will normally be supported by a bond, similar to the bond which accompanies the Highways Act, s 38 agreement for the making up of new roads and in theory it is the purchaser's responsibility to check the adequacy of the bond although in practice this may be difficult to do. An unexpected negative response to this part of the question does not mean that a s 18 agreement does not exist, since the local authority is not always a party to the agreement they may not at the time of the search have been informed of the existence of the agreement by the regional water authority. In any event, however, further enquiries in relation to the existence of a s 18 agreement should be raised both with the vendor and with the regional water authority.

5.9.5.7 An affirmative answer to Part C of this question should be thoroughly investigated because it will indicate a liability to pay maintenance charges for some or all of the sewers serving the property. The Public Health Act 1936, s 24(4) imposes this liability in respect of certain public sewers which were privately constructed before 1 October 1937 and certain premises which have combined drainage.

5.9.5.8 Where the property is not presently sewered into a public sewer, which will be revealed in response to part A of the question, the property owner may expect to pay for the maintenance of sewers and drains serving his property. In this situation he will also be concerned to know whether there is any likelihood of the property being connected to a public sewer in the future and this may be revealed in response to Part D of the question. The local authority can only require the property to be connected to a public sewer if (inter alia) there is a public sewer on a level which makes it reasonably practicable to construct a drain to connect with it lying within 100 feet of the building. The local authority may only inist on the connection of the property to a public sewer more than 100 feet in distance from the building if they agree to bear the additional expense of the connection.

If the local authority do not have sufficient information available in order to answer this part of the question, enquiries should be raised with the regional water authority. A full structural survey of the property may also reveal the existence and routes of sewers and drains.

Where the answer to this part of the question is given in the affirmative, this will indicate that the local authority would be in a position to require the property owner to pay for the connection of the property to a nearby public sewer under their powers contained in the Public Health Act 1936, s 37, but should not be taken as meaning that the local authority *will* insist on such a connection being made.

5.9.5.9 An affirmative answer to Part E of the question may impose a financial liability on the property owner in relation to payment for the construction of a sewer to serve a public highway. Although the Public Health Act 1936, ss 12 and 13 only apply to premises built after

3 October 1961 a similar liability arising under a local act could apply to property built at any time. On 1 April 1974 the power to pass resolutions of this nature vested in the regional water authority, and thus the local authority may not be aware of the passing of such a resolution made since this date. Resolutions of this type are usually registered as local land charges, although it is not compulsory for them to be so registered. It is understood that regional water authorities do not intend to use their powers to charge frontagers with the cost of sewering the highways, but if the purchaser is concerned with this aspect of sewerage charges, further enquiries may be made with the appropriate regional water authority.

5.9.5.10 Where the property drains into a private sewer, the purchaser's solicitor should check the existence and extent of an easement to use the private sewer.

5.9.5.11 The addresses of the regional water authorities are contained in ch 21, below, which also gives further details of searches to be made with the water authorities. Searches in respect of pipe-lines and cables are dealt with in ch 22, below.

5.9.6 Question 6 (enforcement of planning control)

5.9.6.1

6. (A) Except as shown in the Official Certificate of Search, or in the Register kept pursuant to s 92A of the Town and Country Planning Act 1971, has any enforcement or stop notice under s 87 or s 90 of the Town and Country Planning Act 1971 been authorised by the Council for issue or service (other than notices which have been withdrawn or quashed)?
(B) Are there any entries in the Register kept pursuant to s 92A of the Town and Country Planning Act 1971?
(C) Where can the Register be inspected?
(D) If an enforcement notice has been served or issued, has it been complied with to the satisfaction of the Council?

5.9.6.2 A local planning authority may serve an enforcement notice under the Town and Country Planning Act 1971, s 87 where there has been a breach of planning control. The notice requires the breach to be remedied at the end of the period for compliance specified in the notice (minimum period is 28 days). A stop notice may also be served under s 90 which takes effect between three and 14 days after service. Stop notices may be served in connection with unauthorised changes of use as well as in relation to unauthorised building works. The local authority is generally reluctant to serve either of these notices since they may have to pay compensation to the property owner if the notice is subsequently withdrawn or is defeated on appeal on certain grounds.

5.9.6.3 An enforcement or stop notice which has been issued or served will be registered as a local land charge and will be revealed in answer to the local land charges search. This question is designed to elicit information about enforcement or stop notices which have been authorised but not yet issued or served.

5.9.6.4 The Town and Country Planning Act 1971, s 92A was added to the Act by the Local Government and Planning (Amendment) Act 1981 and requires the local authority to maintain a register of enforcement and stop notices containing details of all such notices which have been issued or served after 27 November 1981 whether or not they have taken effect. An enforcement or stop notice does not take effect whilst an appeal against it is pending. The official certificate of search issued pursuant to the local land charges search will probably not reveal details of enforcement and stop notices which have taken effect since 27 Nobember 1981 but details of such notices will be revealed in response to Part B of this question.

5.9.6.5 It follows that all outstanding enforcement or stop notices will be revealed either in response to this question or in answer to the local land charges search.

5.9.6.6 Part D of the question relates to enforcement notices which remain on the register even though they may have been complied with. The relevance of this part of the question is that by the Town and Country Planning Act 1971, s 93 an enforcement notice continues to be effective even after it has been complied with and, provided it has been registered as a local land charge, may be enforced against any owner or subsequent owner of the land in relation to any future breach of the same planning matter which was specified in the original notice. It is not necessary for the local authority to issue fresh enforcement notices in relation to repeated breaches of the same planning matter.

5.9.6.7 Enforcement notices relating to listed buildings are dealt with by question IV of the Part II enquiries (para 5.10.4, below).

5.9.7 Question 7 (planning policy)

5.9.7.1

7. (A)(i) What stage has been reached in the preparation of a structure plan for the area which includes the property?

(ii) Have the Council made public any proposals for the alteration of an approved structure plan?

(B)(i) What stage has been reached in the preparation of local plans for the area which includes the property?

(ii) Have the Council made public any proposals for the alteration of an adopted local plan?

(iii) Do any of the proposals made public by the Council in relation to local plans:

(a) indicate the primary use for the area which includes the property?

(b) include any provisions for the property?

(C)(i) Is an old style development plan in force in the area which includes the property?

(ii) If so, does the plan:

(a) indicate the primary use for the area?
(b) include any provisions for the property?
(D)(i) Have the Council made public any proposals for the preparation or modification of a non-statutory plan for the area which includes the property?
(ii) If so:
(a) what stage has been reached?
(b) do any proposals indicate the primary use of the area or include any provisions for the property?
(E) Is the property included in any of the categories of land specified in s 71 of the Land Compensation Act 1973?

5.9.7.2 The answer to this question should reveal the planning policy of the local authority. In particular the purchaser will be concerned to see whether the local authority have any proposals which will affect the property. The question is necessarily complicated because not all local authorities have prepared structure and local plans in accordance with the Town and Country Planning Act 1971 (Parts A and B) and in some areas the planning policy is still shown on the development plans (Part C) which were prepared under previous legislation. The answer to this question will reveal the local authority's planning policy for the area and is not concerned with its proposals for individual properties.

5.9.7.3 Terminology

Development plan. This is a plan which was prepared by the local authority under the Town and Country Planning Acts 1947 and 1962, which shows the manner in which the local authority proposed to use the land within its area. These plans are gradually being superseded by the structure and local plans which are to be prepared under Town and Country Planning Act 1971, but remain in force until the structure and local plans for the area are completed.

Structure plans and local plans. The Town and Country Planning Act, 1971 provides for the replacement of the old style development plans by structure and local plans. Although the 1971 Act has now been in force for a number of years, in many areas work on the structure and local plans is not yet complete. By the end of 1981 structure plans for the whole of England and Wales had been submitted to the Secretary of State for approval, but as the local plans cannot formally be adopted until the structure plan for the area has been approved, many of the local plans have not yet come into force. The structure plan is a written policy statement dealing with the major planning issues for the whole of the area covered by a local planning authority. Local plans covering part only of the area show a detailed breakdown of the broad policies shown in the structure plan, as they apply to the smaller area shown on the local plan.

5.9.7.4 Proposals for new roads in the vicinity of the property are dealt with under question 2 (para 5.9.2, above) and will not be revealed in answer to this question.

5.9.7.5 Where a 'primary use' for the area is indicated it is unlikely that planning permission for another type of use would be granted.

5.9.7.6 Some local authorities are currently replying to Part B in extremely general terms which indicate that the local plan for the area does include policies which might affect the property which is the subject of the search. Where a reply in these terms is received it seems that the applicant's solicitor may have to raise further enquiries with the local authority to ensure that the planning policies mentioned in the reply to Part B do not affect the property adversely. A copy of the local plan can usually be bought from the local authority at a relatively modest cost.

5.9.7.7 The Land Compensation Act 1973, s 71 (Part E) refers to land in relation to which the local authority has passed a resolution reserving the land for the purposes of any function of a government department, local authority or statutory undertaker. A blight notice may be served where land is affected by the application of this section.

5.9.7.8 Greater London

Question 7 on form Con 29D is worded slightly differently from the question illustrated in para 5.9.7.1, above. The Greater London Development Plan is the approved structure plan for the whole of Greater London. The Initial Development Plan for Greater London is the London equivalent of the old-style development plan.

5.9.8 Question 8 (article 4 directions)

5.9.8.1

8. Except as shown in the Official Certificate of Search, have the Council resolved to make a direction under article 4 of the Town and Country Planning General Development Order 1977 relating to the restriction of permitted development?

5.9.8.2 Under the Town and Country Planning General Development Order 1977, art 3, 23 classes of development specified in Part I of the Schedule to the Order may be carried out without the need to obtain express planning permission for that development. An authority may resolve to withdraw the effect of the General Development Order either in whole or in part in relation to its area by passing a direction under art 4 of the General Development Order.

Article 4 directions which have already been made will in general be revealed by the local land charges search and this question is directed at the local authority's future proposals to pass an art 4 direction.

5.9.8.3   In Greater London the Greater London Council also have power to make this type of direction and within this area additional enquiries should be made with the Greater London Council.

5.9.9   Question 9 (notices under Town and Country Planning Act 1971)

5.9.9.1
9. Except as shown in the Official Certificate of Search, have the Council resolved to make any order under s 45, s 51 or s 60 of the Town and Country Planning Act 1971?

5.9.9.2   Under the Town and Country Planning Act 1971, s 45 the local authority has power to revoke or modify a planning consent at any time before the operations have been completed. This power is rarely exercised by the local authority since on its exercise substantial compensation may be payable for the loss caused by the making of the order.

5.9.9.3   By s 51 of the 1971 Act the local authority has power to order the discontinuance of a lawful use of the property. Such an order generally requires confirmation from the Secretary of State. The power is rarely exercised since compensation is payable to the land owner affected by the order.

5.9.9.4   Tree preservation orders made under the Town and Country Planning Act 1971, s 60 prohibit the cutting down, lopping, topping or wilful destruction of the trees specified in the order,. Orders may relate to single trees, groups of trees or to woodland and are relatively common, particularly in connection with the development of new estates. Contravention of an order is an offence punishable on summary conviction by a fine of up to £1,000. Existing orders will be revealed in response to the local land charges search. This enquiry will reveal orders which are proposed but which have not yet been registered as local land charges.

5.9.10   Question 10 (compensation for refusal of grant of planning permission)

5.9.10.1
10. Has compensation been paid by the Council under s 169 of the Town and Country Planning Act 1971?

5.9.10.2   In certain circumstances compensation is payable under the Town and Country Planning Act 1971, s 169 where the Secretary of State refuses to grant planning permission for the development of the land or grants it conditionally. Once compensation has been paid, a succeeding owner of the land cannot obtain further compensation in respect of the same matter and thus the amount of compensation payable on a subsequent compulsory acquisition of the property would be substantially reduced. Where following the payment of compensation planning permission for certain types of development is granted, the amount of the compensation may have to be repaid (s 159 of the 1971 Act).

5.9.11 Question 11 (planning applications)

5.9.11.1

11. (A) Are there any entries relating to the property in Part I or Part II of the Register kept pursuant to s 34 of the Town and Country Planning Act 1971?

(B) Where can that Register be inspected?

5.9.11.2 Most planning consents which have been granted in relation to the property will be revealed in answer to the local land charges search. The answer to this question will give details of planning applications which have been made in relation to the property, thus revealing information about pending applications and previous refusals. The information relating to previous refusals gives a useful insight into the local authority's planning policy for the area, and where the purchaser intends to develop the property may provide an indication of the likelihood or otherwise of his obtaining a permission to develop the property. Only brief details of the applications will be given in answer to this question and it may be necessary to obtain copies of the actual applications from the local authority.

5.9.12.2 Where the local authority consider that a particular area is of special architectural or historic interest they may designate the area as a conservation area in order to preserve or enhance the character or appearance of the area. Within such an area special procedures apply in relation to the making of planning applications and permission to demolish or alter the building may be difficult to obtain. The General Development Order only applies to a limited extent within a conservation area. Some individual buildings within a conservation area may be listed as buildings of historic or architectural interest. The designation of an area as a conservation area on or after 31 August 1974 will be registered as a local land charge and will be revealed by the answers to the search. This question only deals with conservation areas which were designated as such before 31 August 1974.

5.9.13 Question 13 (building preservation notice)

5.9.13.1

13. Have the Council authorised the service of a building preservation notice under s 58 of the Town and Country Planning Act 1971?

5.9.13.2 Where the local authority consider that a building which is not listed as such is nevertheless of historic or architectural interest they may serve a building preservation notice on the owner and occupier. The notice lasts for six months during which time the Secretary of State may decide to list the building. A notice which has already been served will be revealed in answer to the local land charges search. This question is designed to reveal proposals for the service of such a notice. While the notice is in force it is an offence to damage or demolish the building or to alter or extend it in such a way as to alter its character without having first obtained listed building consent. (Listed building consents are referred to in para 5.10.4, below.)

5.9.13.3 Within Greater London the Greater London Council has power to issue a similar type of notice and a separate enquiry may be made of the Greater London Council in appropriate circumstances.

5.9.14 Question 14 (compulsory purchase)

5.9.14.1

14. Except as shown in the Official Certificate of Search, have the Council made any order (whether or not confirmed by the appropriate Secretary of State) or passed any resolution which is still capable of being implemented for the compulsory acquisition of the property?

5.9.14.2 A compulsory purchase order is not generally capable of being registered as a local land charge until a notice to treat has been served on the landowner. This question therefore serves as a vital early warning system to obtain advance information about compulsory purchase orders which are either proposed or which have been made but in respect of which no notice to treat has yet been served. Where a purchaser has exchanged contracts to purchase land which is subject to a compulsory purchase order he can be compelled to complete his purchase since the estate in the land still exists and his only remedies would be to obtain compensation from the acquiring authority and/or to seek a remedy against his vendor for non-disclosure.

Since over 50 statutes confer powers of compulsory acquisition on local authorities, if an order is revealed in response to this question the particular statute under which the order has been made must be referred to.

This question will not elicit information relating to compulsory purchase orders made by either the regional water authority or an urban development corporation.

5.9.14.3 In Greater London reference should also be made to enquiry 20 (para 5.9.20, below).

5.9.15   Question 15 (slum clearance)

5.9.15.1
15. (A) Is the property included in a programme of slum clearance which has been submitted or been the subject of a resolution to submit, to the Department of the Environment, or has otherwise been adopted by resolution of the Council?
(B) Except as shown in the Official Certificate of Search, have the Council resolved to define the area in which the property is situated as a General Improvement Area?

5.9.15.2 A local authority may pass a resulution, subject to confirmation by the Secretary of State, to declare part of its area as a slum clearance area. This may only be done where the authority is satisfied that the houses in the area are unfit for human habitation and cause a danger to health and that the most satisfactory way of dealing with the situation is to demolish all the buildings within it. Within such an area the local authority enjoys wide powers of compulsory purchase in respect of which (in general) only limited compensation for the site value will be paid.
5.9.15.3 General improvement areas are those areas defined by the local authority as being areas where living conditions can be improved by improving amenities or dwellings with the assistance of statutory powers. Within such an area special grants may be available to assist with the improvement of property. The local authority also has special powers of compulsory purchase in these areas.

5.9.16   Question 16 (smoke control)

5.9.16.1
16. Except as shown in the Official Certificate of Search, is the property included in an area for which the Council have passed a resolution to make or vary a smoke control order under s 11 of the Clean Air Act 1956?

5.9.16.2 Existing smoke control orders are registered as local land charges and will be revealed in answer to the local land charges search. This question is designed to reveal the existence of proposals for future orders. Where a smoke control order is in force it is an offence to emit smoke from the chimney of any building within the area and the use only of authorised fuels is permitted, eg coke, anthracite.

5.9.16.3 *Property within the City of London*
A special question is added to Con 29D relating to properties within

188

the City of London, the whole of which area is a smokeless zone. The Common Council of the City of London may pass a resolution exempting any specified premises from the effects of the smoke control legislation.

5.9.17   Question 17 (General Rate Act)

5.9.17.1

17. Is a resolution in force bringing into operation Schedule 1 to the General Rate Act 1967, as to rating of unoccupied property? If so, please specify:
   (i) the categories of properties affected;
   (ii) the effective date of the resolution;
   (iii) the proportion of the rate due.

5.9.17.2   As a general principle rates are levied on the occupier of premises so that no rates can be payable in respect of unoccupied premises. However, where a local authority has resolved to bring into force the General Rate Act 1967, Sch 1 within its area, rates become payable on property which has been vacant for a continuous period of three months. The amount of empty rate is in the discretion of the local authority and may vary from the full rate to a small proportion of that rate. The amount may also be different for different categories of property. No rates are payable in respect of property which is vacant by reason of a legal prohibition, eg a closing order, and rates do not become payable on a newly constructed dwelling house until it has been unoccupied for six months.

5.9.17.3   Under the Rating (Exemption of Unoccupied Industrial Hereditaments) Regulations 1984 (SI 1984/231) no rates are payable on unoccupied factories, mills and similar industrial buildings which if previously used were last used for an industrial purpose.

5.9.17.4   Within the City of London powers exist under the City of London Sewers Act 1848, s 177 as amended to levy half rates on empty properties within this area.

5.9.18   Question 18 (registration of title)

5.9.18.1

18. Is the property situated in an area where registration of title under the Land Registration Acts is compulsory on sale? If so, please specify the District Registry and the date of compulsory registration.

5.9.18.2   The information revealed in response to this question may already be known to the prospective purchaser either through the terms of the draft contract or from the result of a public index map search (ch 6). The question does however serve two purposes:
   (a) Where the answer to the question is in the affirmative, and the property is not yet registered, the question serves to remind the

189

purchaser that compulsory registration of title will be required on completion of the sale;

(b) the date of the coming into effect of the compulsory registration order is stated so that the purchaser may check whether land which is currently being offered for sale with an unregistered title should previously have been registered. Within an area where registration of title is compulsory, an application for the registration of the title to the land must be made within two months of the date of a conveyance on sale of the freehold estate, or the grant of a lease for a term of at least 40 years, or within two months of the assignment on sale of a lease having at least 40 years still unexpired. Failure to register in an appropriate case renders the conveyance or transfer of the legal estate in the land void. If it appears to the purchaser that the land ought previously to have been registered he should require the vendor to correct this defect without delay.

5.9.18.3 Within the Greater London Area registration of title is compulsory and question 18 on form Con 29D is differently worded from the question shown above, to take account of this fact. On form Con 29D the question asks the name of the district registry concerned and the date of the compulsory registration order.

5.9.19 Question 19 (London only: outstanding notices)

5.9.19.1

19. Are there any outstanding statutory or informal notices (other than notices shown in the Official Certificate of Search and notices served consequent on an order made or a resolution passed to acquire the property recorded in reply to Enquiries 14 or 20) which have been issued by the Council under the Public Health Acts, Housing Acts, Highways Acts or London Building Acts?

5.9.19.2 This question is similar in nature to question 3 (para 5.9.3, above). The effect of any notice revealed in response to this question should be checked by reference to the statute under which the notice has been issued. It should be noted that notices under the London Building Acts are also liable to be disclosed under this question. The London Building Acts apply within the Inner London boroughs where they have a similar effect to the Building Regulations.

5.9.20 Question 20 (London only: compulsory acquisition)

5.9.20.1

20. Has any order been made (whether or not confirmed by the appropriate Secretary of State) other than an order referred to in Enquiry V(B) in Part II or has any resolution been passed which would involve the acquisition of the property?

5.9.20.2   In addition to question 14 (para 5.9.14, above) this question also seeks to elicit information relating to compulsory purchase orders. Orders made under enquiry V(B) of the Part II enquiries relate to compulsory purchase orders made in respect of listed buildings (para 5.10.5, below).

5.9.21   Question 21 (London only: improvement of roads)

5.9.21.1

21. (A) Have any proposals (other than such as are referred to in Enquiry 2) for the improvement, widening, alteration or construction of a metropolitan road been approved, which, if implemented, would involve the acquisition of the property?

5.9.21.2   In addition to question 2 (para 5.9.2, above) this question deals with proposals for the construction or improvement of metropolitan roads within the Greater London area. Further enquiries relating to any information revealed by this question should be raised with the Greater London Council.

5.10   ANALYSIS OF PART II ENQUIRIES ON FORMS CON 29A AND CON 29D

Note: The wording of all the Part II enquiries is identical on both forms.

5.10.1   Question I (footpaths)

5.10.1.1

1. Has any public path or road used as a public path or byway which abuts on or across the property been shown in a draft, provisional or definitive map or a draft revision or revised map, whichever may be the later, prepared under Part IV of the National Parks and Access to the Countryside Act 1949, Schedule 3 to the Countryside Act 1968 or Part III of the Wildlife and Countryside Act 1981?

5.10.1.2   Under Part IV of the National Parks and Access to the Countryside Act 1949 all county councils and the former county borough councils were required to carry out a survey of footpaths and bridleways in their area. Footpaths confer a right of way on foot only, whilst a bridleway confers a right of way on foot or on horseback. A road used as a public path is a byway open to vehicles. As a result of this survey draft maps showing the routes of all footpaths and bridleways were prepared. Provisional maps were then prepared from the draft maps after objections or representations on the form of the draft map had been considered by the Secretary of State. The definitive map prepared from the modified provisional map is conclusive evidence of the public rights of way over the footpaths and bridleways shown on the map.

This question should be raised in connection with the purchase of rural properties. A note to the printed question draws attention to the fact that the council cannot be deemed to know the boundaries of the property unless a plan of the property is submitted with the search application.

5.10.2 Question II (diversion of roads or footpaths)

5.10.2.1

II. Have the Council approved any proposals for the stopping up or diversion of any of the roads or footpaths referred to in the Description of the Property?

5.10.2.2 Question 2 contained in the Part I enquiries relates only to the construction of or making of improvements to roads and will not give details of proposals to stop up or divert the route of existing roads. The local authority might consider the stopping up or diversion of existing roads, eg to provide safe access to a major new road which is being constructed within the vicinity of the property or as part of a newly created one way system within a town centre. This question could be of relevance to the purchase of any type of property but will probably only be raised in connection with property where it is known that proposals for a major new road or for a one way system are to be implemented.

5.10.3 Question III (advertisement control)

5.10.3.1

III. (A) Are there any entries relating to the Property in the Register kept by the Council pursuant to the Town and Country Planning (Control of Advertisements) Regulations 1969?
(B) Where can that Register be inspected?
(C) Except as shown in the Official Certificate of Search:
  (i) has any notice been given by the Secretary of State or served under Regulation 15 of the Regulations?
  (ii) have the Council resolved to serve a discontinuance notice under Regulation 16?
  (iii) if a discontinuance notice has been served, has it been complied with to the satisfaction of the Council?
  (iv) have the Council resolved to make an order defining the area which includes the property as an area of special control under Regulation 26?

5.10.3.2 A register is maintained by the local authority which contains details of applications for consent to display advertisements. The register is similar to the register of planning applications and details of the entries in the register will be revealed in the same way (para 5.9.11, above). Express permission to display an advertisement is not required where the advertisement falls within the ambit of the Town and

Country Planning (Control of Advertisements) Regulations 1984, reg 14 but the Secretary of State may give notice under reg 15 to the owner of land to withdraw the effect of reg 14 either within a particular area or in any particular case. A notice given under reg 15 is similar in effect to an article 4 direction (para 5.9.8, above). Even where reg 14 applies the local authority may serve a notice under reg 16 requiring the display of an advertisement to cease. Failure to comply with such a notice is an offence. In an area of special control under reg 26 consent to display an advertisement will only be granted in very limited circumstances. This question is mainly of concern to the purchaser of commercial or industrial premises.

The 1969 Regulations referred to in the question have been superseded by the 1984 Regulations referred to above.

5.10.4   Question IV (listed buildings)

5.10.4.1
IV. (A) Have the Council or the Secretary of State granted or refused any listed building consents under s 55 of the Town and Country Planning Act 1971?

(B) Except as shown in the Official Certificate of Search, have the Council resolved to serve a listed building enforcement notice under s 96 of the Town and Country Planning Act 1971?

(C) If a listed building enforcement notice has been served, has it been complied with to the satisfaction of the Council?

5.10.4.2   The result of the local land charges search will reveal whether or not a building is listed as being of special historic or architectural interest and this question deals with the special planning provisions contained in the Town and Country Planning Act 1971 which relate to such buildings. At the time when the form of additional enquiries is submitted to the local authority the result of the local land charges search will not usually be available to the purchaser, and it is suggested, therefore, that consideration should be given to raising this question where the property being purchased is either known to be a listed building or it is thought possible that the property may be listed. It should be borne in mind that some buildings of comparatively recent construction (eg 1930s cinemas) are listed buildings.

5.10.4.3   *Listed building consents*
It is an offence under the Town and Country Planning Act 1971, s 57 to damage a listed building and by s 55 of the Act an offence is committed if without listed building consent a listed building is altered or extended in such a way as to damage its character, or demolished. Listed building consent may be granted by the local planning authority but will obviously be granted (if at all) subject to stringent conditions. Where demolition of a listed building is proposed notice also has to be

given to the Royal Commission on Historical Monuments who must be allowed access to the building prior to its demolition in order to record the building.

5.10.4.4   *Enforcement notices*

Where the provisions restricting alterations and works to listed buildings have not been complied with the local planning authority may serve an enforcement notice under the Town and Country Planning Act 1971, s 96. The Secretary of State also has power to serve an enforcement notice under s 100 of the 1971 Act, but it seems that the service of such a notice may be outside the scope of this question. The enforcement notice will specify certain works which must be executed to restore the building. Failure to comply with such a notice is an offence under s 98 of the 1971 Act. An appeal against an enforcement notice lies to the Secretary of State within the period before the notice takes effect, which must be not less than 28 days after service of the notice.

5.10.5   Question V (repairs notice; compensation where property to be compulsorily acquired)

5.10.5.1

V. (A) To the knowledge of the Council has the service of a repairs notice under s 115 of the Town and Country Planning Act 1971 been authorised?

(B) If the Council have authorised the making of an order for the compulsory acquisition of the property under s 114 of the Town and Country Planning Act 1971, is a 'minimum compensation' provision included, or intended to be included in the order?

5.10.5.2   *Repairs notice*

A repairs notice under the Town and Country Planning Act 1971, s 115 can only be served in relation to a listed building. Where a local authority considers that a listed building is falling into disrepair they may serve notice on the owner requiring specified works to be done to the building within a period of two months. Failure to comply with a repairs notice will enable the local authority to acquire the property compulsorily.

5.10.5.3   *Minimum compensation provisions*

Where a compulsory purchase order has been made in relation to a listed building under the Town and Country Planning Act 1971, s 114 a direction of minimum compensation may be included in the order, which will detrimentally affect the amount of compensation payable when the building is acquired by the local authority. A minimum

compensation direction will only be made where there is evidence that the building has deliberately been allowed to fall into disrepair in order to justify its demolition and the subsequent redevelopment of the site.
5.10.5.4   An applicant should consider raising this question in connection with the proposed purchase of an existing building which is known or thought to be listed as a building of historic or architectural interest and which is currently in a poor state of repair.

5.10.6   Question VI (completion notice)

5.10.6.1
VI. Have the Council resolved to terminate any of the planning permissions in force by means of a completion notice under s 44 of the Town and Country Planning Act 1971?

5.10.6.2   A completion notice may be served by a local planning authority where work commenced under a planning consent which specified a time limit for the commencement of the work has not been completed and the local planning authority envisage that the development will not be completed within a reasonable time. A completion notice will require the completion of the works within a further specified period of not less than 12 months, failing which the planning consent will cease to have effect. An appeal against a completion notice lies to the Secretary of State.

At the time when the form of additional enquiries is submitted to the local authority, the purchaser will probably not have had the opportunity to inspect a copy of any planning permission relating to the property which he is buying. It may therefore be a wise precaution to raise this question in connection with the purchase of any property which is being purchased with the benefit of an existing planning permission.

5.10.7   Question VII (National Parks and Access to Countryside Act)

5.10.7.1
VII. Has any order under s 87 of the National Parks and Access to the Countryside Act 1949, been made relating to an area which includes the property?

5.10.7.2   An order made under the National Parks and Access to the Countryside Act 1949, s 87 designates a particular area as being of outstanding natural beauty. Such an order enables the Countryside Commission to make byelaws for the control of the area, and in particular will require the local authority to consult with the Commission before taking any steps with regard to property within the area. Planning permission for new development or for the alteration of existing buildings within such an area may therefore be difficult to obtain or may be granted subject to stringent conditions.

This question should be considered in relation to the purchase of existing property or land for development within a rural area.

5.10.8 Question VIII (pipe-lines)

5.10.8.1
VIII. Has a map been deposited under s 35 of the Pipe-lines Act 1962, or s 39 of the Gas Act 1972, showing a pipe-line within 100 feet of the property?

5.10.8.2 Any person who wishes to construct a pipe-line which is to extend for ten miles or more in length must obtain an authorisation for the construction from the Secretary of State under the Pipe-Lines Act 1962, s 1. A similar authorisation is required for the diversion of an existing pipe-line. In all cases where an authorisation has been granted a map showing the position of the pipe-line must be deposited with the local authority under the Pipe-lines Act 1962, s 35. Similar provisions contained in the Gas Act 1972, s 39 apply to gas pipe-lines owned by the British Gas Corporation. The deposited maps are available for public inspection free of charge. This question only deals with pipe-lines for which an authorisation has been granted and will not reveal details of other pipe-lines within the vicinity of the property. The purchaser of a property situated in a rural area will be concerned to raise this question because the existence of such a pipe-line or a proposal to construct such a pipe-line may give rise to compulsory purchase powers in favour of the pipe-line owner. It is also necessary to obtain ministerial consent for the construction of a building which will be within ten feet of the surface of the land over the pipe-line. There is no particular significance in the '100 feet' distance mentioned in the question, but the existence of a pipe-line situated at a greater distance than 100 feet would be unlikely to interfere with the amenity value of the property being purchased.

5.10.9 Question IX (houses in multiple occupation)

5.10.9.1
IX. Is the property included in a registration of houses scheme (houses in multiple occupation) under s 22 of the Housing Act, 1961, containing control provisions as authorised by s 64 of the Housing Act 1969?

5.10.9.2 The Housing Act 1961, s 22 enables the local authority to require the registration of houses which are in multiple occupation and to refuse or vary such a registration where either the house is unsuitable for multiple occupation or the person having control of the house is considered unfit to manage the house. As a condition of registration the authority may require specified works to be done to the house. Under the Housing Act 1969, s 64 it is an offence to contravene a registration scheme. This question is clearly only of relevance to houses which are or which are intended to be used for multiple occupation.

5.10.10 Question X (noise abatement)

5.10.10.1
X. (A) Have the Council made, or resolved to make, any noise abatement zone order under s 63 of the Control of Pollution Act 1974 for the area which includes the property?
(B) Is there any entry in relation to the property recorded in the Noise Level Register kept pursuant to s 64 of the Control of Pollution Act 1974?
(C) Where can the Register be inspected?

5.10.10.2 The local authority may make a Noise Abatement Order under the Control of Pollution Act 1974, s 63 which designates the area affected by the order as a noise abatement zone. The order specifies the classes of premises to which it relates. Within such a zone the local authority records the noise levels emanating from premises, which levels must not be exceeded without the consent of the local authority. Section 66 of the Act empowers the local authority to require a reduction in noise levels and under s 67 the local authority may specify an acceptable noise level for a proposed new building. The noise level register is open to public inspection free of charge and copies of the entries may be obtained on payment of a fee.

This question may be relevant where the property to be purchased is either industrial or commercial property where the nature of the business to be undertaken will involve the use of noisy machinery or equipment.

5.10.11 Question XI (urban development areas)

5.10.11.1
XI. If the property is situated in an area designated as an urban development area under Part XVI of the Local Government, Planning and Land Act 1980, please specify the name of the urban development corporation and the address of the principal office.

5.10.11.2 Under the Local Government, Planning and Land Act 1980 the Secretary of State may, if he considers it to be in the national interest, designate an area as an urban development area. An urban development corporation is then set up to secure the regeneration of the area. Where a property is within such an area some planning enquiries should be directed to the urban development corporation whose address will be revealed in response to this question. There is some difficulty for an applicant's solicitor in knowing whether or not a property is situated within such an area and therefore in deciding whether or not this question should be asked. It is suggested that the question may be asked where the property which is being purchased is situated in an area containing older property (eg property built before about 1920) within the urban area of a city or large town.

5.10.12   Question XII (enterprise zones)

5.10.12.1

XII. Is the property situated in an area designated as an enterprise zone under Part XVIII of the Local Government, Planning and Land Act 1980?

5.10.12.2   Under the Local Government, Planning and Land Act 1980 the Secretary of State may designate an area as an enterprise zone. The purpose of declaring an enterprise zone is to encourage the introduction of new industry and commerce into the area and considerable incentives are provided for developers within these areas in the form of freedom from planning control and fiscal advantages, such as exemption from general rates on individual buildings. Some difficulty exists in knowing whether a particular property will lie within such an area. It is suggested that this question should be asked where it is proposed to purchase a vacant site or existing building for development within a run-down area of an inner city or major town.

Although the enterprise zone authority, from whom further information would have to be obtained, may be the local planning authority itself, the name and address of the enterprise zone authority will not be revealed in response to this question and where question XII is asked, it is suggested that a supplementary question requesting the name and address of the enterprise zone authority should also be raised.

5.10.13   Question XIII (improvement areas)

5.10.13.1

XIII. Have the Council resolved to define the area in which the property is situated as an improvement area under s 4 of the Inner Urban Areas Act 1978?

5.10.13.2   Where property is situated in an area which has been defined as an improvement area special grants may be available for the improvement of the property. These grants are usually more generous in financial terms than the standard improvements grants. It is suggested that this question should be raised when the property being purchased is an older property within an inner city area or inner urban area of a large town.

5.10.14 Check list of relevance of Part II enquiries

5.10.14.1 Set out below is a check list of the situations in which the Part II enquiries or some of them should be raised. The check list is provided for guidance and merely indicates situations in which the raising of various Part II enquiries may be considered.

5.10.14.2 Checklist

Type of property	*Consider the questions below*		
Property in rural area	I	VII	VIII
Where proposals for new roads (urban or rural) or for implementation of one way system are known to exist	II		
Commercial and industrial premises	III	X	XII
Old buildings or buildings thought to be listed	IV	V	
Property bought with benefit of existing planning permission	VI		
Houses in multiple occupation or proposed to be used for such purpose	IX		
Property in inner urban areas	XI	XII	XIII

5.11 SUPPLEMENTARY QUESTIONS

5.11.1 Although it is not suggested that questions supplementary to those printed on the standard forms should be raised in every transaction, there will be situations in which it will be relevant to raise such questions and some thought should always be given to the subject of raising supplementary questions before the standard form is submitted to the local authority. The subject matter of the supplementary questions will vary depending on the nature of the transaction being undertaken and the suggestions outlined below do not purport to comprise a comprehensive list to cover all situations. Supplementary questions may be raised in the space provided on the Con 29 form, or may be raised by letter following the receipt of the answers to form Con 29 from the local authority.

5.11.2 Roads

5.11.2.1 *Ownership of roads*

Printed enquiry 1 only refers to roads which are maintainable at the public expense under the Highways Acts. The local authority may, however, be responsible for the maintenance of roads in some other capacity, eg as landowner or housing authority. Where property owned or known to have previously been owned by the local authority is being purchased (eg a council house) it may be advisable to raise a supplementary question asking whether the local authority is responsible for the maintenance of the roads in some capacity other than under the Highways Acts.

5.11.2.2 New roads
Printed question 2 deals with proposals for new roads within a radius of 200 metres from the property. If this radius is considered to be inadequate because, eg disturbance from noise of a new trunk road may penetrate beyond 200 metres, a supplementary enquiry extending the range of question 2 to 400 metres (or further if required) may be considered to be appropriate.

5.11.2.3 New private roads
The answer to printed question 2 will only reveal proposals for new public roads to be constructed within the vicinity of the property and proposals for the construction of new private roads are not covered by the scope of this question. A supplementary question enquiring about proposals for new private roads may therefore be considered.

5.11.3 Footpaths
Question 1 in Part II of the printed form relates only to designated footpaths in rural areas. A supplementary question asking whether the council is aware of the route of or any disputes concerning a non-designated footpath which abuts on or crosses the property may be considered desirable.

5.11.4 Planning
5.11.4.1 *Permitted use*
No question on the current forms Con 29A or D asks for information relating to the permitted use of the property under the Town and Country Planning (Use Classes) Order 1972. If such information is required it will be necessary to raise a specific supplementary question.

5.11.4.2 Copies of planning applications and consents
The planning enquiries on the printed form will give details of planning applications relating to the property. It is often necessary to obtain copies of these applications or consents and it may save time if a supplementary question is added to the printed form asking the local authority to supply copies of such documents when returning the answers to the search. It will be necessary to include in the question an undertaking to pay the local authority's reasonable charges for the supply of the copy documents. In cases where it is anticipated that there may be a large number of planning applications registered, it

may be wise to restrict the undertaking to an upper financial limit, or to limit the request to specified types of planning applications.

5.11.5 Subsidence
A supplementary question enquiring whether the local authority is aware of any current or potential cause of subsidence, land erosion or similar problems affecting the property may yield information which will indicate that further searches and enquiries, eg mining searches, may be necessary.

5.11.6 Enterprise zones
Where enquiry XII is to be raised a supplementary question requesting the name and address of the enterprise zone authority should be raised since this information is not revealed by the printed enquiry.

5.11.7 Development in the vicinity of the property
A question asking whether the local authority is aware of any proposals for future development within the vicinity of the property will yield useful information from some local authorities. Others will decline to answer the question on the basis that it is too wide to be capable of specific answer.

5.11.8 Urban development corporations
Urban development corporations enjoy special powers of compulsory purchase the exercise of which will not be revealed in response to printed enquiries 14 or XI. Where it is thought that the property may be situated within an urban development area a supplementary question seeking confirmation that the Urban Development Corporation have no proposals for the compulsory acquisition of the property may be considered. If this question is raised on form Con 29 it will only produce a response where the local authority is also the urban development corporation. Where some other authority acts as the urban development corporation the enquiry should be raised separately with them.

5.11.9 Pipe-lines
Printed enquiry VIII will only reveal information relating to pipe-lines in respect of which an authorisation has been granted. If information about all pipe-lines within 100 feet of the property is required the scope of question VIII will have to be extended by raising an appropriate supplementary question.

5.12 CHECKLIST OF STANDARD ANSWERS TO PART I ENQUIRIES ON FORMS CON 29A OR CON 29D
5.12.1 Set out below is a checklist of the standard answers which an

applicant's solicitor might expect to receive in response to a search made in respect of an established residential property in a suburban area. The check list is provided as a guideline only and is not intended to be a substitute for a thorough check of the search answers. It should also be stressed that the table set out below has been compiled on the basis of a search made against established residential property in a suburban area and the answers to the search must be expected to differ for other types of property.

The answers to Part II enquiries will vary depending on the circumstances and no check list is provided in respect of these.

5.12.2   Check list of standard answers

Topic	Question number	Expected answer	Comment
Roads	1 A	Yes	A negative answer indicates the road is not maintainable at public expense; and if the answer to 1B and 1C are also negative road charges will probably be payable
	1 B	N/A	
	1 C	N/A	
Proposals for new roads	2 A(1)	NO	An affirmative answer to any part of question 2 indicates a proposal for a new road or the improvement of an existing road within 200 metres of the property. Either proposal will probably have a detrimental effect on the value of the property
	2 B(i)	NO	
	2 B(ii)	NO	
	2 C	NO	
	2 D	NO	
Outstanding notices	3	NO	An affirmative answer should be carefully investigated to ascertain the liability involved
Breach of Building Regulations	4	NO	If affirmative, vendor should be asked to remedy breach

Topic	Question number	Expected answer	Comment
Drains and sewers	5 A(i)(a)	YES	If property does not drain into public sewer, property owner could be responsible for cost of upkeep of sewer
	5 A(i)(b)	Drain & private sewer/drain alone	Either answer is acceptable
	5 A(ii)(a)	YES	If negative answer, owner of property may be liable for maintenance
	5(a)(ii)(b)	YES	As above
	5(a)(ii)(c)	Drain & private sewer/drain alone	Either answer is acceptable
	5(a)(iii)	NO	An affirmative answer may indicate a liability for maintenance of the drain or sewer
	5 B(i)	NO	An affirmative answer
	5 B(ii)	N/A	should only appear in relation to a property under construction or a very recently built property
	5 C	YES	If negative answer to C and
	5 D	N/A	affirmative to D the land owner may be required to pay the cost of connection of the property to a public sewer
	5 E(i)	NO	An affirmative answer to any part of 5 E will involve a payment by the landowner towards the expenses of construction of sewers
Enforcement of planning control	6 A	NO	If the answer is in the affirmative the vendor should be required to remedy the breach
	6 B	NO	
	6 C	Offices of local authority	

5.12.2 *Additional enquiries of the local authority*

Topic	Question number	Expected answer	Comment
	6 D	N/A	If answer is 'NO', vendor must be required to remedy the breach
Planning policy	7 A-D	Answers will vary from authority to authority	Ensure that answers to 7 B(iii)(b), 7 C(ii)(b), 7 D(ii)(b) are all negative
	7 E	NO	An affirmative answer may indicate a future compulsory acquisition of the land
Article 4 direction	8	NO	If affirmative, check the contents of the direction
Notices under Town and Country Planning Act 1971	9	NO	S 45—resolution to modify or revoke planning permission. If affirmative answer, check carefully S 51—discontinuance of use and alteration or removal of buildings. If affirmative check carefully S 60—tree preservation orders. If affirmative check which trees are affected
Compensation for refusal of grant of planning permission	10	NO	Dwelling houses are excluded from the provisions of s 169
Planning applications	11 A	Only as revealed by official search	Planning consents granted in relation to the property will be revealed in response to the LLC1 search. If answer to this question is affirmative, details of the entries (which will be applications for or refusals of planning permission) should be obtained
	11 B	At offices of local authority	
Conservation areas	12	NO	If affirmative answer, planning permission to develop the property may be difficult to obtain or may be granted subject to various conditions

Topic	Question number	Expected answer	Comment
Building preservation notice	13	NO	An affirmative answer indicates that the building will probably become a listed building in the near future
Compulsory purchase	14	NO	If answer is affirmative, it is unlikely that the proposed purchase will be able to proceed. A full investigation of the answer, and the client's instructions are needed
Slum clearance	15 A	NO	An affirmative answer may lead to compulsory acquisition of the property
	15 B	NO	Property which is situated in an improvement area is eligible for special grants towards the improvement of the property *but* under Housing Act 1969 the local authority also have special compulsory purchase powers within an improvement area
Smoke control	16	YES/NO	In urban and suburban areas the answer to this question is more likely to be in the affirmative, in which case the client must be told of the restrictions on burning certain fuels within a smoke control area
General Rate Act	17	YES/NO	If the answer is in the affirmative a proportion of rates will become payable on the property if it is left vacant for a continuous period of three months. The amount of the empty rate will be specified in the answer

Topic	Question number	Expected answer	Comment
Registration of title	18	YES/NO	Answer will depend on whether a compulsory registration order is in force. If answer is affirmative and property is presently unregistered check that no disposition for value has been made since the date of the order
	CON 29D only		(*London*)
Outstanding notices	19	NO	This question is similar to question 3 (above)
Compulsory acquisition	20	NO	An affirmative answer will probably prevent the transaction from proceeding further.
Improvement of roads	21	NO	This question is similar to question 2 (above)

5.13 THE RESULT OF THE SEARCH

5.13.1 The form of the answers

Local authorities do not follow a standard practice in supplying the results to the form of additional enquiries. Some local authorities write or type the answers on the printed form of enquiry itself; others supply a printed sheet which repeats the questions and sets out the answers alongside the respective questions. Either of these practices is convenient for the applicant's solicitor who may quite easily check off the answers against the relevant questions. It is, however, fairly common for a local authority to supply the answers to additional enquiries by sending to the applicant a printed sheet which bears only the question numbers and the relevant answers to those questions. In such a case the applicant's solicitor must cross refer the question sheet to the printed enquiry form in order to check the answers. This approach is inconvenient for the applicant's solicitor, particularly where the search was made on the short form of enquiries which does not contain the wording of the questions. Whichever method has been employed by the local authority in supplying the answers, the applicant's solicitor must thoroughly check the answers supplied against the questions asked. Further enquiries may need to be made either of the local authority or of the vendor if an answer to a particular question is unsatisfactory. It should also be borne in mind that the answers to some of the questions on the additional enquiry form may indicate that further searches and enquiries of other bodies should be undertaken, eg where it is revealed that a property lies within a mineral consultation area consideration may be given to undertaking some 'form of mining search (see for example chs 28–32).

5.13.2 Protection afforded by the search

The local authority is under no statutory obligation to reply to the form of additional enquiries, although by convention it will do so. No statutory form of protection or compensation exists for a purchaser who suffers loss as the result of having relied on a search result which turns out to be inaccurate; but the local authority would be liable in negligence for an inaccurate search result provided that negligence, in the tortious sense of the word, could be established. (See headnote (3) to form Con 29A and headnote (2) to form Con 29D, paras 5.4 and 5.6, above.) A discussion of liability on searches is contained in ch 2, above.

5.14 UPDATING THE SEARCH

5.14.1 Although some of the information revealed in answer to these enquiries will alter over a period of time, most of the information given will not change during the normal interval which occurs between the receipt of the result of the search and completion. This search need not therefore be repeated prior to completion unless a long delay occurs between the receipt of the result of the search and completion. If a second search is made it must be submitted to the local authority in sufficient time to ensure that the result of the search is received before completion.

5.14.2 Relying on a search made by a third party

Where a prospective purchaser's solicitor has obtained the answers to an official search and his client subsequently withdraws from the transaction, the purchaser's solicitor may offer the answers to his search to the vendor's solicitor for use by another prospective purchaser. Where the second purchaser wishes to effect an exchange of contracts fairly quickly he may choose to rely on the result of search obtained by the earlier purchaser. Since the information revealed by the search is unlikely to change over a short period of time, there is little danger to the second purchaser in relying on the earlier search provided the second purchaser's solicitor is satisfied that the earlier search was properly made and that not too long an interval has elapsed since the issue of the result of the search. If a period exceeding three months has elapsed since issue of the search certificate, the second purchaser should be advised to make a fresh search. Although it may in the circumstances outlined above be possible to rely on the result of an additional enquiries search made by a third party, the result of a previous local land charges search made by a third party should not be relied on and a fresh local land charges search should always be made.

In a few cases where the purchaser's mortgagee is separately represented in the transaction, the solicitor for the mortgagee may insist on a separate local land charges search and form of additional enquiries being made on the mortgagee's behalf. A second purchaser, sub-purchaser or mortgagee who acquired his interest in reliance on a search made by another person would have the same right to sue the council in negligence for loss caused by an erroneous search result as if he had requisitioned the search himself.

5.14.3 Notification of change of ownership
As a matter of courtesy, and for rating purposes, the local authority should be informed of the change of ownership of the property after completion. The vendor may choose to notify the local authority himself as a precaution against future assessment for rates or other charges on the property, but more commonly the notification is effected by the purchaser. Many local authorities include with the replies to the local search and additional enquiries a standard form for notification of the change of ownership which they ask the purchaser to complete and send to them after completion.

5.15 SEARCH SUMMARY

Application	Form Con 29A (outside London) Form Con 29D (Greater London) *or* Form Con 29AX (short form, outside London) Form Con 29DX (short form, Greater London)
Plan	Only required if property cannot clearly be identified by postal address
Fee	Part I enquiries (one parcel only) £9.65 Each additional parcel of land £2.40 Part II printed enquiries £0.75 per question Supplementary questions £1.80 each question
Address	Appropriate district council or London borough council
Special points	
Area affected	All transactions to acquire an interest for value in land except perhaps the grant of a short lease where no premium is payable.

Part III

Other common searches

Chapter 6

Public index map search

6.1 The public index map search is one of the few searches which may be made at HM Land Registry without the authority of the registered proprietor of the land.[1]

6.2 WHEN TO MAKE THE SEARCH

6.2.1 Unregistered land
This search should always be made at an early stage in an unregistered transaction, its purpose being to ensure that no part of the land has already become registered, and that no priority notice or caution against first registration exists which might inhibit a registration of the title. The search will also reveal whether or not a compulsory registration order has been made affecting the area. If required the search may be repeated close to completion of the transaction to confirm that no priority notice or caution has been lodged since the date of the earlier search certificate.

6.2.2 Registered land
It is generally thought that there is no particular merit in making this search in connection with a registered estate since most of the information revealed by the search certificate will already be known to the purchaser. It is possible however that the search could reveal some irregularity in the title (eg a discrepancy in the physical area of land registered or in the title number) of which the purchaser would otherwise be unaware and thus the search should not be considered to be totally irrelevant when dealing with registered land.

6.3 HOW TO MAKE THE SEARCH
Form 96 should be completed and forwarded to the appropriate district land registry.[2] Where the property lies within a compulsory registration area and can be clearly identified by reference to its postal address a plan may be dispensed with. In all other cases two copies of a plan which is of sufficient scale to clearly show the property and its surrounding area and outlining the property in a colour should accompany the search application. The current fee for the search is £2.

6.4 *Public index map search*

6.4 FORM 96

Form 96
HM Land Registry

Land Registry Acts 1925 to 1971

**APPLICATION FOR AN OFFICIAL
SEARCH OF THE INDEX MAP**

Numbers in brackets relate to notes overleaf.

The box below must be completed using BLOCK
LETTERS and inserting the name, **full address and
postal code** to which the official certificate of result
search is to be sent.

FOR OFFICIAL USE ONLY	Land Registry fee stamps to be affixed here.

Key number

Applicants ref.[1]

Telephone no.

Administrative county

I/We hereby apply under rule 286 of the Land
Registration Rules 1925, for an official search of the
Index Map and Parcels Index, including the list of
pending applications for first registration, in respect of
the land referred to and shown

District or London borough

Property description

edged/coloured ....on
the attached plan[2].

Payment of fees[3]

Please put an X in the appropriate box

☐ I am/We are authorised credit account holder(s) and request that the appropriate fee be debited to my/our account.

☐ A cheque/postal order is enclosed or Land Registry adhesive fee stamp(s) are affixed in the space above.

Signed..Date...

This application should be sent to the appropriate district land registry[4].

**OFFICIAL CERTIFICATE
OF RESULT OF SEARCH**

To be completed by HM Land Registry

*N.B. Please enclose this result of search and any plan annexed
thereto with any correspondence or application for first
registration relating to the above property.*

It is hereby certified that the official search applied for above has been made with the following result.
ONLY the statements in the boxes marked X apply.

☐ The land is not registered and is not affected by any caution against first registration or any priority notice.

☐ The land is registered freehold under Title no. ....

☐ The land is registered leasehold under Title no. .... held under a lease dated ....

and made between ....

....

Term.........................years..............................[less..................................days] from ....

☐ A rentcharge is registered under Title no. ....created by a deed dated ....

and made between ....

.... Amount payable £...........................

☐ The land is affected by a *caution against first registration/priority
notice* registered under Title No. ....

OFFICIAL STAMP

☐ The land is in a compulsory area.

☐ The land is in a non-compulsory area[5].

In accordance with your above request the fee of £ .... has been debited to your account.

212

NOTES

1. Any reference should be limited to ten digits (including oblique strokes and punctuation).

2. The plan accompanying this application must contain sufficient details of the surrounding roads and other features to enable the land to be identified satisfactorily on the Ordnance Map. However, a plan can normally be dispensed with if the land is situated in an area where registration of title is compulsory on sale and the property can be identified by postal description. Nevertheless, the Chief Land Registrar reserves the right to require a plan to be supplied where he deems it necessary.

3. The fee must be paid in accordance with the current Land Registration Fee Order. An applicant who has been granted credit account facilities may request that the fee be debited to his account provided his key number is entered overleaf. A cheque or postal order should be made payable to "HM Land Registry". Land Registry fee stamps can be purchased at any main Post Office, (postage stamps are not acceptable).

4. The application should be forwarded to the appropriate district land registry shown below.

5. All purchases of public sector housing made under the right to buy provisions of the Housing Act 1980 are compulsorily registrable.

District Land Registry	Areas served on 1 April 1981*
The Birkenhead District Land Registry 76 Hamilton Street, BIRKENHEAD, Merseyside L41 5JW (Telephone No. 051 647-5661)	Counties of Cheshire and Merseyside.
The Croydon District Land Registry Sunley House, Bedford Park, CROYDON, CR9 3LE (Telephone No. 01-686 8833)	Greater London south of the River Thames (including the London Borough of Richmond upon Thames.)
The Durham District Land Registry Southfield House, Southfield Way, DURHAM, DH1 5TR (Telephone No. Durham (0385) 66151)	Counties of Cleveland, Cumbria, Durham, Humberside, Northumberland, North Yorkshire, and Tyne and Wear.
The Gloucester District Land Registry Twyver House, Bruton Way, GLOUCESTER, GL1 1DQ (Telephone No. Gloucester (0452) 28666)	Counties of Berkshire, Gloucestershire, Oxfordshire, Warwickshire and West Midlands.
The Harrow District Land Registry Lyon House, Lyon Road, HARROW, Middlesex HA1 2EU (Telephone No. 01-427 8811)	Greater London north of the River Thames, but excluding the London Boroughs of Barking and Dagenham, Havering, Newham, Redbridge, Richmond upon Thames and Waltham Forest.
The Lytham District Land Registry Birkenhead House, LYTHAM ST ANNE'S, Lancs. FY8 5AB (Telephone No. Lytham (0253) 736999)	Counties of Greater Manchester and Lancashire.
The Nottingham District Land Registry Government Buildings, Chalfont Drive, NOTTINGHAM, (Telephone No. Nottingham (0602) 291111) NG8 3RN	Counties of Derbyshire, Nottinghamshire, South Yorkshire, Staffordshire and West Yorkshire.
The Peterborough District Land Registry Aragon Court, Northminster Road, PETERBOROUGH, (Telephone No. Peterborough (0733) 46048) PE1 1XN	Counties of Cambridgeshire, Leicestershire, Lincolnshire, Norfolk, Northamptonshire and Suffolk.
The Plymouth District Land Registry Plumer House, Tailyour Road, Crownhill, PLYMOUTH, (Telephone No. Plymouth (0752) 701234) PL6 5HY	Counties of Avon, Cornwall, Devon, Dorset, Somerset and Wiltshire.
The Stevenage District Land Registry Brickdale House, Danestrete, STEVENAGE, Herts. (Telephone No. Stevenage (0438) 314488) SG1 1XG	London Boroughs of Barking and Dagenham, Havering, Newham, Redbridge and Waltham Forest. Counties of Bedfordshire, Buckinghamshire, Essex and Hertfordshire.
The Swansea District Land Registry 37 The Kingsway, SWANSEA, SA1 5LF (Telephone No. Swansea (0792) 476677)	Counties of Hereford, Worcester and Shropshire. All the counties in Wales.
The Tunbridge Wells District Land Registry Curtis House, TUNBRIDGE WELLS, Kent TN2 5AQ (Telephone No. Tunbridge Wells (0892) 26141)	Counties of East Sussex, Kent and Surrey.
The Weymouth District Land Registry 1 Cumberland Drive, WEYMOUTH, Dorset DT4 9TT (Telephone No. Weymouth (03057) 76161)	Counties of Hampshire, Isle of Wight and West Sussex.

* Changes occurring after this date will be the subject of a statutory instrument. Explanatory leaflet No. 9 is obtainable free of charge from any district land registry; it contains a complete list of all areas of local government in England and Wales and indicates the district land registry currently serving each. The dates on which compulsory registration was introduced to each area are also shown.

213

6.5 WHAT THE SEARCH WILL REVEAL
  (a) Whether or not the land lies within a compulsory registration area;
  (b) whether the freehold is registered and if so under which title number;
  (c) whether a leasehold interest is registered and if so the title number and brief details of the lease;
  (d) whether the land is affected by a rent charge;
  (e) whether the land is affected by a caution against first registration or a priority notice.

6.6 Where the transaction in respect of which the search was made leads to first registration after completion, the index map search and plan should be enclosed with the application for first registration. All purchases of public sector housing made under the right to buy provisions of the Housing Act 1980 are subject to compulsory registration.

6.7 PAYMENT OF FEES ON LAND REGISTRY SEARCHES
Fees may generally be paid by any of the following methods:
  (a) by monthly credit account ('key number' must be inserted on application form);
  (b) by cheque or postal order;
  (c) by Land Registry stamps obtained from main post offices and affixed to the search application form.

NB The same methods of payment are applicable to fees payable to HM Land Charges Registry.

6.8 SEARCH SUMMARY

Application	Form 96
Plan	Plan in duplicate
Fee	£2
Address	Appropriate district land registry
Special points	
Area affected	Any unregistered land

---

1 Land Registration Rules 1925, r 286.
2 See Appendix I, below for addresses.

Chapter 7
Pre-contract Central Land Charges search

7.1 This search is normally made prior to the completion of a transaction involving unregistered land but may in certain circumstances be considered desirable as a precautionary step prior to exchange of contracts. By the Law of Property Act 1969, s 24 a purchaser is not deemed to have knowledge of an incumbrance which is registered at HM Central Land Charges Registry merely by virtue of the existence of the registration. At the pre-contract stage in the transaction s 24 of the 1969 Act displaces the general 'registration is notice' rule imposed by the Law of Property Act 1925, s 198, and places the onus of disclosing such registered charges on the vendor, thus in general relieving the purchaser of his obligation to make this search prior to exchange of contracts.

As this search is made against the names of the estate owners of the land, which will often not be known to the purchaser until he receives the abstract of title after exchange of contracts, it is often impracticable for the purchaser to make a full search at this stage in the transaction.

7.2 WHEN TO MAKE THE SEARCH

The principal occasion when it will be necessary to make the search prior to contract is when the legal estate is held in the name of a single estate owner and it is known or suspected that the property is occupied by the estate owner and his spouse. A non-owning spouse may have rights of occupation under the Matrimonial Homes Act 1983 which may have been registered as a class F land charge and a search against the present estate owner will reveal such registration. If such a registration is revealed by a search made at this stage the purchaser will be able to negotiate for the removal of the registration, or if this seems not to be possible, to withdraw from the transaction without having the complication in many cases of already being committed to a binding contract to sell his own house. If the class F land charge was not discovered until the pre-completion search was made, there would be little time in which to negotiate for the removal of the charge and a delayed completion would usually be inevitable even if the registration was ultimately removed.

The Matrimonial Homes Act 1983, s 4 provides that where a class F registration exists and the vendor contracts to give vacant possession it is a term of the contract that the vendor will procure the cancellation of the charge before completion and that failure to do so entitles the purchaser to withdraw from the contract, but this provision is of little practical consolation to a purchaser who despite being able to retire from his purchase contract finds that he is irrevocably committed to a contract to sell his own house.

A clear land charges search obtained prior to contract does not guarantee that the property is totally free from third-party rights of occupation. A class F charge could be registered by a non-owning spouse at any time up to completion and thus for absolute certainty the search should be repeated at a later stage in the transaction.

Equitable beneficial interests in the property, as distinct from rights of occupation, will not be revealed by this search and separate enquiry (usually by way of preliminary enquiry, see ch 3, above) should be made in relation to these.

Where the draft contract reveals the existence of restrictive covenants which will either be onerous or which will impede the purchaser's proposed user of the property, it may be prudent to make a Central Land Charges search against the covenantor to check whether or not the covenants have been registered as D(ii) land charges. It is unlikely in most circumstances to find that the covenants have not been registered, but the lack of registration would invalidate their enforceability and would thus influence the purchaser in deciding how to deal with the covenants.

Where a Central Land Charges search is being undertaken prior to contract it would seem sensible to make the search against all estate owners currently known to the purchaser (the names of some of the previous estate owners may be revealed to the purchaser in the draft contract) and of course it is increasingly common for an abstract of title to be delivered to the purchaser before exchange of contracts.

If entries are revealed by a search made at this time, there will be enough time in which to consider and deal with the matters revealed by the search. In the case of previous estate owners a further pre-completion search against the same names will be unnecessary.

7.3 CHAIN TRANSACTIONS

In any situation where the purchaser knows that he is involved in a chain of transactions a pre-contract Central Land Charges search may be undertaken as a precautionary step to ensure that no bankruptcy proceedings have been registered against the vendor. The existence of such proceedings discovered after contract will not usually allow the purchaser to withdraw from the contract, but the inevitable delay to the transaction while awaiting the appointment of a trustee in bankruptcy will cause severe disruption to the synchronisation of the chain.

This early warning of the pending bankruptcy, obtained by making a Central Land Charges search will give the purchaser time to decide whether or not to proceed with the proposed purchase.

7.4 HOW TO MAKE THE SEARCH
7.4.1 Form K15 listing the names of the estate owners together with their periods of ownership should be submitted to the Central Land Charges Department. A fee of 50p per name is charged.
7.4.2 This search may also be made by telex or telephone (see ch 34, below for further details of this search).

7.4.3 Payment of fees
See para 6.7, above.

7.5 SEARCH SUMMARY

Application	K15
Plan	No
Fee	50p per name
Address	Central Land Charges Department Burrington Way Plymouth
Special points	
Area affected	Unregistered land only

Chapter 8

Company search

8.1 It is recommended that a company search be undertaken when buying land or taking a lease from a company registered under the Companies Act 1948. Frequently this search is made at the pre-completion stage of the transaction, but it is probably more sensible to make the search prior to contract in order that any problems revealed by the search may be resolved in good time before completion. A search made prior to contract may be updated or repeated just before completion.

8.2   REASONS FOR SEARCH

8.2.1   To discover registered charges

The Companies Act 1948, s 95, requires a company to register a fixed or floating charge created over its assets within 21 days of the creation of the charge. Failure to register renders the charge void against a creditor or the liquidator of the company. The requirement to register under s 95 applies irrespective of whether the charge is also registrable at HM Land Registry, or HM Land Charges Registry or is supported (in unregistered land) by a deposit of title deeds. Although floating charges are capable of registration at HM Land Registry or HM Land Charges Registry this is not generally done and evidence of their existence can usually only be obtained by making a company search. The existence of a floating charge will not prevent the company from selling the assets over which the charge has been taken until crystallisation of the charge occurs. Crystallisation will take place when a receiver is appointed, when a winding up commences, when the company ceases to carry on business or on the happening of any other specific event named in the deed creating the charge. On discovery of a floating charge a purchaser should require the vendor to produce on completion evidence of non-crystallisation of the charge in the form of a certificate from the company or the mortgagee. To be conclusive the certificate should be given by the mortgagee although in practice a certificate given by the company seems to be commonly accepted.

The terms of the floating charge may contain restrictions on the company's power to create further fixed or floating charges. Such a restriction should be checked by an intending mortgagee.

8.2.2 To check the company's proper name, address and power to convey or borrow

A company must use its proper name as shown on its certificate of incorporation. A company's proper address is its registered office, details of which are filed on the register at Companies House.

The company's power to buy, sell or hold land or to borrow money on the security of land is contained in its memorandum of association, a copy of which is filed at Companies House. A transaction which is outside the scope of the powers given in the memorandum is ultra vires and void. The European Communities Act 1972, s 9 allows a person who deals in good faith with the company to enforce an otherwise ultra vires contract against the company provided the contract was one which the directors of the company had decided it was in the best interests of the company to make. The precise extent of the protection accorded by this section is unclear and in order to avoid doubt and subsequent litigation it is prudent to check the company's ability to convey or borrow by means of a company search.

The memorandum or articles of the company may limit the company's borrowing powers either by imposing an upper financial limit on the amount of money borrowed or by restricting the purposes for which a loan may be obtained. Both of these matters should be checked by an intending mortgagee.

In the course of making a company search the articles of the company should be checked to verify the directors' authority to conduct the transaction and the requirements of the articles relating to the sealing of documents by the company.

8.2.3 Insolvency

A resolution to wind up the company voluntarily must be filed at Companies Registry under the Companies Act 1948, s 143. Where a company is being wound up compulsorily no record of this will appear on the company's file until the winding up order has been made and if doubt exists a search should be made for the presentation of a petition at either the Company's Court or in the *London Gazette* (see paras 8.7 and 8.8, below).

The appointment of a receiver or liquidator should be revealed by a company search. Where a receiver has been appointed or a voluntary liquidation is in progress a purchase transaction may normally proceed subject to delay while the documentation is amended to include the receiver or liquidator as a party to the contract or conveyance.

In the case of a compulsory liquidation the Companies Act 1948, s 227 provides that any disposition of a company's property made after the commencement of a winding-up is void unless the court otherwise orders.

8.3 REGISTERED LAND

The effect of the Land Registration Act 1925, s 60 is that a purchaser is not bound by a charge created by a company over a registered estate unless that charge is registered at HM Land Registry, and regardless of whether the charge is otherwise registered under the Companies Act 1948, s 95. The Chief Land Registrar will also have ascertained prior to registering the company as proprietor of the land that the company has power contained in its memorandum to buy, sell or hold land. It may therefore be argued that insofar as a purchaser is dealing with registered land he may rely on the Land Registration Act 1925, s 60 and may dispense with a company search. It has however already been noted (para 8.2.1, above) that the existence of floating charges will not normally be registered at the Land Registry neither will a Land Registry search reveal an impending liquidation. It is therefore suggested that a company search should still be made when dealing with registered land.

8.4 HOW TO MAKE THE SEARCH

8.4.1 Personal search

A personal search may be made by attending at the public search rooms of the Companies Registration Office in Cardiff between the hours of 9.30 am and 4 pm or at Companies House in London between 9.45 am and 4 pm (addresses in para 8.11, below). The first requirement for a personal search is to obtain the company's correct name and number from the public index. A search application form (fee £1) may then be purchased from the control counter (Cardiff) or index room (London) which when completed is exchanged for a tab allocating a seat number in the reading room at which the company record will be delivered within a short time of presenting the search application. The company record on microfilm contains the entire contents of each live company's file except for annual returns and accounts which were more than three years old at the time of initial filming and changes in directors and secretaries which were more than seven years old at the time of initial filming.

A warning fiche is inserted in a company's file to advise of newly filed documents relating to mortgages, liquidation or the appointment of a receiver where those documents have not yet reached the fiche record. Newly filed documents can be inspected at the control counter (Cardiff) or the general counter (London).

Full size copies of any page from the microfilm record may be obtained by filling in an application form obtained in the reading room (fee £0.10 per page). Certified copies of filed documents are available at a cost of £0.40 per page.

Full details of the personal search service are contained in a leaflet entitled *A Guide to Public Search* published by the Companies Registration Office.

8.4.2 Agency services
Most solicitors practising outside London or Cardiff will not be able to use the personal search facilities outlined above. In these cases a company agent or local firm of solicitors may be employed to carry out the search on the solicitor's behalf. The names of agencies willing to carry out such searches may be obtained from advertisements appearing in the *Law Society's Gazette* and other legal publications. Many company search agencies carry out a 24-hour search service and may be instructed by letter, telephone or telex.

Clear and comprehensive instructions must be given to the agent making the search, including

(a) the full name of the company to be searched;

(b) details of the information required, eg whether full company search required or only details of charges or registered office;

(c) copies of any documents required.

The agents fee, in addition to the £1 search fee will vary depending on the type of search undertaken.

8.4.3 *Updating the search*
Where a company search was made prior to contract it would be wise to update the search just before completion to check that no further documents have been filed which will affect the transaction being undertaken. Many company search agencies offer an updating service which will be less expensive than repeating the whole search.

8.4.4 Although company files are open to public inspection it should be noted that there is no 'official search' procedure and no priority period is conferred by a company search. It should also be noted that the company records kept at the Companies Registry tend not to be totally up to date (particularly with regard to filed accounts) and that the records kept at the London Office are 24 hours behind those kept at Cardiff.

8.5 SCOTTISH COMPANIES
The records for companies registered in Scotland are kept at Companies Registration Office, 102 George Street, Edinburgh, EH2 3DJ (031 2255 774) where the microfilm files may be inspected. The files for Scottish companies may be ordered for inspection in London or Cardiff but there will inevitably be a delay and it is usually easier to instruct Scottish agents to conduct the search.

8.6 OVERSEAS COMPANIES
A company incorporated outside England and Wales but having a

place of business within Great Britain is required to be registered in the Register of Overseas Companies maintained by the Companies Registry under the Companies Act 1948, Part X, although this requirement is sometimes not complied with. Where an overseas company is not registered under Part X of the 1948 Act but nevertheless does have an established place of business within Great Britain, a charge created by that company must be delivered for registration to the Companies Registry in order for the charge to be enforceable under English law.[1] Such a charge cannot actually be *registered* (because the company itself is not registered) but is entered by the Registry on a non-statutory register (called 'the Slavenburg Register') which may be inspected free of charge.

8.7 SEARCH AT COMPANIES COURT
It would be wise to make a search at Companies Court if there is any suspicion that the company may be in financial difficulty.

A compulsory winding-up commences when a petition is presented against the company, and the Companies Act 1948, s 227 provides that any disposition of a company's property made after the commencement of winding-up is void unless the court otherwise orders.

The records of all winding-up petitions, whether presented to the High Court or a county court, are now kept at Companies Court in London. The search may only be made by telephone (01 430 0630). No fee is charged and there is no provision for an official certificate of search and no priority period is given.

8.8 LONDON GAZETTE
All winding-up petitions are required to be advertised in the *London Gazette* which may be inspected for details of such petitions. This search may be made instead of searching at Companies Court, but it is suggested that since there is some danger of overlooking entries in the *London Gazette* a Companies Court search is preferable.
8.8.1 *London Gazette*
  Room 403
  HMSO Publications Centre
  51 Nine Elms Lane
  London SW8 5DR
  (01 211 6314)

8.9 DISQUALIFIED DIRECTORS
A register of company directors who have been disqualified from so acting under the Insolvency Act 1976 is maintained at the Companies Registry. The register is open to inspection on payment of a search fee (£0.05).

8.10 ACTING FOR A LANDLORD

A landlord intending to grant a lease to a company or to grant licence
to assign in favour of a company assignee should carry out a company
search as outlined in paras. 8.2 and 8.4, above. In addition to the
information contained in para 8.2, above it may in these circumstances
be prudent also to inspect the filed accounts of the company.

8.10.1 See also Infolink (para 26.8.4, below).

8.11 SEARCH SUMMARY

Application	Form supplied by Companies Registry
Plan	
Fee	£1
	(plus agent's fee if agent used)
Address	Companies Registration Office
	Crown Way
	Maindy
	Cardiff
	(0222 388588) *or*
	London Search Room
	Companies House
	65–71 City Road
	London EC1
	(01 253 9393)
Special points	–
Area affected	–

1   *NV Slavenburg's Bank v Intercontinental Natural Resources Ltd* [1980] 1 All ER 955,
[1980] 1 WLR 1076.

Chapter 9

Commons registration search

9.1 Following recommendations in the report of the Royal Commission on Common Land 1955–58[1] the Commons Registration Act 1965 was enacted in order to preserve common land for public access and enjoyment and to enable schemes for management and improvement of common land to be implemented. At the time of the Royal Commission's report it was thought that approximately one-and-a-half million acres of land in England and Wales could be classified as common land but the precise extent of ownership and the nature of the common rights affecting such land were largely unknown. Thus the Commons Registration Act 1965 required all common land, together with details of its ownership and rights enjoyed over the land to be registered within a period of three years following the commencement of the Act. The period for registration expired on 2 January 1970 since when no further registrations have been possible.

9.2 COMMON LAND

Common land is privately owned land (although the name of the owner may be unknown) which is subject to rights of common, whether these rights are exercisable at all times or only during limited periods. The definition, contained in the Commons Registration Act 1965, s 22 also includes the waste land of a manor whether or not that land is subject to rights of common. Town and village greens do not fall within the definition of 'common land' but are registrable under s 3 of the Act in a separate register maintained by the registering authority (county council or Greater London Council).

9.2.1 Rights of common

The definition of rights of common under the 1965 Act extends beyond the common law definition of such rights. At common law a right of common is a right which one or more persons may have to take or use in common with the owner some portion of that which another man's soil naturally produces.[2] One essential feature of a right of common is that it is exercised jointly with the owner of the land. In contrast to this a sole right is a right which is exclusive to the owner of the right and is exercised to the exclusion of the owner of the land. The definition of rights of common under the Act includes some rights which at common law would be classified as sole rights.

9.2.2 Examples of rights of common included in the Act

(a) Common of pasture	
(b) Common of piscary	(the right to fish)
(c) Common of turbary	(the right to dig turves or peat)
(d) Common of estovers	(the right to take wood)
(e) Other rights in the soil	eg the extraction of gravel or stone
(f) Cattlegates or beastgates	(a sole right occurring mainly in the North of England entitling the owner of the right to pasture for a limited number of animals)
(g) Sole rights of vesture or herbage	(the right to take corn, grass, underwood, sweepage and the like from land to the exclusion of the owner of the land. (Sweepage means all that can be swept up with a scythe))
(h) Sole rights of pasture	(Similar to (g) but confined to what can be taken by the mouths of animals)

9.3 WHEN TO MAKE THE SEARCH

A search should be made prior to contract whenever land is being bought which either is or is adjacent to

(a) land which has never been built on;

(b) land which at one time may have belonged to the lord of the manor;

(c) a town or village green.

9.3.1 The search is not confined only to rural areas since many small vacant pieces of urban land are subject to registered common rights. The search may, however, be dispensed with where the property being purchased is in a fully developed urban area.

9.3.2 Many registrations affect only very small areas of land, eg the grass verge between the garden of a house and the publicly maintained highway. It is particularly important to search even over these small areas, since if rights were registered over eg a grass verge it would not be possible to obtain planning permission to alter the access way to the property.

9.3.3 Common rights are overriding interests in registered land under the Land Registration Act 1925, s 70(1)(a). Therefore the search is of equal application to both registered and unregistered land.

9.4 HOW TO MAKE THE SEARCH
Form CR21 should be completed in duplicate and sent with two copies of a plan of the land to be searched and the fee of £3.00 to the appropriate county council or for land in London, to the Greater London Council.

The scale of the plan used should be of sufficient size for the council to be able to identify clearly the land being searched. A large scale plan (eg 6 inches to mile) is desirable where a narrow strip of land such as a grass verge is the subject of the search.

9.4.1 For information on obtaining large scale plans see para 11.7, below.

9.5 FORM CR 21
This form is reproduced on pp 227–228, below.

9.6 COMMENT ON FORM CR 21
9.6.1 The form is supplied in duplicate and both copies must be completed together with two plans of the land.
9.6.2 Registering authorities are required to keep two separate registers, the register of common land, and the register of town or village greens. Form CR 21 makes application for a search in both registers.
9.6.3 Initial registration under the Act was provisional only. After the period allowed for registration had elapsed a further period was allowed for objections to the registration to be lodged. If no objections to the registration had been lodged by the closing date the registration became final. Although the period for lodging objections has now expired some registrations are still listed as provisional because the objections to the registration have not yet been resolved by the Commons Commissioners.
9.6.4 Section 13 of the Act relates to registrations which have been made pursuant to an amendment of the register under that section.
9.6.5 Section 4 of the Act precludes the registration of ownership of land (inter alia) where it is already registered under Land Registration Acts 1925–71 or where the application to register was made after 2 January 1970.

9.7 WHAT THE SEARCH REVEALS
9.7.1 The result of the search will reveal whether the land or any part of it is subject to a provisional or final registration under the Act.
9.7.2 Details of the rights so registered are not revealed by the search and must be obtained by requesting a copy of the registration from the council. A further fee is payable for a copy of the entry.
9.7.3 The existence of rights of common will mean that third parties

COMMONS REGISTRATION ACT 1965
REGISTERS OF COMMON LAND AND TOWN OR VILLAGE GREENS

CR Form 21

(For the use of the registration authority)
Official Number

REQUISITION FOR AN OFFICIAL SEARCH
(For completion by or on behalf of applicant. Please read notes overleaf)

Name and address in BLOCK
LETTERS to which the certificate
is to be sent.

The   County Council/Greater London Council is required to make a search in its Registers of Common Land and Town or Village Greens in respect of land at   shown edged/coloured   on the enclosed plan and duplicate plan. The fee of £   is enclosed.

Signature of applicant (or agent)   Reference

Date   Telephone Number

CERTIFICATE OF OFFICIAL SEARCH

(For the use of the registration authority. (If (a) is deleted, complete (b) to (f) deleting the words in brackets as appropriate. If (a) is not deleted, delete (b) to (f)).

A search has been made in the registers with respect to the land shown on the plan enclosed with the requisition. The result, up to and including the date of this certificate, is as follows:

REGISTER OF COMMON LAND

(a) There are no entries.
(b) (None of the land) (The land) (The part edged/coloured   on the plan herewith) is (provisionally/finally registered) (registered under section 13 of the 1965 Act) (under Unit No(s)   )
(c) (None of the land) (The land) (The part edged/coloured   on the plan herewith) is (provisionally/finally registered) (registered under section 13 of the 1965 Act) as subject to rights of common.
(d) (None of the land) (The land) (The part edged/coloured   on the plan herewith) is the subject of (provisional/final ownership registration) (ownership registration under section 13 of 1965 Act).
(e) (None of the land) (The land) (The part edged/coloured   on the plan herewith) is stated to be registered under the Land Registration Acts 1925 to 1971.
(f) (None of the land) (The land) (The part edged/coloured   on the plan herewith) is exempt from registration under section 4 of the 1965 Act.

REGISTER OF TOWN OR VILLAGE GREENS

(a) There are no entries.
(b) (None of the land) (The land) (The part edged/coloured   on the plan herewith) is (provisionally/finally registered) (registered under section 13 of the 1965 Act) (under Unit No(s)   )
(c) (None of the land) (The land) (The part edged/coloured   on the plan herewith) is (provisionally/finally registered) (registered under section 13 of the 1965 Act) as subject to rights of common.
(d) (None of the land) (The land) (The part edged/coloured   on the plan herewith) is the subject of (provisional/final ownership registration) (ownership registration under section 13 of 1965 Act).
(e) (None of the land) (The land) (The part edged/coloured   on the plan herewith) is stated to be registered under the Land Registration Acts 1925 to 1971.
(f) (None of the land) (The land) (The part edged/coloured   on the plan herewith) is exempt from registration under section 4 of the 1965 Act.

Signed on behalf of the registration authority
Official stamp of the registration authority
giving date of issue of certificate

227

NOTES

1.   A requisition for an official search may be made only on the form overleaf. The form should be completed, together with its duplicate (which may be completed as a carbon copy), and sent by post or delivered personally to the registration authority for the area in which the land is situated. In the absence of special local arrangements the registration authority for land in Greater London is the Greater London Council, and, for land elsewhere, is the council of the county in which the land is situated.

2.   A separate requisition must be made in respect of each parcel of land in relation to which a search is requested except where for the purposes of a single registration or a single transaction a certificate is required in respect of two or more parcels of land which have a common boundary or are separated only by a road, railway, river, stream or canal. By "parcel of land" is meant a piece of land which is or is deemed to be in separate occupation or separately related at the time of the requisition. Unoccupied land is to be deemed to be occupied by the person who receives the rackrent, whether on his own account or as agent or trustee for any other person, or by the person who would receive the rackrent if the land were let at a rackrent.

3.   A requisition must be accompanied by a PLAN, IN DUPLICATE, and by sufficient particulars of the situation of the land to enable the registration authority to identify it.

4.   A certificate of official search includes registrations made up to and including the date of issue, but takes no account of pending applications and confers no protection on a purchaser or intending purchaser.

5.   A certified copy of any entry in a register maintained under the Act may be obtained on payment of the fee.

6.   Certain areas (referred to in section 11 of the Commons Registration Act 1965) were exempt from registration under section 4 of the Act. Parts of such area may however be registered subsequently under section 13 of the Act (which provides for the registration of new common land and town or village greens).

FEES

(All fees must be prepaid)

Official search and certificate

£3.00

Further charge in respect of each additional parcel of land included in the requisition

25p (subject to a maximum additional fee of £5)

Certified copy of an entry in a register, or a certified copy of or extract from any register map

Such reasonable fee as the registration authority may fix according to the time and labour involved.

may be able to exercise certain rights over the land, and that planning permission for the development of the land will not be forthcoming.

9.7.4 An official certificate of search is supplied by the council but the certificate confers no protection on the purchaser.

9.7.5 Since no new registrations can now take place a search made before exchange of contracts need not be repeated prior to completion.

9.8 Where land is registered with a final registration under the Act, that registration is conclusive[3] and despite the provisions of ss 13 and 14 of the Act (allowing for amendment and rectification of the register) no proper machinery exists for challenging a registration. The lack of a machinery for challenging or cancelling an incorrect registration can cause severe inconvenience to a land owner who finds that his land has been wrongly registered under the Act, and because of s 10 he is unable to obtain planning permission to develop the land. It is suggested that it may be possible to challenge an incorrect registration under RSC Ord 53, but this is by no means a guaranteed remedy.

9.9 AREAS EXEMPTED FROM REGISTRATION UNDER THE ACT

9.9.1 Areas exempted by regulation

(If buying land within one of these areas an enquiry about rights of common should be made both of the vendor and of the local area office of the Forestry Commission.)

1 The Links Common, Whitley Bay, Northumberland.

2 The Stray, Harrogate, Yorkshire.

3 Part of West End Road, Recreation Ground, Southampton.

4 Cippenham Village Green Common, Slough, Buckinghamshire.

5 Ten pieces of land known collectively as the 'Coventry Commons,' City of Coventry, Warwickshire.

6 Otterbourne Hill Common, Otterbourne, Hampshire.

7 Victoria Gardens, Portland, Dorset.

8 Cassiobridge Common, Watford, Hertfordshire.

9 Shenfield Common, Brentwood, Essex.

10 Thorpe Green, Egham, Surrey.

11 Ley Hill Common, Coleshill Common, Austenwood Common, Gold Hill Common, Hyde Heath Common, all in Amersham Rural District, Buckinghamshire.

12 Upper Tilt, Lower Tilt, Brook Hill and Leigh Hill Commons, Little Heath Common, Old Common, Downside Common, all in Esher Urban District, Surrey.

13 West Wickham Common (London Borough of Bromley).

14 Kenley Common, partly in the London Borough of Croydon and partly in the Caterham and Warlingham Urban District, Surrey.

15 Coulsdon Common (London Borough of Croydon).

16 Spring Park, West Wickham (London Borough of Bromley).

17 Oxshott Heath, Esher, Surrey.
18 Micklegate Stray, Yorkshire.
19 Farthingdown Common, Coulsdon (London Borough of Croydon).
20 Riddlesdown Common, Purley (London Borough of Croydon).
21 Mitcham Common (London Borough of Merton).

9.9.2 The Forest of Dean

It is thought that the extensive rights to graze sheep in this forest exist by sufferance of the Crown and not as rights of common, hence the exemption of this area from the Act under s 11.

Enquiries relating to land in the Forest of Dean can be made to the Deputy Gaveller, Forestry Commission, Crown Offices, Coleford, Glos (0594 33057).

9.9.3 Epping Forest

Section 11 of the Act excluded Epping Forest from the provisions of the Act because a register of commoners was already in existence under the Epping Forest Act 1878, Sch 4.

Enquiries relating to land in this area should be made by letter to The Superintendent of Epping Forest, The Warren, Loughton, Essex (01 508 2266). A plan showing the extent of the land to be searched is helpful but not essential. No fee is charged for this service.

9.9.4 The New Forest

This area is also exempted by s 11 because the New Forest Atlas kept under the New Forest Act 1949, s 4 contains a register of forest rights relating to this area. There is no register of rights of common relating to land within the New Forest. A search for forest rights may be made in person at the offices of The Clerk to the Verderers, The School House, Emery Down, SO4 7DY (042 128 2052). The offices are open in the mornings only and a fee of £0.05 is charged for a personal search. A postal search may be made by sending a letter to the above address. The fee for a postal search is £10 and a 1:2500 ordnance survey plan showing the extent of the property should be enclosed with the search request.

9.10 SEARCH SUMMARY

Application	CR21
Plan	Duplicate plan (Scale of plan should be large as possible)
Fee	£3
Address	Appropriate county council or Greater London Council

Special points	
Area affected	Land which has never been built on
	Land at one time owned by the lord of the manor
	Town and village greens

1 Cmnd 462.
2 5 *Halsbury's Laws* (3rd edn) 298.
3 Commons Registration Act 1965, s 10.

Chapter 10

Office copy entries

10.1 An application for office copy entries is not strictly a 'conveyancing search' since it is a procedure more usually undertaken by the vendor than the purchaser; there are, however, occasions when a purchaser or his mortgagee may feel that it is necessary to obtain his own set of office copy entries or a copy of a particular document filed at the Land Registry.

10.2 A vendor selling land which has a registered title will normally be required to deduce title to his land under the Land Registration Act 1925, s 110. This section entitles the purchaser to

(a) copies of the subsisting entries in the register;

(b) an authority to inspect the register;

(c) a copy of the filed plan;

(d) copies or abstracts of any documents noted on the register so far as they affect the land being sold.

Section 110 simply requires 'copies' of the documents noted above to be supplied to the purchaser, and where the land or charge certificate is in the vendor's possession, a photocopy of these documents would suffice to comply with the section. Where the land or charge certificate is in the possession of the vendor's mortgagees it will, however, usually be necessary for the vendor to make application for office copies in order both to draft the contract for sale and to supply to the purchaser evidence of his title. It is suggested that a vendor should always apply for office copies since these will be more up to date than the land or charge certificate in his possession and may reveal entries, eg a caution which are not shown on the vendor's certificate. Further, it is a requirement of the Law Society's Conditions of Sale (Condition 12(1)(b)(i)) that office copies be supplied when using this form of contract. Law Society Council Direction (Opinion of the Council of the Law Society 316(1)) also recommends that office copies should be supplied to a purchaser. Office copies (as opposed to photocopies) bear a Land Registry watermark which is visible when the pages are held up to the light.

10.3 A vendor in deducing title to a purchaser will normally supply office copies of the register entries. If he does not do so (and is not obliged by the contract so to do, eg under the National Conditions) the purchaser may consider making application himself in order to check the current state of the register. Any person other than the registered proprietor or his solicitor needs to obtain the written authority of the registered proprietor prior to applying for copies since the register itself is not open to public inspection.

A mortgagee whose mortgage is not concurrent with the owner's purchase of the land will similarly wish to obtain office copies of the entries before completing the loan.

10.4 Title to registered land is normally deduced prior to exchange of contracts, thus the vendor should make his application for copies immediately on receiving instructions to sell the land so that the copies may be supplied to the purchaser with the draft contract.

Where a purchaser needs to make application for copies this again should be done at an early stage in the transaction so that any problems may be resolved before a binding contract is entered into but, as noted above, the purchaser will have to secure the vendor's authority to make this search before sending his application to the Land Registry. The vendor's written authority to search must *accompany* the search application.

10.5 HOW TO MAKE THE SEARCH

Form A44 should be completed and sent to the appropriate district land registry together with the requisite fee.

10.5.1 Usually a complete set of entries with title plan is required for which the current fee is £3. A form 102 certificate may be issued in place of the filed plan where the filed plan is large and complicated. This procedure is used mainly in connection with the sale of plots on building estates (fee £3).

It is possible to obtain copies of part only of the register for which the current fees are as follows:

Register entries only	£1
Title plan only	£1
Form 102 only	£1
Other filed documents	£2 per document

Mortgages and leases are not normally filed on the register and thus are not supplied as part of a 'complete set' of office copy entries. Even where such documents are filed they are not ordinarily supplied as either part of a complete set or as 'other filed documents' unless a special request is made by letter showing why a copy of the document cannot be obtained from the person who holds the original.

10.5.2 Payment of fees
See para 6.7, above.

10.5.3 Addresses of district land registries
See Appendix 1, below.

10.6 *Office copy entries*

10.6 FORM A44

Form A44 HM Land Registry

Application for Office Copies [1]
Numbers in brackets relate to notes overleaf

(Use BLOCK LETTERS)

I/We ....
Name of applicant or solicitor

hereby apply to

.... District Land Registry,[2]

for the office copies specified below and I/We declare that

(Please enter ☐   I am/We are the registered proprietor(s)

X in the ☐   I/We act as solicitor(s) for the registered proprietor(s)

appropriate

box) ☐   the written authority of the registered proprietor(s) (or his solicitors) to inspect the register is enclosed.

FOR OFFICIAL USE ONLY

PARTICULARS OF ACCOUNT HOLDER[3]	
Key Number	Reference

Title number [4]	
County and district (or London borough)	
Short description of property	
Full name(s) of registered proprietor(s)	

Please state in the appropriate box(es) the NUMBER of copies required

A	Complete set[5] with Title plan	C	Register entries	E	Form 102[6]
B	Complete set with form 102	D	Title plan	F	Document(s) referred to on the register as filed[7] Specify here or state "all"

a) Where you have requested a form 102 certificate and an estate plan has been approved enter the plot number(s) in the space opposite.

b) Where no estate plan has been approved a plan MUST be lodged in duplicate[8]

(a) Plot number(s) ....

(b) The certificate is to be issued in respect of the land shown .... on the attached plan

OFFICIAL USE FEE DEBITED

£   p

If you are aware that an application is in the course of registration in respect of the above title and you require office copies back-dated to the day prior to the receipt of that application, enter YES in the box opposite[9]

☐

Signed .... Telephone No. .... Date ....

Reference

Please enter above using BLOCK LETTERS the name, address and reference to whom the office copies are to be sent.

FOR OFFICIAL USE ONLY			
ITEM	NUMBER	FEE DEBITED	
		£	P
Complete set			
Register Entries			
Title Plan			
Form 102 certificate			
Document(s)			
TOTAL FEE DEBITED			

Form A44 **10.6**

FOR OFFICIAL USE ONLY			Dated	No. of copies
Prepare office copies of:				
Register				
Filed plan/GM Negative Positive Tinted				

Deed dated	Marked with title	No. of pages	No. of plans	Tinted	Untinted	No. of copies

Drafted by .... Despatched by...

Date.. Date...

NOTES FOR GUIDANCE OF APPLICANTS

1 Full information on all aspects of applications for office copies is set out in Practice Leaflet No. 13 which is obtainable without charge from any district land registry.

2 The application should be sent to the district land registry serving the area in which the land is situated. A list of addresses of the district land registries is set out below.

3 The fees payable are set out in the current Land Registration Fee Order and also in Practice Leaflet No. 13. In special cases, an enquiry by telephone can be made of any district land registry. Cheques or postal orders should be made payable to "HM Land Registry". Where an applicant, who has been granted credit facilities, wishes to pay by monthly credit account he must also complete the "Particulars of Account Holder" panel. Any reference should be limited to ten digits (including oblique strokes and punctuation). Failure either to supply the credit account details or to send the prescribed fee with this application will usually mean its return to the applicant.

4 A separate application form must be used for each title number in respect of which copies are required.

5 A "complete set" of office copies comprises copies of (a) the entries in the register (b) the title plan (or a certificate in form 102) and (c) any document referred to on the register as being filed in the Land Registry.

6 This is a simpler and quicker alternative to obtaining an office copy of a large title plan for the purpose of a sale or other transaction affecting only a part of the land in the registered title.

7 Mortgages and leases. Original mortgages and leases are not filed in the Land Registry. Where copies are filed, office copies of the filed copies will not be issue save in response to a special request by letter showing why a copy cannot be obtained from the person who holds the original.

8 Any plan accompanying this application must be drawn to a suitable scale (generally not less than 1/2500) and supplied in duplicate. The plan must show by suitable marking the extent of the land affected and, where necessary, figured measurements should be entered on the plan to fix the position of the land by tying it to existing physical features depicted by firm black lines on the plan of the registered title.

9 If there is a pending application and you are applying for an office copy in connection with a further transaction it is possible for negotiations to proceed on the strength of a back-dated office copy of the register which can be brought up-to-date in effect by making a non-priority official search in form 94C in which the date of that office copy is entered as the date of the commencement of the search; a fee under the current Land Registration Fee Order is payable for an official search of this type. The certificate of result of search will reveal details of the pending application for registration and will state officially (if such be the case) that it is in order but has not yet been completed by entry on the register. If negotiations proceed on this basis, and assuming that your prospective transactions is a transfer, lease or charge, the normal search in form 94A or 94B can be made as usual immediately before the completion of the transaction. **If a back-dated office copy is not required, your application for office copies will be held until the completion of the pending application for registration.**

ADDRESSES OF DISTRICT LAND REGISTRIES

District Land Registry	Address	Telephone No.	Telex Call No.
Birkenhead	76 Hamilton Street, Birkenhead, Merseyside L41 5JW	051-647 5661	628475
Croydon	Sunley House, Bedford Park, Croydon CR9 3LE	01-686 8833	917288
Durham	Southfield House, Southfield Way, Durham DH1 5TR	0385 66151	53684
Gloucester	Bruton Way, Gloucester GL1 1DQ	0452 28666	43119
Harrow	Lyon House, Lyon Road, Harrow, Middx. HA1 2EU	01-427 8811	262476
Lytham	Lytham St Annes, Lancs. FY8 5AB	0253 736999	67649
Nottingham	Chalfont Drive, Nottingham NG8 3RN	0602 291111	37167
Peterborough	Aragon Court, Northminster Road, Peterborough PE1 1XN	0733 46048	32786
Plymouth	Plumer House, Tailyour Road, Crownhill, Plymouth PL6 5HY	0752 701234	45265
Stevenage	Brickdale House, Danestrete, Stevenage, Herts. SG1 1XG	0438 314488	82377
Swansea	37 The Kingsway, Swansea SA1 5LF	0792 476677	48220
Tunbridge Wells	Tunbridge Wells, Kent TN2 5AQ	0892 26141	95286
Weymouth	1 Cumberland Drive, Weymouth, Dorset DT4 9TT	03057 76161	418231

oyez The Solicitors' Law Stationery Society plc, Oyez House, 237 Long Lane, London SE1 4PU   F3662 1-84
* * * *

235

10.7 COMMENT ON FORM A44

The title number of the land must be supplied when applying for office copies. If this is not known and the requirement for the copies is urgent it is possible to submit an index map search (see ch 6, above) and form A44 simultaneously, requesting the Land Registry to issue office copies immediately on the result of the index map search. This procedure may be necessary where the charge certificate is in the possession of the vendor's mortgagee who is slow to release the title number.

Where an application for registration of the land is pending, a subsequent application for office copies will be postponed until the pending application for registration is completed, causing undue delay in the issue of the office copies. This delay can be avoided if the purchaser completes the box on the form requesting that the office copies are back dated to the day prior to the date of receipt of the pending application. Office copies issued under this procedure can then be updated by using the non-priority search form 94C (fee £2).

10.8 SEARCH SUMMARY

Application	A44
Plan	
Fee	£3 for complete set
	Fees for other items vary
Address	Appropriate district land registry
Special points	
Area affected	Registered land only

Part IV

Less common searches of general application

Chapter 11

Introduction to less common searches

11.1 Since the decision in *G & K Ladenbau (UK) Ltd v Crawley & De Reya*[1] it seems probable that a purchaser's solicitor would be liable in negligence if he failed to make any of the less usual searches in circumstances where such search or searches would have been appropriate and the client suffered loss as a result of this omission.

11.2 The solicitor's main difficulty if he is not personally familiar with the area in which the property is situated, is in knowing which of the less common searches would be appropriate to the circumstances of the transaction with which he is presently dealing.

11.3 When taking instructions as much information as possible should be obtained from the client about the locality of the property, eg whether the boundary of the property backs on to a railway or river or adjoins common land.

The estate agent's particulars of the property may also yield useful information relating to the locality of the property. Additionally information relating to the locality may be requested from the vendor by means of a preliminary enquiry and the vendor may be asked to supply a plan of the property showing details of the surrounding neighbourhood.

11.4 INSPECTION OF THE PROPERTY

Frequently the relevance of a particular search will only be revealed by an inspection of the property. Where it is not possible for the solicitor to make such inspection, the client's surveyor, or failing that the client himself should be asked to inspect the property. When an inspection is carried out the following matters should so far as possible be checked:

(a) rights of non-owning occupiers;
(b) rights of way and other easements;
(c) building extensions to the property (because of planning and building regulation consents);
(d) fixtures and fittings;
(e) boundaries;
(f) routes of services.

11.4.1 Leasehold property

On buying a leasehold property the state and condition of the property should be noted: It is usual on the sale of a leasehold property to modify the covenants for title implied by the Law of Property Act 1925, s 76.[2] The effect of this modification is that the purchaser will take over any outstanding liability for breach of repairing covenant and will not be able to claim indemnity from the vendor in respect of such breach.

Where a newly-built or converted property is being sold on the grant of a lease the vendor's solicitor should inspect the property prior to drafting the lease in order to check rights of way and easements.

11.5 SURVEYS

The vendor's duty of disclosure does not extend to physical aspects of the property in respect of which the caveat emptor rule applies. The majority of purchasers do not commission an independent survey of the property preferring instead to rely on the building society's valuation, which most building societies will now allow the purchaser to see. It is argued that the purchaser's and the mortgagee's respective interests in the property are very similar, in that if there were anything radically wrong with the property it would not be a wise investment for the purchaser nor a safe security for the mortgagee. The mortgagee's primary concern is to ensure that the property is worth the amount which is being lent on mortgage; thus where a high proportion of the purchase price is being borrowed it is probably true to say that the purchaser and his mortgagee's interests do largely coincide. This will not, however, be true where only a small percentage of the purchase price is being loaned and in these circumstances an independent survey is highly desirable. A survey is also to be highly recommended in relation to an older property regardless of the amount being taken on mortgage. Most building societies and banks are now participating in the House Buyer's Valuation and Survey Scheme initiated by the Royal Institute of Chartered Surveyors which enables a combined survey on behalf of both mortgagee and purchaser to be carried out. The cost of this scheme is greater than a building society valuation but less than a full structural survey. The House Buyer's Valuation and Survey does not comprise a full structural survey of the property but it probably provides an adequate safeguard for a client buying ordinary residential property.

In the case of *Yianni v Edwin Evans & Sons*[3] the purchaser brought a successful action in negligence directly against the surveyor who conducted the survey on behalf of the mortgagee. There is also a possibility that the purchaser might be able to sue his own solicitor in negligence if the solicitor failed to advise the client about the importance of having an independent survey done. Despite the fact that there is no decided case law on the solicitor's duty in relation to surveys, the possibility of liability in this area cannot be entirely discounted.

11.6 Searches in Part IV of this book

Part IV contains a number of less usual searches which although not applicable to every transaction could be encountered in any area throughout England and Wales. The tables in Appendices 2 and 3, below give a general guideline as to when the various searches in Part IV may be appropriate.

11.7 PLANS

Many of the less usual searches require a plan of the property to be submitted with the application and in some cases a large scale plan is needed.

Large scale plans can be obtained from the British Library, The Map Library, Great Russell Street, London, WC1, (01 636 1544) who operate a postal service. The charge is between £2.50–£9.70 depending on the size and quality of the plan. No money should be enclosed with the request for the plan, an invoice will be sent with the plan.

The general licence to reproduce ordnance survey maps which solicitors can hold does not cover the royalty on copies made by the museum and generally copyright permission from Copyright Branch, Ordnance Survey, Romsey Road, Maybush, Southampton SO9 4DH (0703 775555) must be obtained (fee £2–£4) prior to submitting the request for copies to the British Library. (Alternatively large scale maps are obtainable through branches of HM Stationery Office.)

---

1   [1978] 1 All ER 682, [1978] 1 WLR 266.
2   See Law Society Condition 8(5) National Condition 11(7).
3   [1982] QB 438, [1978] 3 All ER 592.

Chapter 12

Railways

12.1 OVERGROUND RAILWAYS

Where land is bordered by an existing or disused railway, or railway lines cross through the land being purchased, an enquiry by letter should be made of the area surveyor at the appropriate regional office of British Railways Property Board to ascertain the liability to maintain the boundaries which abut on to the railway. It is common to find that British Rail have undertaken responsibility for the maintenance of the boundaries and they may also have reserved rights to enter the property in order to carry out their maintenance obligations.

12.1.1 This enquiry should be made before exchange of contracts but need not be repeated prior to completion since the information revealed is unlikely to alter in the intervening period.

12.1.2 A plan of sufficient scale to show clearly the land involved should accompany the search request. The Board should also be asked to state whether or not the railway lines in question belong to them, and if not to whom they do belong; whether or not the Board is responsible for the maintenance of the boundaries; and whether or not the Board has reserved any rights of entry over the land now being purchased. A fee assessed in accordance with the amount of time taken by the Board to investigate the query is charged for the supply of this information.

12.1.3 British Rail Regional Offices

Southern	Denison House
	296/298 Vauxhall Bridge Road
	London
	SW1V 1AG
South Western	Temple Gate House
	Temple Gate
	Bristol
	BS1 6PX
Midland	Stanier House
	10 Holliday Street
	Birmingham
	BT1 1TG

Eastern	King's House
	236/240 Pentonville Road
	London
	N1 9JZ
North Eastern	Headquarters Offices
	York
	YO1 1HP
North Western	34 High Street
	Manchester
	M4 QB
Scottish	Buchanan House
	58 Port Dundas Road
	Glasgow
	G4 0HG

12.1.4 Some overland railways are owned by the local passenger transport executive in which case an enquiry by letter enclosing a plan of the land should be sent to the civil engineering department of the Passenger Transport Executive. The request for information is the same as that outlined in para 12.1.2, above and a fee is charged on a time spent basis.

12.1.5 Addresses of passenger transport executives

London (Regional Transport) Transport Executive	55 Broadway
	Westminster
	London
	SW1H 0BD
	(01 222 5600)
Manchester, Greater	PO Box 429
	County Hall
	Piccadilly Gdns
	Manchester
	M6O 1HX
	(061 273 3322)
Merseyside	24 Hatton Garden
	Liverpool
	L3 2AN
	(051 227 5181)
Midlands, West	16 Summer Lane
	Birmingham
	B19 3SD
	(021 622 5151)
Tyne and Wear	Cuthbert House
	All Saints
	Newcastle upon Tyne
	NE1 2DA
	(0632 610431)

12.1.5 *Railways*

Yorkshire, South	Exchange St
	Sheffield
	S2 5SZ
	(0742 78688)
Yorkshire, West	Metro House, West Parade,
	Wakefield
	Yorks
	WF1 1NS
	(0924 378234)

12.1.6 A few railways are now owned and maintained by private railway companies. In these cases enquiries similar to those outlined above should be directed to the particular company which owns the railway.

12.2 UNDERGROUND RAILWAYS

Where it is known or suspected that an underground railway or tunnel passes underneath or close to the land being purchased a search may be necessary to enquire about the existence of such a tunnel, its ownership, the depth of the tunnel from the surface, and whether the owners of the tunnel claim any rights over the property being purchased in relation to the maintenance of the tunnel.

12.2.1 The existence of an underground railway may give rise to subsidence or structural problems in relation to an existing or proposed building. Specific advice from a surveyor or structural engineer may be necessary in such cases.

12.2.2 The search should be made before exchange of contracts by letter enclosing a plan of the property. A fee will be charged on a time spent basis.

12.2.3 Where to make the search

Underground tunnels of overground railways	British Rail (see para 12.1.3, above)
London Underground	London Regional Transport (see para 12.1.5, above)
Newcastle Metro	Tyne and Wear Passenger Transport Executive (see para 12.1.5, above)

12.3 SEARCH SUMMARY

Application	By letter
Plan	Yes
Fee	Assessed on time spent basis

Address	Generally to Area Surveyor British Railway Property Board (see paras 12.1.3 and 12.1.5, above)
Special points	
Area affected	Land bordering railway or where railway crosses through or under land

Chapter 13

Sites of Special Scientific Interest (SSSIs)

13.1 DEFINITION

A Site of Special Scientific Interest (SSSI) is an area of land or water which has been designated by the National Conservancy Council (NCC) as being of outstanding value for its wildlife or geology.

Once an area has been so designated the owners or occupiers of the land are notified of the exact location and features of the site. Any specific operations on that land which might damage the site are also listed and notified to the owners or occupiers. A criminal offence is committed if a listed operation is undertaken or permitted to be undertaken on the site without the consent of the NCC. Although operations on the land which would require planning consent are not contained in the list of specific operations notified to the owner or occupier, the local planning authority on receipt of a planning application which concerns a SSSI is bound to consult with and to take the advice of the NCC in determining that planning application. It is therefore unlikely in most cases that a planning application which involved the destruction of the site would succeed.

13.2 The first indication that an area of land is designated as a SSSI will normally come to light through the answer to question 7(e) on the standard form of additional enquiries of the local authority (see ch 5, above). A further enquiry should then be raised with the local authority by letter to obtain precise details of the listing. SSSIs are also registrable as local land charges in Part 4 of the Register (para 4.9.7.1, above).

13.2.1 An approach should be made to the vendor to obtain the list of operations which have been prohibited and to enquire whether consent to any of the listed operations has been given by the NCC either in writing or under the terms of a management agreement. Management agreements are registrable as local land charges under Part 4 of the Register.

13.2.2 Where an intending purchaser proposes to obtain planning permission for land which includes the SSSI an approach should be made to the NCC to discuss the planning proposals with them. Consultations with the NCC before a formal planning application is submitted to a local authority will usually save both time and expense in the subsequent planning application.

13.2.3 The further enquiries of the vendor, the local authority and
the NCC should be made prior to exchange of contracts so that any
problems encountered may be resolved before a binding contract is
entered into. In view of the difficulties which are likely to be encountered in obtaining planning permission over land affected by a SSSI a
client who intends to develop the land may consider that a conditional
contract may be appropriate in these circumstances.

13.3 Once an area has been listed as a SSSI the listing is final and
not subject to appeal. Certain grants and tax exemptions may be
applicable to such land.

13.3.1 Further reading: *Code of Guidance for sites of Special Scientific
Interest* (HMSO).

13.3.2 Areas of archaeological interest are subject to similar provisions
to those contained in this chapter.

13.4 SEARCH SUMMARY

Application	By letter
Plan	No – provided land is identified
Fee	–
Address	Nature Conservancy Council 19/20 Belgrave Square London SW1X 8PY (01 235 3241) *or* Regional officer – address in local telephone book
Special points	Advice service only
Area affected	Areas listed as SSSIs

Chapter 14

Agricultural credits search

14.1 A fixed or floating charge made by a farmer in favour of a bank over agricultural stock or assets is void against anyone other than the farmer himself unless the charge is registered within seven days of its execution (Agricultural Credits Act 1928, s 9).

14.2 A purchaser engaged in buying farming stock or assets or a mortgagee lending money on the security of such items should make an agricultural credits search at an early stage in the transaction in order to check the existence and validity of subsisting charges.

14.3 HOW TO MAKE THE SEARCH
Form AC6 should be completed in duplicate and submitted to The Superintendent, Agricultural Credits Department, Burrington Way, Plymouth.

The search is made against the farmer's full name and no description of the property or plan is required.

14.3.1 Fees
£0.50 per name searched. Fees must be prepaid. An additional fee of £0.80 is payable if the result of the search is to be sent by telephone.
14.3.2 No personal or telephone search facilities exist.

14.4 FORM AC6
This form is reproduced on pp 249–252, below.

14.5 WHAT THE SEARCH REVEALS
An official certificate of search, which is conclusive, is normally issued on the day of the receipt of the application and will reveal registrations made up to and including the date of the search. The certificate will reveal the date of the charge, whether the charge is fixed or floating, the sum secured by the charge and the name and address of the bank in whose favour the charge is registered.
14.5.1 Copies of any entries on the register may be obtained by applying to the Agricultural Credits Department on form AC5 (fee £0.50 per entry).
14.6 The search should be repeated just before completion in order to ensure that no further entries have been effected since the date of the previous search. No priority period is given by the official search certificate.

Form AC6
(Duplicate)

Agricultural Credits Act. 1928

| Land Registry stamps
to be affixed here |

Application for an Official Search

Official Number...

This duplicate must also be completed; a carbon copy will suffice.

| THE SUPERINTENDENT,
AGRICULTURAL CREDITS DEPARTMENT,
BURRINGTON WAY,
PLYMOUTH, PL5 3LP. | This panel is printed so that if desired the form can be enclosed in a standard window envelope. |

I/We hereby apply for an Official Search to be made in the Agricultural Charges Register for any subsisting entries therein under the undermentioned names, and request that the result of search be

*...

Signature of Applicant .... Date ....

Telephone Number.. Telegraphic Address..

N.B. Insert "posted", "telegraphed" or "telephoned" as required and enclose any additional fee.

NAMES TO BE SEARCHED (Please use block letters)	
Forename(s)	
Surname	
Address	
Forename(s)	
Surname	
Address	
Forename(s)	
Surname	
Address	
Forename(s)	
Surname	
Address	

A separate form must be used if additional space is required

This form should be sent by **prepaid post** and should bear the prescribed adhesive Land Registry Fee Stamp which may be purchased at Head Post Offices. The envelope should be addressed to the AGRICULTURAL CREDITS SUPERINTENDENT, Agricultural Credits Department, Burrington Way, Plymouth, PL5 3LP. **NO COVERING LETTER IS REQUIRED.**

| | Reference | This panel must be completed using BLOCK LETTERS, and inserting the name and address to which the official certificate of result of search is to be sent. |
| | Telephone No. | |

14.4 *Agricultural credits search*

Official Certificate of the result of search in the Agricultural Charges Register under the names and addresses specified overleaf

The Search reveals

Name and Address of Farmer	Date and Ref. No. of Registration	Date of Instrument	Sum secured by the Charge	Floating or Fixed Charge	Name and Address of Bank in whose favour the Memorandum of Charge is registered

FOR OFFICIAL USE ONLY	
1st Name . . .	Searched by .... Checked by ....
2nd Name . . .	Searched by .... Checked by ....
3rd Name . . .	Searched by .... Checked by ....
4th Name . . .	Searched by .... Checked by ....

Printed in England by Beeston Printers Limited, Beeston, Nottingham and published by Her Majesty's Stationery Office
10p each or 25 for £2 (exclusive of tax)

Dd 599683 K560 7/79

ISBN 0 11 390214 X

Form AC6

Agricultural Credits Act, 1928

Affix
fee stamps
on attached
duplicate

Application for an Official Search

Official Number..

The attached duplicate must also be completed; a carbon copy will suffice.   Please see notes overleaf.

THE SUPERINTENDENT,
AGRICULTURAL CREDITS DEPARTMENT,
BURRINGTON WAY,
PLYMOUTH, PL5 3LP.

This panel is printed so that if desired the form can be enclosed in a standard window envelope.

I/We hereby apply for an Official Search to be made in the Agricultural Charges Register for any subsisting entries therein under the undermentioned names, and request that the result of search be

*...

Signature of Applicant ....   Date ....

Telephone Number..   Telegraphic Address..

*N.B. Insert "posted", "telegraphed" or "telephoned" as required and enclose any additional fee.

NAMES TO BE SEARCHED (Please use block letters)	
Forename(s)	
Surname	
Address	
Forename(s)	
Surname	
Address	
Forename(s)	
Surname	
Address	
Forename(s)	
Surname	
Address	

A separate form must be used if additional space is required

This form should be sent by **prepaid post** and should bear the prescribed adhesive Land Registry Fee Stamp which may be purchased at Head Post Offices. The envelope should be addressed to the AGRICULTURAL CREDITS SUPERINTENDENT, Agricultural Credits Department, Burrington Way, Plymouth, PL5 3LP. **NO COVERING LETTER IS REQUIRED.**

	Reference
	Telephone No.

This panel must be completed using BLOCK LETTERS, and inserting the name and address to which the official certificate of result of search is to be sent.

Official Certificate of the result of search in the Agricultural Charges Register under the names and addresses specified overleaf

The Search reveals

Name and Address of Farmer	Date and Ref. No. of Registration	Date of Instrument	Sum secured by the Charge	Floating or Fixed Charge	Name and Address of Bank in whose favour the Memorandum of Charge is registered

NOTES

Normal time for issuing Official Search Certificates

1. Certificates of official search are normally posted on the day of the receipt of the application therefor if received before 12 noon. Under Rule 8(2) of the Agricultural Credit Rules, 1928, the certificate extends to registrations effected during the day of the date of the certificate, and may be issued only after the Office is closed for registrations of that date.

Certified copy of any entry may be obtained

2. If the Certificate shows that there is an entry in the Register and further information respecting it is desired, a certified copy of the Memorandum filed thereunder can be obtained on application therefor duly stamped (Form AC5).

14.7 SEARCH SUMMARY

Application	AC6
Plan	–
Fee	£0.50 per name
Address	The Superintendent
	Agricultural Credits Department
	Burrington Way
	Plymouth
	PL5 3LP
	(0752 779831)
Special points	
Area affected	Purchase of agricultural land or assets

Chapter 15

Rent registers

15.1 REGULATED TENANCIES
15.1.1 A regulated tenancy is a tenancy (not a mere licence) of a house or part of a house which is let as a separate dwelling and which enjoys the protection of the security of tenure provisions of the Rent Act 1977.
15.1.2 Either landlord or tenant (or both together on a joint application) may apply to the rent officer for the area for registration of a fair rent which, once registered, becomes the maximum legally recoverable rent for those premises and unless there is a change in the circumstances of the tenancy, cannot be altered on an individual application for a period of two years from the date of registration.
15.1.3 A landlord may (and in the case of the grant of a protected shorthold tenancy within Greater London, must) apply for a rent to be registered prior to the grant of a tenancy, when a certificate of fair rent will be issued. The restrictions on the recovery and increase of rent outlined in the preceding paragraph apply equally to a rent registered under a certificate of fair rent.
15.1.4 A search should be made to discover whether or not a rent has been registered in relation to a particular tenancy, the amount of the registered rent, and the date of registration in order to know when an application may be made to increase the rent.

15.2 WHEN TO MAKE THE SEARCH
The search should be made as early as possible in the transaction in the following situations:
(a) when acting for a client who is purchasing, leasing or taking a mortgage on property which is or will be subject to a regulated tenancy;
(b) when acting for landlord or tenant in making or challenging an application to register a fair rent (see para 15.4.1, below).
15.2.1 Since the registered rent cannot usually be altered for two years from the date of registration it will not be necessary to repeat the search prior to completion of the transaction.
15.3 The search is made with the office of the local rent officer whose address and telephone number will be listed in the local telephone directory under the heading 'Local authority'. The addresses of local

rent officer services are also listed in the *Directory of Local Authorities* (1983 Oyez).

15.4 HOW TO MAKE THE SEARCH

The procedure varies from area to area. Some offices will answer queries over the telephone. Others prefer to deal with queries sent in by letter specifying details of the property to be searched.

15.4.1 Personal search

All offices will allow a personal inspection of the register and will permit the searcher to make notes of details of the register entries.

A personal search is preferable when acting for a landlord or tenant who is seeking to register a rent or to challenge such an application, since the register will reveal details of rents registered for comparable properties in the locality, which information may be of assistance to the client's application.

15.4.2 No fee is charged for the search, however made, but a fee of £1.00 is charged for each copy of an entry supplied. Form RR25 may be used to request copies of the entries.

15.5 WHAT THE SEARCH REVEALS

In relation to each registration the following information will be revealed:

(a) the amount of the registered rent;
(b) date of registration;
(c) details of the property comprising the tenancy;
(d) name and address of landlord and tenant;
(e) address of the property;
(f) commencement date, term and rental period of the tenancy;
(g) details of repairing obligations;
(h) details of services or furniture supplied by the landlord;
(i) other terms of the tenancy which were taken into account in assessing the fair rent.

15.6 RESTRICTED CONTRACTS

A restricted contract is a tenancy or licence within the Rent Act but which does not enjoy the full protection of Rent Act security of tenure. A limited form of security of tenure is available to these contracts but rent control similar to that afforded to regulated tenancies exists. The principal situations in which a restricted contract is to be found are:

(a) where the resident landlord exception applies (see the Rent Act 1977, s 12 as amended by the Housing Act 1980, s 65);
(b) where the tenant shares essential living accommodation with the landlord (Rent Act 1977, s 12);
(c) where the rent under the licence or tenancy includes a substan-

tial payment by the tenant which is attributable to services (not board) provided by the landlord.

15.6.1 Rent control under restricted contracts

Either party to a restricted contract may apply to a rent tribunal for the assessment of a reasonable rent for the property. The reasonable rent so fixed becomes the maximum legally recoverable rent for the premises and generally may only be reviewed after a two-year period has elapsed since the date of the registration.

15.6.2 The reasons for making the search, when to make the search and what the search will reveal are broadly similar to the information contained in the preceding paragraphs relating to regulated tenancies (see paras 15.1.4, 15.2, 15.5, above).

15.7 WHERE TO MAKE THE SEARCH

The search is made at the offices of the rent assessment panel for the area.

15.7.1 Addresses of rent assessment panels

Bristol	2nd Floor, Prudential Buildings
	Wine Street
	Bristol
	BS1 2PR
	(0272 299431)
Cambridge,	Cresta House
Chiltern and Thames	Alma Street
	Luton
	LU1 2SW
	(0582 25152)
Devon and Cornwall	Phoenix House
	Notte Street
	Plymouth
	PL1 2RA
	(0752 266864)
East Midland	Chaddesden House
	77 Talbot Street
	Nottingham
	NG1 5GN
	(0602 473825)
Eastern	St Clare House
	Greyfriars
	Ipswich
	Suffolk
	1PI 1LU
	(0473 56721)

Greater Manchester and Lancashire	6th Floor, Michael House Longridge Place Corporation Street Manchester M4 3AN (061 832 9661)
London	Newlands House 37–40 Berners Street London W1P 4BP (01 580 2000)
Merseyside and Cheshire	1st Floor, Port of Liverpool Building Pier Head Liverpool L3 1BY (051 236 3521)
Northern	4th Floor, Warwick House Grantham Road Newcastle on Tyne NE2 1QX (0632 326081)
South Eastern	Anston House 137–139 Preston Road Brighton Sussex BN1 6AF (0273 506381)
Southern	Queen's Park House 2–8 Queen's Terrace Southampton SO1 1BP (0703 25626)
West Midland	5th Floor, Somerset House 37 Temple Street Birmingham B2 5DP (021 643 8336)
Yorkshire	4 South Parade Leeds LS1 5RF (0532 39744)

Wales   2nd Floor, Williamson House
                                              17 Newport Road
                                              Cardiff
                                              CF2 1AA
                                              (0222 486408)

15.8   HOW TO MAKE THE SEARCH

15.8.1   A search of the register may be made in person for which no fee is charged.

A personal search is to be preferred if information about properties within a general locality is required.

15.8.2   By letter giving details of the information required.

15.8.3   On form Con 29E.

15.8.4   A fee of £2.00 is payable for a search made by letter or on form Con 29E.

£1.00 is payable for each copy of an entry on the register.

15.9   FORM CON 29E

This form is reproduced on p 259, below.

15.10   SEARCH SUMMARY

	Regulated tenancies	*Restricted contracts*
Application	In person, by telephone or letter	In person or by letter or on form Con 29E
Plan	–	
Fee	Fee for copies only (£1.00)	No fee for personal search Other searches £2.00 £1.00 per copy
Address	Local rent officer service	See para 15.7.1, above
Special points		
Area affected	Tenanted residential property	

1983 EDITION

To be submitted in duplicate

REQUEST FOR A SEARCH OF THE REGISTER KEPT PURSUANT TO SECTION 79 OF THE RENT ACT 1977

Address and Description of the Property

RE...

....

....

....

....

ADDRESS OF RENT ASSESSMENT PANEL
The President

Local authority:..

....

Fees of £2.00 are enclosed.

Signed...

Solicitors.

Dated...

HEADNOTES

(1) Cheques should be made payable to the appropriate Rent Assessment Panel.

(2) The replies are furnished in the belief that they are correct but on the distinct understanding that neither the President nor any member of his staff is legally responsible therefor, except for negligence. Any such liability for negligence shall extend not only to the person by or on whose behalf the enquiry is made but also to a person (being a purchaser for the purposes of Section 10(3) of the Local Land Charges Act 1975) who or whose agent had knowledge, before the relevant time as defined in the said section, of the replies to these enquiries.

(3) This form of request was settled following consultations with The Law Society and the Department of the Environment.

(4) A copy of an entry in the Register will not be supplied unless there is a further written request accompanied by a fee of 50p.

ENQUIRY	REPLY
Are there any, and if so what, subsisting entries in the Register in respect of the above property or any part of it kept pursuant to Section 79 of the Rent Act 1977, as amended by Paragraph 43 of Schedule 25 to the Housing Act 1980?	

Signed ....

For and on behalf of the President.

NAME AND ADDRESS (IN BLOCK LETTERS) TO WHICH THIS FORM IS TO BE RETURNED

SOLICITORS' REFERENCE..

....

....

TELEPHONE NUMBER...

....

TELEX ....

259

Chapter 16

Corn rent and corn rent annuities

16.1 Corn rent and corn rent annuities were not abolished under the provisions which extinguished tithe redemption annuity and some land near ancient parish churches is still affected by this charge, although the amounts involved in the payment are usually very small.

16.2 Corn rents were created by the various Inclosure Acts and some local Acts and were payments in lieu of tithe liabilities the amount of which varied according to the price of corn.

Corn rent annuities were tithe rent charges redeemable by annuity over a fixed period of years.

16.3 WHEN AND WHERE TO MAKE THE SEARCH

16.3.1 An appointment should be arranged by telephone prior to making a personal search at the address below. No facilities exist for searches to be made by telephone nor by correspondence.

16.3.2   Public Record Office
Bourne Avenue
Hayes, Middlesex
(01 571 3831)
Opening hours 10 am – 5 pm on Tuesdays and
Thursdays only.

16.3.3 Although these charges used to be common over rural land most have now been redeemed. Consideration should be given to making the search when land is being purchased which is near to an ancient parish church.

16.4 FEES

No fee is charged for making a search but the cost to the client of undertaking a personal search or of employing an agent to do so may be expensive. In view of the fact that the incidence of the charge is rare and the amount payable thereunder is usually small, the client's specific instructions to undertake the search should be obtained before proceeding with the search.

16.4.1 Copies of documents which are kept at the Hayes office may be ordered either through the Hayes office or by contacting the Public Records Office at Kew (01 876 3444).

A document which is needed urgently should be ordered through the Kew Office since orders placed at Hayes are sometimes subject to delay.

Fees in accordance with SI 1534/1951 are charged for copies of documents.

16.5 WHAT TO LOOK FOR WHEN MAKING THE SEARCH
16.5.1 It may be of assistance to take with you a plan showing the land to be searched and the surrounding area.
16.5.2 The first step to take when making a search is to refer to the parish list in order to find the correct tithe district in which the land in question is situated. The parish list is based on the boundaries of parishes where were in existence in 1836 since when many boundaries have changed and it will normally not be possible to rely on a modern postal address in order to locate the correct tithe district.
16.5.3 The district record map should then be consulted which will identify the field numbers of any tithe fields included in that district. Land colour edged on the map will have or have had a liability to some sort of tithe. The tithe map microfilm may also need to be consulted to obtain the correct field numbers.

16.5.4 Corn rent
Only limited records exist in relation to this charge. The corn rent index and documents relating to altered apportionments of corn rents should be inspected. Where the corn rent index shows evidence of a corn rent it will usually give details of the Inclosure Act under which the charge was created and will indicate the location of the relevant documents. The index will not establish whether the charge has been redeemed.

16.5.5 Corn rent annuities
The relevant tithe apportionment microfilm will indicate whether the land being searched is affected by a corn rent annuity. Affected fields are distinguished by a marginal notation of the letters R^A followed by a number. The number refers to the certificate of redemption by annuity from which the period for which the annuity was to be payable may be ascertained. In the majority of cases the annuity period will have expired and thus no further sum will be payable. In a few cases the charge is still extant.
16.5.6 The lists of tithe districts may also contain information showing land which has been subject to corn rent or corn rent annuity, but the information contained in these lists is not guaranteed to be accurate.

16.6 WHAT THE SEARCH WILL REVEAL
No official search procedure exists and no protection or priority is conferred on a purchaser who makes a search. By searching the records

it will be possible to determine that land is definitely *not* affected by corn rent or a corn rent annuity, but it may not be possible to conclude that land is so affected because the records kept at Hayes are incomplete and do not show the precise boundaries of the areas subject to the charge.

16.6.1 If it is suspected that such a charge may exist over the land a specific preliminary enquiry to this effect should be raised with the vendor. Inspection of the local parish records may also yield further information.

16.7 Rights arising under corn rents and corn rent annuities are rights to which the provisions of the Limitation Act 1980 apply. Where no demand has been made for payment during the past 12 years it is probable that the rights have been extinguished by the Limitation Act 1980.

16.8 TITHE REDEMPTION ANNUITY

Although these charges have been compulsorily redeemed under the Finance Act 1977, s 56 some queries still remain in relation to them. Enquiries should be addressed to:

Inland Revenue Central Accounting Office
Barrington Road
Worthing
West Sussex.

16.9 SEARCH SUMMARY

Application	Personal search only
Plan	May be helpful to take plan with you to identify land
Fee	No fee for search
	Fees charged for copy documents
Address	Public Records Office
	Bourne Avenue
	Hayes
	Middlesex
	UBT 1RF
	(01 573 3831)
Special points	No search by telephone or letter
Area affected	Some land near ancient parish churches

Chapter 17

Chancel repairs

17.1 HISTORY
The history of chancel repair liability is both ancient and complex, having existed in England and Wales from some date prior to the accession of King Richard I in 1189. By custom the responsibility for the upkeep of the church used to be divided between the rector and the parishioners, the latter being responsible originally for the maintenance of the western end of the church, the chancel being the responsibility of the incumbent. The parishioners' responsibility to repair the western end passed eventually into the hands of the church and does not affect modern conveyancing. The liability for chancel repairs is closely connected with the (now defunct) right to collect tithes. During the thirteenth to fifteenth centuries many rectories were acquired by monasteries who thus took over the right to collect the tithes together with liability to repair the chancel of the church, but with the dissolution of the monasteries during the reign of Henry VIII much of the monasterial property fell into lay hands.

Steps were taken from the end of the seventeenth century to eliminate tithes and this was in part achieved under the various Inclosure Acts by which common land enjoyed by a village was 'enclosed' and at the same time part of the enclosed land was appropriated to the rector in return for the extinction of the tithe. Thus the rector's newly acquired land became rectoral property and chancel repair liability accordingly became attached to the ownership of that land. Since this time much of the land owned by the monasteries and rectors has passed into private ownership and although tithe liability (subsequently converted into tithe redemption annunity) has ceased to exist[1] the liability to repair the chancel of a church still remains in whole or in part attached to that land.

The incidence of this liability is not infrequent and may be found to be attached even to quite ordinary dwellings on a housing estate. The absence of any 'notice' procedure relating to this charge within the modern system of conveyancing makes it extremely difficult to find out whether or not a particular property is affected by this charge. Insofar as the liability attaches to land in private ownership the payment is not always regularly enforced. However, where the liability is enforced it may require the payment of a large sum of money, eg the Land Commission's working paper on chancel repairs[2] cites as an example a landowner who was called upon to pay a five figure sum for the repair of the chancel of his parish church.

17.2   LAND WHICH MAY BE AFFECTED BY LIABILITY

It is impossible to define with precision the land which may be affected by liability. The charge will only affect land within a parish which has a church which dates from the mediaeval period or earlier, thus liability is more likely to occur in rural areas than in urban ones. In this context a 'church' means a parish church of the Church of England only. If land falls into any of the categories below there is a possibility that chancel repair liability may still exist. The following list is intended as a guideline only and is not exhaustive:

(a) land which has at some time been owned by the rector of a parish;

(b) glebe land (land other than the parsonage and its grounds which has at some time formed part of the benefice whether belonging to a rector or vicar);

(c) land which in 1936 had the benefit of a rent charge owned by a rector, the Church Commissioners, the Ecclestiastical Commissioners, the Dean and Chapter of a Cathedral, the Colleges of Oxford, Cambridge and Durham Universities, or by Winchester or Eton Colleges;

(d) land still in the ownership of any of the bodies listed in (c) above;

(e) land which in 1936 was subject to a tithe which had been extinguished by the merger of ownership of the liability to pay and the right to receive payment of the tithe;

(f) land affected by tithes which had been extinguished by Inclosure Acts or other legislation prior to 1936;

(g) land which is or has been subject to a corn rent or corn rent annuity.

17.2.1   It will usually be necessary to check the tithe and corn rent records to find out whether land does fall into one of the above categories. Tithe searches are made in the same way as corn rent searches (see ch 16, above) and can be time consuming and expensive and will not necessarily yield conclusive information.

17.3   SEARCHING FOR CHANCEL REPAIR LIABILITY

If land is thought to come within one of the categories listed in the preceding paragraph a personal search may be made at the Public Records Office, Bourne Avenue, Hayes, Middlesex (01 573 3831). It is necessary to make an appointment by telephone prior to visiting this office.

It will first be necessary to identify the tithe district which includes the area of the land now being investigated (see para 16.5, above) and then to check the record of ascertainments which will show whether a liability exists in that district and will give details of the apportionment of that liability between the various parcels of land affected. The record of ascertainments will only show the proportionate liability of the land, the actual amount of liability will not be known until the total cost of repairs to a particular chancel is calculated. The records of ascertainment are not complete in that they do not cover all land in England and Wales and in some cases the description of the land given in the record may be insufficient to enable a precise identification of the land to be made. The boundaries of the land detailed in the record may not bear any resemblance to modern boundaries but some reconciliation of the two may be made by inspecting the district record maps which show the boundaries of former tithe areas on modern maps.

A further complication arises where (as is likely) the ownership of the land originally affected by liability has become fragmented and it may now be extremely difficult to ascertain the exact proportion of liability attaching to a particular property.

17.3.1 This search is likely to be time consuming and costly to the client particularly if an agent has to be employed to make the personal search. It is therefore suggested that the client's specific instructions are obtained prior to making the search.

17.3.2 Public Record Office leaflet No 61 provides a guide to these searches.

17.3.3 County archive records may in some cases contain information which will confirm the existence of liability.

17.4 LAND AFFECTED OR THOUGHT TO BE AFFECTED BY LIABILITY

17.4.1 Where an outstanding liability is discovered during the course of the purchase of land, an attempt should be made to obtain an express indemnity from the present vendor, because the implied covenants for title will not extend to cover this type of liability.

17.4.2 An owner of land which is known to be subject to liability may consider taking out an insurance policy to cover his liability.

17.4.3 Liability may affect both unregistered and registered land since chancel liability repair is an overriding interest in the latter under the Land Registration Act 1925, s 70(1).

17.5 THE NATURE OF THE LIABILITY

Where liability does exist the demand for payment which is unlimited in financial terms is enforceable against the freehold land owner irrespective of whether he has notice of the existence of the liability.

A demand for payment in full for the cost of repairs may be made to the owner of any part of land which is affected by the charge. In such circumstances the owner, having made payment in full can seek contributions from the owners of other affected land within the same parish if he can identify them. Unless express provision has been made in the conveyance or transfer no indemnity can be sought from a previous owner of the land because the liability for chancel repairs is not covered by the covenants for title implied by the Law of Property Act 1925, s 76.

17.6   WALES
The provisions affecting chancel repair liability in Wales differ from those relating to English churches due to the disestablishment of the Church of Wales in 1920. Most chancel repair liability falls to the Representative Body of the Church of Wales but there may be rare exceptions where land still in private ownership is affected by the charge.

17.7   THE LAW COMMISSION'S PROPOSALS
The Law Commission's Working Paper No 86 entitled *Transfer of Land Liability for Chancel Repairs* outlines the history and nature of chancel repair liability and makes proposals for the reform of the law in this area. The provisional conclusion of the report recommends the gradual abolition of the liability phased over a 20-year period with no provisions for compensation. No steps have yet been taken to implement this proposal.

17.8   SEARCH SUMMARY

Application	Personal search only by prior appointment
Plan	Not required but it may assist to take one with you
Fee	Free
Address	Public Records Office Bourne Avenue Hayes Middlesex (01 573 3831)
Special points	A tithe or corn rent search may also be necessary
Area affected	Chiefly land in ancient rural parishes

1 Finance Act 1977, s 56.
2 Transfer of Land, Liability for Chancel Repairs Working Paper No 86.

Chapter 18

Enrolled deeds

18.1   The validity of some deeds is dependent on their having been enrolled or recorded in a register. If such a document is encountered during the course of investigating title to unregistered land its validity must be authenticated at this stage in the transaction. Deeds requiring enrolment do not take effect if they are not enrolled but this does not preclude the vendor from making title to the land under the Limitation Act 1980.

Most deeds to which this requirement applies will bear a stamp, seal or endorsement which will confirm that the enrolment requirement has been fulfilled, and further investigation is required only where conspicuous evidence of the enrolment is missing. The requirement for enrolment applies to very few modern documents, the principal examples of which are listed in the following paragraphs.

18.2   CHARITIES
Assurances to charities prior to the Charities Act 1960 were required to be enrolled, the records of which are now kept at the offices of the Charities Commissioners, 14 Ryder Street, St James's, London, SW1Y 6AH (01 214 6000).
18.2.1   A search may be made by letter which should specify the location of the land, the date of the deed and the name of the charity.
18.2.2   A personal search may be made at the offices of the Charity Commissioners, but solicitors are asked to write or telephone in advance so that the documents may be made available for inspection.
18.2.3   No fee is charged for a search whether made by telephone or letter. A fee of £0.08 is charged for each page of copy documents supplied.

18.3   POWERS OF ATTORNEY PRIOR TO 1971
A search will only be necessary if the original or an examined abstract of the power is not contained in the abstract of title.

A search made in person or by letter for which no fee is charged, may be made at Royal Courts of Justice (Room 84), Strand, London, WC2 (01 405 7641).

18.4 DEED POOLS RELATING TO CHANGE OF NAME

If the original deed or an examined abstract thereof is not supplied with the abstract of title a search for a deed poll made less than four years ago may be made in person at Room 81, Royal Courts of Justice, Strand, London, WC2 (01 405 7641). A fee of £0.13 is charged for each name searched against. Deed polls are no longer *required* to be enrolled, therefore not all such deeds will have been filed with the High Court. Documents over four years old are kept by the Public Record Office at Kew (see para 18.6, below).

18.5 DISPOSITIONS BY THE DUCHIES OF LANCASTER AND CORNWALL

Dispositions of land made by the Duchies are void unless enrolled with the appropriate Duchy Office within six months. A deed which has been so enrolled will bear a conspicuous endorsement, thus an enquiry of the respective Duchy Offices will only be necessary if the endorsement is absent or the deed has been lost.

18.5.1 Enquiries may be made by letter or in person (after a prior telephone call). In either case the date of and parties to the deed, and a description of the land affected should be given.

18.5.2 Duchy of Lancaster Office, 1 Lancaster Place, Strand, London, SW2E 7ED (01 836 8277).

18.5.3 Duchy of Cornwall Office, 10 Buckingham Gate, London, SW1E 6LA (01 834 7346).

18.5.4 A special central land charge search procedure is available for searches against land which is or has been held by the Duchies (see ch 34, below).

18.6 DEEDS HELD BY THE PUBLIC RECORD OFFICE

An appointment should be made by telephone if it is required to inspect any of the deeds or records listed below. The telephone call should initially be made to Public Record Office, Kew, Richmond, Surrey, TW9 4FU (01 876 3444), although some documents are held at the Public Record Office in Chancery Lane, London, WC2. No fee is charged for inspection of documents but a fee is charged for copies.

In some cases the permission of the Crown Estates Commissioners will need to be obtained prior to making a search.

18.6.1 A very large number of documents of many different types is held by the Public Record Office. Amongst those which may be relevant to conveyancers are the following:

(a) deed polls over four years old;

(b) grants from the Crown;

(c) counterpart leases of foreshore in Durham;

(d) records relating to tithes and chancel repairs (see chs 16 and 17, above);

(e) manorial records;

(f) some ancient private (eg not Crown grant) conveyances (details in Leaflet No 25 published by Public Record Office);

(g) powers of attorney made prior to 1937.

18.7 SEARCH SUMMARY

Application	By letter or in person
Plan	–
Fee	Various
Address	See appropriate paragraph
Special points	
Area affected	Generally only relevant to unregistered land where an original deed needs to be verified

Chapter 19

Index of proprietors

19.1 The Index of proprietors is part of the registered land system and comprises a list of names of registered proprietors together with a description of all the land held by each proprietor. The register also contains limited information relating to charges affecting registered titles but does not contain details of charges made in favour of building societies, local authorities or government departments.

One function of this index is to enable the Chief Land Registrar to trace the name and title number of land belonging to a debtor where the Registrar is required to place a creditor's notice on the register for bankruptcy purposes.

19.2 THE RIGHT TO SEARCH
The registered proprietor of land is entitled to make this search against his own title, but presumably would only wish to do so in order to check that the registered details of his own land and address were correct.

Any other person who can satisfy the Chief Land Registrar that he is interested generally in the property of the proprietor whose name is being searched against may make a search. The search is usually only made by personal representatives or by a trustee in bankruptcy who wish to find out what land, if any, is registered in the name of the deceased or bankrupt.

19.3 HOW TO MAKE THE SEARCH
Application *must* be made on form 104 accompanied by the fee (£2.00 per name searched against).

The register is maintained by reference to proprietors' names and there is no need to supply a description of the land or title number. The register is kept at HM Land Charges Registry, Burrington Way, Plymouth and no facilities exist for personal searches.

19.4   FORM 104

(Not available from Law Stationers).

> FORM 104 APPLICATION FOR AN OFFICIAL SEARCH IN THE INDEX OF PRO-
> PRIETORS' NAMES. (RULE 9)
> To: The Chief Land Registrar, HM Land Registry, Burrington Way,
> Plymouth, PL5 3LP.
> [*Name of applicant*] hereby applies for an official search to be made in the
> index of proprietors' names in respect of:
> FULL NAME
> ADDRESS(ES)
>
> [*In any case where the search is required in a name other than that of the applicant*
>   The applicant is interested generally in the property of the above-
> named person [*here state the nature of the applicant's interest*, 'as trustee in
> bankruptcy', 'as personal representative', *or as the case may be*]].
> Signature of applicant or his solicitor
> [Name of solicitor]
> Address of applicant or solicitor
>
> Date
> *Note:* Separate applications should be made in respect of any former or
> alternative names. Every address which may have been used as an
> address for service for entry on the register should be stated.

19.5   WHAT THE SEARCH REVEALS

The search will reveal the description and title number of any land
held by the proprietor against whose name a search has been made.
Limited details of charges may also be given (see para 19.1, above).

19.6   SEARCH SUMMARY

Application	Form 104
Plan	
Fee	£2 per name
Address	HM Land Charges Registry Burrington Way Plymouth PL5 3LP
Special points	Generally only of use to PRs or trustee in bankruptcy
Area affected	Registered land only

Chapter 20

Index of minor interests

20.1 The Index of minor interests was set up as part of the registered land system under the 1925 legislation but is quite separate from the ordinary register of titles and is of no concern to a person who is dealing with the legal estate in the land because a registered dealing for value will over-reach the interests protected by the index.[1]

20.1.1 The index exists solely to regulate the priority of dealings with the beneficial interests under a trust or settlement. These interests are protected on the Index by the registration of a priority caution or priority inhibition.

20.1.2 The Law Commission's Report on Property Law: Land Registration[2] has recommended that the minor interests index should be abolished, but no steps have yet been taken to implement this proposal.

20.2 WHERE TO MAKE THE SEARCH
A search should be made when there is a prospective dealing with a beneficial interest in the land.

20.3 THE RIGHT TO SEARCH
The Chief Land Registrar must permit any person to inspect the register if that person would have been entitled to inspect notices served on a trustee of the trust.[3] In general the authority of the trustees of the trust should be obtained and submitted with the search application.

20.4 HOW TO MAKE THE SEARCH
An application should be made by letter to HM Land Registry, Croydon (wherever the land is situated). The authority to inspect and fee of £1.00 which must be pre-paid, should accompany the application. Although it is not necessary to supply a description or plan of the land, the land to be searched must be identified by its title number. If the title number is not known the minor interests search will have to be preceded by a public index map search in order to obtain this information (see ch 6, above).

20.5 WHAT THE SEARCH REVEALS
The reply to the search is by letter which will reveal details of priority cautions and inhibitions (if any) registered against the title.

20.5.1 Office copies of the register entries may be obtained (fee £1.00).

20.6 SEARCH SUMMARY

Application	By letter
Plan	–
Fee	£1 must be pre-paid
Address	HM Land Registry Sunley House Bedford Park Croydon CR9 3 LE (01 686 8833)
Special points	Authority to inspect required
Area affected	Purchase or mortgage of beneficial interests in registered land only

1 Land Registration Rules 1925, r 11.
2 Law Com No 125.
3 Land Registration Rules 1925, r 290(2).

Chapter 21

Water authorities

21.1 RIVERS AND STREAMS

Regional water authorities have control over most rivers and streams in England and Wales and have statutory powers to grant licences or consents in relation to the use of water and the discharge of waste material into inland and certain coastal waters.

21.2 WHEN TO MAKE THE SEARCH

21.2.1 Land bordered by a river or stream or which is traversed by a river or stream

A search should be made to discover whether the owner of the land is responsible for the maintenance of the river banks and whether a notice of disrepair has been or is likely to be served in relation to such want of repair. If a notice of disrepair has been served or is imminent an appropriate indemnity may be sought from the vendor. Where the water authority itself is responsible for repair and maintenance they may have reserved rights to enter the property in order to carry out their maintenance obligations.

The water authority will also on request supply details of previous flooding of the land, but they will be reluctant to predict the likelihood of future flooding. Evidence of previous flooding may affect the insurance of the property.

21.2.2 Low-lying land close to a river or stream

Enquiries relating to past flooding should be made.

21.2.3 Pipes and sewers running under land where planning permission for building works is contemplated

A search should always be made before building plans are finalised to discover the routes of water pipes and sewers passing underneath the property. The consent of the water authority will have to be obtained if it is proposed to divert or re-lay the route of an existing sewer. Building Regulation consent from the local authority is required where it is proposed to erect a building over an existing sewer.

21.2.4 Property discharging trade effluent
The discharge of trade effluent whether into a sewer (public or private) or into inland waters, estuaries, tidal waters, coastal waters or into undergound strata containing water is prohibited except under licence from the regional water authority. The existence and terms of such a licence should be checked with the authority, who should also be informed of any change of ownership of the land.

21.2.5 Impoundment of water
An impoundment licence under the Water Resources Act 1963 is required whenever it is proposed to impound water within a watercourse. The licence is required regardless of the purpose of the proposed impoundment. Such a licence is therefore necessary even for the purpose of building a dam to create an ornamental pond or in order to create a pond as a source for spray irrigation of crops by a farmer.

The benefit of such a licence does not pass with the ownership of the land. An intending purchaser must however investigate the terms of the existing licence in order to be satisfied that impounding works have been carried out in accordance with the terms of the licence.

21.2.6 Property relying on a natural source for its water supply
A number of agricultural or industrial properties rely wholly or in part on a natural source for their water supply. The use of water from a natural source, except for domestic use, whether that source is a spring, river, well or borehole is only permitted where a licence to use the supply has been obtained under the Water Resources Act 1963. Although it is possible to transfer the benefit of the licence to a purchaser of the land the assignment of the licence will only be effective if the water authority is notified of the change of ownership within one month of the assignment. Failure to notify within this time limit causes the licence to lapse and there is no guarantee that a new licence will be granted to the new owner of the land. Loss of the licence may have serious consequences for the client and the expenses connected with the grant of a new licence (if forthcoming) may be high. It is therefore important in these circumstances to investigate the existence and terms of the current licence both with the vendor and with the water authority before exchange of contracts. The client's file should be marked with a reminder to notify the authority of the change of ownership after completion.

Where the new owner takes over part only of the land which has the benefit of a licence he does not take over the right to abstract water under the previous owner's licence. A new licence must be applied for within one month of the change of ownership.

The detailed provisions relating to the transfer of licences are contained in Water Resources (Succession to Licences) Regulations 1969.

21.3 WHERE TO MAKE THE SEARCH

The search should be made with the appropriate regional water authority. If there is doubt over which authority is responsible for a particular area the National Water Council, 1 Queen Anne's Gate, London, SW1H 9BT (01 222 8111) will supply this information.

21.3.1 Addresses of regional water authorities

Anglian	Ambury Road
	Huntingdon
	PE18 6NZ
	(0480 56181)
North West	Dawson House
	Great Sankey
	Warrington
	WA5 3LW
	(092 572 4321)
Northumbrian	Northumbria House
	Regent Centre
	Gosforth
	Newcastle-upon-Tyne
	NE3 3PX
	(0632 843151)
Severn-Trent	Abelson House
	2297 Coventry Road
	Sheldon
	Birmingham
	B26 3PS
	(021 743 4222)
South West	3–5 Barnfield Road
	Exeter
	EX1 1RE
	(0392 50861)
Southern	Guildbourne House
	Chatsworth Road
	Worthing
	BN11 1LD
	(0903 205252)
Thames	New River Head
	Rosebery Avenue
	London
	EC1R 4TP
	(01 837 3300)·

Wessex

Wessex House
Passage Street
Bristol
BS2 0JQ
(0272 290611)

Yorkshire

West Riding House
67 Albion Street
Leeds
LS1 5AA
(0532 448201)

Wales

Cambrian Way
Brecon
Powys
LD3 7HP
(0874 3181)

21.4 HOW TO MAKE THE SEARCH

A letter should be sent to the area engineer of the appropriate regional water authority enclosing a plan which shows the extent of the area to be searched. The search should be made before exchange of contracts but need not be repeated prior to completion. Where appropriate enquiries should be raised to deal with the following matters:

(a) the routes of water mains passing under the property;

(b) whether the authority claims any rights over the property;

(c) the existence of any liability on the owner of the property in relation to maintenance and repair of river banks;

(d) whether a notice of disrepair has been served or is likely to be served in relation to (c);

(e) details of past flooding;

(f) the existence, extent and method of transfer of any licence or consent relating to the property.

21.4.1 No fixed fee is charged for answering these enquiries. Some authorities will make a small charge, others provide the service free.

21.5 CHANGE OF OWNERSHIP

A letter notifying the water authority of the change of ownership of land is essential in cases where a licence or consent from the authority affects the land. The notification will normally be made by the purchaser after completion, but the vendor may consider giving notice himself in order to avoid any future liability for breach of the terms of the licence or consent. Standard form Con 46G accompanied by a plan identifying the land may be used for notification and should be sent in duplicate to the appropriate regional authority.

It is not standard conveyancing procedure for the purchaser to notify change of ownership in relation to ordinary domestic property. However, the water authorities do encourage solicitors to notify them of such changes. This notification is of great assistance to the authorities, particularly in view of the fact that water and sewerage charges are now assessed separately from general rates.

Apportionment of water and sewage charges is usually made on the completion statement and not dealt with through the authority concerned.

21.6 CANALS

Canals are the responsibility of British Waterways Board, but some private liability may exist in relation to the maintenance of banks and towpaths. Where a property abuts on to a canal or is situated near to a canal it may also be necessary to make enquiries relating to the previous flooding of the land.

Before contracts are exchanged a letter enclosing a plan of the property should be sent to the estates officer of the appropriate area office of British Waterways Board. If it is not known which office is responsible for the area in which the land is situated this information may be obtained from the national headquarters of the Board.

21.6.1 The enquiries raised by the letter should encompass the items mentioned in notes (b)—(e) inclusive of para 21.5, above. A fee may be charged for answering the enquiries.

21.6.2 Addresses of British Waterways Board

National Headquarters	Melbury House
	Melbury Terrace
	London
	NW1 6JX
	(01 262 6711)
Principal Estate	PO Box 9
Officer (North)	1 Dock Street
	Leeds
	LS1 1HH
	(0532 436741)
Estate Office	Willow Grange
(South East)	Church Road
	Watford
	Herts
	WD1 3QA
	(92 26422)
Estate Officer	Dock Office
(South West)	The Dock
	Gloucester
	GL1 2 EJ
	(0452 25524)

278

21.7 WATERWAYS IN EAST ANGLIA

Some small waterways in East Anglia are not covered by the provisions mentioned in the preceding paragraphs, but are controlled by local drainage boards to whom enquiries relating to ownership and maintenance should be directed. The drainage boards will answer queries sent in by letter and there is generally no fee for this service. A plan showing the land should accompany the enquiry. The drainage board should also be notified after completion of the change of ownership of the land. Where land adjoins a navigable part of the Norfolk Broads enquiries relating to the maintenance of the banks and navigation rights should be made to the Rivers Officer, Great Yarmouth Port and Haven Commissioners, 21 South Quay, Great Yarmouth (0493 55151). Enquiries may be made by letter accompanied by a plan showing the land and no fee is charged for this service. The Commissioners are normally consulted by the local planning authority when an application is made to build on land adjacent to the Broads and planning permission may be refused if the proposed building would interfere with the wind flow over the water. It may therefore be prudent to seek the views of the Commissioners with regard to a client's proposals for development prior to submitting a formal planning application.

21.8 SEARCH SUMMARY

Application	By letter
Plan	Yes
Fee	No fixed fee Varies from authority to authority
Address	Regional water authority (rivers) British Waterways Board (canals)
Special points	
Area affected	Any land bounded by a river, stream or canal or which has a river, stream or canal passing through or nearby the property

Chapter 22

Pipe-lines and cables

22.1 A client who is concerned with developing or redeveloping land will need to obtain information about the routes of pipe-lines and cables which lie underneath the property to be developed. Such information should be obtained prior to contract in a case where the land is currently being purchased, in other cases the information should be obtained before the plans for the proposed building work are finalised.

22.2 SEWERS
Information relating to the existence and type of sewers serving the property will be given by the local authority in response to question 5 on the standard form of additional enquiries (ch 5, above).

The route of public sewers is not revealed by the above search but may be ascertained by a personal inspection of the map of sewers maintained by the local authority (district council or London borough council) under the Public Health Act 1936, s 32. This map is available for inspection by any person at all reasonable hours free of charge.

Sewers which are reserved for foul water only or for surface water only may not be shown on this map.

22.3 WATER PIPES
Enquiries relating to the routes of water pipes should be addressed to the regional water authority (see ch 21, above).

22.4 ELECTRICITY CABLES
Enquiries relating to equipment maintained by the Central Electricity Generating Board should be made by letter addressed to the Engineering Department at the appropriate area office. No fee is charged for this service. A plan showing the situation of the land will assist the board in answering the enquiries.

The board maintains a map showing the location of all existing mains, service lines, underground works and street boxes which is open to public inspection on payment of a fee of £0.05. A charge of £0.25 is made for copies.

22.4.1 Area offices of Central Electricity Generating Board

South West (including Wales)	Bedminster Down Bridgwáter Road Bristol BS13 8AN
South East (including London and Home Counties)	Bankside House Sumner Street London SE1
Midlands	Haslucks Green Road Shirley Solihull West Midlands B90 4PD
North East	Beckwith Knowle Otley Road Harrogate HG3 1PS
North West	Europa House Bird Hall Lane Cheadle Heath Stockport SK3 0XA

22.4.2 Enquiries relating to equipment maintained by the regional electricity boards should be sent by letter to the engineering department of the appropriate area offices.

22.4.3 Electricity Board area offices

London	Templar House 81–87 High Holborn London WC1V 6NU
Eastern	PO Box 40 Whearstead Ipswich 1P9 2Q
East Midlands	PO Box B4 North PDO 398 Coppice Road Arnold Nottingham NG5 7HX
Merseyside and North Wales	Sealand Road Chester CH1 4LR

Midland	Muckland Hill
	Halesowen
	Worcestershire
	B62 8BP
North East	Carliol House
	Newcastle on Tyne
	NE99 15E
South East	Grand Avenue
	Hove
	Sussex
	BN3 2LS
Southern	Southern Electricity House
	Littlewick Green
	near Maidenhead
	Berks
	SL6 3QB
South Wales	St Mellons
	Cardiff
	CF3 9XW
South West	Electricity House
	Colston Avenue
	Bristol
	BS1 4TS
Yorkshire	Wetherby Road
	Scarcroft
	Leeds
	LS14 3HS

22.5   PIPE-LINES

Plans of pipe-lines authorised to be constructed under the Pipe-lines Act 1962 are maintained by the local authority (district council or London borough council) and are open to inspection at reasonable hours free of charge. Pipe-lines and cables laid by the gas and electricity boards and by the United Kingdom Atomic Energy Authority are not shown on this map.

22.6   GAS PIPES

A letter accompanied by an ordnance survey map (scale 1:1250) should be sent to the legal department or engineering department of the appropriate area offices of the British Gas Corporation. The location of any pipes, plant or machinery will be marked on the map and returned to the enquirer. This service is provided free of charge.

22.6.1 Addresses of Area Boards

British Gas Corporation	Rivermill House 152 Grosvenor Road London SW1V 3JL
East Midlands	PO Box 145 De Montfort Road Leicester
Eastern	Star House Potters Bar EN6 2PD
North Eastern	New York Road Leeds
North Thames	North Thames House London Road Staines Middlesex
North West	Welman House Altringham Cheshire
Northern	Nor Gas House Killingworth Newcastle on Tyne
South East	Segas House Catherine Street Croydon Surrey
South West	Riverside House Temple Street Keynsham Bristol
Southern	St Mary's Road Southampton SO5 5AT
West Midlands	Wharf Lane Solihull West Midlands
Wales	Snelling House Bute Terrace Cardiff

22.7 TELECOMMUNICATIONS

The appropriate area office of British Telecom will answer enquiries made by letter free of charge. A plan showing the extent of the land may assist the area office in answering the enquiries.

22.8   SEARCH SUMMARY

Application	By letter or in person
Plan	May be required
Fee	Usually free
Address	See appropriate paragraph
Special points	
Area affected	Any land where it is necessary to ascertain the route of pipes and cables. Particularly relevant to land which is to be developed

Chapter 23

Building societies and friendly societies

23.1 WHEN TO MAKE THE SEARCH
It may from time to time be necessary to check the rules of a building society or friendly society, or to obtain evidence of the change of name of a society, eg on an amalgamation. It is also possible to search for details of the assets and commitments of a society, the address of its chief office and the names of its directors and secretary.

23.1.1 A mortgage receipt given by a building society using the form of wording prescribed by the Building Societies Act 1962 acts as a sufficient discharge of the mortgage. Where the statutory form of wording is used it is therefore unnecessary to check the rules of a particular society to ascertain the correct procedure for discharge.

23.2 HOW TO MAKE THE SEARCH
A personal search may be made at the Registrar of Friendly Societies, 15 Great Marlborough Street, London, W1 (01 437 9992). No facilities exist for personal searches. A fee of £2.50 per file is charged and a minimum charge of £1.50 is made for copies of entries.

23.3 Information similar to that outlined in para 23.1, above is also kept by the Registrar of Friendly Societies in relation to industrial and provident societies and certified loan societies.

23.4 CHARITIES
Records relating to registered charities are kept at the offices of the Charity Commissioners where a search may be made in order to check the constitution of the charity, its name or change of name and financial status.

A letter requesting a search may be sent to the offices of the Commissioners at 14 Ryder Street, London, SW1. No fee is charged for the search but a fee of £0.08 per sheet is charged for copies of the file entries. A personal search may also be made at the above address. A prior appointment made by telephone is appreciated.

23.5 TRADE UNIONS
The records of trade unions are kept at the Certification Office, 15–17 Ormond Yard, Duke of York Street, London, SW1Y 6JT (01 214 8292). A personal search may be made at this address or the enquiry

can be dealt with by letter. A fee of £1.25 per file is charged but the search fee is waived if copies of documents are taken. The normal charge for copy documents is £0.20 per page.

23.6 SEARCH SUMMARY

	Building societies and friendly societies	*Charities*	*Trade unions*
Application	Personal search only	By letter or personal search	By letter or personal search
Plan	–	–	
Fee	£2.50 per file	No fee	£1.25 per file
Address	Registrar of Friendly Societies 15 Great Marlborough Street London W1	Charity Commissioners 14 Ryder Street London SW1	Certification Office Ormond Yard Duke of York Street London SW1
Special points	–	–	–
Area affected	–	–	–

Chapter 24

Bankruptcy

24.1 BANKRUPTCY PETITIONS
24.1.1 County court
A bankruptcy petition may be presented in the county court in whose jurisdiction the debtor carries on business or lives. The register of petitions is open to public inspection by making either a personal search or by sending a letter to the appropriate county court specifying the full name of the debtor. A fee of £0.50 is charged for each name searched.

24.1.2 High Court
The bankruptcy department of the High Court (Room 901 Thomas More Building, Royal Courts of Justice, Strand, London, WC2) maintains a register of bankruptcy petitions presented against debtors who carry on business or live within the Greater London area. The register is open to public inspection by personal search only on payment of a fee of £1.10 for each name against which a search is made.

24.2 RECEIVING ORDERS
A receiving order made by a county court will be registered in that court and will be revealed by making a search of the register as outlined in para 24.1.1, above.

A central register of all receiving orders made in England and Wales is maintained by the bankruptcy department of the High Court (address in para 24.1.2, above). A personal search of this register may be made on payment of a fee of £1.10 for each name against which a search is made.

24.3 SEARCH IN THE CENTRAL LAND CHARGES REGISTER
A bankruptcy petition is automatically registered as a pending action under the Land Charges Act 1972 in the Central Land Charges Department, Burrington Way, Plymouth, PL5 3LP (0752 779831) whether or not the debtor is known to own any land. A receiving order in bankruptcy is similarly registered as a writ or order. These entries will be revealed by making a Central Land Charges search on form

K16 against the name of the debtor. The fee is £0.50 for each name searched.

24.3.1 This search is more fully discussed in ch 34, below.

24.3.2 Payment of fees see para 6.7, above.

24.4 REGISTERED LAND

Where a bankruptcy petition is presented against the proprietor of registered land the Chief Land Registrar will enter a creditor's notice on the register of the title(s) affected. A bankruptcy inhibition will be placed on any affected title on the making of a receiving order. These entries would be revealed by making a search against the title, but such a search may generally only be made with the authority of the registered proprietor himself (see ch 35, below). A search made at the Central Land Charges Department on form K16 will reveal bankruptcy entries against the proprietor of registered land since the land charges entries are made irrespective of the ownership of land.

24.5 SEARCH SUMMARY

Application	K16
Plan	–
Fee	£0.50 per name
Address	Central Land Charges Department Burrington Way Plymouth PL5 3LP
Special points	The K16 search is the most commonly made search for bankruptcy entries but others also exist, see text for details
Area affected	

Chapter 25

Boundaries

25.1 No formal search procedure exists to ascertain the position of boundaries but the burden of discovering their identity and ownership will usually lie with the purchaser since both Law Society Condition 13 and National Condition 13 relieve the vendor of his obligation to define precisely their route or to prove title to their ownership. Such a contractual condition is necessary in order to protect the vendor because the exact delineation of the boundaries of his land may not be evident from the title deeds or the register of title. It is frequently the case that title deeds show general boundaries only and thus reference may need to be made to the common law general boundaries rules in order to clarify the position.

25.2 COMMON LAW REBUTTABLE PRESUMPTIONS RELATING TO BOUNDARIES

25.2.1 The ad medium filum rule
A person who owns land abutting on a private or public highway is presumed to own the soil or sub-soil respectively of the highway up to the middle line. The surface of a public highway is vested in the highway authority.

25.2.2 The hedge and ditch rule
Where two properties are separated by a hedge and an artificial ditch, the boundary line is presumed to lie on the far side of the ditch from the hedge.

25.2.3 Foreshore
In the absence of contrary evidence the boundary of land adjoining the sea lies at the top of the foreshore. The foreshore is that part of the shore lying between the ordinary high and lower water marks. Land below the medium line of the foreshore belongs to the Crown. Where the sea advances or recedes so that the high water mark is changed, the boundary of land adjacent to the sea-shore will also change.

N.B. Counterpart leases of the foreshore in Durham are registered at the Public Record Office (see para 18.6, above).

25.2.4 Non-tidal rivers and streams

The *ad medium filum* rule applies so that the owners of the properties on either bank of the river or stream own the bed up to the middle of the river or stream. The owner of the river bed is also presumed to own the right to fish in the stream, but this presumption may be rebutted and it is common to find that fishing rights have been alienated.

25.2.5 Tidal rivers and sea inlets

The bed and foreshore of a tidal river or sea inlet is prima facie vested in the Crown subject to the public's rights of navigation and fishing. The Crown's right extends to the point in the river where the tide ebbs and flows, beyond which point the *ad medium filum* rule applies.

25.2.6 Lakes

Where a lake is entirely within the boundaries of one piece of land, the bed of the lake belongs to the owner of the surrounding land. There is no clear authority or presumption to state where the boundary lies when the lake is bounded by properties in different ownership, but possibly the *ad medium filum* rule applies.

25.2.7 Buildings divided horizontally and vertically

There is no presumption to determine the horizontal boundary between the floors of a building, although it is commonly accepted that the structures dividing flats and maisonettes are party structures and should be maintained as such. The conveyance or lease of a ground floor or basement will not impliedly include the sub-soil. The conveyance or lease of a building divided horizontally or vertically will include the external walls enclosing the property conveyed or demised.[1] These matters apart, there is great uncertainty at common law over the ownership of dividing strata in buildings and it is essential that the parcels clause of the conveyance or lease makes express provision for their ownership and maintenance. Normally the beams and floorboards of a floor should belong to the owner of an upper flat or unit and the ceiling should belong to the owner of the lower flat or unit.

25.2.8 Trees

A tree belongs to the owner on whose land it was planted even if its trunk, roots or branches extend into a neighbouring property. Where it cannot be established who planted the tree, eg because the trunk traverses the boundary of the land, ownership may be inferred from the circumstances. Regular lopping or topping by one person is indicative of ownership by that person.

25.3 ORDNANCE SURVEY MAPS
25.3.1 The practice of the ordnance survey is to show the centre line

of a boundary feature as the boundary. Thus the boundary line shown on the map gives a good general indication of the line of the boundary but may not be of assistance if it is required to define the boundary with precision. For example, where the boundary of land is marked by a hedge and artificial ditch, the ordnance survey map will show the boundary as running along the centre line of the hedge which is at variance with the common law hedge and ditch rule (para 25.2.2, above). Unless there is evidence to the contrary, eg where the conveyance is made by reference to an ordnance survey map, the common law will prevail over the boundary shown on the ordnance survey map.

25.3.2 In some cases it may be necessary to obtain an old plan or map showing the property in order to establish the situation of the boundaries. Copies of all editions of the ordnance survey maps (dating from 1870) are kept at the British Library, who will supply copies on request. Unless the map is to be used in pending court proceedings or is over 50 years old, copyright permission for the reproduction of the plan must be obtained from ordnance survey before applying to the British Library for a copy. Details of the British Library Service and the address of the copyright branch of ordnance survey are contained in para 11.7, above.

25.3.3 There are primarily two series of ordnance survey maps, the County Series, based on an original survey dated from 1870, and the National Grid Series dating from 1945. Both series are published in various scales ranging from 1:1250 to 1:1250 000.

25.3.4 Ordnance survey maps are not generally admissible in evidence as proof of private boundaries unless a plan with the title deeds has been based on an extract from such a map.

25.3.5 Further reading

(a) J.B. Harley *Maps for the Local Historian: a Guide to the British Sources* (1972, National Council of Social Service for the Standing Conference for Local History);

(b) J.B. Harley and C.W. Phillips *The Historian's Guide to Ordnance Survey Maps* (1965, National Council of Social Service for the Standing Conference for Local History).

25.3.5.1 Both the above books contain details of the series of published ordnance survey maps and may be helpful in deciding which particular edition of a map would be relevant to the determination of a boundary query.

25.4 REGISTERED LAND

25.4.1 It is possible to apply to the Chief Land Registrar under the Land Registration Rules 1925, r 276 to have the position of the boundaries of registered land fixed, but this is a time consuming and expensive procedure which is rarely used. Of the 8 million titles now registered less than 100 are registered with fixed boundaries, the remainder being registered with general boundaries only under the Land Registration Rules 1925, r 278.

Where the boundaries to land are fixed this is noted on the property register of the title.

25.4.2   The Land Registration Rules 1925, r 278 provides as follows:

> (1) Except in cases in which it is noted in the Property Register that the boundaries have been fixed, the filed plan or General Map should be deemed to indicate the general boundaries only.
>
> (2) In such cases the exact line of the boundary will be left undetermined as, for instance, whether it includes a hedge or wall and ditch, or runs along the centre of a wall or fence, or its inner or outer face, or how far it runs within or beyond it; or whether or not the land registered includes the whole or any portion of an adjoining road or stream.
>
> (3) When a general boundary only is desired to be entered in the register, notice to the owners of the adjoining lands need not be given.
>
> (4) This rule shall apply notwithstanding that a part or the whole of a ditch, wall, fence, road, stream, or other boundary is expressly included in or excluded from the title or that it forms the whole of the land comprised in the title.

25.4.3   The common law presumptions relating to boundaries (para 25.2, above) therefore generally apply also to registered land.

25.4.4   Land Registry filed plans are based on ordnance survey maps which may not themselves show the true boundaries of the land (see para 25.3, above). Common law presumptions will prevail over the filed plan unless there is evidence to the contrary.

25.4.5   If there is an appreciable discrepancy between the true boundaries and those shown on the filed plan a claim for compensation under the Land Registration Act 1925, s 83 would lie if the registered proprietor had suffered loss as a result of the discrepancy.

25.4.6   Ownership of boundaries

As far as the ownership of boundaries is concerned, the register can be relied on to show the true position. Provided that provisions relating to ownership were clearly set out in the documentation involving first registration, this will be recorded on the register of the title and the ownership of a boundary shown by a 'T' mark on the filed plan.

25.4.7   Registered titles do not show ownership of the sub-soil to the centre of a road even where there has been an express conveyance including these rights.

25.4.8   Where registered land adjoins the seashore, rights over the foreshore may be shown on the property register of the title.

25.4.9   The Law Commission Report on Property Law: Registered Land (Law Com No 125 (1983)) has recommended the retention of the general boundaries rule.

25.5 LOOKING FOR EVIDENCE OF BOUNDARIES
Since no formal search procedure exists, evidence of the true position
and ownership of boundaries can generally only be established by a
certain amount of detective work coupled with common sense. The
following sub-paragraphs contain a non-exhaustive check list of the
type of enquiry which it may be relevant to undertake when seeking
evidence of the ownership and true position of boundaries.

(a) An on-site inspection of the property by the client, or preferably
by the solicitor or surveyor;

(b) application of the common law presumptions (para 25.2, above).

(c) preliminary enquiries of the vendor in the course of the purchase
of the land;

(d) an inspection of pre-root title deeds may yield information relating to the ownership and position of boundaries which is not
revealed by the modern deeds. For this reason the pre-registration
deeds to registered land should be preserved;

(e) inspection of old ordnance survey maps (para. 25.3, above);

(f) a public index map search at HM Land Registry (see ch 6,
above). In the case of unregistered land a plan of the land to be
searched must be submitted with the search application except that
the submission of a plan is not necessary within areas of compulsory
registration provided the property can be clearly identified by its
postal address. However, where evidence of boundaries is sought it
is recommended that a plan should always be submitted with the
search application so that any discrepancy between the submitted
plan and the Land Registry ordnance map will be revealed. The
Land Registry will supply a copy of its own plan on request (fee
£0.50) which will only show general boundaries but which may
assist in establishing the line of the boundary;

(g) where the boundary of land is marked by a fence it is usual for
the fencing posts to be placed on that side of the fence which enjoys
both the right of ownership and the burden of maintenance of the
boundary. There is, however, no legal presumption in support of this
theory;

(h) acts of ownership, eg maintenance of a fence or cutting of a
hedge by one party may be admissible in evidence in support of
ownership of the boundary but may be rebutted where the boundary
feature in dispute is governed by a common law presumption.[2]

25.6 PLANS
25.6.1 If the description of the property in the contract affords a
sufficient and satisfactory identification of the land without a plan the
purchaser cannot insist on having the property conveyed by reference
to a plan.[3]
25.6.2 A plan should be used where the boundaries of the land are

not self evident on inspection of the property and is highly desirable on the sale of part only of the vendor's title. A sale of part only of a registered title must generally be transferred by reference to a plan.[4]
25.6.3 Where the property is described by reference to a plan and the plan is referred to as being 'for identification purposes only', the verbal description in the deed will prevail over the plan in the event of a conflict between the plan and the verbal description. A plan so described need not be drawn to scale but even if it is drawn to scale it does little to assist in the proper identification of the property. Where the verbal description in the deed does not refer to a plan, but a plan is nevertheless annexed to the deed, the plan may still be referred to in order to resolve ambiguities. Where the verbal description in the deed refers to the property as being 'more particularly delineated on the plan' the plan will prevail over the verbal description in the event of conflict. Such a plan must be accurately drawn to scale, and the scale must be of sufficient magnitude to enable the property to be clearly identified. A scale of 1:1250 is commonly used for plans but this scale is not sufficiently large to enable detailed boundaries to be identified. Particularly in relation to estate conveyancing or on the sale of part of a property a larger scale (eg 1:500) should be used. In the case of *Scarfe v Adams*[5] a plan of the scale of 1:2500 was used in connection with the conveyance of part of a house. The court found it impossible to ascertain the boundaries of the properties from the plan and admitted extrinsic evidence comprising an architect's plan in order to ascertain the intentions of the parties. O'Connor LJ in his judgment in that case made the following statement pertaining to the use of plans 'If a house is to be divided and a plan is to form part of the material describing the boundary, it is essential that there should be a large scale plan of the house showing the rooms and the walls. That is particularly so when there is a reference in the deed to a party wall'.

Scale plans may be based either on ordnance survey maps or on architects' drawings. Solicitors may obtain licences to copy ordnance survey maps on payment of annual fee.[6] Alternatively in the case of registered land the plan may be based on the filed Land Registry plan, subject to the scale being appropriate for the purpose for which the plan is being used. The copyright in Land Registry plans is vested in the Crown, thus a licence from the Director General of the Ordnance Survey is required if such a plan is to be used.

Where a conveyance of land leads to first registration of the title it is helpful if the plan used on the conveyance co-ordinates with the filed plans used by the Land Registry. Provided the scale is appropriate the plan obtained from a search of the public index map may be used for this purpose.

25.6.4 Details to be shown on plans

Plans should indicate the scale to which they are drawn. This may be shown in imperial or metric measurements (but not a mixture of the two), although metric measurements are preferred by HM Land Registry. The dimensions of the land and an indication of the compass points should also be included.

The Land Registry adheres to a code of colour reference for use on filed plans and in view of the continuing extension of the areas of compulsory registration of title it may be sensible to follow the Land Registry's colour coding system even when dealing with land that is not presently within a compulsory registration area. The Land Registry's code is as follows:

Red edging is used to show the extent of the land within the title. Green edging indicates land that was at one time within the title but which has been removed. Green tinting shows excluded islands of land within the land edged red, that is, parcels of land which are physically surrounded by land within the title, but which do not form part of it. Brown tinting or hatching indicates the benefit of a right of way, while blue tinting or hatching is used to show the part of a registered title which is the subject of a right of way.

If additional colour references are needed for plans the Registry suggest the following (provided such colours have not already been utilised):

Tinting in pink, yellow and mauve; edging in blue, yellow or mauve; hatching in any colour except red, black and green; and numbering or lettering small self-contained areas.

25.6.5 Signature of plans

The Law Society recommends that a plan should bear a memorandum signed by the parties who have executed the conveyance, clearly identifying the document to which the plan is annexed.[7] In registered land transactions the plan must be signed by the transferor and by or on behalf of the transferee.[8]

25.6.6 A plan annexed to a deed will normally only indicate the extent of the property at ground level. By the principle *usque ad caelum et usque ad inferos* the owner of land is presumed to own the space above ground level and the soil below. Therefore a ground level plan may sometimes govern the ownership of overhanging features (eg eaves) or underlying features.[9]

25.7 Further reading

(a) J.F. Garner *Rights of Way* (4th edn 1982, Oyez);
(b) V. Powell-Smith *The Law of Boundaries and Fences* (1967, Butterworths).

25.8 SEARCH SUMMARY

Application	No formal search procedure – see para 25.5, above
Plan	–
Fee	–
Address	–
Special points	–
Area affected	Any land where boundaries are unclear

1 *Sturge v Hackett* [1962] 3 All ER 166, [1962] 1 WLR 1257, CA.
2 *Henniker v Howard* (1904) 90 LT 157.
3 *Re Sharman''s Contract* [1936] Ch 755, [1936] 2 All ER 1547.
4 Land Registration Rules 1925, r 98.
5 [1981] 1 All ER 843, CA. See also *Mayer v Hurr* (1983) Times, 23 April.
6 See (1971) 68 LS Gaz 405.
7 LS Digest, Vol 1, p 157.
8 Land Registration Rules 1925, rr 79 and 113.
9 But see *Truckell v Stock* [1957] 1 All ER 74, [1957] 1 WLR 161, CA.

Chapter 26

Miscellaneous registers and records

26.1 BIRTH, MARRIAGE AND DEATH CERTIFICATES
Copies of these certificates may be obtained either by post or by making a personal search at St Catherines House, 10 Kingsway, London, WC2 (01 242 0262). Where a request for a copy certificate is submitted by post the fullest details available should be specified giving at least the date and place of the event and the full name(s) of the parties involved. A certificate sent by post costs £10. The fee for a certificate obtained after a personal search is £5.

26.2 ADOPTION CERTIFICATES
Copies of certificates showing the date and court of adoption, the name of the child as adopted and the full names and addresses of the adoptive parents may be obtained from St Catherines House, 10 Kingsway, London, WC2. The procedure for obtaining such certificates and the fees are the same as those contained in para 26.1, above.

26.3 WILLS
Copies of wills of deceased persons may be obtained by writing to the Record Keeper, Correspondence Department, PRFD, Somerset House, Strand, London, WC2R 1LP (01 405 7641). The full name of the deceased, date of death and the last known address of the deceased must be stated in the letter. A handling fee of £1.00 is charged and a fee of £0.24 per page of the will is payable for copies. Where a request is submitted by post a delay of up to one month in receiving the copy may be experienced. A personal search (free of charge) may be made at Somerset House. A fee of £0.25 is charged if the will is read in situ. Copies may be ordered (delay four days) at the fee of £0.25 per page.

26.4 PARISH RECORDS
It may be necessary to consult parish records for evidence of births, marriages and deaths, or in some cases for confirmation of the existence of corn rent annuities or chancel repair liability (see chs 16 and 17, above).

The incumbent of the parish should be contacted to request an inspection of the records. If the incumbent does not have the appropriate records an application can be made to the county records office or the diocesan records office for the area.

26.5 BILLS OF SALE

Bills of Sale must be registered at the Central Office of the Supreme Court (Room 81, Royal Courts of Justice, Strand, London, WC2 (01 405 7641)). A personal search of the records may be made (fee £0.05 for each period of five years which is searched) and copies of bills obtained at the cost of £0.25 per page. There is no procedure for postal searches, but an official search may be requisitioned by attending personally at Room 81 and requesting a court official to make the search. The official search costs £2.00.

26.6 DEEDS OF ARRANGEMENT

Most deeds of arrangement need to be registered with the Department of Trade, Gavrelle House, 2–14 Bunhill Row, London, EC1 (01 606 4071) within seven days of their execution. Failure to register renders them void. If the arrangement affects land it should also be registered at the Central Land Charges Registry (unregistered land) or protected as a caution at HM Land Registry (registered land). Failure to make the appropriate registration against the land will render the deed void against a purchaser.

A search may be made for deeds of arrangement which have been registered with the Department of Trade at the above address. The search, which must specify the full name of the debtor, may be made by post or in person. A fee of £1.10 is charged for each name searched. A charge is also made for copies of deeds.

26.7 CONSUMER CREDIT

Any person or organisation who in the course of business extends credit, arranges credit for another or negotiates for the settlement of a debt must obtain a licence from the Director General of Fair Trading. When granted a licence lasts for ten years and can be renewed on expiry but is not transferable, eg on the take-over of a business or company. The absence of a licence will render any subsequent credit contract unenforceable except with leave of the Director General of Fair Trading. Mortgages which are taken out concurrently with the purchase of the land secured by the charge, or which exceed £15,000, or which are granted by building societies, insurance companies or other lenders specified by statutory instrument as being exempted from the Act are not affected by the provisions of the Consumer Credit Act 1974. The Act does apply to land mortgages which do not fall into one of the above categories and will mainly be of relevance in relation to second and subsequent mortgages. Where the Act does apply it may be necessary to check whether the lender (and mortgage broker where relevant) hold a current licence and further that the notice procedures under s 58 of the Act have been followed. Failure to comply with s 58 of the Act renders the agreement unenforceable without a court order. A search to check the existence and validity of a licence may be made in person or by post at the Consumer Credit Public Register, Government Buildings, Bromyard Avenue, Acton, London, W3 7BB (01 743 5566 ext 3086). The search fee is £1.00. Copies of the licence may be obtained at the cost of £0.30 per sheet on a personal search. Where a postal search is made a minimum charge of £1.50 is made for copies.

26.8   HIRE-PURCHASE AND CREDIT AGREEMENTS

26.8.1   Where a contract for the sale of land includes fittings, enquiries should be made of the vendor to confirm that any subsisting hire-purchase or credit agreement relating to the fittings will be discharged on or before completion. A warranty of freedom from incumbrances is contained in National Condition 4 but is absent from the Law Society Conditions of Sale.

26.8.2   No central register of credit agreements exists and it is not generally possible for a member of the public to check the existence of a subsisting credit agreement over chattels.

26.8.3   HP Information PLC, Greencoat House, Francis Street, London, SW1 (01 828 0851) maintain a voluntary register of hire-purchase and related agreements relating to major consumer purchases (mainly vehicles) financed through finance companies, but access to this register is normally only available on subscription, although the company will assist by providing information to solicitors who are acting for clients involved in proceedings where the title to goods is disputed.

26.8.4   Infolink (United Association for the Protection of Trade, Ltd, 89 London Road, Croydon, Surrey, CR9 2SY (general enquiries 01 686 5644)) keep a register of credit agreements voluntarily registered with them by their members. They also provide a search service by post, telephone, telex or remote computer terminal for their members on payment of a fee. Membership (£25 per annum) is not available to private individuals but is open to traders and to solicitors. A search will reveal details of existing credit agreements, default, county court judgments and insolvency registered against either individuals or corporate bodies. In the case of companies details of the registered office, borrowing, and consumer credit licence number may also be registered. Some information relating to creditworthiness may be available from this source, which is not available from inspection of public records.

Although the search facility is not totally comprehensive because, eg the registration of credit agreements is a voluntary step taken by the creditor, the instantaneous methods of search provided by this company make this search worthy of consideration as an alternative to searching in the official register for such items as the registered office of a company, a consumer credit licence or county court judgment.

26.9 JUDGMENT DEBTS

The Registry of County Court Judgments, 99–101 Red Cross Way, Borough, London, SE1 1EE (01 407 1044) maintains records of all county court judgments which exceed £10. A personal search of the register (fee £1.00) may be made or a request for a search, specifying the full name of the person against whom the search is to be made may be submitted by post. Where a postal search is made a fee of £2 per name is charged for the first five years of records searched. If it is necessary to search for a period of more than five years the fee is £4 per name.

No current register of High Court judgments exists.

26.10 PATENTS

A search for details of an existing patent may be made free of charge at the Science Reference Library, 25 Southampton Buildings, London, WC2A 1AN (01 405 8721) or at the patents section of public libraries in major provincial cities throughout the British Isles. The Patent Office (at the above address) does not conduct searches on behalf of applicants but it is possible to obtain information from this office (by personal inspection or by post) relating to the name of the present proprietor of a particular patent. The classification of patents is both complex and highly technical and a personal search made by a person who is unfamiliar with the classification system is likely to be time-consuming and possibly inconclusive. A list of professional search agents is available for consultation in the Science Reference Library. A list of patent agents is available from the Chartered Institute of Patent Agents, Staple Inn Buildings, London, WC1V 7P2. The leaflet *Patents, a source of technical information* published free of charge by the Patent Office contains an outline of the classification system and search procedure.

The Official Journal (Patents) which is published weekly contains details of all patents and applications for patents published in a given week. The journal is available from the sales counter of the Patent Office or by post from Sales Branch, The Patent Office, Orpington, Kent BR5 3RD.

26.11 TRADE MARKS

26.11.1 Any person may make a personal search of the Trade Marks Index at the Patent Office, 25 Southampton Buildings, London, WC2 (01 405 8721). A fee of £0.85 is charged for each period of 15 minutes spent in the search room. A search for conflicting marks may also be made on application to the Registrar on form TM29 (not illustrated in the text). An application on form TM29 must be accompanied by two representations of the mark to be searched each mounted on A4 size paper and the fee of £8.00. The Manchester branch office of the Patent Office at Baskerville House, Browncross Street, New Bailey Street, Salford, M3 5FU has a duplicate index showing textile marks only. Search facilities are also available at this office.

The Index comprises a classified index of devices, and alphabetical indexes of words occurring as trade marks or parts of trade marks arranged according to their beginnings and endings. The Index includes pending applications as well as those marks already protected by registration.

26.11.2 The leaflet entitled *Applying for a Trade Mark*, obtainable free from the Patent Office, contains a summary of the main provisions of the Trade Marks Act 1938 together with the procedure applicable for registering a trade mark and the search procedure outlined above.

26.12 REGISTERED DESIGNS

26.12.1 The protection of new industrial designs is provided for by registration under the Registered Designs Acts 1949–1961. Additionally such designs may enjoy copyright protection (without registration) under the Copyright Act 1956 as amended by the Design Copyright Act 1965.

26.12.2 Particulars relating to registered designs are kept at the Designs Registry, 11th Floor, State House, High Holborn, London, WC1R 4TP, enquiries to Room 1124A (01 405 8721). These particulars include the dates of applications for registration, names and addresses of proprietors, notices of licences and assignments and other documents affecting proprietorship, the nature of articles for which the designs are registered and notices of extensions of the original five-year period of protection. Illustrations of designs are not included. A register of designs for textile articles only, which contains duplicates of the entries kept at the London registry, is kept at the Manchester branch of the registry, Baskerville House, Browncross Street, New Bailey Street, Salford, M3 5FU.

26.12.3 How to make a search

A personal search of entries in the Register of Designs may be made on payment of a fee of £1.00.

Registered designs themselves are available for inspection after a certain time limit has elapsed since their registration. The fee for inspection is £1.00 per design.

Where a personal search of the Register is made or a postal search on form 20 (for which the fee is £4.00) it is necessary to know the design registration number of the item. This information may be obtained by searching the card index of proprietors of registered designs which is held in the Science Reference Library, 25 Southampton Buildings, London, WC2A 1AW.

Where the design registration number is not known, a search application may be submitted on form 21 for which the fee is £17.00.

Copies of registered documents may be obtained on payment of a fee of £0.11 per page.

26.12.4 A weekly list of new designs registered (except textile articles) is published in *The Official Journal (Patents)* (see para 26.10, above).

26.12.5 The search application forms referred to above are not illustrated in the text, but are available from the Designs Registry. The leaflet *Protection of Industrial Designs* obtainable free of charge from the Designs Registry contains details of the registration and assignment of designs and of the search procedure.

26.13 COPYRIGHT

26.13.1 Stationers' Hall Registry

The Stationers' Company has since 1924 maintained a register of books and fine arts voluntarily registered by copyright owners for purposes of record. The register also includes maps, charts, music, circulars, patterns, photographs and engravings.

A search of the register, in order to check the existence of copyright, may be made by applying by letter to The Registrar, Stationers' Hall, Ludgate Hill, London, EC4M 7DD (01 248 9279). As much information as possible about the item to be searched should be included in the letter. A fee of £5.00 is charged for a search. A copy of an entry in the register may be obtained on payment of a further fee of £7.00. No personal search facilities exist.

Registration with the Stationers' Company is voluntary, thus a negative result of the search should not be regarded as conclusive evidence of lack of copyright protection.

26.13.2 The British Library

The British Library, as the principal copyright library, enjoys the right of deposit of all printed material, including maps, published in the United Kingdom. It is therefore possible by making a personal search to check whether copyright in a printed work exists. It is also possible to obtain from the British Library a photographic, photostat or microfiche copy of any page(s) of a book, map, manuscript or music which has been deposited there. Standard charges are made for copies, the amount of which depends on the size and quality of the reproduction. Applications for copies may be made in person or by post (British Library, Great Russell Street, London, WC1B 3DG (01 636 1544)). The written permission of the copyright owner is normally required before a copy can be made of any work which was first published or whose author was living within the last 50 years. The onus of tracing the copyright owner rests with the applicant. However, a single copy of the following may be supplied without prior copyright permission for the purposes of research or private study:

(a) a single article from a single issue of a periodical publication;

(b) an extract from non-periodical work (except music, maps and manuscripts) not exceeding (in general) 4,000 words.

26.14 LICENSED DEALERS IN SECURITIES

The names and addresses of the holders of principals' licences to deal in securities are published annually by HM Stationery Office (price £6.00).

Part V

Less usual searches applicable to specific geographical areas

Chapter 27

Introduction to Part V

27.1 This section deals with a number of searches the relevance of which is confined to particular geographical areas of England and Wales and which therefore are only of concern when dealing with properties in those areas.

If there is doubt whether a particular search dealt with in this section would be required, advice may be sought from a surveyor practising in the locality or from the land charges department of the local district council.

27.2 The tables in Appendices 2 and 3, below, show the approximate delineation of the areas affected by these searches.

27.2.1 Although every attempt has been made to locate all the searches which are peculiar to certain areas of the country, the searches contained in this section of the book should not be regarded as a comprehensive list of all possible searches.

27.3 Specific locality searches dealt with in other chapters

27.3.1 Epping Forest
Register of commons: see para 9.9.3, above.

27.3.2 The New Forest
Register of forest rights: see para 9.9.4, above.

27.3.3 The Forest of Dean
Special procedure for enquiries relating to rights of common: see para 9.9.2, above.

There are also some coal and iron workings in this area in relation to which enquiries may be made of the local area office of the Forestry Commission.

27.3.4 Newcastle on Tyne
Underground railway enquiries: see para 12.2.3, above.

27.3.5 Dispositions by the Duchies of Lancaster and Cornwall
Deeds void unless enrolled: see para 18.5, above. Special central land charges search procedure: see para 34.6, below.

27.3.6   East Anglia
Smaller waterways in control of local drainage boards: see para 21.7, above.

27.4   OIL
Onshore oil exploration is a relatively new venture in the United Kingdom. Where proposals to extract oil from land are evidenced by a planning application or consent, these will be revealed in the answers to the standard from of additional enquiries of the local authority. There is no central register of current or proposed sites for oil exploration. The only areas currently affected by this problem are Dorset and parts of Sussex, Kent and Surrey where, if it is suspected that oil exploration is or may be taking place in the future an inspection of the site is advisable and consideration should be given to raising enquiries with British National Oil Corporation (01 235 8020) or with the Department of Energy.

27.5   SAND AND GRAVEL
Sand and gravel extraction is localised but widespread throughout England and Wales. The presence of a working pit in the locality of the property will be evident from an inspection of the property. Settlement and subsidence of land in the vicinity of present workings is not normally a major problem since these workings are comparatively shallow. The presence of workable deposits beneath the land will normally be revealed in response to additional enquiries of the local authority. A property which is built over a disused and filled-in pit may suffer from subsidence. The fact that the property is built on the site of a filled-in pit may be revealed by the answers to a local search since the act of in-filling will have required planning permission. Local planning authorities now lay down very stringent requirements for the construction of buildings on the site of filled-in pits thus subsidence problems are likely to be less acute with a recently built property than with an older building. No central register of working pits or of filled-in sites exists but the building inspector of the appropriate local authority may have details of all such sites within his area.

If it is suspected that a property has been built on the site of an in-filled pit the client should be advised to commission a full structural survey of the property, and specific additional preliminary enquiries should be raised with the vendor.

A survey will afford some protection for the client since an action may lie against the surveyor in negligence. If it were established that subsidence had occurred owing to the construction of inadequate foundations an action might also lie against the vendor/builder under the Defective Premises Act 1972 or against the local planning authority under the principle established in *Dutton v Bognor Regis UDC*[1] (approved by the House of Lords in *Anns v Merton London Borough Council*[2].

27.6 MINERAL CONSULTATION AREAS

A number of county councils have designated land which is rich in mineral deposits as 'mineral consultation areas'. When an area is so designated this will be revealed in response to the standard additional enquiries of the local authority. In such a case the authority has undertaken to consult with the local mineral extraction industries before granting planning permission to develop the land. Planning permission will generally be refused if the proposed development would impede the future extraction of the minerals.

In other areas the county council maintains a minerals local plan, inspection of which would reveal whether an area of land contained unexploited minerals beneath the surface. In this situation no formal consultation exists between the authority and the local mineral industries when a planning application is submitted.

27.7 QUARRIES

The presence of an existing or disused quarry underneath or in the vicinity of the land to be purchased should be revealed in response to the standard form of additional enquiries of the local authority. In some parts of the country land in the vicinity of a quarry may be designated as a mineral consultation area which may adversely affect an application for planning permission to develop the land. It may be possible to make further enquiries of the quarry company itself relating to its future proposals to work the land or to subsidence but no formal search procedure exists. A full structural survey should be recommended where property has been built on the site of a filled-in quarry.

---

1   [1972] 1 QB 373, [1972] 1 All ER 462, CA.
2   [1978] AC 728, [1977] 2 All ER 492, HL.

Chapter 28

Coal mining

28.1 Most coal and coal mines are owned by the National Coal Board. However, the surface of the land may be in private ownership in which case the surface owner may have common law rights of support for his land and a right to compensation for damage caused by subsidence. In certain cases the National Coal Board has the right to withdraw support from the surface of the land to such an extent as is necessary to enable them to work the coal. Before withdrawing support the Board are required to give notice to this effect in the *London Gazette*. If it is desired to erect a building on land in respect of which the Board has given notice withdrawing rights of support, plans of the proposed buildings must be submitted to the Board who can request special work to be done to the foundations.

The present law relating to compensation for subsidence is complex and in some cases payment is at the discretion of the Board and not as of right.

28.2 HOW TO MAKE THE SEARCH
A search should be made before exchange of contracts when buying property which is situated in a traditional coal mining area. Some mining tunnels extend for a considerable distance underneath the land surrounding a mine. This search is therefore of relevance to all properties within a mining area and not just to those properties within the immediate vicinity of the mine. The search is made by letter enclosing an ordnance survey plan of the property, addressed to the appropriate area surveyor of the National Coal Board.

A fee of £13 is charged for searches made in respect of dwellings. Part of the fee may be refunded if the property is discovered to be outside the mining area. Where the search is made in relation to larger parcels of land the fee is assessed by the Board.

28.3 NATURE OF ENQUIRIES
Enquiries should be directed to such of the following information as is thought to be relevant to the property:
  (a) does the property lie within an area affected by
   (i) old mine workings;
   (ii) current mine workings;

(iii) future proposals for workings?
If the answer is 'yes' please supply details of the workings or proposed workings;
(b) is the property liable to subsidence?;
(c) has any claim been made relating to subsidence damage? If so please supply details;
(d) has any notice been published withdrawing rights of support for the land? If so please supply details;
(e) is the property liable to flooding caused by mining subsidence? If so please supply details;
(f) is there any old shaft within the vicinity of the property? If so please supply details including the condition of the shaft;
(g) is the property near or within the vicinity of:
 (i) any disused tip;
 (ii) any current tip;
(iii) the site of a proposed tip?
If the answer is yes, please supply details;
(h) does the National Coal Board claim any rights of way or other surface rights over the property? If so please supply details;
(i) is the property affected by:
 (i) past opencast workings;
 (ii) present opencast workings;
(iii) proposals for future opencast workings?
If so please supply details.

28.4   Addresses of National Coal Board area offices
(In the case of doubt the National Coal Board London Survey Department (Mining Branch) (01 235 2020) will confirm which area office should be contacted.)

Barnsley	Grimethorpe Barnsley South Yorkshire S72 7AB (0226 710000)
Doncaster	St Georges Thorne Road Doncaster South Yorkshire DN1 2JS (0302 66733)
Kent	1–3 Waterloo Crescent Dover Kent (0304 201401)

North Derbyshire	Bolsover Near Chesterfield Derbyshire S44 6AA (0246 822231)
North	Coal House Team Valley Gateshead Tyne and Wear NE11 0JD (0632 878822)
North Nottinghamshire	Edwinstowe Mansfield Notts NG21 9PR (0623 822481)
North Yorkshire	PO Box 13 Allerton Bywater Castleford North Yorkshire WF10 2AL (0977 5565)
South Midlands	Coleorton Hall Coleorton Leicester LE6 4SA (05304 3131)
South Nottinghamshire	Bestwood Nottingham NG6 8UE (0602 273711)
South Yorkshire	Wath-upon-Dearne Rotherham South Yorkshire S63 7EW (0709 873331)
Western	Staffordshire House Berry Hill Road Stoke-on-Trent Staffs ST4 2NH (0782 48201)

South Wales

Coal House
Ty-Glas Avenue
Llanishen
Cardiff
CF4 5YS
(0222 753232)

Opencast Executive

200 Lichfield Lane
Berry Hill
Mansfield
Notts
NG18 4RG
(0623 22681)

28.5 The Board's reply is in the form of a report. Technical information relating to ground movement associated with current or future workings is not revealed by the search but can be obtained on payment of an additional fee.

28.5.1 Where there is likelihood of subsidence it may be advisable to ask a mining surveyor to report on the property.

28.5.2 The report is not conclusive and contains a disclaimer of liability.

28.5.3 Where opencast mining affects the land or its neighbourhood further enquiries may need to be made with the opencast coal executive (address in para 28.4, above).

28.6 NEW COALFIELDS

Apart from the established coal mining areas new mines have recently gone into production in the Vale of York and are likely to do so in the near future at Belvoir in Leicestershire. Other areas which may be affected in future include land in Oxfordshire and Warwickshire. As and when these new pits come into production coal mining searches will be relevant to properties in these areas.

The rights to compensation for subsidence in these new areas may differ slightly from those applicable to established mining areas, since in many cases the amount of compensation will be assessed by reference to the withdrawal of common law rights of support and will not be limited by the provisions of the Coal Mining (Subsidence) Acts 1950 and 1957. It is anticipated that a bill which will simplify and consolidate the compensation legislation will be introduced into Parliament in the near future.

28.7 MINING WITHIN THE FOREST OF DEAN

Coal and iron mining have for centuries been carried on within the Forest of Dean, although the extent of current workings is very small. In addition to making enquiries of the National Coal Board, an enquiry relating to land in this area should also be sent to the Deputy Gaveller,

Forestry Commission, Crown Office, Coleford, Gloucestershire (0594 33057).

28.8 SEARCH SUMMARY

Application	By letter
Plan	Ordnance Survey plan
Fee	£13 for dwelling Fee assessed for larger areas
Address	Area surveyor National Coal Board See para 28.4, above
Special points	
Area affected	Coal mining areas

Chapter 29

Tin mining

29.1 Tin and arsenic mining were in the past major industries in Cornwall and South West Devon. Despite the fact that only a few mines are now operational the danger of subsidence from old workings remains.

29.2 HOW TO MAKE THE SEARCH
A general indication that a property lies within a tin mining area will be revealed in answer to the standard form of additional enquiries of the local authority. The local authority is unable to supply information relating to subsidence but a search may be made by writing to the Cornish Chamber of Mines, Mount Wellington, Fernys Platt, Chacewater, Cornwall, TR4 8RJ (0872 863110). A 1:2500 ordnance survey map on which the property should be clearly marked should accompany the search request. A fee of £30 is charged where the search relates to one property only. Where the search relates to land which is to be developed as, eg a building estate, a fee of £60 is charged.

29.3 WHAT THE SEARCH REVEALS
If the property lies within the area of a disused mine the search is made by the Chamber of Mines and will reveal whether or not there are any shafts underneath the property, whether there are any mine workings near or under the property, and in the event that there are, whether these are any danger to the property or to any proposed development of the land. Where the property lies within the perimeter of a working mine the search is forwarded by the Chamber of Mines to the mine itself whose surveyor reports directly to the applicant. Many of the Cornish mines are very ancient in origin and complete records of their workings and boundaries do not exist, thus the result of this search should not be regarded as conclusive. The Records Office, County Hall, Truro will, on request, supply a list of mining surveyors whose specialist advice may be sought in a case where there is danger of subsidence.

29.4 MINERAL CONSULTATION AREAS
Where unexploited mineral deposits exist underneath land the land may be designated as a mineral consultation area. This designation of

land will be revealed in answer to the standard form of additional enquiries of the local authority. In such a case the local authority has undertaken to consult with the Cornish Chamber of Mines before granting planning permission over the property. The Chamber of Mines will determine whether a proposed development would be likely to impede any future mining underneath the land. Planning permission may therefore be difficult to obtain within such an area.

29.5 SEARCH SUMMARY

Application	By letter
Plan	1:2500 ordnance survey
Fee	£30 (£60 for development land)
Address	Cornish Chamber of Mines Mount Wellington Fernys Platt Chacewater Cornwall TR4 8RJ
Special points	Search not conclusive
Area affected	Cornwall and South West Devon

Chapter 30

Clay

30.1 Substantial deposits of ball clay and china clay exist and continue to be quarried in parts of Devon, Dorset and Cornwall, in which areas it is possible to make a search relating to land affected with the respective companies who produce clay in those areas. Such a search will reveal whether the land searched is affected by clay deposits, whether these deposits are likely to be worked in the future and whether there is any danger of subsidence from past workings. The presence of mineral deposits underneath the land should be revealed initially in response to the standard form of additional enquiries of the local authority. Devon and Cornwall also operate a policy of mineral consultation areas (see para 27.6, above) which may affect the grant of planning permission to develop the land.

Clay is also worked, but less extensively, in other parts of the country, where specific enquiries of the clay producing company may yield information, but no formal search procedure exists.

Property which is built on heavy clay may suffer from subsidence during prolonged periods of dry weather.

30.2 HOW TO MAKE THE SEARCH

Enquiries should be sent by letter enclosing a large scale plan of the property (1: 2500) to the appropriate company (see below). In general no fee is charged for answering these enquiries.

30.2.1 Cornwall
Assistant Area Estates Surveyor
English Clays
John Keay House
St Austell
Cornwall
(0726 4482)

30.2.2 **Devon and Dorset**

The quarries are likely to be owned by one of two companies:

Watts Blake and Bearne	English Ball Clays
Park House	Broadway Road
Courtenay Park	Newton Abbot
Newton Abbot	Devon
Devon	
(0626 2345)	

30.3 SEARCH SUMMARY

Application	By letter
Plan	1:2500 Ordnance survey
Fee	Generally free
Address	Appropriate producing company (see para 30.2, above)
Special points	
Area affected	Devon, Dorset, Cornwall

Chapter 31

Brine

31.1 Parts of Cheshire are affected by past and present workings for the extraction of brine. These workings can cause subsidence to the surrounding land, compensation for which may be available under the Cheshire Brine Pumping (Compensation for Subsidence) Act 1952 as amended.

31.2 AREAS AFFECTED
Alsagar
Bucklow
Crewe
Congleton
Knutsford
Lymm
Macclesfield
Nantwich
Northwich
Runcorn
Sandbach
Winsford

31.3 Where property is being purchased in any of the areas listed in the preceding paragraph a search may be made before exchange of contracts with Cheshire Brine Subsidence Compensation Board, 41 Chester Way, Northwich, Cheshire, CW9 5JE (0606 2172).

31.4 HOW TO MAKE THE SEARCH
Under the Cheshire Brine Pumping (Compensation for Subsidence) Act 1952 s 39 the Board is required to keep records and plans showing particulars of property in respect of which claims for compensation have been lodged. These records are open to public inspection free of charge but will not normally yield sufficient information to satisfy a prospective purchaser of the land. Further information may be obtained by making a search either in person or by post at the above offices. The fee of £6.00 should be sent with the search application.

The Board can usually identify an established property by reference to its postal address and their own plans and only require a plan to be sent to them where enquiries relate to a newly built property. It would, however, be prudent to enclose a plan of the property with all search requests in order to avoid delay.

The present owner of the land must give his permission to make the search, thus an authority to inspect should be obtained from the vendor's solicitors and submitted with the search request.

31.4.1 The search request should ask the Board for the following information:

    (a) whether salt mining or brine extraction has been, is now, or will in the foreseeable future be carried on underneath or in the vicinity of the property;

    (b) whether there is any danger of subsidence to the property;

    (c) whether any claim for compensation for subsidence exists or has been filed and if so the outcome of that claim;

    (d) in relation to proposed new development, whether any special recommendations relating to the laying of foundations for a building should be followed.

31.5 SEARCH SUMMARY

Application	By letter or personal search
Plan	Not always required but would assist
Fee	£6
Address	Cheshire Brine Subsidence Compensation Board 41 Chester Way Northwich Cheshire CW9 5JE
Special points	An authority to inspect given by present owner of land must accompany application
Area affected	Parts of Cheshire

Chapter 32

Limestone

32.1 Despite the fact that limestone mining was discontinued in the West Midlands during the 1930s a small risk of subsidence still exists in the areas immediately around the disused workings and a mining search should therefore be made to discover whether the property is likely to be affected by subsidence.

32.2 AREAS AFFECTED
Dudley Metropolitan Borough
Metropolitan Borough of Sandwell
Walsall Metropolitan Borough
Wolverhampton Metropolitan Borough

32.2.1 Only a small number of properties in Wolverhampton are situated in the vicinity of the disused workings and it is suggested that a telephone call is made to the Borough to check the likelihood of the land being affected before submitting a search. In the Borough of Sandwell the properties affected are mainly council houses or large industrial holdings. The Boroughs of Dudley, Sandwell and Walsall all recommend that a search should be undertaken in connection with the sale of council houses.

32.3 HOW TO MAKE THE SEARCH
The four boroughs named above all operate different procedures.

32.3.1 Dudley
Enquiry should be made by letter (and not as an additional enquiry on form Con 29) addressed to the assistant borough solicitor at Council House, Dudley, West Midlands, DY1 1HF (tel 0384 55433). Technical enquiries (as opposed to legal queries) should be addressed to Public Works Department, Council House, Mary Stevens Park, Stourbridge, West Midlands, DY8 2AA (0384 392111).

32.3.2 Sandwell
This borough will only answer mining queries if an additional enquiry is added to Part II of the Con 29 form using the following wording:

   'Is the property affected by limestone workings?'

The appropriate additional enquiry fee (currently £1.80) is charged for answering this question.

Address: Town Hall, West Bromwich, West Midlands, B70 8DX (021 569 2571).

32.3.3 **Walsall**

A purchaser's solicitor making additional enquiries of this borough will automatically be informed by means of a letter attached to the local search and enquiry replies whether or not the property is affected by limestone workings. No specific enquiry on the Con 29 form is necessary and no fee is charged for this service. General legal enquiries connected with limestone workings should be addressed to Head of Legal Services, Civic Centre, Walsall, WS1 1TP (tel 0922 21244). Technical enquiries should be made to the Director of Engineering and Town Planning at the same address.

32.3.4 **Wolverhampton**

This authority prefers to deal with queries which are raised by letter addressed to the Structural Department of the Council and does not make a charge for answering queries raised in this way. They will deal with limestone searches as an additional enquiry on form Con 29 (where the standard fee of £1.80 is payable) but it is administratively more convenient for them if the matter can be dealt with under separate cover.

Address: Structural Department, Civic Centre, St Peters Square, Wolverhampton, WV1 1RG (tel 0902 27811).

32.4 FURTHER INFORMATION

A detailed consultant's report on the limestone workings was commissioned by the Department of the Environment in 1981 and is available for inspection at the offices of the local authorities mentioned above. A summary of the report may be obtained from the Department of the Environment, West Midlands, Regional Office, Five Ways Tower, Frederick Road, Birmingham 15 (021 643 8191 ext 2572, 2568 or 2591) at the price of £1.50. The conclusion reached by the report is that in general the risk of subsidence is low. Most building societies are willing to lend money on properties situated in limestone areas but insurance against subsidence should be considered if the property is likely to be affected.

32.5 SEARCH SUMMARY

Application	Dudley: by letter
	Sandwell: additional enquiry on Con 29
	Walsall: not needed. See para. 32.3.3, above
	Wolverhampton: by letter

Plan	Not required
Fee	Dudley: No fee Sandwell: £1.80 Walsall: No fee Wolverhampton: No fee
Address	Respective borough councils addresses given in text above
Special points	–
Area affected	West Midlands

Part VI

Pre-completion searches

Chapter 33

Probate

33.1 BUYING DIRECTLY FROM A PERSONAL REPRESENTATIVE

By the Administration of Estates Act 1925, s 37 a conveyance by a personal representative to a purchaser remains valid despite the subsequent revocation of the grant of probate or letters of administration. This section affords substantial protection to a purchaser who is dealing with a personal representative but the use of the word 'subsequent' in the section implies that the protection of the section only applies where the grant has not been revoked until after completion has taken place. Although revocation of a grant is a relatively infrequent occurrence it has been suggested that a purchaser should make a search as close to the completion date as possible to ensure that the grant has not been revoked.

A further reason for making this search is that the Administration of Estates Act 1925, s 27 (2) which provides that a payment of money made in good faith to a personal representative acts as a good discharge, ie receipt to the payer, only operates to protect the purchaser where the grant was valid and had not been revoked at the time of payment.

The vendor's capacity as personal representative will be revealed at the draft contract stage in the transaction and the purchaser may choose to carry out a probate search prior to contract in order to avoid entering into a contract which might later have to be rescinded. If a pre-contract search is made, the search should ideally be repeated prior to completion to ensure that the grant has not been revoked since the first search was made.

33.2 WHERE THE GRANT FORMS PART OF THE CHAIN OF TITLE

When a personal representative conveys to a purchaser the original grant will normally be produced on completion of that transaction, and if not handed over at completion either an examined copy or an examined abstract of the grant will then form part of the purchaser's title to the land. The existence of a copy grant or examined abstract supplied to a subsequent purchaser suggests that the grant had not been revoked at the time of the earlier conveyance by the personal representative (see above) and in the absence of suspicious circumstances it is suggested that a probate search need not be made.

If there is no proof of the existence of the grant at the time of the conveyance by the personal representative a search for non-revocation for the period immediately preceding the conveyance or assent should be made.

If personal representatives have made an assent in favour of a beneficiary, the latter should be in possession of an examined copy of the grant bearing the date of the assent. In this event it is suggested that a subsequent purchaser from that beneficiary need make no enquiry concerning revocation in the absence of suspicious circumstances.

33.2.1 To suggest that such a search should be made in every case where title to unregistered land is to be made by personal representatives would it is considered to be going too far. It appears that where a general grant is revoked the original grant is called in, which suggests that it would be advisable to make the search if the original grant cannot be produced by Vendor personal representatives. Further, in the not very common case of a limited grant, it may be necessary to enquire whether the grant has expired.

33.3   REGISTERED LAND

33.3.1   Buying from a personal representative who is the registered proprietor of land

A personal representative who seeks to become registered proprietor of the land in place of the deceased will have to produce the grant of representation to the Chief Land Registrar at the time of his application for registration. The Chief Land Registrar is under no duty to investigate the validity of a grant lodged with him[1] and once the personal representative has been registered as proprietor of the land a purchaser from the personal representative will take good title unless the revocation of the grant is actually noted on the register.

33.3.2   Buying from a personal representative who is not registered as proprietor of the land

In most cases a personal representative will not himself apply to be registered as the proprietor of the deceased's land and will deal directly with the purchaser who will on production of the land or charge certificate, transfer and office copy or certified copy of the original grant of probate or letters of administration apply to be registered as proprietor in place of the deceased. Even in this situation the Chief Land Registrar is under no duty to investigate the validity of the grant, thus it seems that the purchaser will in any event become the registered proprietor of the land notwithstanding the prior revocation of the grant.

If it were subsequently discovered that the grant had been

revoked prior to completion the question would arise as to whether or not rectification of the register could be obtained against the purchaser. Although there is no authority on this point, it is argued that in view of the absence of obligation on the Chief Land Registrar to investigate the grant it would be inequitable to rectify against the purchaser in these circumstances. If, however, rectification were ordered against the purchaser, he would be able to claim indemnity for loss suffered provided that he had not caused or contributed to his own loss by fraud or lack of proper care.[2] A probate search made prior to completion, which did not reveal the revocation of the grant would prevent the purchaser from being debarred from compensation on the grounds of lack of proper care.

33.4 WHERE TO MAKE THE SEARCH
The search should be made at the Principal Probate Registry. If it is known that the grant was issued by a district registry enquiries should also be made of the appropriate district registry.

33.4.1 Addresses of probate registries

Principal Registry of the Family Division	Somerset House Strand London WC2R 1LP (01 405 7641)
Probate Registry of Scotland	Sheriff's Clerk HM Commissary Office Sheriff's Court House 16 North Bank Street Edinburgh EH1 2NJ (031 226 7181)
Probate Registry of Wales	49 Cardiff Road Llandaff Cardiff CF5 2YW (0222 562422)
Birmingham	Cavendish House Waterloo Street Birmingham B2 5PS (021 236 6263)
Brighton	28 Richmond Place Brighton BN2 2NA (0273 684071)

Bristol	The Crescent Centre
	Temple Back
	Bristol
	BS1 6EP
	(0272 23915)
Ipswich	17–19 Cornhill
	Ipswich
	IP1 1DF
	(0473 53724)
Leeds	Devereux House
	East Parade
	Leeds
	LS1 2BA
	(0532 431505)
Liverpool	3rd Floor
	India Buildings
	Water Street
	Liverpool
	L2 0QR
	(051 236 8264)
Manchester	9th Floor
	Astley House
	23 Quay Street
	Manchester
	M3 4AT
	(061 834 4319)
Newcastle-upon-Tyne	2nd Floor
	Plummer House
	Croft Street
	Newcastle-upon-Tyne
	NE1 6ND
	(0632 328543)
Oxford	10A New Road
	Oxford
	OX1 1LY
	(0865 241163)
Winchester	4th Floor
	Cromwell House
	Andover Road
	Winchester
	SO23 7EW
	(0962 53046)

33.5 HOW TO MAKE THE SEARCH

33.5.1 In person
The year book for the year of the grant should be searched. If the grant has been revoked a note of the revocation will have been entered next to the entry recording the issue of the grant.

The records are computerised for grants issued after 1 January 1981.

No fee is charged for a personal search. Copies of the entry may be obtained by filling in an application form. The fee for copies is £0.25 per page.

33.5.2 By post
A letter, together with the search fee of £1 should be sent to the Registry, specifying the full name of the deceased, the date of death, and the last known address. of the deceased.

The result of a postal search will normally take between seven and ten days and this delay should be anticipated if the search is to be made close to completion.

33.6 SEARCH SUMMARY

Application	Personal search or by post
Plan	–
Fee	Personal search free
	By post £1
Address	Principal Registry of the Family Division
	Somerset House
	Strand
	London
	WC2R 1LP
	(01 405 7641)
Special points	
Area affected	Generally only applicable to unregistered land

---

1 Land Registration Rules 1925 (SR & O 1925/1093), r170 (5).
2 Land Registration Act 1925, s 83 (5) (a).

Chapter 34

Pre-completion searches in the Central Land Charges Register

34.1 THE CONTENTS OF THE REGISTER

34.1.1 The register of pending actions

This register contains details of pending land actions and bankruptcy petitions. By the Land Charges Act 1972 s 17(1) a pending land action is any action or proceeding pending in court relating to land or any interest in or charge on land. An action seeking a declaration of entitlement to a share in the proceeds of sale of land is not capable of registration within this category.[1]

Bankruptcy petitions are registered irrespective of whether the debtor is known to own any land.

34.1.2 The register of writs and orders

This contains details of:

(a) any writ or order affecting land which has been issued for the purpose of enforcing a judgment (including charging orders over land);

(b) an order appointing a receiver of land;

(c) a receiving order in bankruptcy, whether or not it is known to affect land.

34.1.3 The register of deeds of arrangement

A deed of arrangement which affects land should be registered in this register under the Land Charges Act 1972, s 71(1). Registration lapses after five years but is renewable for a further period of five years. Deeds of arrangement are also required to be registered under the Deeds of Arrangement Act 1914 (see para 26.6, above).

34.1.4 The Register of Annuities

The registration of certain annuities and rent charges under the Judgments Act 1855 was transferred to this Register under the Land Charges Act 1925. No new entries have been possible on this register since 31 December 1925 and the register will be closed when all existing registrations have been vacated.

Registrable annuities created since 1925, and those created before 1926 which were not registered before 1926 are registrable as class C(iii) or class E land charges respectively (see para 34.1.5, below).

34.1.5 The Register of Land Charges

Land charges are divided into six classes comprising charges on or obligations affecting land, other than local land charges. A charge on land does not include a charge on or over the proceeds of sale of land.[2] Some uncertainty exists as to the precise scope of some of the classes.

34.1.5.1 *Class A*

This comprises financial charges on land created pursuant to the application of some person under the provisions of a statute, eg a charge obtained by a landlord in respect of compensation paid to a tenant for improvements to business premises. Other examples are given in the Land Charges Act 1972, Sch 2.

34.1.5.2 *Class B*

These charges are similar in nature to class A charges but are imposed automatically by statute and not by the application of some person (cf class A). Most of the matters which would otherwise fall into this category are registrable as local land charges and are registered as such. Few class B registrations exist, the most common being a charge in favour of the Law Society for a contribution to the Legal Aid Fund under the Legal Aid Act 1974, s 9(6).

34.1.5.3 *Class C*

This comprises various types of mortgages or charges affecting land, whenever created, but charges created before 1926 are generally only registrable if acquired under a conveyance made after 1925.[3]

C(i) Puisne mortgage.   Legal mortgages not supported by the deposit of title deeds.

C(ii) Limited owner's charge.   Any equitable charge acquired by a tenant for life or statutory owner under the Finance Act 1975 or any other statute, by reason of his discharge of capital transfer tax or other liabilities.

C(iii) General equitable charge.   Any other equitable charge which is not secured by a deposit of the title deeds to the legal estate and which does not arise or affect an interest under a trust for sale or a settlement and is not included in any other class of land charge. This category of charge is not therefore clearly defined, although the definition expressly *excludes* the matters mentioned in the preceding sentence and also charges given by way of indemnity against rent equitably apportioned or charged on land.

The following appear to be registrable within this class:
(a) equitable charges of a legal estate not protected by deposit;
(b) a vendor's lien for unpaid purchase money where he has parted with the title deeds;

(c) annuities charged on land created after 1925;

(d) equitable rentcharges.

C(iv) Estate contract. An estate contract is a contract by an estate owner or by a person entitled at the date of the contract to have a legal estate conveyed to him to convey or create a legal estate, including a contract conferring either expressly or by statutory implication a valid option to purchase, a right of pre-emption or any other like right.[4]

The following are therefore registrable within this category:

(a) a contract for the sale of land;

(b) an agreement for a lease;

(c) an option to purchase land or to take a lease;

(d) an option to renew a lease;

(e) a contract to make a settlement of land;

(f) a contract to grant a legal easement;

(g) a desire notice served under Leasehold Reform Act 1967.

Rights of pre-emption are expressly included in the statutory definition but such a right does not apparently create an interest in land.[5]

An equitable mortgage not supported by the deposit of title deeds may strictly speaking be registrable within this category as a contract to create a legal mortgage. There is no direct authority on this point,[6] but such mortgages are more commonly found to be registered under class C(iii). So far as an intending purchaser is concerned, the precise category of registration of such a charge is probably irrelevant since, however it appears on the register, he has notice of it and will call for its discharge.

34.1.5.4 *Class D*

The following charges fall within this class.

D(i) Charge for capital transfer tax. The Commissioners for Inland Revenue may register a charge for capital transfer tax over freehold land. This is rarely done in practice.

D(ii) Restrictive covenants. A covenant or agreement restrictive of the user of land entered into after 1925 is registrable within this category. Restrictive covenants entered into before 1926, even if repeated in a later conveyance, are not registrable but are enforceable through the doctrine of notice. Positive covenants and covenants by way of indemnity are not registrable neither are restrictive covenants made between lessor and lessee.

D(iii) Equitable easements. This category is defined as 'an easement right or privilege over or affecting land created or arising on or after 1 January 1926 and being merely an equitable interest'.[7] The precise extent of this category is uncertain[8] but does include the grant of an easement for life. The category probably does not include the following:

(a) a licence to occupy land;
(b) a right of access by estoppel;
(c) a right to remove fixtures;
(d) an equitable right to re-enter land.

34.1.5.5 *Class E*

Annuities created before 1926 but not then registered in the register of annuities are registrable within this class.

34.1.5.6 *Class F*

The Matrimonial Homes Act 1983 gives a spouse who has no legal estate in the matrimonial home certain statutory rights of occupation during the subsistence of the marriage. Such rights are registrable within this class. The right to register a Class F charge exists whether or not the spouse also has an equitable interest in the property.

34.1.6 Agricultural charges

A register of charges under the Agricultural Credits Act 1928 is maintained but is separate from the main registers. A central land charges search will not reveal entries in this register but a search may be made on form AC6 (see ch 14, above).

34.1.7 Summary of matters not capable of registration

(a) interests which are capable of being overreached;
(b) equitable easements created before 1926;
(c) restrictive covenants created before 1926;
(d) restrictive covenants between lessor and lessee (options to renew and to purchase the reversion are registrable);
(e) land charges created by a conveyance which leads to registration of title;
(f) equitable interests arising under a bare trust;
(g) estoppel interests and contractual licences;
(h) mere equities.

34.1.8 The effects of registration

Registration of a matter in the Central Land Charges Registry does not confer any validity on the matter registered but, subject to the Law of Property Act 1969, s 24, constitutes 'actual notice of such instrument or matter ... to all persons and for all purposes connected with the land affected'.[9] As a result of this rule a purchaser of land will be bound by all matters affecting the land which are registered as land charges whether or not he has made a search of the register or has otherwise been notified of the incumbrance. There is a limited right to compensation for undisclosed pre-root land charges (see ch 2, above).

34.1.9   The effects of non-registration
The effects of non-registration vary according to the class of land charge in question.

34.1.9.1   *Land charges classes C(iv) and D*
Non-registration renders the charge void against a purchaser of a legal estate for money or money's worth.

34.1.9.2   *All other classes of land charge*
Non-registration renders the charge void against a purchaser of the land or of any interest in the land for valuable consideration (including marriage).

34.1.9.3   *Writs and orders (except bankruptcy) deeds of arrangements, annuities*
These are void against a purchaser unless registered.

34.1.9.4   *Pending land actions (except bankruptcy)*
Non-registration avoids a pending land action only if a purchaser of the land is without express notice of the action.

34.1.9.5   *Bankruptcy petitions and receiving orders*
Non-registration renders these void against a purchaser of a legal estate in good faith for money or money's worth without notice of an available act of bankruptcy.

34.1.10   Consequences of non-registration
Lack of registration does not affect the validity of the charge as between the original contracting parties.

Once a land charge has been avoided against a purchaser by non-registration it remains unenforceable against his successors in title regardless of whether these successors in title give value for the land. It is thought that once a charge has become void for want of registration its validity cannot be revived by a purported late registration.[10]

It should be remembered that lack of registration will generally only render a charge void against a purchaser for value (class C(iv) and D—money or money's worth), thus non-registration will not affect the validity of a charge against a donee, devisee or squatter. The definition of purchase in the Land Charge Act 1972, s 17(1) does not require 'good faith' but the courts will not allow a sham transaction to defeat a non-registered charge.[11] Despite non-registration a charge may still be indirectly enforceable by the doctrine of estoppel[12] or through a chain of indemnity covenants.

34.1.11   A comparative table showing how land charges in unregistered land are protected on the title of registered land is contained in para 35.21, below.

34.2 WHEN TO MAKE THE SEARCH

34.2.1 The land affected

In general the matters which are registered at the Land Charges Department only affect unregistered land. Anything which in the case of unregistered land would be so registered will, where the land is registered, be protected either as a minor interest, appearing on the register itself or will take effect as an overriding interest. There is therefore no need to make a central land charges search when buying land which is registered with an absolute title. However, where land is registered with a title other than absolute, certain matters are expressed to be excluded from the effect of registration and such matters could be affected by entries registered at the land charges department. Therefore such a search should in theory be made when dealing with land which is registered with a title other than absolute. In practice, such a search may not be practicable since to obtain full protection in these circumstances a search should be made (or be available) against estate owners of the land during the 15 years prior to the date of the present contract, and these names are not usually revealed by the office copy entries, nor will the vendor have such information. A search in these circumstances will therefore be impossible.

34.2.2 Bankruptcy

The register contains details of all bankruptcy petitions presented and receiving orders made against individuals whether in the High Court or county court and irrespective of whether the individual is known to own any land. A search in the land charges department is therefore the most comprehensive type of search which can be made for bankruptcy entries and is relevant to both registered and unregistered land.

A solicitor who is acting for a proposed mortgagee of property will normally be required to obtain a clear certificate of the result of a bankruptcy search against the borrower's name before the mortgage funds are made available to the borrower. Details of the search are contained in para 34.8, below.

34.2.3 Pre-contract search

It may in certain circumstances be desirable to make a full search or a bankruptcy only search before exchange of contracts (see ch 7, above).

34.2.4 Pre-completion search

When the title to unregistered land has been investigated a full search in the land charges register should be made against the names of all estate owners who appear in the abstract of title unless previous satisfactory search certificates have been supplied with the abstract. The search should be conducted as close to contractual completion date as possible in order to take full advantage of the priority period given by the search (para 34.7.7, below).

Where a search is to be made by post the search application should be sent to the Registry approximately seven days before contractual completion date to allow for delays in the post. Where the search is to be made in person, by telephone or telex it may be possible to postpone making the search until a day or two before the completion date, but it should be remembered that the confirmatory certificate of the result of the search (which is the conclusive result of the search) will be sent to the applicant by post and this certificate should be obtained by the applicant prior to actual completion.

34.2.5   Certificates of search supplied with the abstract of title

Although the vendor is not required to do so, he may include with the abstract of title supplied to the purchaser copies of land charges search certificates which have been obtained by him or by his predecessors in title during the course of a previous dealing with the land.

It is only possible to register a land charge against an estate owner for the time being of the land, thus once an estate owner has disposed of his interest no further entries can be made against the name of that estate owner in relation to that particular parcel of land. Provided therefore that a previous search certificate supplied by the vendor shows that the previous search was made against the correct name of an estate owner, and for the full period of his ownership of the land and the subsequent conveyance was dated within the priority period afforded by the search it will not be necessary for the purposes of the current transaction to repeat the search made against the earlier estate owner. For the same reason, if a search has been made before exchange of contracts against the name of previous estate owners it is not necessary to repeat that search prior to completion, but it will be necessary to update a pre-contract search made against the present vendor.

34.2.6   Estate owners

34.2.6.1   The following are estate owners against whom a search may have to be made:

sole owners in fee simple;
co-owners;
mortgagees;
trustees;
trustee in bankruptcy;
official receiver;
personal representatives;
the President of the Family Division (the legal estate of a person dying intestate vests in him on death);

tenants for life;
lessees.

34.2.6.2 The following are not estate owners and no search need be made against them:

liquidators of companies (except where an order has been made under the Companies Act 1948, s 244);

receivers for debenture holders or mortgagees;

receivers appointed under the Mental Health Act 1983;

attorneys;

trustees of Settled Land Act Settlements (unless they are statutory owners).

34.3 HOW TO MAKE THE SEARCH

34.3.1 Personal search

A search may be made by personal attendance at the Land Charges public counter in either Plymouth or at HM Land Registry, Croydon, between the hours of 11 am and 3 pm from Monday to Friday. The applicant must complete a form K15 and pay the appropriate fee in cash or by Land Registry stamps. The form is then handed to a land charges operator who conducts the search on the applicant's behalf. The result of the search is displayed on a visual display unit for the applicant to see whether or not any entries are revealed. An official certificate of the result of the search is then prepared and is posted to the address supplied by the applicant. The certificate cannot be handed over the counter to the applicant. The personal search procedure is not available for bankruptcy only searches, but a full search made against an individual's name will reveal bankruptcy entries.

34.3.2 Postal searches

An application form (K15, or K16 for bankruptcy only) should be completed and sent together with the appropriate fee to the land charges department (address in para 34.12, below).

34.3.3 Searches made by telephone

Provided the applicant holds a credit account with the land charges department a full search may be made by telephone on Plymouth 0752 701171, between the hours of 10 am and 4 pm. When making a telephone search the applicant should supply the following information which will be requested by the telephone operator in the land charges department in the order given below.

(a) applicant's key number, name, address and reference;

(b) the particulars of the search to be made

  (i) county (and former county);

  (ii) the full forenames and surname of the name to be searched;

  (iii) the period in whole years to be covered by the search.

Where less than ten entries are revealed by the search the operator will give details of these to the applicant. In other cases the operator will state the number of entries revealed but will not supply details. Following the call the official certificate of search will be printed and posted to the applicant by first class post.

34.3.4 Searches made by telex

Holders of credit accounts may apply for a search by telex (LANDCHG 45431) using the standard form telex shown below. The result of the search is posted to the applicant.

34.3.4.1 *Standard form telex*

Each item should commence on a new line with double spacing between the lines:

(a) applicant's answer back code and telex number; date in brackets;

(b) the word SEARCH;

(c) the name to be searched (forenames should precede the surname and be separated from the former by an oblique stroke);

(d) the letters PD followed by the period to be searched. The years should be typed in numerals for the inclusive period to be covered by the search and should be separated by the word TO;

(e) steps (c) and (d) should be repeated for each additional name to be searched;

(f) the letters CO followed by the county. Any former county should be typed on the same line but enclosed in brackets;

(g) the letters DES followed (if required) by a short description of the land. Any former description of the land should be typed on the following line and be enclosed in brackets;

(h) the letters KN followed by the applicant's key number;

(i) the letters REF followed by the applicant's reference.

34.3.5 Summary of arrangements for searching

Method of lodging search	Type of Search	Method of paying fees	Address to which re. will be sent
Postal or delivery by hand	Full and bankruptcy	Fee stamps or credit account	Applicant's addres or specified alternative
Telephone	Full only	Credit account only	Applicant's addres only
Telex	Full only	Credit account only	Applicant's addres only
Personal attendance	Full only	Cash or fee stamps	Applicant's addres only

34.3.6　A booklet entitled *Computerised Land Charges Department, A Guide for Solicitors* is available free of charge from the Land Charges Department.

34.4　FEES FOR LAND CHARGES APPLICATIONS

Registration of a land charge	50p	per	Name
Renewal	,,	,,	,,
Rectification	,,	,,	,,
Cancellation of entries	,,	,,	,,
Priority notices	,,	,,	,,
Office copies	,,	,,	,,
Postal searches	,,	,,	,,
Official search by telephone	80p	,,	,,
Official search by teleprinter	70p	,,	,,
Official search by personal attendance at Plymouth	80p	,,	,,

For detailed information, reference may be made to the Land Charges Fees Order 1975 (SI 1975/1315) obtainable from HM Stationery Office.

34.4.1　Payment of fees
See paras 6.7 and 34.3.5, above.

34.4.2　Credit account payment
Where an application for a search or for office copies of an entry is made by telex or telephone payment of fees must be made by credit account. In all other cases payment may be made by credit account.

34.5　FORM K15
This form is reproduced on pp 342–343, below.

34.6　COMMENT ON FORM K15

34.6.1　Names of individuals to be searched
The conclusiveness of the search certificate depends inter alia on the search having been made against the correct names of the estate owners of the land, ie the names as they appear in the title deeds. It is necessary to supply the full forenames and surname of an individual and to insert these correctly on the designated lines on the search form. Insertion of the forenames and surname on the correct lines is essential because some names can be reversed (eg STEVEN HENRY; HENRY STEVEN) and an incorrect insertion of the name would result in the search being made against the wrong individual. Where there is any discrepancy in the spelling of a name contained in the title deeds, the search should be made against all variations of that name to ensure that a proper search is carried out. For example, an individual is described variously in the deeds as JOHN WILLIAM SMITH and

Form K15   Land Charges Act 1972

Payment of fee
(see note 3 overleaf)

EITHER
Insert a cross (X)
in this box
if the fee is
to be paid through a
credit account

OR
affix stamps in this space

● **APPLICATION FOR AN OFFICIAL SEARCH**

NOT APPLICABLE TO REGISTERED LAND

Application is hereby made for an official search in the index to the registers kept
pursuant to the Land Charges Act 1972 for any subsisting entries in respect of the
under-mentioned particulars.

For Official Use only		IMPORTANT: Please read the notes overleaf before completing this form			

IMPORTANT: Please read the notes overleaf before completing this form

For Official Use only		NAMES TO BE SEARCHED (Please use block letters and see note 4 overleaf)	PERIOD OF YEARS (see note 5 overleaf)	
STX			From	To
	Forename(s)			
	SURNAME			
	Forename(s)			
	SURNAME			
	Forename(s)			
	SURNAME			
	Forename(s)			
	SURNAME			
	Forename(s)			
	SURNAME			
	Forename(s)			
	SURNAME			

COUNTY (see note 6 overleaf)

FORMER COUNTY

DESCRIPTION OF LAND
(see note 7 overleaf)

FORMER DESCRIPTION

Particulars of Applicant (see notes 8, 9 and 10 overleaf)		[Name and address for despatch of certificate] (Leave blank if certificate is to be returned to applicant's address)
KEY NUMBER	Name and address	

Applicant's reference:	Date	FOR OFFICIAL USE ONLY

NOTES FOR GUIDANCE OF APPLICANTS

The following notes are supplied for assistance in making the application overleaf. For further information on procedures for making applications to the Land Charges Department, see the booklet (36 pages) "Computerised Land Charges Department: a practical guide for solicitors", obtainable on application at the address shown below.

1. Effect of search. The official certificate of the result of this search will have no statutory effect in relation to registered land (see Land Registration Act 1925, s. 59 and Land Charges Act 1972, s. 14).

2. Bankruptcy only searches. Form K16 should be used for Bankruptcy only searches.

3. Fee payable. A fee is payable for each name searched. If you have been granted a credit account, you may ask for the fee to be debited to your account. Otherwise, you must affix Land Registry adhesive fee stamps for the appropriate sum in the fee panel provided overleaf. These stamps can be purchased from any head post office or from a sub-post office where the demand is sufficient to warrant stocks being held. Cheques and postal orders are not usually acceptable (but see the guide referred to above).

4. Names to be searched. The forename(s) and surname of each individual must be entered on the appropriate line in the relevant panel overleaf. The name of a company or other body should commence on the forename line and may continue on the surname line (the words "forename(s)" and "surname" should be crossed through). If you are searching more than 6 names, use a second form.

5. Period of years to be searched. The inclusive period to be covered by a search should be entered in complete years e.g. 1970–1977.

6. County names. The name of the county borough must not be entered as the name of the county. Searches affecting land within the Greater London area should state "Greater London" as the county name. ANY RELEVANT FORMER COUNTY SHOULD ALWAYS BE STATED (see the guide referred to above for the list of county names).

7. Land description. It is not essential to provide a land description but, if one is given, any relevant former description should also be given (see the guide referred to above).

8. Key number. If you have been allocated a key number, please take care to enter this in the space provided overleaf, whether or not you are paying fees through your credit account.

9. Applicant's name and address. This need not be supplied if the applicant's key number is correctly entered in the space provided overleaf.

10. Applicant's reference. Any reference must be limited to 10 digits, including any oblique strokes and punctuation.

11. Despatch of this form. When completed, send this application to the address shown below, which is printed in a position so as to fit within a standard window envelope.

THE SUPERINTENDENT,
LAND CHARGES DEPARTMENT,
SEARCH SECTION,   (see note 11 above)
BURRINGTON WAY,
PLYMOUTH PL5 3LP.

JOHN SMITH. If a search is made only against the name of JOHN
WILLIAM SMITH the computer will search against
  JOHN WILLIAM SMITH
  J.W. SMITH and
  SMITH
but it will not search against
  JOHN SMITH
  J. SMITH
  J. WILLIAM SMITH
  WILLIAM SMITH or
  W. SMITH
Where abbreviated forenames (eg JAS. THOS.) are included in the
search application they will be searched as written on the application
form and will not be converted into the full versions of those names.
Particular care should be taken with hyphenated, double barrelled or
prefixed names. If a person is commonly known by an alternative name
or is known to have changed his or her name, eg by deed poll or
marriage, a separate entry is required for each alternative name. A
title, eg Sir or Duke should be entered in brackets before but on the
same line as the individual's forenames. Where the name of an individual or of a corporation sole (eg a mayor or bishop) contains a reference to a territorial designation this should be included in the name to
be searched and the words 'forename' and 'surname' in the boxes on
the application form should be deleted. Where an individual bears a
title a registration may have been effected either by reference to the
title or by reference to the individual's forename and surname alone.
  In order to accommodate both these possibilities a search should be
undertaken against both the title and the common name of the individual. Service ranks, civic and academic designations, decorations and
degrees should not be entered on the search form.

34.6.2 The purchaser of land under a sub-contract
Where A has contracted to sell land to B and B has, before completion
of his purchase from A contracted to re-sell the land to C, C's estate
contract can only be registered against the name of the current estate
owner (A) and the search should be made against A. A registration of
a C(iv) charge against the name of B is ineffective.[13]

34.6.3 Companies and firms
The words 'forename' and 'surname' should be deleted from the
application form and the name of the firm or company inserted commencing on the forename line and continuing into the surname line if
necessary. It is not essential to include the word 'THE' where it appears
as the first word of a name.

34.6.3.1 *Public companies*
Under the Companies Act 1980 public companies which had previously
been registered under the Companies Acts 1948–67 were required to
register either as public limited companies (PLC) or as private companies. A time limit was specified during which this re-registration was
to take place. Although this time limit has now expired it has in some
cases been possible during the years 1980–85 for a registration to be
effected against either the old or new name of a re-registered company.
When searching against a limited company for the period 1979–85
enquiries should be made as to whether the company has re-registered
during this period and, if so, a search should be made against both the
old and new names of the company. If, however, the *only* change in
the name of the company is the alteration from 'Ltd' to 'PLC' a single
search which identifies the company either as 'Ltd' or 'PLC' will reveal
charges registered against both variations of the name.

35.6.4 Local authority names
The names of local authorities are in practice expressed in several
different ways. Provided the place name and status of the authority are
correctly described the search can be carried out.

34.6.5 Other corporations
Where a search is to be made against a corporation other than a
limited company (eg a building society or bishop) care must be taken
to search against the correct version of the name as an incorrectly made
search will afford no protection for the applicant.

34.6.6 Unincorporated bodies
Land held by unincorporated bodies is normally vested in trustees. The
search should therefore be made against the collective name of the
body in the same style as that used for searching against limited companies, eg 'TRUSTEES OF XYZ CHARITY'.

34.6.7 Land held by the Sovereign

34.6.7.1 *The Sovereign in right of the Crown*
The Crown Estate Commissioners do not normally deduce title when
property belonging to Her Majesty in Right of Her Crown is sold and
the following special procedure for searching is provided. If application
is made for a search in the name of 'The Crown Estate Commissioners'
and the reference number 10000168 is quoted in the left hand margin
of form K15, then a search will be made not only in the name of the
Commissioners (and their predecessors, The Commissioners of Crown
Lands and The Commissioners of Woods, Forests and Land Revenues)

but also in the name of Her Majesty the Queen and of His Majesty the King and in the names of every Sovereign since 1855.

34.6.7.2   *The Sovereign in right of the Private Estates*
Normally, when any part of the Crown's Private Estates is being purchased from HM Queen Elizabeth II, the purchaser is advised to search against the sovereigns mentioned below, quoting the appropriate reference numbers. However, if a title is deduced and this shows that the land came into the ownership of the Sovereign on or after 6 February 1952, the search need be made against HM Queen Elizabeth II only (quoting the appropriate reference number) and any previous owners who may be disclosed by the title so deduced. In either case the ensuing certificate of the result of search will disclose any relevant entries, no matter what form of names was employed to describe the Sovereign in the application for registration. (It should be observed that no entries under the Land Charges Act have been registered against Their Majesties Queen Victoria or King Edward VII.)

Reference No	Name	Period	
		From	To
1000555	HM KING GEORGE V	1910	1936
1000652	HM KING EDWARD VIII	1936	1936
1000749	HM KING GEORGE VI	1936	1952
1000846	HM QUEEN ELIZABETH II	1952	(current year)

34.6.8   The Duchy of Cornwall

If application is made for a search in the name of 'The Duchy of Cornwall' and the reference number 1000458 is quoted in the left hand margin of form K15, then a search will be made not only in the name of the Duchy but also in the name of His Royal Highness the Prince of Wales, the name of the Duke of Cornwall and in the names of every Duke of Cornwall since 1855 and, because there have been periods when there was no Duke, in the name of every sovereign since 1855.

34.6.9   The Duchy of Lancaster

The Chancellor and Council of the Duchy of Lancaster do not normally deduce title when property belonging to Her Majesty in Right of Her Duchy of Lancaster is sold and the following special procedure is provided. If application is made for a search in the name of 'The Duchy of Lancaster' and the reference number 1000361 is quoted in the left hand margin of form K15, then a search will be made not only in the name of the Duchy (and of the Chancellor and Council of the Duchy) but also in the names of Her Majesty the Queen, His Majesty the King, the Queen's Most Excellent Majesty, the King's Most Excellent Majesty, and in the names of every sovereign since 1855.

34.6.10   Livery companies, Oxford and Cambridge colleges, certain colleges and schools

A special search procedure, using a given reference number is available for making searches against these bodies. Details of the appropriate reference numbers are given in Land Charges Department Practice Leaflet No 2, the text of which is reproduced below.

34.6.10.1   Land Charges Department Practice Leaflet No 2

Official Searches Against Certain Livery Companies Colleges and Schools

The Practical Guide for Solicitors on the procedures which operate under computerisation in the Land Charges Department refers, at paragraph 23, to arrangements for searching certain special names. These include Livery Companies, the Colleges of Oxford and Cambridge Universities and certain other schools, colleges and institutions. Although, in strictness, the names of the bodies should be specified in extenso in any application, in order to simplify searching in these particular instances, the Chief Land Registrar undertakes to make a search against the full formal title whenever the commonly used shortened version of the name is given in the application, provided that the appropriate reference number set opposite the name is also quoted in the box in the left-hand margin (although it is headed 'For Official Use Only').

The list is not exhaustive. It comprises bodies against which entries made under the Land Charges Act are known to exist.

Livery Companies

Ref No	Shortened Version of Name	Full Name
1001040	Society of Apothecaries	The Master, Wardens and Society of the Art and Mistery of Apothecaries of the City of London
1001137	Armourers' and Brasiers' Company	The Worshipful Company of Armourers and Brasiers in the City of London
1001234	Bakers' Company	The Master Wardens and Commonalty of the Mystery of Bakers of the City of London

Livery Companies

Ref No	Shortened Version of Name	Full Name
1001331	Brewers' Company	The Master and Keepers or Wardens and Commonalty of the Mistery or Art of Brewers of the City of London
1001428	Carpenters' Company	The Master, Wardens and Commonalty of the Mistery of Freemen of the Carpentry of the City of London
1001525	Clothworkers' Company	The Master Wardens and Commonalty of Freemen of the Art or Mistery of Clothworkers of the City of London
1001622	Worshipful Company of Cooks	The Masters or Governors and Commonalty of the Mistery of Cooks of London
1001719	Coopers' Company	The Master Wardens or Keepers of the Commonalty of Freemen of the Mystery of Coopers of the City of London and the Suburbs of the Same City
10001816	Drapers' Company	The Master and Wardens and Brethren and Sisters of the Guild or Fraternity of the Blessed Mary the Virgin of the Mystery of Drapers of the City of London
1001913	Farriers' Company	The Worshipful Company of Farriers
1002010	Fishmongers' Company	The Wardens and Commonalty of the Mistery of Fishmongers of the City of London
1002107	Founders' Company	The Worshipful Company of Founders
1002204	Girdlers' Company	The Master and Wardens or Keepers of the Art or Mystery of Girdlers, London
1002301	Goldsmiths' Company	The Wardens and Commonalty of the Mystery of Goldsmiths of the City of London
1002495	Gold and Silver Wyre Drawers' Company	The Master Wardens Assistants and Commonalty of the Art and Mystery of Drawing and Flatting of Gold and Silver Wyre and making and spinning of Gold and Silver Thread Stuff

Livery Companies

Ref No	Shortened Version of Name	Full Name
1002592	Grocers' Company	The Wardens and Commonalty of the Mistery of Grocers of the City of London
1002689	Haberdashers' Company	The Master and Four Wardens of the Fraternity of the Art or Mystery of Haberdashers in the City of London
1002786	Worshipful Company of Innholders	The Master, Wardens and Society of the Art of Mystery of Innholders of the City of London
1002883	Ironmongers' Company	The Master and Keepers or Wardens and Commonalty of the Mystery or Art of Ironmongers London
1002980	Leathersellers' Company	The Wardens and Society of the Mistery or Art of the Leathersellers of the City of London
1003077	Mercers' Company	The Wardens and Commonalty of the Mystery of Mercers of the City of London
1003174	Merchant Taylors' Company	The Master and Wardens of the Merchant Taylors of the Fraternity of St John the Baptist in the City of London
1003271	Pewterers' Company	The Master and Wardens and Commonalty of the Mystery of Pewterers of the City of London
1003368	Poulters' Company	The Master Wardens and Assistants of Poulters of London
1003465	Saddlers' Company	The Wardens or Keepers and Commonalty of the Mystery or Art of Saddlers of the City of London
1003562	Salters' Company	The Master, Wardens and Commonalty of the Art or Mistery of Salters, London
1003659	Skinners' Company	The Master and Wardens of the Guild or Fraternity of the Body of Christ of the Skinners of London

Livery Companies

Ref No	Shortened Version of Name	Full Name
1003756	Tallow Chandlers Company	The Worshipful Company of Tallow Chandlers of the City of London
		or
		The Master, Wardens and Commonalty of the Mistery of Tallow Chandlers of the City of London
1003853	Tylers' and Bricklayers' Company	The Worshipful Company of Tylers and Bricklayers of London
1003950	Vintners' Company	The Master Wardens and Freemen and Commonalty of the Mystery of Vintners of the City of London

Cambridge University Colleges and Halls

Ref No	Shortened Version of Name	Full Name
1057785	Cambridge University	The Chancellor Master and Scholars of Cambridge University
1005017	Christ's College, Cambridge	The Master, Fellows and Scholars of Christ's College in the University of Cambridge
1005114	Clare College, Cambridge	The Master, Fellows and Scholars of Clare College in the University of Cambridge
1005308	Corpus Christi College Cambridge	The Master, Fellows and Scholars of the College of Corpus Christi and the Blessed Virgin Mary in the University of Cambridge
1005405	Downing College, Cambridge	The Master, Fellows and Scholars of Downing College in the University of Cambridge
1005502	Emmanuel College, Cambridge	The Master Fellows and Scholars of Emmanuel College in the University of Cambridge
1005696	Fitzwilliam College, Cambridge	The Master, Fellows, and Scholars of Fitzwilliam College in the University of Cambridge
1005793	Girton College, Cambridge	The Mistress, Fellows and Scholars of Girton College

Cambridge University Colleges and Halls

Ref No	Shortened Version of Name	Full Name
1005890	Gonville and Caius College, Cambridge	The Master and Fellows of Gonville and Caius College in the University of Cambridge founded in honour of the Annunciation of Blessed Mary the Virgin
1005987	Jesus College, Cambridge	The Master or Keeper and Fellows and Scholars of the College of the Blessed Virgin Mary St John the Evangelist and the Glorious Virgin Saint Radegund Commonly called Jesus College in the University of Cambridge
1006084	King's College, Cambridge	The Provost and Scholars of the King's College of our Lady and Saint Nicholas in Cambridge
1006181	Magdalene College, Cambridge	The Master and Fellows of Magdalene College in the University of Cambridge founded in honour of St Mary Magdalene
1006278	New Hall, Cambridge	The President and Fellows of New Hall in the University of Cambridge
1006569	Pembroke College, Cambridge	The Master, Fellows and Scholars of the College or Hall of Valence-Mary, commonly called Pembroke College, in the University of Cambridge
1006666	Peterhouse, Cambridge	The Master Fellows and Scholars of Peterhouse in the University of Cambridge
1006763	Queen's College, Cambridge	The President and Fellows of the Queen's College of St Margaret and St Bernard, commonly called Queen's College, in the University of Cambridge
1006860	St Catherine's College, Cambridge	The Master and Fellows of St Catherine's College or Hall in the University of Cambridge
1006957	St John's College, Cambridge	The Master Fellows and Scholars of the College of St John the Evangelist in the University of Cambridge

351

34.6.10.1 *Pre-completion searches in the Central Land Charges Register*

Cambridge University Colleges and Halls

Ref No	Shortened Version of Name	Full Name
1007054	Selwyn College, Cambridge	The Master, Fellows, and Scholars of Selwyn College
1007151	Sidney Sussex College, Cambridge	The Master Fellows and Scholars of the College of the Lady Frances Sidney Sussex in the University of Cambridge
1007248	Trinity College, Cambridge	The Master Fellows and Scholars of the College of the Holy and Undivided Trinity Within the Town and University of Cambridge of King Henry the Eighth's Foundation
1007345	Trinity Hall, Cambridge	The Master Fellows and Scholars of the College or Hall of the Holy Trinity in the University of Cambridge

Oxford University Colleges and Halls

Ref No	Shortened Version of Name	Full Name
1029849	Oxford University	The Chancellor Masters and Scholars of the University of Oxford
1008024	All Souls College, Oxford	The Warden and College of the Souls of All Faithful People Deceased in the University of Oxford
1008121	Balliol College, Oxford	The Master and Scholars of Balliol College in the University of Oxford
1008218	Brasenose College, Oxford	The Principal and Scholars of the Kings Hall and College of Brasenose in Oxford
1008315	Corpus Christi College, Oxford	The President and Scholars of Corpus Christi College in the University of Oxford
10084212	Exeter College, Oxford	The Rector and Scholars of Exeter College in the University of Oxford
1008509	Hertford College, Oxford	The Principal Fellows and Scholars of Hertford College in the University of Oxford
1008606	Jesus College, Oxford	The Principal, Fellows and Scholars of Jesus College, within the City and University of Oxford, of Queen Elizabeth's Foundation

Oxford University Colleges and Halls

Ref No	Shortened Version of Name	Full Name
1008703	Keble College, Oxford	The Wardens Fellows and Scholars of Keble College in the University of Oxford
1008897	Lady Margaret Hall, Oxford	The College of the Lady Margaret in Oxford Commonly known as Lady Margaret Hall
1008994	Lincoln College, Oxford	The Warden and Rector and Scholars of the College of the Blessed Mary and All Saints Lincoln in the University of Oxford commonly called Lincoln College
1009091	Magdalen College, Oxford	The President and Scholars of the College of St Mary Magdalen in the University of Oxford
1009188	Merton College, Oxford	The Warden and Scholars of the House or College of Scholars of Merton in the University of Oxford
1009285	New College, Oxford	The Warden and Scholars of St Mary College of Winchester in Oxford commonly called New College in Oxford
1009382	Oriel College, Oxford	The Provost and Scholars of the House of the Blessed Mary the Virgin in Oxford commonly called Oriel College of the Foundation of Edward the Second of Famous Memory sometime King of England
1009479	Pembroke College, Oxford	The Master, Fellows, and Scholars of Pembroke College in the University of Oxford
1009576	Queen's College, Oxford	The Provost and Scholars of the Queens College in the University of Oxford
1009673	St Catherine's College, Oxford	St Catherine's College in the University of Oxford
1009770	St Edmund Hall, Oxford	The Principal Fellows and Scholars of Saint Edmund Hall in the University of Oxford

34.6.10.1 *Pre-completion searches in the Central Land Charges Register*

Oxford University Colleges and Halls

Ref No	Shortened Version of Name	Full Name
1009867	St John's College, Oxford	The President and Scholars of Saint John Baptist College in the University of Oxford
1009964	Somerville College, Oxford	The Principal and Fellows of Somerville College in the University of Oxford
1010061	Trinity College, Oxford	The President Fellows and Scholars of the College of the Holy and Undivided Trinity in the University of Oxford of the Foundation of Sir Thomas Pope Knight Deceased
1010158	University College, Oxford	The Master and Fellows of the College of the Great Hall of the University commonly called University College in the University of Oxford
1010255	Wadham College, Oxford	The Warden Fellows and Scholars of Wadham College in the University of Oxford of the Foundation of Nicholas Wadham, Esquire and Dorothy Wadham
1010352	Worcester College, Oxford	The Provost, Fellows and Scholars of Worcester College in the University of Oxford

Schools and Colleges

Ref No	Shortened Version of Name	Full Name
1011031	Christ's Hospital	The Mayor and Commonalty and Citizens of the City of London Governors of the Possessions Revenues and Goods of the Hospitals of Edward late King of England the Sixth of Christ Bridewell and St Thomas the Apostle as Governors of Christ's Hospital
1011128	Dulwich College	The Estate Governors of Alleyn's College of God's Gift at Dulwich

Schools and Colleges

Ref No	Shortened Version of Name	Full Name
1011225	Eton College	The Provost of the College Royal of the Blessed Mary of Eton near unto Windsor in the County of Buckinghamshire commonly called The King's College of our Blessed Lady of Eton nigh or by Windsor in the said County of Buckinghamshire and the same college
1011322	Harrow School	The Keepers and Governors of the Possession Revenues and Goods of the Free Grammar School of John Lyon within the Town of Harrow on the Hill in the London Borough of Harrow (formerly in the County of Middlesex)
1011419	Highgate School	The Wardens and Governors of the possessions of the Free Grammar School of Sir Roger Cholmeley Knight in Highgate
1011516	Winchester College	Saint Mary College of Winchester near Winchester (the seal is referred to as 'The Common Seal of the Warden and Scholars Clerks of St Mary College and Winchester near Winchester')

LAND CHARGES DEPARTMENT

E.J. PRYER
Chief Land Registrar

34.6.11 Accepted abbreviations

(a) The following words are treated as being the same, within each group, for the purposes of a search:

&	Co	Ld
And	Cos	Ltd
	Coy	Limited
	Coys	
Ass	Comp	
Assoc	Comps	Soc
Assocs	Company	Socs
Associate	Companies	Socy
Associated	Cyfyngedig	Socys
Associates	Cyf	Society

Association	Public Limited Company	Societys
Associations	PLC	Societies
	Cwmni Cyfyngedig	
	Cyhoeddus	
	CCC	
	Cwmni Cyf Cyhoeddus	
Brother		St
Bro	Dr	Street
Brothers	Doc	St
Bros	Doctor	Saint

(b) The singular and plural of the following words (but not others) are treated as being the same:

Broker	Contractor	Enterprise	Industry	School
Builder	Construction	Estate	Investment	Son
Charity	Decorator	Garage	Motor	Store
College	Developer	Holding	Production	Trust
Commissioner	Development	Hotel	Property	Warden

34.6.12 Names incorporating numbers

Some company names contain numbers which, when printed, appear either as numerals or as spelt words. Names will be searched precisely as they appear in the application and it is, therefore, essential to ensure that each name is correctly presented. If a name happens to contain a number, this must be specified in the form in which it is required to be searched, that is, either with numerals (19th Century Land Co Ltd) or alphabetical characters (Nineteenth Century Land Co Ltd). Alternative forms will be searched only when they are separately specified in the application and a fee is paid for each name.

34.6.13 The period to be searched

The period to be searched should be that during which each named estate owner owned the land and should be stated in whole calendar years.

34.6.14 County

Entries in the register are grouped according to the county name stated in the original application for registration. When changes in county boundaries have occurred which affect the land to be searched the name of the former county should be inserted on the application form.

For searches in the Greater London area 'Greater London' should be given as the county to be searched. However, whenever it is possible that an original registration may have referred to a former county, such as Surrey, Kent or Middlesex, then that county must be specified as the former county in the application for search. This is because an entry held in the index under, eg Surrey, will not be revealed by a search referring only to Greater London. If London was specified as the county in the original registration, this entry will be revealed by a search referring to Greater London.

34.6.14.1 *List of county names*
Any county name used on the application form should conform with the list shown below which is issued by the Land Charges Department. Variations and abbreviations of county names should be avoided.
(a) County names up to and including the 31 March 1974

England

Bedfordshire	*Hampshire	Nottinghamshire
Berkshire	Herefordshire	Oxfordshire
Buckinghamshire	Hertfordshire	Rutland
*Cambridgeshire	*Huntingdonshire	Salop (or Shropshire)
Cheshire	Kent	Somerset
*Cornwall	Lancashire	Staffordshire
Cumberland	Leicestershire	*Suffolk
Derbyshire	*Lincolnshire	Surrey
Devon	Middlesex	*Sussex
Dorset	Norfolk	Warwickshire
Durham	Northamptonshire	Westmorland
Essex	Northumberland	Wiltshire
Gloucestershire		Worcestershire
Greater London		*Yorkshire

Wales

Anglesey	Flintshire	Radnorshire
Brecknockshire	Glamorgan	
Caernarvonshire	Merionethshire	
Cardiganshire	Monmouthshire	
Carmarthenshire	Montgomeryshire	
Denbighshire	Pembrokeshire	

* NB For the purpose of the index:

Cambridgeshire	includes the Isle of Ely
Cornwall	includes the Isles of Scilly
Hampshire	includes the Isle of Wight
Huntingdonshire	includes Peterborough
Lincolnshire	includes the Parts of Holland, Kesteven and Lindsey
Suffolk	includes East and West Suffolk
Sussex	includes East and West Sussex
Yorkshire	includes the three Ridings and the City of York

(b) County names on and after 1 April 1974

England

Avon	Greater Manchester	Nottinghamshire
Bedfordshire	Hampshire	Oxfordshire

Berkshire	Hereford &	Salop
Buckinghamshire	Worcester	**Shropshire
Cambridgeshire	Hertfordshire	Somerset
Cheshire	Humberside	South Yorkshire
Cleveland	*Isle of Wight	Staffordshire
Cornwall	Kent	Suffolk
Cumbria	Lancashire	Surrey
Derbyshire	Leicestershire	Tyne and Wear
Devon	Lincolnshire	Warwickshire
Dorset	Merseyside	West Midlands
Durham	Norfolk	*West Sussex
*East Sussex	North Yorkshire	West Yorkshire
Essex	Northamptonshire	Wiltshire
Gloucestershire	Northumberland	
Greater London		

Wales

Clwyd	Mid Glamorgan
Dyfed	Powys
Gwent	South Glamorgan
Gwynedd	West Glamorgan

If the period to be searched includes the year 1974 or earlier then every application for search must include not only the county given above but also any relevant former county name (see the first list).

* In particular, the application for search must refer to:
Isle of Wight as being formerly Hampshire
East Sussex as being formerly Sussex
West Sussex as being formerly Sussex

** A search against Salop or Shropshire will reveal entries registered against either name.

34.6.15 *Postal address differs from actual address*
Where the postal address of a property describes land as being in a different county from its actual address the search should be made against the actual county in which the land is situated, eg postal address 'Rogate, Petersfield, Hampshire', but the village of Rogate is actually in the county of West Sussex. The search should describe the county as West Sussex.

34.6.16 **Description of land**
It is not essential to include a description of the land in the search application because a search of the register is based primarily upon the names of estate owners. Unless an accurate description (and where relevant, former description) of the land can be included in the application it is preferable to leave this section of the form blank, since it is

safer to accept the task of having to read through and dismiss a number of irrelevant entries revealed by the computer than to take the risk of a registration not being revealed because an incorrect description of the land was included in the search form.

34.6.17 Registers of pending actions, writs and orders and deeds of arrangement
These registers are arranged differently from the register of land charges and entries recorded against the names to be searched will be revealed regardless of any period of ownership or description of the land included in the search form.

34.6.18 Great care should be exercised when completing the search application form since the certificate of search will not protect a purchaser who has incorrectly described the land or who has failed to specify the correct name of the estate owner.[14]

34.7 WHAT THE SEARCH REVEALS
34.7.1 A certificate of the result of the search revealing no subsisting entries is delivered on form K17.

34.7.2 Where subsisting entries relating to any of the matters listed in paras 34.1.1–34.1.5 exist the certificate of search is delivered on form K18. The details of any entry which is revealed are printed on the certificate using the following code numbers to distinguish the several component elements of the entry:

(a) Code 1   type of registration (including in the case of land charges the class and sub-class of the charge), the registration number and date of registration;
(b) Code 2   a short description of the land affected by the charge;
(c) Code 3   the parish, place or district;
(d) Code 4   the county;
(e) Code 5   any additional information relating to the entry, eg reference to a priority notice;
(f) Code 6   the name of the chargor;
(h) Code 7   the chargor's address, when recorded in the index.

34.7.3 Infrequently a charge relating to defunct tithes previously payable to the Church Commissioners or their predecessors in title may appear on the result of the search. In such a case a letter should be sent to the Church Commissioners, 1 Millbank, London, SW1P 3U2 (01 222 7010), to inform them of the charge. The Commissioners will then issue a standard letter which is accepted by the Central Land Charges Registry as sufficient evidence to discharge the entry.

34.7.4 Charges registered against limited companies
A fixed charge created by a company before 1 January 1970 was not capable of registration under the Land Charges Act 1925 and so will

not be revealed by this search. Floating charges, whenever created are not generally registered as land charges and so similarly will not commonly be revealed.

Both of the above types of charge must be registered at the Companies Registry under the Companies Act 1948, s 95 and a company search should be undertaken in order to reveal their existence and details (see ch 8, above).

34.7.5 Office copies of entries

An office copy of a land charges entry consists of a copy of the application form which was submitted when the charge was registered.

An application for an office copy of an entry in a register may be made by post on form K19.

An application by telephone for an office copy may only be made if it arises whilst a telephone search is being made.

An application for office copies may be made by telex, using the Land Charges Department's recommended form of wording shown below.

34.7.5.1 *Standard form of telex for requesting office copy entries*
Each item should commence on a new line with double spacing between lines.

    (a) applicant's answer back code and telex number; date in brackets;
    (b) the words 'Office Copy';
    (c) the title of the register affected, eg Land Charges;
    (d) the official reference number and date of registration;
    (e) the name against which the entry is registered;
    (f) the letters REF followed by the applicant's reference;
    (g) the letters KN followed by the applicant's key number;
    (h) the name and address to which the copy is to be sent.

34.7.6 Examining the result of the search

In some cases, eg where an extremely common name has been searched against, or an imprecise and very general description of the land was included in the search application, the computerised search certificate will reveal a large number of entries which do not relate to the land being purchased. These inapplicable entries may be disregarded and no further action need be taken in respect of them.

Where an entry clearly does relate to the property being purchased, the vendor may already have supplied information which relates to the entry, eg disclosure of restrictive covenants or the existence of a second charge over the property, in which case the search certificate will merely confirm the information which has been previously disclosed by the vendor. If the search certificate reveals the existence of an incumbrance not previously disclosed by the vendor it will be necessary to obtain further details of the incumbrance by obtaining an office copy of the entry. A copy of the search certificate and of the office copy of the entry should then be sent to the vendor with a request that he supplies further details of the charge and either procures its cancellation or certifies on the search certificate that the entry does not affect the land being purchased.

In a few cases it may be unclear from the search certificate whether or not the entry does relate to the land being purchased, eg where the purchase is of a single plot on a building estate a charge registered against the estate may be revealed with no indication given as to which particular plots on that estate are affected by the charge.

An office copy of the entry may be obtained and sent with a copy of the search certificate to the vendor with a request for further information as above. The office copy will usually reveal the name and address of the solicitors who lodged the application for registration. It may occasionally be possible to obtain further details of the registration from them.

If having made further enquiries it is still unclear whether or not the charge affects the land, the client should be informed and a defective title insurance policy may be taken out to cover the defect.

34.7.7 Priority period

Where an official certificate of search has been obtained, any entry which is made in the register after the date of the certificate and before the completion of the purchase and is not made pursuant to a priority notice, will not affect the purchaser, provided the purchase is completed before the expiration of the fifteenth working day after the date of the certificate. The date on which the priority period ends is clearly shown on the certificate of the result of the search. Protection under the search will end on the date of completion of the purchase if that date is within the 15-day period.

Where completion is to be delayed beyond the priority period given by the search a further search should be undertaken. Since an entry in the land charges register can only be made against an estate owner during his period of ownership of the land the new search need only be against the present estate owner for the period since the last search.

34.7.8 Priority notices

A person who intends to register a land charge may give notice of his intention prior to the actual creation of the charge by lodging notice on form K6 at the Central Land Charges Department at least 15 working days before completion of the matter giving rise to the charge. A priority notice is then entered in the register to which the intended application will relate. Provided the application to register the land charge is made within 30 working days of the date of the priority notice, the registration will take effect from the date of completion of the matter giving rise to the charge and not from the (later) date when the application to register the charge was received by the Land Charges Department. This procedure is of particular importance when new restrictive covenants are to be created on the sale of part of land. Unless the person imposing the covenants (usually the vendor) lodges a priority notice before completion, the registration of the covenants will not be effected at the time when the purchaser's mortgagee acquires his interest in the land, and will therefore not bind the mortgagee or a subsequent purchaser from him.

Since the priority of registerable mortgages also depends on the date of their registration, this procedure is of similar importance when acting for a second or subsequent mortgagee.

Arguably the priority notice procedure should be used whenever it is sought to register a land charge but except in the two situations outlined above this procedure is little used in practice. As has been noted above (para 34.7.7) a purchaser of land who obtains an official certificate of search will take his interest subject to any land charge which is duly registered pursuant to a priority notice which is revealed on his search certificate.

34.7.9   An official certificate of search is conclusive in favour of the applicant and probably also in favour of the applicant's successors in title. Thus an entry which is registered, but which is not revealed by the result of a correctly made search will not bind a purchaser. Where the result of a search is obtained by telephone or telex, the confirmatory printed certificate, not the telephone or telex reply, is the conclusive document. Where, however, an entry has not been revealed to the purchaser because the name against which the registration was effected was behind the statutory root of title or behind the actual root of title revealed to the purchaser, whichever is earlier, the purchaser will be bound by the entry but may in certain circumstances be entitled to compensation. A discussion of liability on searches is contained in ch 2, above.

34.8   BANKRUPTCY SEARCHES

34.8.1   Duration of registration
The registration of a bankruptcy petition, receiving order or deed of arrangement lasts for a period of five years after which the registration lapses if not renewed.

34.8.2   On form K15
Where a full search against the name of an individual is made on form K15 bankruptcy entries will automatically be revealed in the certificate of result of the search irrespective of the description of the land or period of ownership included in the search application.

A solicitor who is acting for a proposed mortgagee will usually be required to obtain a clear certificate of search against the name of the borrower before the mortgage funds are released to the borrower. Such a search may be made on form K15 in which case the period to be searched should be stated as the current year only, eg 1985–1985. Where the mortgagee's solicitor is also acting for the purchaser of unregistered land it will probably be convenient to simply add the purchaser/borrower's name to the end of the full K15 search which he is making in the course of his investigation of title.

34.8.3   On form K16
Where a bankruptcy only search is being made form K16 should be used.

It is only possible to do a bankruptcy only search by post. If it is desired to make the search in person by telephone or telex a full search must be undertaken.

34.8.4   Registered land
It is not necessary to make a bankruptcy search against the vendor of registered land since bankruptcy entries registered against him will be revealed by a pre-completion search at HM Land Registry (see ch 35, below).

A solicitor who is acting for a proposed mortgagee where the mortgage is being taken out concurrently with the purchase of the registered land will need to make a bankruptcy only search against the prospective borrowers.

Where for any reason the title to registered land is not deduced (eg on the grant of a short lease) a bankruptcy only search may be considered worthwhile against the vendor/lessor since in these circumstances a Land Registry search will not be possible.

34.9   FORM K16
This form is reproduced on pp 364–365, below.

34.10   COMMENT ON FORM K16
The names of individuals should be inserted using the same guidelines as are prescribed for the completion of form K15 (para 34.6, above).

There is no need to give a description of the land nor to state a period of years to be searched. The result of the search will reveal any bankruptcy petitions, receiving orders, or deeds of arrangement registered or renewed during the five years prior to the search application.

Form K16

Land Charges Act 1972

Payment of fee
(see Note 2 overleaf)

EITHER

Insert a cross (X) in this box if the fee is to be paid through a credit account

OR

affix stamps in this space

●

APPLICATION FOR AN OFFICIAL SEARCH
(BANKRUPTCY ONLY)

Application is hereby made for an official search in the index to the registers kept pursuant to the Land Charges Act 1972 in respect of the under-mentioned names for any subsisting entries of:

(i) petitions in bankruptcy in the register of pending actions
(ii) receiving orders in bankruptcy in the register of writs and orders
(iii) deeds of arrangement in the register of deeds of arrangement

For Official Use only			
#			**IMPORTANT: Please read the notes overleaf before completing the form.**

NAMES TO BE SEARCHED
(Please use block letters and see note 3 overleaf)

Forename(s)	
SURNAME	
Forename(s)	
SURNAME	
Forename(s)	
SURNAME	
Forename(s)	
SURNAME	
Forename(s)	
SURNAME	
Forename(s)	
SURNAME	

Particulars of Applicant
(see notes, 4, 5 and 6 overleaf)

Name and address for despatch of certificate
(Leave blank if certificate is to be returned to applicant's address)

KEY NUMBER	Name and address

Applicant's reference:	Date	FOR OFFICIAL USE ONLY

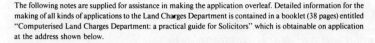

NOTES FOR GUIDANCE OF APPLICANTS

The following notes are supplied for assistance in making the application overleaf. Detailed information for the making of all kinds of applications to the Land Charges Department is contained in a booklet (38 pages) entitled "Computerised Land Charges Department: a practical guide for Solicitors" which is obtainable on application at the address shown below.

1. Effect of search. The official certificate of the result of this search will have no statutory effect in relation to registered land (see Land Registration Act 1925, s. 59 and Land Charges Act 1972, s. 14).

2. Fee payable. A fee is payable for each name searched. If you have been granted a credit account you may ask for the fee to be debited to your account. Otherwise, you must affix Land Registry adhesive fee stamps for the appropriate sum in the fee panel provided overleaf. These stamps can be purchased from any head post office or from a sub-post office where the demand is sufficient to warrant stocks being held. Cheques and postal orders are not usually acceptable, (but see the 'guide' referred to above).

3. Names to be searched. The forename(s) and surname of each individual must be entered on the appropriate lines in the relevant panel overleaf. If you are searching more than 6 names, use a second form.

4. Key number. If you have been allocated a key number, please take care to enter this in the space provided overleaf, whether or not you are paying fees through your credit account.

5. Applicant's name and address. This need not be supplied if the applicant's key number is correctly entered in the space provided overleaf.

6. Applicant's reference. Any reference must be limited to 10 digits, including any oblique strokes and punctuation.

7. Despatch of this form. When completed, send this application to the address shown below, which is printed in a position so as to fit within a standard window envelope.

THE SUPERINTENDENT,
LAND CHARGES DEPARTMENT,
SEARCH SECTION,
BURRINGTON WAY,
PLYMOUTH PL5 3LP.

(see note 7 above)

oyez The Solicitors' Law Stationery Society plc, Oyez House, 237 Long Lane, London SE1 4PU

F4091 5-84
* * * * *

34.11 TABLE OF MAIN DIFFERENCES BETWEEN LAND
CHARGES REGISTRY SEARCHES AND LAND REGISTRY
SEARCHES

Item	Land Charges	Land Registry
Against land	Mainly unregistered land	Registered land only
Bankruptcy	Entries registered irrespective of ownership of land	Only registered if bankrupt is proprietor of registered land
Who may search	Open to public inspection	Authority of registered proprietor generally need in order to make search
Where to search	All searches made at Plymouth	Appropriate district land registry
Subject of search	Search against name of estate owner	Search against title number of land
Fees	£0.50 for each name searched against	No fee
Result of official search	Conclusive in favour of applicant	Not conclusive in favour of applicant
Priority period	15 working days from date of search certificate provided completion takes place before the expiry of this period. NB Priority period ends on date of completion if this is earlier than the 15-working-days' priority period.	30 working days from date of search certificate provided completion takes place and correctly completed application for registration is lodged before the expiry of this period
Priority notice	May be lodged prior to completion to protect proposed registration of charge	No equivalent procedure

34.12 SEARCH SUMMARY

Application	K15
	K16 (bankruptcy only)
Plan	
Fee	£0.50 per name
Address	The Superintendent
	Land Charges Department
	Search Section
	Burrington Way
	Plymouth
	Devon
	PL 3LP
	(0752 779831)
	Telex LANDCHG 45431
	Telephone searches (0752 701171)
Special points	
Area affected	Bankruptcy searches irrespective of ownership of land
	Land searches—unregistered land only

1 *Taylor v Taylor* [1968] 1 All ER 843, [1968] 1 WLR 378. Cf an application under the Matrimonial Causes Act 1973.
2 *Georgiades v Edward Wolfe & Co Ltd* [1965] Ch 487, [1964] 3 All ER 433, CA.
3 Land Charges Act 1972, s 2(8).
4 Land Charges Act 1972 s 2(4).
5 *Pritchard v Briggs* [1980] Ch 338, [1980] 1 All ER 294, CA.
6 See Barnsley *Conveyancing Land and Practice* (2nd edn) p 386.
7 Land Charges Act 1972 s 2(5).
8 See *Shiloh Spinners Ltd v Harding* [1973] AC 691, [1973] 1 All ER 90, HL.
9 Law of Property Act 1925, s 198(1).
10 See *Emmet on Title* (17th edn) p 657.
11 *Ferris v Weaven* [1952] 2 All ER 233, but see *Midland Bank Trust Co Ltd v Green* [1981] AC 513, [1981] All ER 153, HL.
12 *ER Ives Investment Ltd v High* [1967] 2 QB 379, [1967] 1 All ER 504, CA.
13 *Barrett v Hilton Developments* [1975] Ch 237, [1974] 3 All ER 944, CA.
14 See *Du Sautoy v Symes* [1967] Ch 1146, [1967] 1 All ER 25; *Oak Co-operative Building Society v Blackburn* [1968] Ch 730, [1968] 2 All ER 117, CA.

Chapter 35

Search of Register at HM Land Registry

35.1 This search is only relevant to land with a registered title. Where land is registered with a title other than absolute it may also be appropriate to carry out a search at HM Land Charges Registry (see para 34.2.1, above.)

35.2 WHEN TO MAKE THE SEARCH

An authority to inspect the Register given by the registered proprietor of the land is usually required in order to make a search at the Land Registry. Since this authority is not normally supplied to the purchaser before exchange of contracts, it will not usually be possible to make this search until contracts have been exchanged. Unless there are suspicious circumstances the search should be made as close to contractual completion date as possible in order to obtain the benefit of the priority period conferred by the search certificate. The official certificate of the result of the search should be obtained by the purchaser's solicitors before actual completion; thus where a search is to be made by post the application should be submitted approximately seven days before contractual completion date. In the case of searches made by telephone or telex it may be possible to postpone making the search until a little nearer the completion date.

35.3 HOW TO MAKE THE SEARCH

35.3.1 Authority to inspect

The contents of the Land Register are not open to public inspection and generally the written consent of the registered proprietor is required before a search can be made. This authority is usually supplied to the purchaser on exchange of contracts and may take the form of a condition contained in the contract for sale (see Law Society Conditions of Sale, Special Condition E), a letter signed by the vendor or his solicitor, or may be given on Oyez form 201.

35.3.2 Occasions when authority to inspect is not required

   (a) Where the applicant is the registered proprietor or the solicitor for the registered proprietor;

(b) where the applicant is the proprietor of a registered charge or incumbrance;

(c) personal representatives of a deceased proprietor may search on production of the grant of probate or letters of administration;

(d) a person who is 'interested' in the land or in adjoining land may search without authority provided:

  (i) he can satisfy the Chief Land Registrar that there are reasonable grounds for allowing the inspection; and

  (ii) the registered proprietor does not object. Applications of this type are rarely granted. An example of such an application which might succeed would be where a lessee does not know who his freeholder is but needs this information in order to know to whom to pay his rent. On receiving such a request the Chief Land Registrar will notify the registered proprietor who is given ten days in which to lodge his objection;

(e) a judgment creditor may inspect the register on production of an office copy of an order for the enforcement of a judgment against the land. A judgment creditor also has the right to apply to the court by summons for an order for inspection of the register. On production of the court order a search may be made;

(f) the official receiver and trustee in bankruptcy may search the register of title of the bankrupt without an authority to inspect;

(g) in certain circumstances government departments (eg the Commissioners of Inland Revenue) and local authorities may be given permission by the Chief Land Registrar to inspect the register without the authority of the registered proprietor;

(h) any person may apply to the High Court (or in certain circumstances the Crown Court) for an order to allow inspection without the consent of the registered proprietor. Such an order is rarely granted.

35.3.3 Where to make the search

The search is made at the appropriate district land registry for the area. The addresses of the district registries are listed in Appendix I, below.

35.3.4 Postal searches

The search application form should be completed in duplicate and sent to the appropriate district land registry. A search which is sent to the wrong registry will be returned to the applicant and is not forwarded to the correct address by the registry.

35.3.5 Personal searches

A personal search of the register may be made by the registered proprietor or by any person authorised by him so to do. The authority to inspect, where required, must be produced at the time of making the application for the personal search.

A search of the register or map may only be made at the particular district land registry where the land is registered.

No fee is payable when the search is made by the registered proprietor himself. In other cases a fee of £1 is payable.

Personal searches confer no priority and thus are seldom made.

35.3.6   Searches made by telephone

Provided a written authority to inspect (where required) is held by the applicant a search may be made by telephoning the appropriate district land registry. The following undertaking and particulars should be given:

(a) an undertaking that an appropriate search application will be sent forthwith by post together with the fee of £3.00. The fee may be paid by credit account;

(b) the title number and a short description of the property;

(c) the full name of the registered proprietor;

(d) the name, address, telephone number and reference of the solicitor making the application;

(e) the full name of the person for whom the solicitor is acting;

(f) the date from which the search is to be made.

The result of the search will be telephoned to the applicant and will include the title number, a statement as to whether the search relates to the whole or only part of the land comprised in the title, a short description of the property, the date from which the search has been made, and details of any adverse entries on the register or the word 'Nil' if no entries appear.

The result of a telephone search confers no priority on the applicant, although the official certificate of search issued as a result of the subsequent postal application will.

35.3.7   Searches made by telex

Provided the applicant holds a written authority to inspect (where required) a search may be made by telex to the appropriate district land registry. The same information and undertaking must be given as is required for a search made by telephone (para 35.3.6, above). In particular, the telex search must be followed by a postal application for a search and the fee of £3.00.

The abbreviated form of telex prescribed by the Land Registration (Official Searches) Rules 1981, Sch 2 (set out below) must be used when making a search by this method.

35.3.7.1   *Prescribed form of telex*

A. The title number;

B. a short description of the property followed by the words 'Whole Search' or 'Part Search' as appropriate;

C. the date from which the search is to be made;

D. the full name of the registered proprietor;

E. the name and telex address of the solicitor making the application;

F. the name of the person on whose behalf the application is made;

G. the words 'Undertaking Given'.

The reply will be transmitted to the applicant by telex and will contain the following information:

A. title number;

B. 'Whole' or 'Part' to indicate the type of search made, followed in the case of a part search by a brief description of the land;

C. the date from which the search has been made;

D. the word 'Nil' if no entries are revealed, or details of the adverse entries.

A search made by telex confers no priority on the applicant, but a priority period will be given when the official certificate of search is issued in pursuance of the postal application which is submitted to comply with the undertaking given by the applicant's solicitor.

35.3.8 Leases

For the purposes of making a search an intending lessee is included within the ambit of the word 'purchaser' and will therefore make his search in the same way as a purchaser of a freehold interest in the land. However, under the Law of Property Act 1925, s 44, a prospective lessee has no right to call for the deduction of the freehold reversionary title and unless the contract provides to the contrary the prospective lessee will be unable to obtain an authority to inspect the register from the owner of the freehold.

35.3.9 Sub-sales

Where A has contracted to sell land to B, and B has before completion of his purchase from A contracted to sell the land to C, C will not be able to make a pre-completion search against B until B has become the registered proprietor of the land after having completed his own purchase from A. Unless it is intended that the sub-sale between B and C should not be completed until B has acquired his own title through registration, provision must be made for A to supply an authority to inspect to C. Failing this C may have to complete in reliance on B's pre-completion search which, from C's point of view is unsatisfactory, since he will derive no protection from B's search certificate.

35.4   SEARCH OF THE WHOLE OF A REGISTERED TITLE

A search of the whole of a registered title on behalf of an applicant who intends to purchase the land, take a lease of the land, or to lend money on the security of a charge over the whole of the land should be made on form 94A. The form should be completed in duplicate. No plan is required and no fee is payable for making the search, except where the form is submitted after a telephone or telex search has been made.

35.5   FORM 94A
This form is reproduced on pp 373–376, below.

35.6   COMMENT ON FORM 94A
35.6.1   The county and district (or London borough) and title number may be ascertained from the copy entries of the register supplied by the vendor under the Land Registration Act 1925, s 110.
35.6.2   The full name(s) of the registered proprietor(s) as shown on the proprietorship register of the copy entries must be inserted.
35.6.3   The applicant must specify a date from which the search is to be made. This date will normally be the date of the issue of the office copy entries which have been supplied to him by the vendor. The date of issue of the office copies is printed on the bottom right hand corner of each page of the copies. If the vendor merely supplied photocopies of the land or charge certificate in his possession the date from which the search is to be made will be the date on which the land or charge certificate was last brought up to date by comparison with the register. This date is stamped on the inside cover of the land or charge certificate. The vendor will supply this information where he is required to do so by means of a standard question on the requisitions on title form.
35.6.4   The full name of the applicant on whose behalf the search is made must be inserted. Where a solicitor is acting both for the purchaser and his mortgagee the search should be made in the name of the mortgagee. The purchaser may then take the benefit of the result of the search made in the mortgagee's name. A search made in the name of the purchaser affords no protection to his mortgagee.
35.6.5   Where a solicitor is acting for the applicant he must certify either that he acts for the registered proprietor, or that he holds the written authority of the registered proprietor to make the search. The authority itself need only be submitted with the search application where the applicant is not represented by a solicitor.
35.6.6   The application form must be signed (not rubber stamped) by the applicant.
35.6.7   A separate search form must be used for each title number to be searched.

35.7   SEARCH OF PART ONLY OF A REGISTERED TITLE
A search of part only of a registered title made on behalf of an applicant who intends to purchase, take a lease of, or lend money on the security

Form 94B HM Land Registry   **Land Registration (Official Searches) Rules 1981**

Application by Purchaser (¹) for Official Search with priority in respect of PART of the land in a title

(Numbers in brackets relate to notes over- leaf.)

....District Land Registry(²)

The attached duplicate must also be completed (A carbon copy will suffice).

(For an official search of whole of the land in a title, use form 94A).

FOR OFFICIAL USE

County and district (or London borough)	
Title number(³)	
Enter full name(s) of the registered proprietor(s)(⁴)	
Application is made to ascertain whether any adverse(⁵) entry has been made in the register affecting the undermentioned property since the date shown opposite being EITHER the date on which an office copy of the subsisting entries in the register was issued OR the last date on which the land or charge certificate was officially examined with the register.	
Enter full name(s) of the applicant(s) *(i.e. purchaser(s) lessee(s) or chargee(s))*	

I/We *as solicitors acting for* (⁶) the above mentioned applicant(s) certify that the applicant(s) intend(s) to:—

(Enter X in the appropriate box opposite)

P	purchase	the undermentioned PART of the land in the above title
L	take a lease of	
C	lend money on the security of a registered charge on	

Property to be purchased, leased or charged. State either

(a) where an estate layout plan has been approved in the Land Registry
   (i) the plot number(s) (⁷) and
   (ii) the date of approval of the estate plan

or (b) IN ALL OTHER CASES

the short description of the property referring to a plan(⁸). *Please attach a copy of the plan to the duplicate search.*

(a)   Plot number(s)

                                             Date of approval

(b) ....

shown ....on the attached plan.

A   WHERE A SOLICITOR IS ACTING FOR THE APPLICANT(S)

I/We certify that I/We hold the duly signed written authority of (or of the solicitor(s) for) the above mentioned registered proprietor(s) to inspect the register of the above title OR that I/We also act as solicitor(s) for the registered proprietor(s).

Indicate this by entering X in this box   **A**

B   WHERE A SOLICITOR IS NOT ACTING FOR THE APPLICANT(S)

The duly signed written authority of (or of the solicitor(s) for) the registered proprietor(s) to inspect the register of the above title accompanies this application.

Indicate this by entering X in this box   **B**

Key number(⁹)	This panel must be completed using BLOCK LETTERS and inserting the name, **full address and postal code** to which the official certificate or result of search is to be sent.

Signed:..

Date:..

Solicitor's reference(¹⁰)							

Telephone number:.......................................

Form 94D   HM Land Registry   Land Registration (Official Searches) Rules 1981

This page is to be completed only by HM Land Registry

Official Certificate of the Result of Search

It is hereby certified that the official search applied for has been made with the following result:

Since .... 19 .....

N.B.—To obtain priority(⁹), the application for registration in respect of which this search is made must be delivered to the proper office at the latest by 11 am on the date when priority expires.

NOTES

(1)   "Purchaser" means any person who, in good faith and for valuable consideration, acquires or intends to acquire a legal estate in land, so it includes a lessee or a chargee but not a depositee of a land or charge certificate. An official search made by such a depositee or by any person other than a "purchaser", as so defined, should be made in form 94C and a fee is payable.

(2)   The application should be sent to the district land registry serving the area in which the land is situated. A list of addresses of the district land registries is set out on page 4 of this application form.

(3)   A separate form must be used for each title number to be searched.

(4)   The name(s) of the registered proprietor(s) should be entered as they appear on the evidence of the registered title supplied to the applicant. If there has been a change of name(s) the new name(s) should also be entered in brackets.

(5)   Any entry made in the register since the date of commencement of this search but subsequently cancelled will not be revealed.

(6)   Where no solicitor is acting delete all or some of the words in italics as appropriate to the particular situation.

(7)   Where a key number has been allocated it should be used.

(8)   This should be restricted to a maximum of 10 digits including oblique strokes and punctuation.

(9)   The period of priority reserved for the registration of the disposition protected by the official search certificate will be shown either by a stamp impressed in the result of search above or on a separate computer printed result.

(10)   Where a first registration is pending, an official search certificate cannot be issued unless and until the first registration of the title to the land affected has been completed.

(11)   Fuller information about the official search procedure is contained in Practice Leaflet No. 2, entitled "Official searches of the Register", and Practice Leaflet No. 7, entitled "Development of registered building estates" which are obtainable free of charge from any district land registry.

Form 94A   HM Land Registry
(Duplicate)

Land Registration (Official Searches) Rules 1981

Application by Purchaser for Official Search with priority in respect of the WHOLE of the land in a title

.... District Land Registry

(For an official search of part of the land in a title, use form 94B).

County and district (or London borough)	
Title number	
Enter full name(s) of the registered proprietor(s)	
Application is made to ascertain whether any adverse entry has been made in the register since the date shown opposite being EITHER the date on which an office copy of the subsisting entries in the register was issued OR the last date on which the land or charge certificate was officially examined with the register.	
Enter full name(s) of the applicant(s) *(i.e. purchaser(s) lessee(s) or chargee(s))*	

I/We *as Solicitors acting for* the above mentioned applicant(s) certify that the applicant(s) intend(s) to:–

(Enter X in the appropriate box opposite)

P	purchase	⎫ the WHOLE of
L	take a lease of	the land
C	lend money on the security of a registered charge on	⎭ in the above title

A WHERE A SOLICITOR IS ACTING FOR THE APPLICANT(S)
I/We certify that I/We hold the duly signed written authority of (or of the solicitor(s) for) the above mentioned registered proprietor(s) to inspect the register of the above title OR that I/We also act as solicitor(s) for the registered proprietor(s).

Indicate this by entering X in this box | A |

B WHERE A SOLICITOR IS NOT ACTING FOR THE APPLICANT(S)
The duly signed written authority of (or of the solicitor(s) for) the registered proprietor(s) to inspect the register of the above title accompanies this application.

Indicate this by entering X in this box | B |

Key number(7)	This panel must be completed using BLOCK LETTERS and inserting the name, **full address and postal code** to which the official certificate or result of search is to be sent.
Solicitor's reference(8)									

Signed:...

Date:...

Telephone number:...

Form 94D   HM Land Registry   Land Registration (Official Searches) Rules 1981

This page is to be completed only by HM Land Registry

Official search no. to be impressed here:

Official Certificate of the Result of Search

It is hereby certified that the official search applied for has been made with the following result:

Since .... 19 ....

Date stamp	Pending official searches	Pending dealings	Remarks

Search drafted ....   Search checked ....

ADDRESSES OF DISTRICT LAND REGISTRIES

District Land Registry	Address	Telephone No.	Telex Call No.
Birkenhead	76 Hamilton Street, Birkenhead, Merseyside L41 5JW	051-647 5661	628475
Croydon	Sunley House, Bedford Park, Croydon CR9 3LE	01-686 8833	917288
Durham	Southfield House, Southfield Way, Durham DH1 5TR	0385 66151	53684
Gloucester	Bruton Way, Gloucester GL1 1DQ	0452 28666	43119
Harrow	Lyon House, Lyon Road, Harrow, Middx. HA1 2EU	01-427 8811	262476
Lytham	Lytham St Annes, Lancs. FY8 5AB	0253 736999	67649
Nottingham	Chalfont Drive, Nottingham NG8 3RN	0602 291111	37167
Peterborough	Aragon Court, Northminster Road, Peterborough PE1 1XN	0733 46048	32786
Plymouth	Plumer House, Tailyour Road, Crownhill, Plymouth PL6 5HY	0752 701234	45265
Stevenage	Brickdale House, Danestrete, Stevenage Herts. SG1 1XG	0438 314488	82377
Swansea	37 The Kingsway, Swansea SA1 5LF	0792 476677	48220
Tunbridge Wells	Tunbridge Wells, Kent TN2 5AQ	0892 26141	95286
Weymouth	1 Cumberland Drive, Weymouth, Dorset DT4 9TT	03057 76161	418231

oyez   The Solicitors' Law Stationery Society plc, Oyez House, 237 Long Lane, London SE1 4PU   F3784 3/84

of part of the land should be submitted on form 94B which must be completed in duplicate. No fee is payable for making the search except where the application is submitted pursuant to a search made by telephone or telex.

35.8 FORM 94B
This form is reproduced on pp 378–379, below.

35.9 COMMENT ON FORM 94B
35.9.1 Except as outlined in the following sub-paragraph, this form is completed in the same manner as form 94A (para 35.6, above).

35.9.2 Where the land forms part of a building estate and an estate lay-out plan has been approved by the registry it is sufficient to state the date of approval of the estate plan and the plot number or numbers to be searched. In some cases a house with a separately built garage may be shown under two different plot numbers on the estate lay-out plan. The vendor will supply the purchaser with the date of approval of the plan either in answer to preliminary enquiries or in response to the purchaseer's requisitions on title. In all other cases a verbal description of the land must be inserted on the search application and two copies of a plan which clearly identifies the area of land to be searched must be attached to the application form. The Registry prefer the plans to be to the scale of 1:2500 and to contain sufficient dimensions to define the part of the title affected and to identify the land to be searched in relation to existing physical features, eg road junctions, fences or walls. Ideally the plan should be a copy of the one which is intended to be used in the engrossment of the transfer, lease or mortgage.

35.10 NON-PRIORITY SEARCHES ON FORM 94C
35.10.1 The official searches of the register on forms 94A and B described above are only available to a purchaser, lessee or chargee who in good faith and for valuable consideration intends to acquire a legal interest in the land. Although forms 94A and B cover most situations there are circumstances in which an applicant is not entitled to use one of these two forms of search and must instead make his application on form 94C. This form is not therefore widely used and should only be used where the applicant is not permitted to use one of the other search forms because, as its title indicates, the certificate of result of this search does not confer any priority period on the applicant.

35.10.2 Circumstances in which form 94C must be used
(a) When acting for the purchaser of an equitable interest in the land;

(b) by a mortgagee who seeks to protect his charge by a notice of deposit;

Form 94B HM Land Registry Land Registration (Official Searches) Rules 1981

Application by Purchaser (¹) for Official Search with priority in respect of PART of the land in a title

(Numbers in brackets relate to notes overleaf.)

..............................District Land Registry(²)

The attached duplicate must also be completed (A carbon copy will suffice).

(For an official search of whole of the land in a title, use form 94A).

FOR OFFICIAL USE

County and district (or London borough)	
Title number(³)	
Enter full name(s) of the registered proprietor(s)(⁴)	
Application is made to ascertain whether any adverse(⁵) entry has been made in the register affecting the undermentioned property since the date shown opposite being EITHER the date on which an office copy of the subsisting entries in the register was issued OR the last date on which the land or charge certificate was officially examined with the register.	
Enter full name(s) of the applicant(s) *(i.e. purchaser(s) lessee(s) or chargee(s))*	

I/We *as solicitors acting for* (⁶) the above mentioned applicant(s) certify that the applicant(s) intend(s) to:—

(Enter X in the appropriate box opposite)

P	purchase	the undermentioned
L	take a lease of	PART of the land
C	lend money on the security of a registered charge on	in the above title

Property to be purchased, leased or charged. State either
(a) where an estate layout plan has been approved in the Land Registry
(i) the plot number(s) (⁷) and
(ii) the date of approval of the estate plan
or (b) IN ALL OTHER CASES
the short description of the property referring to a plan(⁸). *Please attach a copy of the plan to the duplicate search.*

(a) .... Plot number(s)

.... Date of approval

(b) ....

shown....................on the attached plan.

A WHERE A SOLICITOR IS ACTING FOR THE APPLICANT(S)

I/We certify that I/We hold the duly signed written authority of (or of the solicitor(s) for) the above mentioned registered proprietor(s) to inspect the register of the above title OR that I/We also act as solicitor(s) for the registered proprietor(s).

Indicate this by entering X in this box

A

B WHERE A SOLICITOR IS NOT ACTING FOR THE APPLICANT(S)

The duly signed written authority of (or of the solicitor(s) for) the registered proprietor(s) to inspect the register of the above title accompanies this application.

Indicate this by entering X in this box

B

Key number(⁹)	This panel must be completed using BLOCK LETTERS and inserting the name, **full address and postal code** to which the official certificate or result of search is to be sent.

Signed:....................

Date:....................

Solicitor's reference(¹⁰)

Telephone number:....................

Form 94D   **HM Land Registry**   **Land Registration (Official Searches) Rules 1981**

This page is to be completed only by HM Land Registry

Official Certificate of the Result of Search

It is hereby certified that the official search applied for has been made with the following result:

Since .... 19 ....

N.B.—To obtain priority([11]), the application for registration in respect of which this search is made must be delivered to the proper office at the latest by 11 am on the date when priority expires.

NOTES

(1)   "Purchaser" means any person who, in good faith and for valuable consideration, acquires or intends to acquire a legal estate in land, so it incudes a lessee or a chargee but not a depositee of a land or charge certificate. An official search made by such a depositee or by any person other than a "purchaser", as so defined, should be made in form 94C and a fee is payable.

(2)   The application should be sent to the district land registry serving the area in which the land is situated. A list of addresses of the district land registries is set out on page 4 of this application form.

(3)   A separate form must be used for each title number to be searched.

(4)   The name(s) of the registered proprietor(s) should be entered as they appear on the evidence of the registered title supplied to the applicant. If there has been a change of name(s) the new name(s) should also be entered in brackets.

(5)   Any entry made in the register since the date of commencement of this search but subsequently cancelled will not be revealed.

(6)   Where no solicitor is acting delete all or some of the words in italics as appropriate to the particular situation.

(7)   The application must be made by reference to a plan in all cases save where, in a registered building estate, the estate layout plan has already been approved by the Department for use in connection with official searches. It will then suffice if the application refers to the plot number(s) shown on the approved plan and the date of approval of that plan. If the official search procedure is to operate effectively. however, it is essential that the plot number(s) are stated correctly, particularly where one property comprises two or more separately numbered plots or parcels (eg. a house in a block of dwellings with its garage in a separate garage block).

(8)   The plan accompanying an application must be drawn to a suitable scale (generally not less than 1/2500) and supplied in duplicate. Where necessary, figured dimensions must be entered on the plan, so as to define the extent of the land affected and to fix its position by tying it to those existing physical features which are depicted by firm black lines on the official plan for the registered title.

(9)   Where a key number has been allocated it should be used.

(10)   This should be restricted to a maximum of 10 digits including oblique strokes and punctuation.

(11)   The period of priority reserved for the registration of the disposition protected by the official search certificate will be shown either by a stamp impressed in the result of search above or on a separate computer printed result.

(12)   Where a first registration is pending, an official search certificate cannot be issued unless and until the first registration of the title to the land affected has been completed.

(13)   Fuller information about the official search procedure is contained in Practice Leaflet No. 2 entitled "Official searches of the Register", and Practice Leaflet No. 7. entitled "Development of registered building estates" which are obtainable free of charge from any district land registry.

(c) in order to up-date office copy entries which have been obtained whilst an application for registration of the land is pending (see para 10.7, above).

35.11 FORM 94C
This form is reproduced on pp 381–382, below.

35.12 COMMENT ON FORM 94C
35.12.1 The form must be completed in duplicate and except where payment of the fee is to be made by credit account the fee of £2.00 must accompany the search application.
35.12.2 Except as noted below the form is completed in the same way as form 94A (para 35.6, above).
35.12.3 The applicant's name need only be inserted if the application is submitted on behalf of a person other than the registered proprietor.
35.12.4 Form 94C is used for all applications for non-priority searches irrespective of whether the search is of the whole or part only of the title. Where the search is of part only of the title two copies of a plan will be required in the same circumstances as for form 94B (para 35.9.2, above).

35.13 MORTGAGEE'S SEARCH ON FORM 106
This search is of limited application and may only be used by the proprietor of a charge whose interest is already protected by an entry on the register of the title.

  The purpose of the search is for the mortgagee of a dwelling house to ascertain whether any notice has been entered on the register to protect a non-owning spouse's rights of occupation under the Matrimonial Homes Act 1983. Such a mortgagee must serve notice of an action to enforce his security on a spouse whose interest is protected on the register.

Form 94C   HM Land Registry   **Land Registration (Official Searches) Rules 1981**

Application for Official Search without priority of the entries in the Register

(Numbers in brackets relate to notes over-leaf.)

....District Land Registry(¹)

The attached duplicate must also be completed (A carbon copy will suffice).

County and district (or London borough)	
Title number(²)	
Enter full name(s) of the registered proprietor(s)(³)	
Application is made to ascertain whether any adverse(⁴) entry has been made in the register affecting the undermentioned property since the date shown opposite being EITHER the date on which an office copy of the subsisting entries in the register was issued OR the last date on which the land or charge certificate was officially examined with the register.	
Enter full name(s) of the applicant(s) (*if other than the registered proprietor(s)*).	

For a search in respect of the WHOLE of the land in the above title enter X in this box ☐

For a search in respect of PART of the land in the above title state either

(a) Where an estate layout plan has been approved in the Land Registry
  (i) the plot number(s)(⁵) and
  (ii) the date of approval of the state plan

or (b) in ALL OTHER CASES the short description of the property referring to a plan(⁶). Please attach a copy of the plan to the duplicate search.

(a) _____ Plot number(s)

(b) _____ Date of approval

  ....
  ....
  shown .... on the attached plan

State the method by which the fee(⁷) *payable under the current Land Registration Fee Order is paid by entering X in the appropriate box opposite.*

Credit account ☐

Cheque, postal order or Land Registry fee stamps ☐

A   WHERE A SOLICITOR IS ACTING FOR THE APPLICANT(S)

I/We certify that I/We hold the duly signed written authority of (or of the solicitor(s) for) the above mentioned registered proprietor(s) to inspect the register of the above title OR that I/We also act as solicitor(s) for the registered proprietor(s).

Indicate this by entering X in this box
A

B   WHERE A SOLICITOR IS NOT ACTING FOR THE APPLICANT(S)(⁸)

The duly signed written authority of (or of the solicitor(s) for) the registered proprietor(s) to inspect the register of the above title accompanies this application.

Indicate this by entering X in this box
B

Key number (⁹)	This panel must be completed using BLOCK LETTERS and inserting the name, **full address and postal code** to which the official certificate or result of search is to be sent.

Signed: ....

Date:...

Solicitor's reference(¹⁰)	☐☐☐☐☐☐☐

Telephone number:...

Form 94D   HM Land Registry   **Land Registration (Official Searches) Rules 1981**

This page is to be completed only by HM Land Registry

Official Certificate of the Result of Search

It is hereby certified that the official search applied for has been made with the following result:

Since .... 19......

Note: This certificate confers no priority for the registration of any dealing.

NOTES

(1) The application should be sent to the district land registry serving the area in which the land is situated. A list of addresses of the district land registries is set out on page 4 of this application form.

(2) A separate form must be used for each title number to be searched.

(3) The name(s) of the registered proprietor(s) should be entered as they appear on the evidence of the registered title supplied to the applicant. If there has been a change of name(s) the new name(s) should also be entered in brackets.

(4) Any entry made in the register since the date of commencement of this search but subsequently cancelled will not be revealed.

(5) The application must be made by reference to a plan in all cases save where, in a registered building estate, the estate layout plan has already been approved by the Department for use in connection with official searches. It will then suffice if the application refers to the plot number(s) shown on the approved plan and the date of approval of that plan. If the official search procedure is to operate effectively, however, it is essential that the plot number(s) are stated correctly, particularly where one property comprises two or more separately numbered plots or parcels (eg. a house in a block of dwellings with its garage in a separate garage block).

(6) Any plan accompanying this application must be drawn to a suitable scale (generally not less than 1/2500) and supplied in duplicate. Where necessary, figured dimensions must be entered on the plan, so as to define the extent of the land affected and to fix its position by tying it to existing physical features depicted by firm black lines on the plan of the registered title. Please attach a copy of the plan to the duplicate search.

(7) If Land Registry fee stamps are used they should be affixed in the space provided on the duplicate opposite. They can be purchased at any main Post Office; postage stamps are not accepted. Failure to prepay the fee will result in the rejection of the application.

(8) This does not apply where the application is made personally by the registered proprietor.

(9) Where a key number has been allocated it should be used.

(10) This should be restricted to a maximum of 10 digits including strokes and punctuation.

(11) Fuller information about the official search procedure is contained in Practice Leaflet No. 2, entitled "Official searches of the Register", and Practice Leaflet No. 7, entitled "Development of registered building estates" which are obtainable free of charge from any district land registry.

35.14 FORM 106

Form 106   HM Land Registry

Land Registration (Matrimonial Homes) Rules 1983

Application by Mortgagee for Official Search

.... District Land Registry(¹)

The attached duplicate must also be completed.
(A carbon copy will suffice)

Small raised numbers in bold type refer to notes overleaf

Enter the following particulars:

County and district **or** London Borough	
Title number(²)	
Property	
Full name of mortgagee(s)	
Particulars of mortgage	Registered charge dated .... numbered .... in the Charges Register **OR** Mortgage dated ....protected by notice entered on(³) .... in the Charges Register **OR** Mortgage dated .... protected by caution entered on(³) .... in the Proprietorship Register

I/We(⁴) *as solicitors acting for* the above mentioned mortgagee(s) apply pursuant to section 112B of the Land Registration Act 1925 for an official certificate of the result of a search of the register of the above title for the purpose of section 8(4) of the Matrimonial Homes Act 1983 to ascertain whether any notice or caution is entered in that register to protect rights of occupation under the Matrimonial Homes Act 1967 or 1983.

This panel must be completed using BLOCK LETTERS and inserting the name, full address and postal code to which the official result of search is to be sent.	Signed ....
	Date ....
	Telephone number ....
Reference(⁵)	Key number(⁶) ....

383

Form 107   HM Land Registry   Land Registration (Matrimonial Homes) Rules 1983

This page is to be completed only by HM Land Registry

Official Certificate of the Result of Search

It is hereby certified that the official search applied for has been made with the following result:

[Notice of]   [Caution to protect]   rights   of   occupation

under the Matrimonial Homes Act [1967] [1983] in favour

of . . . . was

registered on . . . .

OR

There is no entry in the register of a notice or caution

to protect rights of occupation under the Matrimonial

Homes Act 1967 or 1983.

Date . . . .

Notes as to the completion of this form

These notes relate to the items shown by small raised numbers in bold type overleaf

1   The application should be sent to the district land registry serving the area in which the land is situated. A list of addresses of the district land registries is set out on page 4 of this application form.

2   A separate form must be used for each title number to be searched.

3   Enter date of registration of notice or caution.

4   Where no solicitor is acting, delete the words in italics.

5   This should be restricted to a maximum of 10 digits including oblique strokes and punctuation.

6   Where a key number has been allocated it should be used.

35.15 COMMENT ON FORM 106
35.15.1 The form must be completed in duplicate. No fee is payable.
35.15.2 The title number, county and district (or London borough) and a description of the property may all be obtained from the charge certificate which will be in the mortgagee's possession.
35.15.3 Details of the mortgagee's charge including its method of protection on the register must be supplied on the application form.
35.15.4 The result of a search made on form 106 confers a priority period of 15 days.

35.16 THE RESULT OF THE SEARCH
35.16.1 The search certificate may reveal the following:
(a) entries affecting the land made in the register since the date specified in the application;
(b) pending applications for registration;
(c) unexpired official certificates of search.

35.16.2 Entries affecting the land

35.16.2.1 *Notices*
A notice is an entry made on the charges register of the title to protect third-party rights over the land (other than over-riding interests which by definition are incapable of registration).

In general, a notice may only be entered on the register with the consent of the registered proprietor of the land, ie the proprietor's land or charge certificate must be on deposit at the Registry or must accompany the application for noting. As an exception to the general rule a notice to protect a non-owning spouse's rights of occupation under the Matrimonial Homes Act 1983 may be registered without production of the land or charge certificate. An application to register a notice is usually made on form A4 together with the document concerned and a certified copied of that document.

Matters which are commonly protected by notice include the following:
(a) the noting of certain leases against the reversionary title;
(b) restrictive covenants;
(c) the grant of easements;
(d) an estate contract;
(e) rights of occupation under the Matrimonial Homes Act 1983;
(f) creditor's notice to protect a bankruptcy petition.
The entry of a notice does not confer validity on the claim, but subject to this a purchaser of registered land will take subject to all matters which are so registered.

35.16.2.2 *Cautions*

A caution is used to protect third-party rights which cannot be entered in the charges register of the title because the registered proprietor will not consent to the entry of a notice by allowing his land or charge certificate to be produced to the Registry. A caution will therefore usually protect the same type of rights as those listed in the preceding sub-paragraph; however, the registration of a caution does not provide the cautioner with total protection of his interest; and generally will not affect dispositions by the proprietor of a registered charge. When a caution has been lodged the cautioner is given notice by the Registrar of any application for a dealing with the land, but unless he substantiates his claim within 14 days of the 'warning' given by the Registrar, he will lose his rights over the land and the pending dealing will proceed to be registered free of the caution.

A caution appears in the proprietorship register of the title. The protection accorded by the caution is personal to the cautioner and cannot be assigned. Before the land is registered a caution against first registration may be lodged which will give the cautioner notice of a first application to register the land. Once the land has become registered the caution will be most commonly lodged against dealings with the land but can also be used against dealings with a charge or against conversion of the title.

35.16.2.3 *Restrictions*

The entry of a restriction on the proprietorship register is a method of curtailing the registered proprietor's powers of disposition of the land and serves as notice to all persons that the proprietor is not an absolute owner of the land. No dealing with the land will be allowed to proceed to registration unless it complies with the terms of the restriction. In some cases a restriction is automatically entered by the registry. In other cases it is necessary to make an application for a restriction to be entered.

Restrictions are commonly found in the following circumstances:

(a) where the beneficial ownership of land is held by tenants in common;

(b) land held by limited companies;

(c) land held by charities;

(d) land held on a Settled Land Act settlement.

35.16.2.4 *Inhibitions*

An inhibition is an entry on the proprietorship register of the title which is used to curtail the proprietor's powers of disposition of the land. The entry of an inhibition is rare and in most cases where it is sought to limit the proprietor's powers of disposition a restriction will be entered on the register. In two particular cases, however, an inhibition will be used:

(a) to give notice of a receiving order in bankruptcy;

(b) where the incumbent of a benefice is registered as the proprietor of land in his corporate capacity.

35.16.2.5 *Registered charges*

The registration of a charge by a mortgagee is the only effective method by which the mortgagee can protect a legal charge over registered land. The entry to protect the charge appears in the charges register of the title and takes effect as a notice.

35.16.2.6 *Notice of deposit*

A notice of deposit may be entered in the charges register of the title by a mortgagee who has taken an equitable mortgage of registered land secured by a deposit of the land certificate. A notice of deposit will not take priority over a subsequent application for registration of a dealing with the land but the person with the benefit of the notice will be given notice of the pending application by the Registrar and will be given an opportunity to protect formally his charge by registration before the pending application relating to the dealing is allowed to proceed.

35.16.2.7 *Charges relating to tithes*

Very infrequently a land registry search will reveal an entry which charges the land with the payment of tithes. Tithe redemption annuity was finally abolished under the Finance Act 1975 and the Church Commissioners (who would otherwise have the benefit of the charge) have reached agreement with the Chief Land Registrar that such entries will automatically be removed from the register on a dealing with the land. No application is required for its removal.

35.17 INFORMATION RELATING TO ENTRY OF A NOTED INTEREST

Where a lessor's title is registered any person who has an interest in a lease (other than as an overriding interest) may apply on form 91 to ascertain whether notice of that lease has been entered in the charges register of the lessor's title.

Where a person has the benefit of an interest other than a lease which is capable of being noted (eg an option) he may apply to the Registry by letter to enquire whether his interest has been noted in the charges register of the appropriate title. Details of the notice will then be supplied by the Registry. Where the benefit of the interest has passed to a third party the same information can be supplied provided the applicant is able to show his entitlement to the benefit.

No fee is charged for this service.

35.18   PROTECTION AFFORDED BY AN OFFICIAL SEARCH

35.18.1   The official certificate of search is not conclusive in favour of the applicant, thus the applicant will take subject to any entries on the register whether or not those entries were revealed by the official certificate of search.[1] Where a purchaser is bound by an entry which has not been revealed by an official certificate of search he may be able to claim compensation for his loss under the Land Registration Act 1925, s 83(3).

35.18.2   **Priority period**

The certificate of the result of an official search made on form 94A or B confers on the applicant a priority period of 30 working days from the date of the certificate. The date of the expiry of the period is stamped on the search certificate. To obtain the protection of the priority period the purchaser must both complete his purchase and lodge a correctly completed application for registration at the offices of the appropriate district land registry by 11 am on the date of the expiry of the priority period.

If completion is delayed to an extent where it is unlikely that the purchaser will be able to lodge his application for registration within the priority period, a further search application may be submitted which will provide a new priority period. It should be noted that even where the two priority periods overlap they cannot be joined together and treated as one. There is therefore the danger in this situation that the purchaser, in relying on the priority period afforded by the second search may find himself bound by an entry which has been registered since the date of the first search certificate.

Where completion has taken place within the priority period but it will not be possible to lodge the completed application for registration because, for example, there is delay in obtaining a form 53, the completed application form, fees and supporting documents should be lodged at the registry within the priority period together with the vendor's solicitor's undertaking (obtained at completion) to forward the form 53. If this procedure is followed the registry will accept the application for registration and will deem it to have been correctly lodged within the time limit and the form 53 may be forwarded to the registry as soon as it is received.

Where it is anticipated that delay will be experienced in the stamping of documents, the application for registration, including the unstamped documents, should be submitted to the registry as soon as possible after completion, together with a certified copy of the document to be stamped, and a request that the registry send back the documents requiring stamping by return and an undertaking by the applicant to re-submit the stamped documents as soon as they are received from the Inland Revenue. In this case also the registry will deem the application for registration to have been lodged within the priority period.

35.19 A table showing the main differences between Land Registry and Land Charges searches is contained in para 34.11, above.

35.20 BANKRUPTCY

Where a bankruptcy petition is presented against the proprietor of registered land the Chief Land Registrar will enter a creditor's notice on the register of the title(s) affected. A bankruptcy inhibition will be placed on any affected title on the making of a receiving order. These entries would be revealed by making a search against the title but such a search may generally only be made with the authority of the registered proprietor. A search made at the Central Land Charges Department on form K16 will reveal bankruptcy entries made against the proprietor of registered land because the land charges entries are made irrespective of the ownership of land.

Where a solicitor is acting for a proposed mortgagee whose mortgage is being taken out concurrently with the purchase of registered land a K16 search should be made in the Land Charges Registry against the name of the proposed borrower.

Where a mortgage is being taken out on the security of land already owned by the prospective borrower a search will be required against the name of the borrower. Since the borrower is already the proprietor of registered land a land registry search will be appropriate in these circumstances. As an additional precaution, a K16 search in the Central Land Charges Registry may be made against the name of the borrower.

35.20.1 Details of Central Land Charges searches are contained in ch 34, above.

35.21 COMPARATIVE TABLE SHOWING HOW LAND CHARGES IN UNREGISTERED LAND ARE PROTECTED ON THE TITLE OF REGISTERED LAND

Item	Unregistered land	Registered land
	Land Charge Class	
Financial charges	A or B	Notice or caution against dealings Often take effect as registered legal charges
Puisne legal mortgage	C (i)	Notice or caution against dealings

35.21 *Search of Register at HM Land Registry*

Item	Unregistered land	Registered land
	Land Charge Class	
Limited owner's charge	C(ii)	Caution against dealings or restriction
General equitable charge	C(iii)	Notice, caution against dealings or notice of deposit
Estate contracts	C(iv)	Notice or caution
Capital transfer tax	D(i)	Notice
Restrictive covenants	D(ii)	Usually by notice
Equitable easements	D(iii)	Usually by notice
Annuities	E	Notice Sometimes by caution or restriction
Rights of occupation	F	Notice
	Pending land action	Caution against dealings, infrequently by inhibition, on bankruptcy by creditor's notice
	Writ or order	Caution against dealings, on bankruptcy by inhibition
	Deeds of arrangement	Caution against dealings may be used but land is usually transferred to the trustee who becomes registered as proprietor

35.22 SEARCH SUMMARY

Application	Form 94A – Search of whole
	Form 94B – Search of part
	Form 94C – non-priority search
	Form 106 – mortgagees search under Matrimonial Homes Act 1983
Plan	Required where search is of part of a registered title only
Fee	Generally no fee, but form 94C–£2.00
	Telephone or telex searches £3.00

Address	Appropriate district land registry (see Appendix 1)
Special points	
Area affected	Registered land only

1   *Parkash v Irani Finance Ltd* [1970] Ch 101, [1969] 1 All ER 930.

Chapter 36

Other pre-completion searches

36.1 LOCAL LAND CHARGES

Where there has been a protracted interval between exchange of contracts and completion it may be prudent to consider making a further local land charges search because the certificate of search issued by the local authority is only valid for the date of issue. Although some academic texts recommend that a repeat local land charges search should always be made prior to completion this is generally not practicable because of the short interval between contract and completion and the sometimes long delay in receiving the local authority's reply. It is suggested therefore that a second search should be considered only in cases where there is an interval of three months or more between exchange and completion. A further additional enquiries search may also be considered in such circumstances but this is of less importance than the local land charges search itself (see chs 4 and 5 for details of these searches).

36.2 COMPANY SEARCH

Where land is being purchased or leased from a company a company search should be made prior to contract so that there is time in hand to resolve any difficulties or irregularities revealed by the search. Since a company search confers no priority period or protection to the purchaser, many solicitors prefer to leave this search until the pre-completion stage, or at least to repeat the search at this stage in the transaction. A search agency may offer an updating service for a previously made search which will be less expensive than making a completely fresh search (see also ch 8, above).

36.3 INSPECTION OF THE PROPERTY

A further inspection of the property should be carried out as near to actual completion as possible and preferably on the day of completion itself. Although it is recognised that it will not be practicable to do this in the course of every domestic conveyancing transaction it should if possible be carried out in any case where there is a possibility of overriding or equitable interests existing through the occupation of a non-owner. It will also be necessary to carry out this inspection in cases where the purchase includes stock-in-trade in order to check the inventory of such items and to value them if this has not previously been done, or where a considerable number of fittings are to be included in the sale. It may be convenient in such circumstances to arrange for completion to take place on the premises themselves. National Condition 5(4) permits completion to take place at the premises so long as reasonable notice of this requirement is given to the vendor (see also para 11.4, above).

36.4 PROBATE SEARCH
The search for non-revocation of grant should be carried out as near to completion as possible (see ch 33, above).

36.5 RENEWAL OF OTHER PRE-CONTRACT SEARCHES
Most of the other pre-contract searches discussed in this book will reveal information which is unlikely to change in the interval which occurs between contract and completion. A repetition of these searches will therefore only be necessary if either there is to be a long interval (eg in excess of nine months) between contract and completion or if there are circumstances which give rise to suspicion.

36.6 AUCTIONS
It will often not be possible to effect full pre-contract searches prior to an auction although where time permits a personal search of the local land charges register should be undertaken. The vendor will often have made a local land charges search with additional enquiries which will be available for inspection at the auction itself. He may also have prepared answers to the standard preliminary enquiries which will similarly be available for inspection. Since the type of property commonly sold at auction is in some way unusual or individual, such of the less usual pre-contract searches as would normally have been undertaken at the pre-contract stage may instead be considered worthwhile at the pre-completion stage of the transaction as a purely precautionary measure.

Appendix I

Addresses of district land registries

District land registry	Address	Telephone No	Telex Call No
Birkenhead	76 Hamilton Street, Birkenhead, Merseyside, L41 5JW	051 647 5661	628475
Croydon	Sunley House, Bedford Park, Croydon, CR9 3LE	01 686 8833	917288
Durham	Aykley Heads, Durham, DH1 5TR	0385 61361	53684
Gloucester	Bruton Way, Gloucester, GL1 1DQ	0452 28666	43119
Harrow	Lyon House, Lyon Road, Harrow, Middx, HA1 2EU	01 427 8811	262476
Lytham	Lytham St Annes, Lancs, FY8 5AB	0253 736999	67649
Nottingham	Chalfont Drive, Nottingham, 3RN NG8	0602 291111	37167
Peterborough	Aragon Court, Northminster Road, Peterborough, PE1 1XN	0733 46048	32786
Plymouth	Plumer House, Tailyour Road, Crownhill, Plymouth, PL6 5HY	0752 701234	45265
Stevenage	Brickdale House, Danestrete, Stevenage, Herts, SG1 1XG	0438 4488	82377

District land registry	Address	Telephone No	Telex Call No
Swansea	37 The Kingsway, Swansea, SA1 5LF	0792 50971	48220
Tunbridge Wells	Tunbridge Wells, Kent, TN2 5AQ	0892 26141	95286
Weymouth	1 Cumberland Drive, Weymouth, Dorset, DT4 9TT	03057 76161	418231

Table of less usual searches by reference to geographical area

Area	Consider the searches listed below	Chapter reference
Cornwall	Land owned by the Duchy	18.5, 34.6
	Tin	29
	Clay	30
Cheshire	Brine	31
Derbyshire	Coal	28
Devon	Tin	29
	Clay	30
Dorset	Oil	27.4
	Clay	30
Durham	Leases of foreshore	18.6.1
Forest of Dean	Special Common rights	9.9.2
	Coal	28
East Anglia	Waterways	21.7
Epping Forest	Special Common rights	9.9.3
Kent	Oil	27.4
	Coal	28
Lancaster	Duchy Property, Coal	18.5, 34.628
Leicestershire	Coal	28
Greater London	Underground railways	12.12.3
Newcastle on Tyne	Underground railways	12.12.3
New Forest	Verderers	9.9.4
Norfolk Broads	Waterways	21.7
Nottinghamshire	Coal	28
Sandwell	Limestone	32
Staffordshire	Coal	28
Surrey	Oil	27.4
East and West Sussex	Oil	27.4
Tyne and Wear	Coal	28
South Wales	Coal	28
Walsall	Limestone	32
Wolverhampton	Limestone	32
Yorkshire	Coal	28

Appendix III

Table of less usual searches by reference to subject matter

Chapter reference	Subject of Search	Approximate areas affected
6	Public index map	All unregistered land
8	Company search	Buying or leasing land from a limited company, granting a mortgage to a limited company
9	Commons registration	Property adjacent to land which has never been built on (including village and town greens)
12	Railways	Land bordering railway or where railway crosses through or under land
13	SSSIs	Where site is indicated as such on answers to local search
19	Index of proprietors	Sometimes necessary when acting for PRs or trustee in bankruptcy
20	Index of minor interests	Dealings with equitable interests in registered land
21	Water authorities	Land bordered by a river or stream or where river or stream runs through the land Also where water is to be impounded, or used from its natural source or where trade effluent is to be discharged into a river or stream
4, 21, 22	Pipe-lines and cables	Where it is necessary to ascertain the routes of pipelines and cables. Particularly relevant where planning permission is sought to build on the land

Table of less usual searches by reference to subject matter

Chapter reference	Subject of Search	Approximate areas affected
23	Building societies, friendly societies, trade unions	Chiefly where information relating to assets of the Society or its change of name is required
14	Agricultural credits	Purchase or mortgage of farming stock or assets
15	Rent registers	Buying residential tenanted property
16	Corn rent and corn annuities	Land near ancient parish churches
17	Chancel repairs	Land in ancient parishes (see para 17.2, above)
18, 23	Charities	May be necessary if buying or leasing land from charity, or if abstract shows dealing with land by a charity
18, 34	Duchies of Lancaster and Cornwall	Only necessary in unregistered land to check validity of a deed if original cannot be authenticated. Note special central land charges search procedure, para 34.6, above
24, 34	Bankruptcy	To check financial status of proposed tenant or mortgagor
25	Boundaries	In any case where boundaries are unclear
26	Birth, marriage, death and adoption certificates, and wills	Where an office copy document is needed in order to prove title
26	Consumer credit	In the context of conveyancing mainly required in connection with second mortgages
26	Hire-purchase	May be required where chattels which could be subject to an undischarged credit agreement are included in the purchase or lease of land
26	Patents, trade marks, registered designs, copyright	Where items which have been so registered are being transferred, eg on the sale of a business as a going concern

Table of less usual searches by reference to subject matter

Chapter reference	Subject of Search	Approximate areas affected
27	Oil	Parts of Dorset, Kent, Surrey and Sussex
27	Sand and gravel	Property built on or near to sand and gravel excavations
28	Coal	Coal mining areas
29	Tin	Devon and Cornwall
30	Clay	Devon, Dorset and Cornwall
31	Brine	Cheshire
32	Limestone	Dudley, Sandwell, Walsall, Wolverhampton
33	Probate	Buying or leasing unregistered land from PRs

Appendix IV

Pre-contract enquiries on Forms E1, E1 (short) and E2. Client questionnaires Forms Q1, Q2 and Q3.

1. The forms of preliminary enquiry published by Stat-Plus and reproduced on pp 402–423 below, were omitted from the main text because the writer was not aware of their existence until the book reached proof stage, an oversight for which the writer owes an apology to the publishers of the forms. Although it has not been possible to include a full commentary on these forms, a brief commentary on their contents appears below.

2. Form E1 comprises a standard set of preliminary enquiries for use in connection with either freehold or leasehold property, covering most of the subject matter contained in both of forms CON 29 (long) and CON 29 (supplementary) (see paras. 3.5 and 3.8 above). By comparison with forms CON 29 (long) and (supplementary) the questions on form E1 are lengthier and more detailed in nature and appear to be phrased in such a way as to discourage the vendor from making elusive or evasive replies to the questions. In common with form CON 29 this form does not ask any specific questions which may assist the purchaser in deciding whether or not to make one of the less usual conveyancing searches (e.g. mining) and does contain some questions which might be considered by the academically minded practitioner to be more in the nature of requisitions on title rather than preliminary enquiries. (See for example question 5 on the discharge of mortgages.) The disclaimer at the foot of the form is in a similar form of wording to that contained in form CON 29 (see paras. 2.2.2 and 3.5.2 above).

   A comparative table of the questions on form E1, forms CON 29 and CON 29 (supplementary) and CONVEY 1 is contained in para. 3.9.14 above.

3. Form E1 Short (reproduced on pp 408–411 below) as its title suggests comprises a shortened version of the long E1 form. The questions on this shortened form are still relatively detailed and would provide an adequate set of questions for the average domestic transaction. This shortened version of the form omits totally the questions relating to the condition of the property (qu. 11, E1) enfranchisement (qu. 25, E1) and to the existence of a residents association (qu. 26, E1). The questions on boundaries, new properties, disputes, notices and outgoings all appear in an abbreviated form on the short form.

4. Form E2 (reproduced on pp 412–415 below) is divided into three sections. The first section dealing with general tenancy enquiries,

the remaining two parts of the form dealing with business and residential tenancies respectively. The contents of the questions are similar in nature to those contained in Form CON 291 (para. 3.11 above) and like form 291, this form does not raise any specific enquiries relating to assured, shorthold or secure tenancies. In relation to residential tenancies questions are included concerning the application to long tenancies of the Leasehold Reform Act 1967, but the questions relating to service charges are restricted to flats and the form does not raise any specific enquiries concerning residential licences. The form is not intended to be used in connection with the purchase of land occupied by an agricultural tenant.

5. Forms Q1 and Q2 (reproduced on pp 416–421 below) are intended for use by the vendor's solicitor or purchaser's solicitor respectively either as check lists when taking instructions from the client relating to matters pertaining to preliminary enquiries, or, because the forms are constructed in non-legal language, they may be sent directly to the client in order to obtain from him the information which will be required in order either to raise or to answer the standard preliminary enquiries (see also para. 3.5.19 above).

6. Form Q3 (reproduced on pp 422–423 below) comprises a client questionnaire solely devoted to the question of which fixtures and fittings are included in the sale or are to be removed from the property. The use of such a form may avoid some of the problems which are frequently encountered in relation to these matters (see also para. 3.5.13 above).

FORM E1

PRE-CONTRACT GENERAL ENQUIRIES
(Freehold and Leasehold Property)

Property

NOTES

1. These Enquiries are for use before any contract is entered into and can be used where the Property is to be sold with vacant possession or fully or partly let but a more comprehensive form of pre-contract Enquiries is available for use in addition where the Property is to be sold subject to any residential and/or business tenancies : see Stat-Plus Form [Conveyancing E2].

2. Where a new house or other building is to be built on the Property, the Vendor should be directed to Enquiry No. 14 (b) (i) before giving his Replies to any of these Enquiries.

Purchaser   Vendor

Purchaser's Solicitors   Vendor's Solicitors

Ref. No.   Ref. No.

ENQUIRIES   REPLIES

(A) RIGHTS AND CLAIMS OF PERSONS OTHER THAN THE VENDOR IN THE PROPERTY

1. Vacant Possession

(a) Will vacant possession of the whole of the Property be given on completion ?

(b) Is the sale dependent upon the Vendor acquiring another Property ?

2. Tenancies
(Delete this section if Stat-Plus Form [Conveyancing E2] Pre-Contract Tenancy Enquiries is used)
If the Property or any part of it will be let on completion, please supply :

(a) full details of all tenancies,

(b) copies of all leases and written tenancy agreements, and

(c) full details of all sub-tenancies if any of which the Vendor is aware.

3. Other Adverse Rights

(a) Please supply full details of any rights or licences to which the Property is subject or will be subject on completion or which otherwise affect the Property (other than any disclosed above or in the draft contract or immediately apparent on inspection) and in particular any rights of way wayleaves easements or any public or common rights ;

(b) Please state :

(i) what persons other than the Vendor are in actual occupation of the Property or in receipt of its rents and profits and their respective ages and

(ii) what legal or equitable interest in or claim in respect of the Property has each of those persons ?

(c) Is the Vendor aware of any other overriding interests (as set out in Section 70(1) of the Land Registration Act 1925) to which the Property is or will on completion be subject ?

4. Restrictions

(a) Please give details of all covenants and restrictions which now or will on completion affect the Property or its use not already disclosed in writing.

(b) In whom and in respect of what land is the benefit of those covenants and restrictions vested or to be vested ?

(c) Is the Vendor aware of any breaches of those covenants and restrictions ?

(d) If so, please give details of those breaches.

(e) Please supply copies of such written evidence as the Vendor has of all consents approvals and waivers given in respect of the covenants and restrictions affecting the Property or its use.

5. Mortgages
Please confirm that the Property will be conveyed on completion free of all mortgages.

(B) RIGHTS AND ADVANTAGES AVAILABLE IN RESPECT OF THE PROPERTY

6.   Access

(a)   Can vehicular and pedestrian access to the Property be had from the highway?

(b)   If not, how is such access to the Property obtained?

(c)   If there is a right of way over neighbouring property:

(i) how was it created?

(ii) on what terms is it exercisable?

(iii) please supply copies of any documents relating to it.

(d)   (i) Are there any charges payable in respect of access to the Property,

(ii) if so, please give details.

7.   Services

(a)   Drainage

(i) Does the Property drain:

(a) directly into a local authority sewer and

(b) without any part of the drains (other than that sewer) passing through any neighbouring property?

(ii) If not:

(a) how is the Property drained?

(b) please supply details of any easement, licence or agreement relating to its drainage and of the charges if any payable in respect thereof.

(b)   Water, gas and electricity

(i) Is the Property served by mains water, electricity and gas?

(ii) Do the pipes and wires supplying those services (where not part of the mains) pass through or over any neighbouring property?

(iii) If so, please supply details of any easement licence or agreement relating to those services or any of them and of the charges if any payable in respect thereof.

8.   Other Facilities

(a)   Please give details of any other subsisting agreements (whether oral or in writing) which affect or relate to:

(i) access for light and air to the Property; and/or

(ii) emergency escape routes from the Property; and/or

(iii) pipes and wires for services not dealt with in Enquiry No. 7: and/or

(iv) rights of entry onto neighbouring property for the purpose of repairing or maintaining the Property; and/or

(v) roads paths ways drains pipes wires and other rights services and facilities which are not public rights and are enjoyed by the Property (either alone or in common with other property) but excluding party structures and any matters already mentioned in any Reply made herein to any earlier Enquiry.

(b)   Please supply copies of all of the agreements in *(a)* above which are in writing.

(c)   Has the Vendor or so far as he is aware any predecessor in title:

(i) made any demand for payment or contribution or any other claim under any such agreement as is mentioned in Enquiry No. 8*(a)* or in respect of any such rights services and facilities as are mentioned therein;

(ii) received any such demand or other claim;

(iii) carried out or been called upon to carry out any works in connection with such agreement or such rights services and facilities?

(d)   If so, please give details.

9.   Guarantees Indemnities etc. and Claims thereunder

(a)   Is the Purchaser to have (whether by assignment or otherwise) any of the following, and if so which:.

(i) any insurance policy indemnity or guarantee in respect of any defect in the title to the Property or breach of any covenant to which the Property is subject;

(ii) any guarantee warranty certificate insurance policy or other agreement relating to any repair or replacement or treatment or improvement of any building or part thereof built on the Property;

(iii) any National House-Building Council Agreement and certificate/policy relating to any such building;

(iv) any covenant indemnity guarantee bond or agreement relating to the maintenance or cost of construction or charges payable on adoption of any road or path over which the owner of the Property has rights of way (not being already disclosed in any Reply herein to any previous Enquiry).

(v) any other insurance policy guarantee indemnity warranty covenant or other agreement relating to the Property;

(b) If so, please supply copies of all relevant documents.

(c) (i) What event has occurred or defect or other matter become apparent which has given or might give rise to any claim under any such document as is referred to in *(b)* above;

(ii) has notice of such event defect or matter been given or received? If so please give details.

(iii) have any claims been made, and if made, settled? Please give details.

(C) BOUNDARIES, CONDITION AND PLANNING USE OF THE PROPERTY

10. Boundaries

(a) To whom do all the boundary walls, fences, hedges and ditches belong?

(b) Has the Vendor maintained or regarded as his responsibility any of the boundary walls, fences, hedges and ditches, and if so, which, and for what reason?

(c) Are any walls or fences party structures, and if so, which and what is the nature of the rights and liabilities in respect thereof?

(d) Has the Vendor (or to his knowledge any predecessor in title) moved any of the boundaries of the Property? If so, please give full details.

(e) If the Property is unregistered, please supply a site plan sufficient to identify the Property.

11. Condition

(a) Has the Property, so far as the Vendor is aware, at any time suffered from (i) flooding (ii) subsidence (iii) rising damp (iv) dry rot, wet rot or other rot (v) woodworm or other timber infestation or (vi) any structural or drainage defect requiring remedial treatment?

(b) If so, please give details of:

(i) the nature of the defect or damage suffered and the date upon which the same became apparent;

(ii) the remedial treatment carried out and any guarantees given in respect thereof. Please supply copies of those guarantees (if not already being supplied pursuant to Enquiry No. 9 *(b)*).

12. Planning Use etc.

(a) What is the present use of the Property and when did it begin?

(b) Has this use been continuous since it began?

(c) During the four years ending with the date of receipt of these Enquiries:

(i) has any building on the Property been built altered or added to?

(ii) has there been any breach in relation to the Property of any planning condition or restriction?

(iii) have there been any other building engineering mining or other operations in on over or under the Property? If so, please give details.

(d) Please supply a copy of any:

(i) planning permission relating to the present use of the Property and any buildings now built or to be built on it;

(ii) bye-law approval or building regulation approval relating to those buildings;

(iii) current fire certificate.

13. Fixtures, fittings etc.

(a) Please specify any fixtures and fittings (including aerials electric fittings and fitted furniture) and any shrubs out-buildings sheds and garden ornaments which the Vendor will remove from the Property on or before completion.

(b) Please confirm that any fixtures fittings and chattels included in the sale are owned absolutely by the Vendor free from any third party rights.

(c) Please confirm that all items mentioned in the Agents particulars are included in the sale.

(d) Has the Vendor (or to his knowledge any predecessor in title) carried out any alterations or additions to the structure of the Property ? If so, please supply details.

(e) When was the electric wiring in the Property last renewed or tested ?

(f) If there is central heating :

(i) How old is it ?

(ii) When was it last serviced ?

(iii) Please confirm that it will be functioning properly on completion.

(iv) Please supply details of any guarantee or service contract.

(v) If there are any oil fired heaters at the Property does the Vendor intend to sell any surplus oil to the purchaser and if so at what price ?

(g) As to telephones :

(i) Does the Vendor intend to transfer the telephone number to a new address ?
If not, please disclose the number.

(ii) Does the Vendor own the telephone receivers and any other equipment ?
If so, will he be removing any such equipment ? and if so please specify.

(iii) Please confirm that the Vendor will not apply for disconnection of the service.

14. New properties

(a) Does the purchase price cover :

(i) the provision of all usual services to the Property;

(ii) fencing of all boundaries;

(iii) laying of all paths and drains; and

(iv) cleaning and levelling the garden ?

(b) Where a new house or other building is to be built on the Property prior to completion :

(i) please confirm that replies to all Pre-Contract General Enquiries are given on the basis that they are not only correct at the date hereof but will be correct on completion;

(ii) Please confirm :
(a) that the Vendor and the Property have been registered with the National House Builders Council (giving the relevant registration number(s));
(b) that until completion the Property will be at the Vendor's risk and that the Vendor will insure the Property against the usual house-owners risks;
(c) on completion the Vendor will clear the Property of all surplus builders material and plant and rubbish and level the garden;
(d) the date on which the Property will be ready for occupation complete in all respects.

(D) MISCELLANEOUS

15. Disputes

(a) Is the Vendor aware of any past or current disputes which relate in any way to the Property its use or any other matter connected with the Property and in particular regarding boundaries easements covenants or any planning matters ? If so, please give details.

(b) Is the Vendor aware of any circumstances which may lead to such disputes as aforesaid ? If so, please give details.

(c) Has the Vendor (or to his knowledge any predecessor in title) had cause to complain about the behaviour of neighbours. If so, please give details.

16. Notices

(a) Please give details of all notices relating to the Property or to matters likely to affect its use or enjoyment in any way whatsoever which the Vendor (or to his knowledge any predecessor in title) has given or received?

(b) Is the Vendor aware of any proposals to develop any adjoining land or carry out any alterations to buildings thereon?

17. Outgoings

(a) What is the rateable value of the Property?

(b) How much is currently paid in general rates?

(c) Have any works or improvements been carried out which may cause the rateable value to be reviewed? If so, please give details.

(d) What water rate is payable in respect of the Property?

(e) Are there any other periodic charges payable in respect of the Property? If so, please give details.

18. Development Land Tax

Is the Vendor's usual place of abode and that of anyone else disposing of an interest in the Property outside the United Kingdom?

19. Completion

When will the Vendor be able to complete the sale of the Property to the Purchaser?

(E) LEASEHOLD ENQUIRIES

(For Leasehold Properties only)

20. The Lease

(a) If not already supplied, please supply a copy of the Lease and of any document varying the same or recording any rent review.

(b) Is the Lease by which the Vendor holds the Property a headlease or an underlease?

(c) Please supply the names and addresses of the landlord and any superior landlord and their respective solicitors.

(d) If the landlord's consent to the proposed assignment is required, what steps have been taken to obtain that consent?

21. Rent and Service Charges

(a) To whom is (i) the rent and (ii) any service charge or other payment made, and in each case where and in what manner has payment been made?

(b) Please give details of all service charges and insurance rents (if any) paid for the last three years, and please supply copies of all written accounts invoices and/or certificates relating to such charges and rents.

(c) Is there any form of reserve or sinking fund? If so, please give details.

(d) Has the Vendor or anyone else to his knowledge challenged any service charges or insurance rents which the landlord has sought to recover for the last three years? If so, please give details.

(e) Has there been any unusually large service charge expenditure in the past or is any contemplated in the future which may substantially increase the service charge contribution payable? If so, please give details.

22. Covenants

(a) So far as the Vendor is aware has the landlord complained or had cause to complain of any breach of covenant on the part of the tenant contained in the lease? If so, please give details.

(b) Has the Vendor complained or had cause to complain of any breach of covenant on the part of the landlord contained in the lease? If so, please give details.

23. Insurance

(a) In practice who insures the Property?

(b) Please supply a copy of the current policy or insurance or full details thereof.

24. Reversionary Title

What documentary evidence of the reversionary title is there with the title deeds of the Property?

25. Enfranchisement

(a) Has the lease been extended pursuant to the Leasehold Reform Act 1967 as amended?

(b) Is the Vendor in a position to enfranchise under the said Act?

(c) Has any notice of enfranchisement been served? If so please supply a copy of it and give details of all steps taken in consequence.

26. Residents Association etc.

(a) Is the Vendor a member of any Residents Association or Management Company relating to the Property and other properties?

(b) If so, please give details of the Vendor's interest and of the constitution and management of the Association or Company and supply copies of all relevant documents?

(c) Please confirm that the Vendor will transfer to the Purchaser on completion of the sale his interest in the Association or Company.

(F) ADDITIONAL ENQUIRIES

The above replies on behalf of the Vendor are believed to be correct but accuracy is not guaranteed, and they do not obviate the need to make appropriate searches enquiries and inspections. The replies are given without responsibility on the part of the Vendor's solicitors their partners or employees.

Signed... Signed...
      (Purchaser's Solicitors)   (Vendor's Solicitors)

Dated... Dated...

Conveyancing Form E1   AHD
© Stat-Plus (Law Stationery)   (These enquiries are copyright and may not be reproduced)

FORM E1 (SHORT)

PRE-CONTRACT GENERAL ENQUIRIES
(Freehold and Leasehold Property)

Property

NOTES

These Enquiries are for use before any contract is entered into and can be used where the Property is to be sold with vacant possession or fully or partly let but a more comprehensive form of pre-contract Enquiries is available for use in addition where the Property is to be sold subject to any residential and/or business tenancies : see Stat-Plus Form [Conveyancing E2].

Purchaser   Vendor

Purchaser's Solicitors   Vendor's Solicitors

Ref. No.   Ref. No.

ENQUIRIES	REPLIES

1. Vacant Possession

(a) Will vacant possession of the whole of the Property be given on completion ?

(b) Is the sale dependent upon the Vendor acquiring another Property ?

2. Tenancies

(Delete this section if Stat-Plus Form [Conveyancing E2] Pre-Contract Tenancy Enquiries is used).

If the Property or any part of it will be let on completion, please supply :

(a) full details of all tenancies,

(b) copies of all leases and written tenancy agreements, and

(c) full details of all sub-tenancies if any of which the Vendor is aware.

3. Other Adverse Rights

(a) Please supply full details of any rights or licences to which the Property is subject or will be subject on completion or which otherwise affect the Property (other than any disclosed above or in the draft contract or immediately apparent on inspection) and in particular any rights of way wayleaves easements or any public or common rights ;

(b) Please state :
(i) what persons other than the Vendor are in actual occupation of the Property or in receipt of its rents and profits and their respective ages and
(ii) what legal or equitable interest in or claim in respect of the Property has each of those persons ?

(c) Is the Vendor aware of any other overriding interests (as set out in Section 70(1) of the Land Registration Act 1925) to which the Property is or will on completion be subject ?

4. Restrictions

(a) Please give details of all covenants and restrictions which now or will on completion affect the Property or its use not already disclosed in writing.

(b) In whom and in respect of what land is the benefit of those covenants and restrictions vested or to be vested ?

(c) Is the Vendor aware of any breaches of those covenants and restrictions ?

(d) If so, please give details of those breaches.

(e) Please supply copies of such written evidence as the Vendor has of all consents approvals and waivers given in respect of the covenants and restrictions affecting the Property or its use.

5. Mortgages

Please confirm that the Property will be conveyed on completion free of all mortgages.

6. Access

(a) Can vehicular and pedestrian access to the Property be had from the highway ?

(b) If not, how is such access to the Property obtained ?

(c) If there is a right of way over neighbouring property :
(i) how was it created ?
(ii) on what terms is it exercisable ?
(iii) please supply copies of any documents relating to it.

(d) (i) Are there any charges payable in respect of access to the Property,
(ii) if so, please give details.

7. Services

(a) Drainage
(i) Does the Property drain :
(a) directly into a local authority sewer and
(b) without any part of the drains (other than that sewer) passing through any neighbouring property ?

408

(ii) If not:
(a) how is the Property drained?
(b) please supply details of any easement, licence or agreement relating to its drainage and of the charges if any payable in respect thereof.

(b) Water, gas and electricity
(i) Is the Property served by mains water, electricity and gas?
(ii) Do the pipes and wires supplying those services (where not part of the mains) pass through or over any neighbouring property?
(iii) If so, please supply details of any easement licence or agreement relating to those services or any of them and of the charges if any payable in respect thereof.

8: Other Facilities

(a) Please give details of any other subsisting agreements (whether oral or in writing) which affect or relate to:
(i) access for light and air to the Property; and/or
(ii) emergency escape routes from the Property; and/or
(iii) pipes and wires for services not dealt with in Enquiry No. 7; and/or
(iv) rights of entry onto neighbouring property for the purpose of repairing or maintaining the Property; and/or
(v) roads paths ways drains pipes wires and other rights services and facilities which are not public rights and are enjoyed by the Property (either alone or in common with other property) but excluding party structures and any matters already mentioned in any Reply made herein to any earlier Enquiry.

(b) Please supply copies of all of the agreements in *(a)* above which are in writing.

(c) Has the Vendor or so far as he is aware any predecessor in title:
(i) made any demand for payment or contribution or any other claim under any such agreement as is mentioned in Enquiry No. 8 *(a)* or in respect of any such rights services and facilities as are mentioned therein;
(ii) received any such demand or other claim;
(iii) carried out or been called upon to carry out any works in connection with such agreement or such rights services and facilities?

(d) If so, please give details.

9. Guarantees Indemnities etc. and Claims thereunder

(a) Is the Purchaser to have (whether by assignment or otherwise) any of the following, and if so which:
(i) any insurance policy indemnity or guarantee in respect of any defect in the title to the Property or breach of any covenant to which the Property is subject;
(ii) any guarantee warranty certificate insurance policy or other agreement relating to any repair or replacement or treatment or improvement of any building or part thereof built on the Property;
(iii) any National House-Building Council Agreement and certificate/policy relating to any such building;
(iv) any covenant indemnity guarantee bond or agreement relating to the maintenance or cost of construction or charges payable on adoption of any road or path over which the owner of the Property has rights of way (not being already disclosed in any Reply herein to any previous Enquiry).
(v) any other insurance policy guarantee indemnity warranty covenant or other agreement relating to the Property;

(b) If so, please supply copies of all relevant documents.

(c) (i) What event has occurred or defect or other matter become apparent which has given or might give rise to any claim under any such document as is referred to in *(b)* above;
(ii) has notice of such event defect or matter been given or received? If so, please give details.
(iii) have any claims been made, and if made, settled? Please give details.

10. Boundaries

(a) To whom do all the boundary walls, fences, hedges and ditches belong?
(b) Has the Vendor maintained or regarded as his responsibility any of the boundary walls, fences, hedges and ditches, and if so, which, and for what reason?

11. Planning Use etc.

(a) What is the present use of the Property and when did it begin?
(b) Has this been continuous since it began?
(c) During the four years ending with the date of receipt of these Enquiries:
(i) has any building on the Property been built altered or added to?
(ii) has there been any breach in relation to the Property of any planning condition or restriction?
(iii) have there been any other building engineering mining or other operations in on over or under the Property?
If so, please give details.

(d)   Please supply a copy of any :
       (i) planning permission relating to the present use of the Property and any buildings now built or to be built on it;
       (ii) bye-law approval or building regulation approval relating to those buildings;
       (iii) current fire certificate.

12.   Fixtures, fittings etc.

(a)   Please specify any fixtures and fittings (including aerials electric fittings and fitted furniture) and any shrubs out-buildings sheds and garden ornaments which the Vendor will remove from the Property on or before completion.

(b)   Please confirm that any fixtures fittings and chattels included in the sale are owned absolutely by the Vendor free from any third party rights.

(c)   Please confirm that all items mentioned in the Agents particulars are included in the sale.

(d)   Has the Vendor (or to his knowledge any predecessor in title) carried out any alterations or additions to the structure of the Property ? If so, please supply details.

(e)   When was the electric wiring in the Property last renewed or tested ?

(f)   If there is central heating :
       (i) How old is it ?
       (ii) When was it last serviced ?
       (iii) Please confirm that it will be functioning properly on completion.
       (iv) Please supply details of any guarantee or service contract.
       (v) If there are any oil fired heaters at the Property does the Vendor intend to sell any surplus oil to the purchaser and if so at what price ?

13.   New properties

(a)   Does the purchase price cover :
       (i) the provision of all usual services to the Property;
       (ii) fencing of all boundaries;
       (iii) laying of all paths and drains; and
       (iv) cleaning and levelling the garden ?

14.   Disputes

Is the Vendor aware of any past or current disputes which relate in any way to the Property its use or any other matter connected with the Property and in particular regarding boundaries easements covenants or any planning matters ?

15.   Notices

Please give details of all notices relating to the Property or to matters likely to affect its use or enjoyment in any way whatsoever which the Vendor (or to his knowledge any predecessor in title) has given or received ?

16.   Outgoings

(a)   What is the rateable value of the Property ?

(b)   Have any works or improvements been carried out which may cause the rateable value to be reviewed ?
If so, please give details.

(c)   Are there any other periodic charges payable in respect of the Property ? If so, please give details.

17.   Development Land Tax

Is the Vendor's usual place of abode and that of anyone else disposing of an interest in the Property outside the United Kingdom ?

18.   Completion

When will the Vendor be able to complete the sale of the Property to the Purchaser ?

ADDITIONAL ENQUIRIES

LEASEHOLD ENQUIRIES
(For Leasehold Properties only)

19. The Lease

(a) If not already supplied, please supply a copy of the Lease and of any document varying the same or recording any rent review.

(b) Is the Lease by which the Vendor holds the Property a headlease or an underlease ?

(c) Please supply the names and addresses of the landlord and any superior landlord and their respective solicitors.

(d) If the landlord's consent to the proposed assignment is required, what steps have been taken to obtain that consent ?

20. Rent and Service Charges

(a) Please give details of all service charges and insurance rents (if any) paid for the last three years, and please supply copies of all written accounts invoices and/or certificates relating to such charges and rents.

(b) Has the Vendor or anyone else to his knowledge challenged any service charges or insurance rents which the landlord has sought to recover for the last three years ?
If so, please give details.

(c) Has there been any unusually large service charge expenditure in the past or is any contemplated in the future which may substantially increase the service charge contribution payable ? If so, please give details.

21. Covenants

(a) So far as the Vendor is aware has the landlord complained or had cause to complain of any breach of covenant on the part of the tenant contained in the lease ?
If so, please give details.

(b) Has the Vendor complained or had cause to complain of any breach of covenant on the part of the landlord contained in the lease ? If so, please give details.

22. Insurance

(a) In practice who insures the Property ?

(b) Please supply a copy of the current policy or insurance or full details thereof.

23. Reversionary Title

What documentary evidence of the reversionary title is there with the title deeds of the Property ?

LEASEHOLD AND ADDITIONAL FREEHOLD ENQUIRIES

The above replies on behalf of the Vendor are believed to be correct but accuracy is not guaranteed, and they do not obviate the need to make appropriate searches enquiries and inspections. The replies are given without responsibility on the part of the Vendor's solicitors their partners or employees.

Signed..
(Purchaser's Solicitors)

Signed..
(Vendor's Solicitors)

Dated..

Dated..

Conveyancing Form E1 Short
© Stat-Plus (Law Stationery)   (These enquiries are copyright and may not be reproduced)   KHD

411

FORM E2

PRE - CONTRACT TENANCY ENQUIRIES

Property	NOTES
	1. These enquiries can be used in conjunction with Pre-Contract General Enquiries Stat-Plus Form [Conveyancing E1] where the Property is wholly or partly let but not in the case of an agricultural holding or an occupation by a person entitled to statutory protection by reason of his or someone else's employment in agriculture.
	2. References in these Enquiries to "lease" or "tenancy" or "tenant" are references to a lease or tenancy of the Property or part of it and to a tenant under such a lease or tenancy.

Purchaser	Vendor

Ref. No.	Ref. No.

ENQUIRIES	REPLIES

(i) GENERAL

1. Present Tenant(s)
Please supply the name and address of each present tenant and (if different) each occupier.

2. Terms of each Lease/Tenancy

(a) Please supply a copy of each existing lease or written tenancy agreement or of any other document which evidences the terms of an existing tenancy and of any document varying the terms of such lease or tenancy including any review of the rent reserved thereby.

(b) Insofar as any of the following terms of any lease or tenancy do not appear from any copy document supplied pursuant to *(a)* above, please give details. The terms are :
(i) the rent currently payable its amount date and manner of payment and whether in advance or in arrear ;
(ii) the premises demised or let ;
(iii) the nature of any rights enjoyed by the tenant over property not included in the premises demised or let ;
(iv) the date upon which the lease or tenancy commenced ;
(v) the date upon which the lease or tenancy is due to expire or otherwise the period or nature of the tenancy ;
(vi) the essential terms of the lease or tenancy.

3. Breaches of covenant

(a) Is the tenant or has he been in arrear in the payment of rent ? If so, please give details.

(b) So far as the Vendor is aware are there any other present or have there been any other past breaches of covenant or obligation by the tenant arising under the terms of any existing lease or tenancy ? If so, please give details.

(c) Has a tenant complained or had cause to complain of any breach of covenant or obligation by the landlord arising under the terms of any existing lease or tenancy ? If so, please give details.

(d) Please supply copies of such written evidence as the Vendor has of all consents approvals and waivers given in respect of the covenants and obligations on the part of the tenant arising under any existing lease or tenancy.

4. Sub-tenancies
Please give full details of any sub-tenancy of all or any part of the Property of which the Vendor is aware, including the name and address (if known) of the present sub-tenant.

5. Notices

(a) Please give full details and supply copies of all notices relating to or affecting the terms of any existing lease or tenancy or the use in any way of the premises subject to such existing lease or tenancy served on or by the local authority or the landlord or the tenant during the currency of such lease or tenancy.

(b) Please give details of all steps taken and/or orders made in consequence of any such notice and please supply copies of all relevant documents.

6. Insurance

(a) Who insures any premises demised or let to a tenant ?

(b) If the tenant, please give details of the existing cover.

7. Alterations

(a) What improvements have been made by any tenant to the premises demised or let to him ?

(b) Are those improvements to be ignored for the purposes of any future rent review ?

(c) Please produce copies of all licences for all alterations carried out by the tenant, and copies of all approved plans.

(d) Have any alterations been carried out by or at the Landlord's expense ? If so, please give details.

(ii) BUSINESS TENANCIES
[NOTE : The Enquiries under this heading do not have to be answered if any existing lease or tenancy or sub-tenancy is not or does not give rise to a tenancy (in this heading referred to as "a business tenancy") to which Part II of the Landlord and Tenant Act 1954 as amended ("the 1954 Act") applies].

8. Identification
Please identify each tenant or sub-tenant (if any) who is a tenant under a business tenancy.

9. Commencement date of business
Upon what date were the premises subject to a business tenancy first occupied for the purpose of the business now carried on from those premises ?

10. New Tenancy
(a) Has a Section 25 Notice or Section 26 Requested under the 1954 Act been served in respect of any current tenancy ?
(b) If so has the tenant duly applied to the Court for a new tenancy in consequence of that Notice or Request ?
(c) If so, what steps have been taken in connection with that application ?
Please supply copies of all documents relevant to the replies given to the above Enquiries.

11. Court Order
Has any order been made in respect of any current tenancy pursuant to Section 38 (4) of the 1954 Act ? If so, please provide a copy.

12. Improvements
(a) Is any tenant under a business tenancy entitled on quitting the premises demised or let to him on the termination of his business tenancy entitled to be paid any compensation for improvements ? If so, please give details.
(b) Has any tenant under a business tenancy made any improvement which is to be ignored in determining a new rent under S.34 (1) (c) of the 1954 Act ? If so, please give details.

13. Rent Reviews
(a) Where rent reviews have taken place or are due to take place, please confirm :-
(i) The rents have been reviewed or are being reviewed strictly in accordance with the terms of the relevant Lease.
(ii) That all notices and applications for arbitration or determination by an expert have been made by the due dates.
(iii) Any reviewed rent has been satisfactorily evidenced and in accordance with any specific terms of the Lease.
(iv) That no rents will be agreed or any evidence given by or on behalf of the Vendor to an expert or arbitrator prior to completion without the Purchaser's consent.
(v) Please specify those Leases where rent reviews are being negotiated or determined.
(b) Please confirm that where no rent review notices have been served and the period for service of such notice specified in the Lease expires prior to the anticipated date of completion the Vendor will serve notice in accordance with the terms of the Lease on the Tenant, after prior consultation with the Purchaser.
(c) Please let us know whether during any rent review negotiation or determination any Tenant or its advisers have used any argument which reflects adversely on the terms or conditions of the Lease or the condition or position of the Property.

(iii) RESIDENTIAL TENANCIES
[NOTE : The Enquiries under this heading do not have to be answered unless the Property or any part of it is occupied by a tenant or sub-tenant as a residence. Each such tenant or sub-tenant is referred to in the Enquiries under this heading as a "residential tenant" and his tenancy and the premises he occupies (whether the whole or part of the Property) are referred to as "residential tenancy" and "residence" respectively].

14. Identification
Please identify each residential tenant.

15. Rent Acts
In case of each residential tenant :
(a) Is the residential tenancy :
(i) regulated or
(ii) a restricted contract or
(iii) treated as a restricted contract by virtue only of the resident landlord exemption (see S.12 of the Rent Act 1977 as amended) ?
(b) What was the Rateable Value of the residence on :
(i) 23rd March 1965 ?
(ii) 22nd March 1973 ?
(iii) 1st April 1973 ?
(c) Is there a registered rent for the residence or any part of it ? If so, please supply a copy of the registration of rent.
(d) What is the current recoverable rent for the residence ?
(e) If a regulated tenancy, is he :
(i) a protected tenant or
(ii) a statutory tenant and if a statutory tenant
(iii) the original tenant
(iv) the first or second successor and if so which ?
(f) If the resident landlord exemption is considered to apply in respect of any residential tenancy :
(i) Please confirm :
(a) that the residential tenancy was granted by a person who at the time when he granted it occupied as his residence another dwelling-house in the same flat or building ;
(b) that since the residential tenancy was granted the interest of the landlord under it has belonged at all times to a person who at the time he owned that interest occupied as his residence another dwelling-house in the same flat or building ;
(c) that the residential tenancy was not granted to a person who immediately before it was granted was a protected or statutory tenant of a dwelling-house in the same building.
(ii) Insofar as such confirmation cannot be given, please state the grounds upon which the Vendor considers that the resident landlord exemption applies.
(g) (i) Does the rent include any amount for the use of furniture or for services ? and if so
(ii) what furniture used by the tenant is provided by the landlord, and on what terms ? and
(iii) what services is the landlord contractually bound to provide ?

16. Long Tenancies
(a) In relation to any long tenancy (as defined for the purposes of the Leasehold Reform Act 1967 as amended) of a house (as defined for the purposes of the same Act).
(i) Is it considered that the tenant under such tenancy is already or may in the future be entitled to enfranchise under the said Act ?
(ii) If it is not so considered, why ?
(b) In relation to such a long tenancy of a house as aforesaid, has a reduced rateable value been agreed or determined for the purposes of the said 1967 Act as amended ? If so please give details.
(c) In relation to such a long tenancy as aforesaid whether of a house or of part of a house, was the tenancy granted as a result of the exercise by a tenant of any statutory right to such a long tenancy ? If so, please give details.

17. Service Charges
In the case of a tenancy of a flat where there is no registered rent (unless the amount registered is entered as a variable amount) and the tenant is liable to pay a service charge :
(a) Is there a recognised tenants' association for the tenants of flats in the building, and if so what is the name and address of its secretary ?
(b) In the last three periods for which a service charge has been payable (including the current period)
(i) has there been any request made for a written summary of costs incurred which are relevant to the service charge ? If so, please give details including information as to the steps taken to comply with such a request ;
(ii) has there been a dispute in connection with the reasonableness of the service charge or that the statutory requirements in connection therewith have not been complied with ? If so, please give details ;
(iii) are any payments of the service charge for those periods currently outstanding. If so, please give details of the amounts currently outstanding, from whom they are outstanding, and the reasons (if any) put forward by the tenants concerned for not paying.
(c) Please confirm that on completion the Vendor will hand over to the Purchaser all estimates and vouchers and other documents which the Purchaser may reasonably require in order to recover payment of any service charge from a tenant whether that service charge is payable in respect of any past present or future period.

(iv) ADDITIONAL ENQUIRIES

The above replies on behalf of the Vendor are believed to be correct but accuracy is not guaranteed, and they do not obviate the need to make appropriate searches enquiries and inspections. The replies are given without responsibility on the part of the Vendor's solicitors their partners or employees.

Signed ....   Signed ....
            (Purchaser's Solicitors)   *(Vendor's Solicitors)*

Dated ....   Dated ....

Ref. No. ....   Ref. No. ....

Conveyancing E2
© Stat-Plus (Law Stationery)   FHD

Pre-contract enquiries and client questionnaires

FORM Q1

CLIENT QUESTIONNAIRE — SALE OF PROPERTY

Solicitor(s):

Our ref:

Client(s)

Telephone No's.	Home
	Work

Property

Postcode

Estate Agent:

SALE PRICE £

QUESTIONNAIRE	PLEASE ANSWER HERE

1. Vacant Possession/Completion

(a) Will you give vacant possession of the whole of the property?

(b) Are there any tenants in any part of the property? If yes, give full details of those persons.

(c) Please give full names and ages of all persons who normally reside in the property this to include yourself, spouse, children and any other persons. State the relationship of those other persons if applicable.

(d) Have completion dates been discussed with the Purchaser and have you a specific date when you would prefer completion? (Whilst we will endeavour to comply please remember your Purchaser may have other commitments.)

2. Adverse Rights

(a) Do any neighbours or others have or exercise any rights (e.g. right of way) with or without permissions or consents whether formal or informal or otherwise over your land?

(b) Are there any wayleave agreements for electricity, telephone, TV lines etc. Please enclose such agreements if any.

(c) Are there any unusual features regarding the land or house or any other matter you are not sure about?

3. Mortgages
Please advise how much is outstanding on:

(a) Your first mortgage — give details of Building Society/Bank etc. and your account number.

(b) A second mortgage or bank charge (if any) — give details and forward any documents in your possession.

4. Restrictions

(a) Have you been notified that you are in breach of any restrictions concerning the property?

(b) Do you know, or have you reason to believe that you are in breach of any such restrictions?

5. Exclusive Facilities
In respect of any roads, paths, party walls, wires, pipes, drains or other facilities used in common with the owners or occupiers of any other properties:

(a) Excluding those roads which are public highways, what documents or agreements regulate their joint use and the liability for repairs, maintenance and replacement? Forward any documents you may have or give details.

(b) Have you or to your knowledge has any former owner or occupier made or received any demands for payment which is still outstanding or is any such demand expected? If so, give details.

416

6. Services
Does the property have:
(a) Mains drainage? If not, give details of drainage system.
(b) Mains water? If not, give details of water supply.
(c) Electricity
(d) Gas
(e) Relay/Cable TV services
(f) If any services are not connected, do you know if they are available?
(g) Does the route of any of these services pass through or over any land that is not yours or that you are not selling? If you do not know, please say so.
(h) Are you aware of any agreements informal or otherwise relating to any of these services or any similar services.

7. Shared Facilities
If you share a roadway, pathway, right of way, drainage or joint facility or service with any neighbour have you ever made payment or been asked to make payment towards the upkeep or to any repair costs?
If so, give details.

8. Guarantees
(a) Do you have an NHBC Agreement or Certificate in your possession? Please enclose.
(b) If you have any Agreement, Certificate, Warranty or Insurance Policy relating to any repair, replacement, treatment or improvement to the fabric of the property, please forward these together with all reports and estimates.
(c) Have any defects covered by any of the above become apparent?
(d) Have you made any claims or given notice of any defects?

9. Boundaries
(a) Which boundaries belong to you or do you believe belong to you?
(b) Have you maintained or made any payments in respect of any boundaries during your ownership?
(c) To your knowledge has the property ever been affected by flooding, dry or wet rot or other similar problems? If yes, give details.
(d) If work has been carried out to rectify the above, please enclose all relative papers.

10. Insulation
If the property has insulation, please enclose details in respect of the Company who undertook the work:
(a) Cavity wall insulation
(b) Roof insulation

11. Disputes
Have you had or are you aware of any previous disputes regarding:
(a) Boundaries
(b) Covenants or restrictions
(c) Any other matter.

12. Planning
(a) Do you know when the property was built?
(b) Have you made any changes or improvements to the property (including the erection of garages, sheds, greenhouses, etc. If yes give details, including the date of the improvement.
(c) Have you made any alterations to the electrical wiring at the property? If yes, give details.
(d) Have you had any dealings with the local planning authority or made any applications to, or received any notice from them?
(e) Please enclose any original, or copy planning permissions, plans or other approvals, including any from the original builder.
(f) Has the property been used solely as a private residence and if so for how long? If not, give details.

13. **Fixtures and fittings**

Please complete the attached Fixtures and Fittings
Questionnaire (Conveyancing Q3). This shows the fittings
which are included in the sale/excluded from the sale and
also those which the Purchaser is buying from you.
Please confirm that:

(a) All items mentioned in the estate agent's particulars are
included in the sale, if not state which items are excluded.

(b) If the Purchaser is paying a sum of money in addition to the
price of the house for any items, please say how much he is
paying.

Central Heating:
Please specify:

(a) Type of system

(b) Date upon which last serviced.

(c) Is the system still under manufacturers/installers
warranty/guarantee? Please enclose agreements.

(d) Is the system subject to a service agreement? If so, please
enclose the service agreement.

(e) Details of fuel supplier.

(f) Has any fuel purchased by you but left unused on
completion being left for the Purchaser? If so for what
price?

Telephone:
Give exchange and number.
Is the telephone being disconnected, or are you taking your
present telephone number with you?

Double Glazing:
Which rooms in the property have double glazing?
When and by whom was it installed?
Is it the subject of manufacturers/installers
warranty/guarantee? If so, enclose agreements.
Is it the subject of any financial charge or loan agreement.

14. **Notices**

Have you received or given any notice relating to the
property or any neighbouring or adjacent properties?

15. **Outgoings**

(a) State the rateable value of your property and to what
authority(ies) do you make payment? Please give names,
addresses and reference numbers.

(b) Please enclose your latest receipt/demand for water and
general (and drainage if appropriate) rates and state if paid
or not or being paid by standing order.

(c) Do you know of any improvements which may affect your
rateable value, i.e. central heating, double glazing) but
which have not been assessed by the rating department.

(d) Do you pay any outgoings (other than general and water
rates, electricity, gas, telephone and ground rent) such as
tithes or drainage rates? If so, please enclose the accounts.

(e) Do you pay an annual ground rent? If so, please enclose
latest receipt/demand.
State whether it has been paid and the name and address of
person to whom it is paid.

16. **Estate Agents' Commission**

Have you agreed the estate agents commission? If yes,
confirm the amount and that we are to discharge it for you.

418

17. Leasehold property only

(a) What is the name and address of your Landlord?

(b) What is the name and address of the Receiver of rent (if it is not paid to the Landlord)?

(c) Please let us have the latest receipts for *(i)* ground rent *(ii)* fire insurance premium (and a copy of the insurance policy if you have one) *(iii)* service maintenance charge.

(d) When was the property last painted
   (i) Inside?
   (ii) Outside?

(e) Did you get the Landlord's consent for any additional buildings or alterations to the property? If so, please send us the consents and approved plans (if any)

(f) If there is a Residents Association or Management Company, please let us know the name and address of its Secretary and send us:-
   (i) Your membership certificate
   (ii) Copies of the past 3 years accounts.

(g) Have you ever had cause to complain of any breach by the Landlord of his covenants under the Lease?

(h) Has the Landlord ever complained of any breach of covenant by you?

(i) Have you ever exercised your rights to obtain information from the Landlord/Management Company as to the amount and breakdown of service charges payable under the Lease.

ADDITIONAL INFORMATION

I/we have read the notes on the first page of this Questionnaire and confirm that the answers which are given are correct to the best of my/our knowledge.

ALL JOINT OWNERS TO SIGN.

....

....

Date ....

General Matters

If you have married or have changed your name since purchasing please provide your marriage certificate or change of name deed. (The document will be returned after production to the Purchasers solicitors).

Please confirm that on completion all your property will be removed from all parts of the property including the loft, gardens and outbuildings. If not, you may be liable for the cost involved in the clearing of your property.

419

FORM Q2

CLIENT QUESTIONNAIRE — PURCHASE OF PROPERTY

Solicitor(s)

PLEASE NOTE
1. The following questions will help us in our preliminary investigations. Please send this form back to us immediately
2. If you cannot reply to some of the questions still complete the form as far as you can. When you have the additional information forward it to us.
3. We advise you not to write any letters except to us and under no circumstances should you give any signed documents to any person.

Our ref:

Client(s)

Telephone No's.	Home
	Work

Present Address

Address of property you are buying:

Freehold ☐   Leasehold ☐

Estate Agent:

PURCHASE PRICE £

PLEASE ANSWER AS FULLY AS POSSIBLE

PLEASE REPLY HERE

PERSONAL DETAILS

1. Give the full names (including all Christian or forenames) in BLOCK LETTERS of all Purchasers.

2. Are all Purchasers aged 18 and over? If not give details.

THE PROPERTY

1. What is the agreed price of the property?

2. Is the property a house, bungalow, flat or maisonette, etc?

3. Is it detached, semi-detached or terraced? (if terraced is it the end house in the terrace?)

4. If there is a garage was it built at the same time as the property? If not, when was it built and of what material? (eg. brick, concrete, wood etc.).

5. Does the property have any unusual features, e.g., cellars, part of the property overhanging adjoining premises etc.

6. Have there been any extensions or alterations made to the property if so, when were such alterations carried out and by whom?

7. Does the entrance drive serve the property only or is it shared with a neighbour?

8. Do neighbours appear to have any rights of way or right of access affecting the front or back gardens?

9. How old is the property?

10. Are you obtaining vacant possession of the whole of the property on completion?

11. Is the property vacant at present?

12. Will you use the property solely as a private residence?

13. Are the adjoining roads, streets and pavements fully made up?

14. Are there any side or back roads, streets, passageways or other rights of way adjoining the property?

15. Are there any telephone poles or similar structures on the property?

16. Does the property have:

    a) Mains water

    b) Mains drainage

    c) Gas

    d) Electricity

17. If the main services are not supplied are there any alternatives?

FIXTURES AND FITTINGS

Please complete the attached Fixtures and Fittings Questionnaire (Conveyancing Q3).

Please show the fittings which are included in the purchase — excluded from the purchase and also those which the vendor is selling to you.

Please confirm that:
a) All items mentioned in the estate agent's price are included in the purchase, if not state which items are excluded.

b) Are there any additional items included? If so please specify.

c) If the vendor is receiving a sum of money from you in addition to the price of the house for any items, please say how much you are paying him.

d) if the property is under construction, have you agreed to pay for any extras? If so please specify.

CENTRAL HEATING

Please specify type of system.

Is the vendor leaving any fuel purchased by him but left unused on completion? If so on what basis?

FINANCIAL

State the amount of mortgage for which you have applied.

Will the mortgage be on an endowment basis? If so supply details of the policies involved or name and address of Broker.

To which building society/bank are you applying for the mortgage.

It is normal for a deposit of 10 per cent of the purchase price to be paid on exchange of contracts. Will you be paying this from your own funds or by means of a bridging loan from your bank?

What is the amount of the deposit that you have given to the estate agents? (Any survey fee is not to be included in this figure).

GENERAL MATTERS

Are you selling your present house?

Have you discussed completion dates? NOTE: The date for occupying the property is normally 3/4 weeks *from exchange of contracts.*

If more than one person purchasing do you wish to purchase so that on the death of one of you, that person's share passes automatically to the survivor, i.e.:- as joint tenants.

Will anyone else be occupying the property, if so, please give full names and ages and confirm, if applicable, that you have informed the Building Society or other Lender of this fact.

We advise you, except in the case of a brand new property, to arrange for an independent structural survey to be carried out since this will often reveal defects which may make you decide to ask for a reduction in the purchase price or withdraw from the purchase altogether.

ALL JOINT PURCHASERS TO SIGN_____

DATE_____   AHE

421

FORM Q3

CLIENT QUESTIONNAIRE — FIXTURES AND FITTINGS

SOLICITOR(S).

1. Please complete this form by giving as much information as you can in the boxes provided.
2. When completed please send this form back to us immediately.

Client(s)

Address

LIST OF FIXTURES AND FITTINGS FOR:			
Address of property			
INTERNAL	INCLUDED	EXCLUDED	PRICE IF TO BE SOLD/PURCHASED
Kitchen storage units			
Other kitchen fittings			
Venetian blinds			
Extractor fans			
Wall mirrors			
Bathroom cabinet			
Shower			
Shower fitings			
Towel rails			
Door chimes/bell			
Curtains			
Curtain Rails			
Carpet(s)			
Electric points			
Wall lights			

P.T.O

422

INTERNAL (Cont'd)	INCLUDED	EXCLUDED	PRICE IF TO BE SOLD/PURCHASED
Ceiling lights			
Dimmer switches			
Electric light bulbs			
Wall heaters			
Immersion heaters			
Hot water cylinder jacket			
Roof insulation			
Telephone handsets			
EXTERNAL			
TV Aerial			
Garden shed			
Greenhouse			
Garden ornaments			
Shrubs			
Plants			
		TOTAL £	

I/We confirm that all items mentioned above are not subject to hire purchase or conditional sale agreements or similar financial charge.

Signed .... Date .... 19 ....

Index

Local land charges—*continued*
register—*continued*
  further reading, 4.9.18
  land compensation charges, 4.9.9
  light obstruction notices, 4.9.14
  listed building charges, 4.9.13
  miscellaneous charges,
    other charges, 4.9.7.2
    planning charges, 4.9.7.1
  new towns charges, 4.9.10
  opencast coal charges, 4.9.12
  Parts 1–12, 4.9.4–4.9.15
  planning charges, 4.9.6, 4.9.7.1,
    4.9.16
  property within Greater London,
    4.9.17
  purpose of, 4.9.1
registration,
  effect of, 4.7
  liability of registering authorities,
    4.7.2
  official certificate of search, advantages of, 4.7.1
restrictions on use, 4.2
search,
  additional information revealed,
    4.6.2.2
  delay, 4.3.2
  details revealed by, 4.6.2
  fees, 4.3.4
  how to make, 4.3
  office copy of entry revealed by, 4.6.1
  official, 4.3.1
  official certificate, 4.5, 4.6, 4.7
  personal, 4.3.3
  reasons for making, 4.2
  result of, 4.6
  summary, 4.11
  updating, 4.8
  when to make, 4.1
Logs
  stocks of, additional enquiries, 3.10.2
Long tenancy. *See* TENANTED PROPERTY
Market garden
  improvements for which conpensation payable, 3.13.9.4
Marriage certificates
  copies of, 26.1
Matrimonial home
  pre-contract Central Land Charges search. *See* CENTRAL LAND CHARGES REGISTRY
Matrimonial Homes Act
  rights under, additional enquiries, 3.10.2

Minerals
  consultation areas, 27.6
Mining
  coal. *See* COAL MINING
  tin. *See* TIN MINING
Minor interests, index of. *See* INDEX OF MINOR INTERESTS
Misdescription
  remedies for, 1.7.1
Misrepresentation
  liability on searches, 2.3.2
  remedies for, 1.7.3
Mortgage
  puisne, register of land charges, 34.1.5.3
Mortgagee
  search of Land Registry. *See* LAND REGISTRY
Multiple occupation
  houses in, additional enquiries of local authority, 5.10.9
National Coal Board
  area offices, 28.4
National House Building Council
  agreement, additional enquiries, 3.10.2
  insurance policy against structural defects, 3.5.7.3
New Forest
  exemption from registration under Act, 9.9.4
New property. *See* PROPERTY
Noise
  abatement, additional enquiries of local authority, 5.10.10
Non-disclsoure. *See* DISCLOSURE
Notices
  building preservation, 5.9.13
  completion, 5.10.6
  Land Registry entries, 35.16.2.1
  outstanding, additional enquiries of local authority, 5.9.3, 5.9.19
  preliminary enquiries of vendor, 3.5.6, 3.9.4
  repairs, 5.10.5.2
  Town and Country Planning Act 1971, under, 5.9.9
Office copy entries
  application for, 10.1–10.4
  fees, 10.5
  Form A44,
    comment on, 10.7
    form, 10.6
  how to make search, 10.5
  search summary, 10.8
Oil
  exploration, 27.4

Order
non-registration, effect of, 34.1.9.3
register of, 34.1.2, 34.6.17
tenanted property, 3.11.6
Ordance survey maps
boundaries, 25.3
Overground railways. *See* RAILWAYS
Overseas company
search, 8.6
Outgoings
preliminary enquiries of vendor, 3.5.14,
3.9.10
supplementary questions, 3.8.7
Owner
limited, register of land charges, 34.1.5.3
Parish records
inspection of, 26.4
Patents
existing, search for details of, 26.10
Pending action
non-registration, effect of, 34.1.9.4
register of, 34.1.1, 34.6.17
Personal representative. *See* PROBATE
Personal search
company, 8.4.1
Land Registry, 35.3.5
local authority, 5.3.2
pre-completion, 34.3.1
probate, 33.5.1
rent register, 15.4.1
Pipe-lines
additional enquiries of local authority,
5.10.8
gas, 22.6
generally, 22.1, 22.5
running under proposed building works,
21.2.3
search summary, 22.8
supplementary questions of local authority, 5.11.9
water pipes, 22.3
Planning
additional enquiries of local authority,
applications, 5.9.11
article 4 directions, 5.9.8
building preservation notice, 5.9.13
compensation for refusal of grant of
planning permission, 5.9.10
completion notice, 5.10.6
compulsory purchase, 5.9.14, 5.9.20
conservation areas, 5.9.12
enforcement of planning control, 5.9.6
General Rate Act, 5.9.17
Greater London, 5.9.7.8
improvement of roads, 5.9.21

Planning—*continued*
additional enquiries of local authority—
continued
notice under Town and Country
Planning Act 1971, 5.9.9
outstanding notices, 5.9.3, 5.9.19
policy, 5.9.7
registration of title, 5.9.18
slum clearance, 5.9.15
smoke control, 5.9.16
tree preservation orders, 5.9.9.4
applications, register of, 4.10.3
development plan, meaning, 5.9.7.3
local land charges, 4.9.6, 4.9.7.1, 4.9.16
local plans, meaning, 5.9.7.3
matters not requiring disclosure, 1.5.4
preliminary enquiries of vendor, 3.5.12
site of special scientific interest, 13.2.2–
13.2.3
structure plans, meaning, 5.9.7.3
supplementary questions of local authority,
copies of applications and consents,
5.11.4.2
permitted use, 5.11.4.1
Plans
boundaries. *See* BOUNDARIES
large scale, 11.7
ordnance survey maps, 11.7
property, of, 11.7
Postal search
Land Registry, 35.3.4
pre-completion, 34.3.2
probate, 33.5.2
Pre-completion search
auctions, 36.6
company search, 36.2
Central Land Charges Register, in. *See*
CENTRAL LAND CHARGES REGISTRY
inspection of property, 36.3
local land charges, 36.1
probate. *See* PROBATE
renewal of, 36.5
**Pre-contract Central Land Charges
search.** *See* CENTRAL LAND CHARGES
REGISTRY
Preliminary enquiries of vendor
additional enquiries,
access to neighbouring property,
3.10.2
age of property, 3.10.2
deposit, 3.10.2
leasehold flats, 3.10.2
leasehold property, 3.10.2
long leases of houses, 3.10.2

Index

Preliminary enquiries of vendor—*continued*
additional enquiries—*continued*
Matrimonial Homes Act, rights under, 3.10.2
NHBC agreement, 3.10.2
names of previous estate owners, 3.10.2
newly built property, 3.10.2
not on printed forms, 3.10
number and type, 3.10.1
removal of rubbish, 3.10.2
stocks of coal, calor gas, logs, 3.10.2
suggested, table of, 3.10.2
telephone, 3.10.2
tenanted property. 3.10.2
water abstraction licences, 3.10.2
adverse rights, 3.5.10, 3.9.7
agricultural tenancies, *see* Form Con 292 *post*
answering, 3.5.19
approach to,
purchaser's solicitor, by, 3.3.1
vendor's solicitor, by, 3.3.2
boundaries, 3.5.4, 3.9.3
business, purchase of, 3.14
chattels, 3.8.6
client questionnaires, Appendix IV
completion, 3.5.15, 3.9.12
development land tax, 3.5.16
disputes, 3.5.5, 3.9.3, 3.11.7
facilities, 3.5.9
fixtures and fittings, 3.5.13, 3.8.6, 3.9.8
Form Convey 1,
adverse rights, 3.9.7
boundaries, 3.9.3
comment, 3.9.2
comparative table of questions, 3.9.14
completion, 3.9.12
disputes, 3.9.3
fixtures and fittings, 3.9.8
form, 3.9.1
leasehold enquiries, 3.9.13
notices, 3.9.4
outgoings, 3.9.10
residency, 3.9.11
restrictions, 3.9.7
semi-detached house, 3.9.9
services to property, 3.9.6
terraced house, 3.9.9
works carried out at property, 3.9.5
Form Con 29 (long),
adverse rights, 3.5.10
boundaries, 3.5.4
comment on, 3.5

Preliminary enquiries of vendor—*continued*
Form Con 29 (long)—*continued*
comparative table of questions, 3.9.14
compared with Form Con 29 (short), 3.7.2
completion, 3.5.1, 3.5.15
development land tax, 3.5.16
disclaimer of liability, 3.5.2
disputes, 3.5.5
facilities, 3.5.9
fixtures and fittings, 3.5.13
form, 3.4
guarantees, 3.5.7
leasehold enquiries, 3.5.18
new properties, 3.5.17
notices, 3.5.6
outgoings, 3.5.14
planning, 3.5.12
restrictions, 3.5.11
services, 3.5.8
Form Con 29 (short),
comment, 3.7
comparative table of questions, 3.9.14
compared with Form Con 29 (long), 3.7.2
form, 3.6
Form Con 291,
business tenancies,
duration of business, 3.11.10
generally, 3.11.9
improvements, 3.11.11
Landlord and Tenant Act 1954, Part II, exemption, 3.11.13
new tenancy, 3.11.12
comment, 3.11.1
disputes, 3.11.7
form, 3.11.1
insurance, 3.11.5
long tenancies, 3.11.19
orders, 3.11.6
rateable value limits, 3.11.15.6, 3.11.15.8, 3.11.15.9
regulated tenancies, 3.11.15.2–3.11.15.3, 3.11.15.7
rent, 3.11.16
rent revision, 3.11.8
resident landlord, 3.11.18
residential tenancies, 3.11.14
restricted contracts, 3.11.15.4
service charge, 3.11.20
statutory rules, application of, 3.11.15
statutory tenancy, 3.11.15.5
sub-letting, 3.11.4
tenant, 3.11.2

Tenancies
disclosure, 1.3.2
Tenanted property
additional enquiries, 3.10.2
business tenancies, 3.11.9–3.11.13
disputes, 3.11.7
Form Con 291,
comment, 3.11.1
form, 3.11.1
improvements, 3.11.11
insurance, 3.11.5
long tenancy,
Landlord and Tenant Act 1954, Part I, 3.11.19.4
Leasehold Reform Act 1967, 3.11.19.3
meaning, 3.11.19.2
secure tenancies, 3.11.19.5
new tenancy, 3.11.12
orders, 3.11.6
rent,
protected shortholds, 3.11.16.4
registered, 3.11.16.1
regulated tenancies, 3.11.16.2
restricted contracts, 3.11.16.3
review, 3.11.8
resident landlord, 3.11.18
residential premises, 3.11.14
service charge,
generally, 3.11.20.1–3.11.20.2
limit on payments, 3.11.20.4
recognised tenants' associations, 3.11.20.5
right to information, 3.11.20.3
statutory rules, application of,
rateable value limits,
appropriate day, 3.11.15.6
classes A–E, 3.11.15.6
Leasehold Reform Act 1967, 3.11.15.8, 3.11.15.9
regulated tenancies. *See* REGULATED TENANCIES
restricted contracts, 3.11.15.4
statutory tenancy, 3.11.15.5
sub-letting, 3.11.4
tenant, 3.11.2
terms of letting, 3.11.3, 3.11.17
Tenants' association
recognised, 3.11.20.5
Terraced house
enquiries prior to contract, 3.9.9
Third party
relying on search made by, 5.14.2
Tied cottage. *See* AGRICULTURAL TENANCY
Tin mining
generally, 29.1

Tin mining—*continued*
mineral consultation areas, 29.4
search,
how to make, 29.2
information revealed by, 29.3
summary, 29.5
Tithes
charges relating to, 35.16.2.7
redemption annuity. *See* CORN RENT
Title
grant of probate forms part of chain of, 33.2
patent defects in, disclosure of, 1.5.1
registration of, additional enquiries of local authority, 5.9.18
reversionary, preliminary enquiries of vendor, 3.5.18.9–3.5.18.10
type and tenure of, disclosure of, 1.3.8
Towns
new, charges, 4.9.10
Trade marks
search, 26.11
Trade unions
search of records, 23.5
search summary, 23.6
Tree preservation orders
additional enquiries of local authority, 5.9.9.4
Underground railways. *See* RAILWAYS
Unregistered land
public index map search, 6.2.1
Urban development areas
additional enquiries of local authority, 5.10.11
Urban development corporation
supplementary question of local authority, 5.11.8
Usual searches. *See* SEARCHES
Vehicles
supplementary questions, 3.8.5
Vendor
disclosure. *See* DISCLOSURE
preliminary enquiries of. *See* PRELIMINARY ENQUIRIES OF VENDOR
solicitor. *See* SOLICITOR
Wales
chancel repair liability, 17.6
Water abstraction licences
additional enquiries, 3.10.2
Water authorities
British Waterways Board, addresses of, 21.6.2
canals, 21.6
change of ownership, 21.5
impoundment of water, 21.2.5